# Belief in God in Our Time

*Foundational Theology, I*

*M. John Farrelly, O.S.B.*

A Michael Glazier Book
THE LITURGICAL PRESS
Collegeville, Minnesota

*To*
*my brothers and sisters, both living and deceased:*

John(+), William(+), Caroline Gross, Elizabeth Kavanagh(+),
Rev. Thomas, Edward Scott, Sister Cordelia, R.S.C.J.(+),
Francis, Peter, Julia McCarthy, and David

Cover design by David Manahan, O.S.B.
Cover photo: Larry Dunmire/Imagery Photography

A Michael Glazier Book published by The Liturgical Press

1    2    3    4    5    6    7    8    9

**Library of Congress Cataloging-in-Publication Data**
Farrelly, John, 1927–
    Belief in God in our time / M. John Farrelly.
        p.   cm — (Foundational theology ; 1) (Theology and life
series ; v. 35)
    "A Michael Glazier book."
    Includes bibliographical references.
    ISBN 0-8146-5706-0
    1. Apologetics—20th century.  2. God.  I. Title.  II. Series.
III. Series: Farrelly, John, 1927–    Foundational theology ; 1.
BT1102.F37   1992
230'.01—dc20                                    91-38572
                                                    CIP

# Contents

Preface . . . . . . . . . . . . . . . . . . . . . . . . . . . . . . . . . . . .    5

1. The Problematic of Mediating Faith in our Time  . .   15
   I. A Sketch of Disbelief and Its Roots in Our Time . .   16
   II. The Task of Foundational Theology . . . . . . . . .   26

2. Models for Theological Mediation of Christian Belief
   in God . . . . . . . . . . . . . . . . . . . . . . . . . . . . . . . . . .   30
   I. Dialogical versus Dialectical Models . . . . . . . . .   31
   II. Vatican II and Mediation of Belief in God . . . . .   44
   III. History and Process: Theory and Practice . . . . .   56

3. Scripture and Our Belief in God . . . . . . . . . . . . . . .   73
   I. The Old Testament . . . . . . . . . . . . . . . . . . . . . .   84
   II. The New Testament . . . . . . . . . . . . . . . . . . . . .   99

4. Soundings in Christian History on the Doctrine of
   Belief in God . . . . . . . . . . . . . . . . . . . . . . . . . . . . .  114
   I. The Patristic Age . . . . . . . . . . . . . . . . . . . . . . .  115
   II. The High Middle Ages Through the Reformation .  127
   III. From the Seventeenth to the Early Twentieth
   Century . . . . . . . . . . . . . . . . . . . . . . . . . . . . . . . .  140

5. Conversion and Human Transcendence . . . . . . . . . .  165
   I. Christian Conversion in the Twentieth
   Century . . . . . . . . . . . . . . . . . . . . . . . . . . . . . . . . .  166
   II. Personal Transcendence . . . . . . . . . . . . . . . . . . .  179
   III. Social Life and Transcendence . . . . . . . . . . . . .  205

6. Grounds for Belief in the Existence of God . . . . . . .   215
    I. Critical Grounding of Faith: An Epistemological
      Question . . . . . . . . . . . . . . . . . . . . . . . . . . . . . . .   216
    II. Experience of Conscience as Testimony to God's
      Existence . . . . . . . . . . . . . . . . . . . . . . . . . . . . . .   234
    III. Intimations of God Mediated by the Physical
      World . . . . . . . . . . . . . . . . . . . . . . . . . . . . . . . . .   243

7. God as Transcendent Personal Being . . . . . . . . . . . .   260
    I.  God as Transcendent Personal Being . . . . . . . .   261
    II. Some Buddhist and Christian Reflections on the
      Ultimate . . . . . . . . . . . . . . . . . . . . . . . . . . . . . . .   277

8. God's Relation to the World and History . . . . . . . .   289
    I. God's Immanence in the World: Symbol and
      Concept . . . . . . . . . . . . . . . . . . . . . . . . . . . . . . . .   290
    II. God's Relation to Change in History . . . . . . . . .   299
    III. The Mystery of Evil . . . . . . . . . . . . . . . . . . . . .   321

9. Faith in God, Religion, and Religious Language  . . .   332
    I.  Faith and Religion as Necessary for Human
      Beings in Our Time . . . . . . . . . . . . . . . . . . . . . .   332
    II. Religious and Theological Language . . . . . . . . .   354

Index of Principal Authors . . . . . . . . . . . . . . . . . . . . . . . .   373

Index of Subjects . . . . . . . . . . . . . . . . . . . . . . . . . . . . . . .   376

# Preface

Scripture calls upon Christians of our time as in previous ages: "Always be ready to give an explanation (*apologia*) to anyone who asks you for a reason for your hope" (1 Pet 3:15). To give an answer to those who question our Christian hope involves giving both an explanation of what our hope is and grounds for our holding that hope. Christians throughout history have given such accounts of their faith, either in a popular way or in a reflective, critical, and systematic fashion that can be properly called theology. The latter is what we attempt in this work. As I understand it, this calls us to give the *meaning* of what we believe as Christians in a way that is genuinely faithful to the norms of Christian faith. To articulate the meaning of our faith demands that we explain both what it signifies (e.g., what "God reveals" signifies) and what its relevance or importance is to our lives (e.g., how belief in God and salvation through Jesus Christ fulfill, liberate, and transform our lives). To answer those who question our Christian hope calls us also to show the grounds or *foundations* for our believing in a way that is genuinely in dialogue with those who have difficulties with such belief, whether these are people who do not hold the Christian faith or Christians who differ very markedly from us in their understanding of the faith and its implications for action.

An attempt to evaluate critically the meaning and grounds of our Christian belief and hope in God in a way appropriate to our time raises many questions. For example, what are major problems with such belief and hope in our time? What is the Christian belief in God that we are seeking to evaluate? What does theological evaluation of such belief involve? In asking here for major problems with such belief, I am speaking from the perspective of the North Atlantic countries and, even more specifically, from the perspective of the United States. If I were writing from the perspectives of East Asia, India, Africa, or Latin America, my priorities would be different; but I hope that what we offer complements rather than contradicts other perspectives. In our age we do live in a world that is becoming progressively smaller; so we cannot neglect major difficulties that are posed to the Christian faith by, for example, other world religions or injustices rampant throughout the world.

One major problem with faith today, as we shall see later, is a religious indifference that is a byproduct of a culture largely dominated by people's autonomous search for meaning in a rapidly changing world heavily influenced by technology and the physical and human sciences. This attitude can so control an individual and a culture that they accept in practice and even in theory a naturalistic historical consciousness that represents, we will claim, a distorted understanding of the self and society. In this environment, many Christians have jettisoned their inherited Christian belief and identities.

The seriousness of the issues addressed in this area of theology is evident not only in the widespread disbelief in our time, but, more immediate to most of us, in differing understandings of God and Jesus Christ among Christians and, we should add, among Catholics—differences that extend beyond the bounds of a genuinely Christian or Catholic pluralism. These differences are apparent, for example, in some of the diverse responses given to Vatican II's reforms. Some differences among Catholics on issues of social justice, sexual morality, and interreligious dialogue reflect differing views of God, humanity, and Christ, as well as differing views of the Church. While some Christians have over assimilated to the secular and non-Christian culture in which we live, there are also some Christians who, while strongly resisting the erosion of faith that surrounds them, at times over identify with an earlier cultural expression of Christian belief, not distinguishing such a cultural expression from what is central to this faith itself. They resist a reinterpretation of the Christian faith that meets the challenges of the Church in its present stage of pilgrimage through history, such as those that come from Eastern religions or our sharper awareness today of the equal dignity of women and men. Thus they present a distorted image of Christian belief and life to the world. This situation is not unique to Christianity but is also found widely in Islam and Asian religions in our time. We find throughout the world many conflicts between forms of fundamentalism or conservatism and forms of modernism or liberalism.

The theological effort to mediate Christian belief in God in a way appropriate to our time is part of what is widely called fundamental or, as I prefer, foundational theology—a section of theology distinct from and introductory to systematic theology. This area of theology has undergone significant shifts in focus in recent decades.[1] In the Catholic Church before Vatican II, most Catholic theologians who wrote in this field of theology presented an apologetics that was, unfortunately, often marked by a certain defensiveness, objectivism, and extrinsecism. That is, they justified belief with reasons that were not intrinsically connected with the content of the message of Christ or the anxieties and difficulties of men and women of our time. The documents of Vatican II, partially under the influence of certain Catholic and Protestant critics of the earlier manualist apologetics, interpreted revelation and faith in a more personal, concrete, historical, and biblical manner and called for a more positive dialogue with modern atheism, nonChristian religions, and particularly with our fellow Christians of other denominations. Since then, there has been a certain fracturing of foundational theology in the Church. For some, it has continued to be primarily an effort to show that belief in Christ is reasonable, though belief and revelation are now interpreted in accord with Vatican II. For others, it has become primarily a theology of revelation, without much atten-

---

[1] Some recent studies of apologetics, fundamental, or foundational theology in the twentieth century are the following: J. Schmitz, "La théologie fondamentale," in R. Vander Gucht and H. Vorgrimler, *Bilan de la théologie au XX<sup>e</sup> siècle* (Tournai-Paris: Casterman, 1971) vol. 2, 9–151; Jean-Pierre Torrell, "Chronique de théologie fondamentale," *Revue thomiste,* periodically from 1964 to the present; H. Stirnimann, "Erwagungen für Fundamentaltheologie. Problematik, Grundfragen, Konzept," *Freiburger Zeitschrift für Philosophie und Theologie* 24 (1977) 291–365; René Latourelle and Gerald O'Collins, eds., *Problems and Perspectives of Fundamental Theology* (New York: Paulist, 1982); Francis Schüssler Fiorenza, *Foundational Theology, Jesus and the Church* (New York: Crossroad, 1984).

tion being given to the apologetic dimension. For still others, it is the study of the foundations of theology rather than of the Christian faith.

In the opinion of many theologians we need an *integrative* view of foundational theology; we need an introductory section of theology that studies in a systematic and critical fashion the meaning and grounds of our faith in God through Jesus Christ—a study that includes such things as an analysis of the meaning of what Christ proclaims to offer us (the kingdom or salvation) and the way he proclaims it (as a revelation) and some grounds for our belief in his mediation of God's salvation and revelation. Along with some other theologians, I think that this study is more properly called foundational theology than apologetics, since it is oriented not primarily to convincing nonbelievers but to a critical evaluation of the meaning and grounds of our own Christian faith—without entailing a foundational*ism*. A study of foundational theology is primarily meant for Christians, though we can hope that some religious seekers who are not Christian will find it helpful. The only meaning and grounds that we can offer others are those that have been adequate for ourselves. This study then, though not directed to nonbelievers, is in dialogue with them, since believers too are deeply affected by difficulties that others in our culture have with the Christian faith, and we are responsible not only for critically grounding our own faith but for presenting it to others.

The above, I suggest, is necessary but not sufficient as a description of foundational theology. In Catholic theology the question of belief in God has usually been treated in another section of theology, namely, in the treatise on "the One and Triune God." But if foundational theology is to evaluate critically the meaning of and grounds for belief in Jesus Christ, it would seem that it must begin with the question of God, since Jesus has meaning only within this context. And perhaps the major problem with acceptance of Christian revelation for many in our time lies in their lack of bases for giving faith in God a primary place in their self-understanding and lives, or in the kind of God they believe in. Jesus proclaimed his message to a people who had already undergone a divine pedagogy leading them to give primacy to God in their lives and to understand somewhat the relation that was appropriate for them to adopt with God. It does seem necessary to have such a section in foundational theology if it is to be in touch with the basic problems undermining the faith of many in our time. However, since the full question of Jesus Christ and the question of the Trinity—the properly Christian belief in God—are addressed in other parts of theology, foundational theology does not presume to give more than an introductory and incomplete critical evaluation of our belief in God and Jesus Christ's mediation of his salvation and revelation.

I am suggesting then that in foundational theology there are two parts, which successively evaluate the meaning and grounds for our belief in God and in Jesus Christ as his mediator. To situate what we are doing here, I should add that there is a further part of foundational theology that deals with the norm of Christian faith and the nature of theology. For Catholics to evaluate critically the norm of Christian faith, it would seem that they must evaluate what Vatican II proclaimed in chapter 2 of its Dogmatic Constitution on Divine Revelation (*Dei Verbum*) and do so in an ecumenical context. This part of foundational theology does not contain the major treatise on the Church, for that is the subject of ecclesiology. We also need, in this part, a section dedicated to the nature of theology. Actually, all of foundational theology contributes to such a study, and not only to a critical evaluation of Christian and Catholic faith, since it treats revelation, faith, Scripture, tradition, and the development of doctrine. But we need a specific section that brings all these elements to bear on the nature of theology. That seems appropriate for the conclusion of foundational theology. Beginning students in theology, to whom foundational theology is usually presented, should have some experience of doing theology before they reflectively examine in detail what theology is. Thus in this interpretation, foundational theology has three parts that critically evaluate in succession: (I) the meaning and grounds of our faith in God, (II) faith in God through Jesus Christ, and (III) the norm of faith and the nature of theology. What we attempt in this book is an evaluation of the current problematic of parts I and II, and a critical evaluation of our belief in God. The reason for treating the problematic of both parts I and II will be evident in chapter 2 where the diversity of theological approaches to this whole question will be recalled.

Our study of the meaning and grounds of our Christian belief in God is not a philosophy or history or sociology or psychology of religion, though it makes some use of these disciplines. As theology it is an "insider's" reflection, namely, the reflection of a believer. The classical theologians were believers who reflected on their faith, and thus it seems that historically there is much reason to restrict the word "theology," as distinct from religious studies more broadly, to the systematic, critical reflection on the faith that is done by believers. Theology is *fides quaerens intellectum,* faith seeking understanding, though we should explicitly acknowledge that this faith that seeks understanding includes hope and charity. Foundational theology uses the Church's teaching, Scripture, and tradition, as we shall see in the first chapters, to show what the faith is that we seek to critically evaluate.

One of the functions of this part of theology is to critically establish what the norm of faith is, though in one sense it already uses this when it shows through Scripture what Christians understand belief in God to be. The teaching of the Church constitutes here not the answer but the problem, for it is this that we seek to critically evaluate. Critical evaluation assumes, of course, that the faith can still develop and so such evaluation corrects some traditional interpretations. Foundational theology differs from the main areas of systematic theology, for it cannot use, especially in its earlier parts, the arguments that rely on faith to defend the *grounds* of belief. Later chapters will show how we attempt to use contemporary experience and reason and modern critical study of Scripture to help evaluate this faith.

By this identification of our project, I show that I understand theology and specifically foundational theology to be an ecclesial discipline. It serves the Christian community, and therefore it seems appropriate for the theologian to reflect critically on the meaning and foundations of belief that are offered by the Christian community. For the Catholic theologian, and especially for one who seeks to prepare people for ministry, this means giving particular attention to a critical reflection on the way the faith was articulated by Vatican II. This Council was influenced by Protestant theologians and exegetes; and, as we shall recall later, the World Council of Church's Faith and Order Commission has also written on the question of relating Christian faith to our world today. So in the first parts of foundational theology, we are not dealing with Church-dividing issues but rather with issues that Christians of differing ecclesial communities face together as we try to mediate the Christian message to our world.

Some may say that if we engage in this study from the background of Christian and even Catholic belief, then we cannot enter into genuine dialogue with nonbelievers or be unprejudiced judges of evidence for or against Christian belief in God. We should certainly acknowledge that acceptance of the Christian faith has frequently in the past been an obstacle to respect for the positions of others who do not share our belief and to dialogue with nonbelievers. But this is not the attitude of Vatican II nor of those who remain faithful to its spirit. Moreover, it takes as much effort and imagination for the nonbeliever to genuinely understand the believer as it does for the believer to understand either the nonbeliever or members of other religious bodies. Whether this book does engage in honest dialogue with modern difficulties with Christian belief in God is something the reader must judge. But in principle, if God has indeed revealed himself definitively though not exclusively through Jesus Christ and the Holy Spirit, then it is not impossible for the Christian theologian to engage in an enterprise such as we are attempting here. Such a theologian can joyously acknowledge truth and goodness wherever they are found.

One of the difficulties that this present enterprise faces is the fact that for Catholic theologians there has been a paradigm shift in theology since Vatican II. Before the council theologians engaged in this kind of study largely under the sign of Thomas Aquinas. Since the council there has been a remarkable flight from Thomas by many Catholic theologians. As part of the acceptance of Thomas before the council was uncritical, so too part of the flight from him since then has perhaps also been uncritical. The Catholic theologian has to take a stand on whether philosophical reflection on contemporary experience calls for a rejection of Thomas' philosophy or a more nuanced evaluation of it that is in part positive and in part transformative of it. Most would probably agree that it calls for both continuity and discontinuity with Thomas' philosophy, but at times in the pages that follow we shall have to address this question in more detail. The present study is conducted within a much broader framework than the thought of Thomas Aquinas, but at times I contrast a Thomistic view and a contemporary view (e.g., on the possibility of metaphysics) and seek to transcend this opposition without reestablishing a basis for the Thomistic view *ab initio.* Thus I acknowledge that my earlier acceptance of Thomas marks philosophical aspects of this dialogue. As the reader will find, I very significantly modify the Thomism I initially accepted, but do not totally abandon it. This book presupposes some knowledge of modern and classical—and specifically Thomistic—philosophy.

This book attempts in the first two chapters to identify the basic problematic of belief in God through Jesus Christ in our time. Then the next seven chapters deal more directly with a theological reflection on the meaning and grounds of our belief in God (Part I). I hope later to write a volume that critically evaluates belief in God specifically through Jesus Christ (Part II).

I have taught the material of this book a number of times over a thirty-year period and have done so particularly, though not exclusively, to students preparing for ministry. The book is proposed simply as an introduction. Many issues that are raised here could and should be treated in much greater depth. There is, however, an advantage in taking a look at the problem as a whole, even when this necessitates a briefer treatment of the parts. The interrelation of the different parts of the study has its own contribution to make to an understanding of the whole. Moreover, I will refer the interested reader to books and articles where particular issues are treated at greater length and depth. These references also show the great debt I owe to many Scripture scholars, theologians, philosophers, historians of religions, and others whose work I use.

I must note here an option I have chosen in reference to the difficult question of inclusive language. I have sought to write in a way that recognizes that women constitute half of the human race and half of the Church. In reference to the use of the personal pronoun of God, I have, along with a number of other theologians, defended in another publication the view that the main symbols of the Holy Spirit in Scripture are feminine, and that therefore it is proper to use the feminine personal pronoun in reference to the Spirit. The main symbol of the Second Person of the Trinity is masculine, for we believe that the Word became flesh in Jesus Christ. However, in this book we are not treating the question of the Trinity, though we do refer to Trinitarian questions in our limited dialogue with Buddhism and Hinduism. The whole of the answer to the question of language about God is not offered, then, in this book. I have chosen, in accord with Christian tradition, to speak of God generally by way of the third person masculine pronoun, understanding this to mean grammatical rather than sexual gender. Though this is an inadequate solution today, it seems to me less inadequate than to speak of God by restrictive impersonal pronouns or names or to constantly use such expressions as "he/she." From those readers who differ from me on this issue, I ask their forbearance.

I cannot conclude this preface without expressing my gratitude to my students through the years, particularly those at De Sales School of Theology in Washington, D.C., who have been the day-to-day dialogue partners in my theological work, and so have contributed much to this present book. I thank my fellow theologians Augustine DiNoia, O.P., and James Buckley for generously reading this work and giving me their much appreciated evaluations of it. I also thank Raymond Studzinski, O.S.B., and William Cenkner, O.P., professors in the School of Religious Studies at The Catholic University of America—the former for reading and evaluating chapter 5, and the latter for reading and evaluating an article I wrote on mysticism West and East that informs what I write here on Buddhism and Hinduism. I am also very grateful to Peter Leonard, O.S.F.S., professor of biology at Allentown College of St. Francis de Sales, for reading the section in chapter 6 where I make use of biology and for making valuable comments on this section. And I thank Sheila Garcia who has read this volume from the perspective of a graduate theology student. She has helped me particularly with inclusive language. It is impossible to give an adequate list of those to whom I am indebted for this volume, since that would demand that I note the many different contexts in which I have dialogued with others concerning issues treated here. To restrict myself to just one such context, I think that the three trips I have had the privilege of taking to East Asia since 1985 for lectures and discussions at international philosophical conferences and smaller symposia in ten cities and seven countries have contributed much to my current theology. For these opportunities I have a special debt of gratitude to George McLean, O.M.I., secretary of the International Society for Metaphysics and of the Council for Research in Values and Philosophy and member of the board of the International Federation of Philosophical Societies, for it was at his invitation that I took the first two of these trips. And finally, I am indebted to James Wiseman, O.S.B., and the late Leonard Vickers, O.S.B., abbots of St. Anselm's Abbey while I was writing this book, for the opportunity I had to complete this work.

M. John Farrelly, O.S.B.
April 21, 1991
Feast of St. Anselm

# 1

# The Problematic of Mediating Faith in Our Time

There are, I suggest, two major contexts for the task of foundational theology. One is found in the difficulties advanced against Christian faith in God in our time; by this we mean particularly those difficulties associated with the culture in which we live, rather than those that are specific to individuals because of their particular experience of the Church. The second context is found in the differences among theologians as they seek to reflect critically on the meaning and foundations of faith. This chapter attempts to identify several major difficulties with Christian faith in God in our time and then gives an initial sketch of what we consider necessary for a theological mediation of such faith in these circumstances. The following chapter compares this model of theological mediation of faith in God with some prominent theological models of the twentieth century and shows in the process how the model we have adopted borrows from these other models and differs from them. At that point we shall suggest that our model is that of Vatican II and that Vatican II's model integrates the positive elements of varied twentieth-century models while overcoming some of their mutual oppositions. This chapter and the next then are an introduction to both part one and part two of foundational theology, namely, critical reflections on the meaning and grounds of our belief in God and belief in God specifically through Jesus Christ. We present this material, as we do the rest of the material in this book, not as a full treatment of these important issues but as an introduction to them.

What then are the major problems that bring people to experience a loss of Christian faith in God in the world today, particularly in the countries of the North Atlantic region, and more specifically in the United States? It is these that we should identify and then address in foundational theology's study of the meaning of and grounds for faith in God. To indicate our interpretation of this situation, we shall first present a brief sketch of the tension and conflict between an identity founded on the belief in God that the Church proposes to people and an identity that is widespread in our modern and postmodern world that, in different degrees, resists this through disbelief or serious doubt. In this latter identity we shall briefly specify two major sources of disbelief and doubt that a critical reflection on faith today should address. Second, we shall give an initial sketch of what we understand the task of a theological mediation of faith in God through Jesus Christ to involve in these circumstances. We should note that the difficulties of belief we will mention exist not only for non-Christians, but for Christians themselves in differing degrees. From our own struggle to believe, we can identify with the difficulties others have.

## I. A Sketch of Disbelief and Its Roots in Our Time

The Church, and this includes not only the Roman Catholic but all the major Christian Churches, professes belief in God more by proclaiming what he has done to save us than by reflecting on his existence. The Church proclaims to the people of the world that God has in his goodness offered humanity salvation through Jesus Christ and the Spirit, a salvation that is mediated by the Church and that is the most significant reality in the lives of individual persons and, indeed, in history. God has offered us liberation from sin (whether personal, social or original), from death, and from Satan; thus he has offered us liberation from the greatest evils that oppress men and women. He offers us this and communion with himself in what Jesus called the kingdom of God. Thus he offers us life with himself and a unity among human beings on this basis—a life that has its fullest expression after our life in history is completed, but that also has its transformative impact here and now for individual and society. This transformative impact leads the Church and Christians to proclaim the good news throughout the world by word and deed in the conviction that it is the answer to our deepest needs. What God offers through Christ and the Spirit, and the Church mediates, is humanity's only genuine fulfillment, because our deepest identity and dignity consists in this orientation toward communion with God; our hearts are restless till they rest in God. This salvation is given to those who believe in God and what he has revealed—a revelation that comes to its fulfillment in Jesus Christ. It is not opposed to men and women's rightful activity in the world, but is the context that gives such activity ultimate meaning and grounds and preserves it from self-destructiveness. God is a transcendent personal being who is also immanent in history and the world by his love, providence, and eschatological saving activity. The conversion of the human person to God is of central importance in the person's life; it is possible to him or her only through God's grace. But it is an act that has supporting evidence; it is not contrary to human experience and reason, if these are properly understood; indeed these testify to God's existence, and history testifies to the Church's claims about Jesus Christ.

There are a great number of people in our time whose parents or ancestors were Christian and who may well have accepted a Christian belief similar to that just sketched, but now feel incapable of believing in the reality and relevance of this belief. In the mid-1970's, a survey concluded that there were eighty million unchurched people in the United States. Among those who profess to be Christians, there are vast numbers who do not accept what the Churches would consider the full Christian understanding of God and its implications for individual and social life. Many who in different degrees have distanced themselves from the Churches do not deny the existence of God, but do not consider a relation to God, and particularly one which is in continuity with the past understanding of the Judaeo-Christian West, central in their lives.

The identities of these people are not formed by the Christian proclamation. Rather they are formed by their society, their own choices, their self-determined goals, and thus by what is much more immediate in their lives. They live in specific circumstances, with differing interests, engagements, and life projects: what concerns them, what has urgency and relevance for them is what has an immediate impact on these. Talk about God does not have this impact or immediacy. Many such people interpret their lives in terms that are very individualistic, seeking achievement, personal experiences, and economic gain that enhance their sense of self. But many too are trying to make a living, raise a family, contribute to their immediate social milieu and even to the larger country and world of which they are a part. They may well try to make use of the knowledge available to them, and indeed they may have a greater sense of social justice than many who claim to be Christian believers. The problems that threaten their lives are matters of health, personal relations, family, economy, politics, environment, crime, international relations, etc. And the relevant ways of achieving an improved life or responding to problems are offered by changes that are specific to these different problem areas. Medical science, psychiatry, economic and political changes, and great contributions of technology are available to us as they were not in previous ages. Practically speaking, meaning in life is found in this life, and the way to gain this meaning is the fulfillment of our needs. The answers of religion are frequently respected and thought appropriate for a previous age and those who still need them, but these other people do not turn to them. If religious answers are thought still helpful, there are religions other than Christianity, there are forms of Christianity that have adapted to the present age, and there are ways to inner peace that do not entail a strong Christian faith commitment (e.g., meditation, therapy, music, fellowship). The needs of the present age, whether individual or social, national or international, are best met by means which specifically address them.

Some people have tried these means to meet current human needs and aspirations and have found them wanting. While many may go to great lengths to assure meaning in history, many too have lost hope because of evils and darkness suffered in their personal lives or because of despair over the larger political, social, and economic forces shaping their society or the larger world. They do not think that Christianity has the answer to their search. For some, the Christian view of God has supported a social order that was unjust to the poor, women, and other marginalized people. For others, a turn to Christianity would be wish fulfillment. It is in many ways opposed to any current understanding of history offered us by the practice of our society and the physical and human sciences. Moreover, in both personal life and twentieth-century history, many things happen with no evident presence of the Christian God. In fact, horrors like World Wars, the Holocaust, and other twentieth-century instances of massive evil are powerful evidences against the existence of the Christian God. For many in our time, reality is ultimately unfriendly and God is absent. This difficulty with Christianity is noted by many who reflect on these issues. For example, Karl Rahner writes: "The real argument against Christianity is the experience of life, this experience of darkness. And I have always found that behind the technical arguments leveled by the learned against Christianity—as the ultimate force and *a priori* pre-judgment supporting these scientific doubts—there are always these ultimate experiences of life causing the spirit and the heart to be sombre, tired and despairing."[1] One can see then that the reasons for unbelief today are not only and perhaps not primarily intellectual. They are tied up with the styles of life of individuals and societies. It is more a question of experience and values than of intellectual knowledge; but it is also a question of knowledge, for it seems to many that the best knowledge we have in our time of the person, society, history, and the physical world is not consistent with Christian views of God's activity (e.g., miracles, providence, life after death). These reasons for disbelief are built into many aspects of our societies and into our psyches. They are manifested not primarily in direct denials of God, but in religious indifference, many degrees of practical irreligion, relativism, and agnosticism.

The great pluralism we are so aware of in our shrinking world leads some to a disengagement from a specifically Christian understanding of God and an acceptance of some Eastern form of religion or some hybrid religion. In some, relativism

---

[1]K. Rahner, "Thoughts on the Possibility of Belief today," *Theological Investigations,* vol. 5 (Baltimore: Helicon, 1966) 6.

can induce this attitude; it would be hubris, they think, for one to proclaim that one's own interpretation of the ultimate context of meaning is equally true for other cultures. In others, a disengagement from the objectives and presuppositions of Western culture, a return to nature, and an unawareness of the spiritual riches of the Christian tradition can lead to an openness to Eastern religions that dissolves Christian faith.

After this brief sketch, we should analytically specify some major sources of the disbelief in Christianity that characterizes this form of modern identity—factors on which we should focus in addressing unbelief in a book such as this. These sources are roots of the great difficulties many of our contemporaries experience with faith in God as articulated by the Christian Churches. The first of these roots, we suggest, is an understanding and acceptance of self and the second is an understanding of God.

Many people of our time have a consciousness of themselves in history that differs from that common among our ancestors.[2] This can be described as a modern historical conscious-

---

[2]The Fathers at the Second Vatican Council present in the Introduction to *Gaudium et Spes* (The Pastoral Constitution on the Church in the Modern World) an interpretation of the situation to which their message is addressed. See Austin Flannery, ed., *Vatican Council II. The Conciliar and Post Conciliar Documents* (Northport, N.Y.: Costello Publishing Co., 1975) 903–911. What they emphasize is the change of our culture and society to a more dynamic one than that to which the Church earlier addressed itself. For example the Council teaches: "Ours is a new age of history with critical and swift changes (*profundae et celeres mutationes*) spreading gradually to all corners of the earth. They are the products of man's intelligence and creative activity, but they recoil upon him, upon his judgments and desires, both individual and collective, upon his ways of thinking and acting in regard to people and things. We are entitled then to speak of a real social and cultural transformation whose repercussions are felt too on the religious level" (4). This current pace of historical change is accompanied by crises of growth or tension, by serious imbalances among peoples, within particular societies and within individuals, and by more insistent aspirations for a life of human dignity. This new culture is largely dependent on the larger influence that is exercised by the mathematical and natural sciences (including the human science) and by the repercussions of technology. For many people all of this calls into question traditional values and religion itself. Thus atheism in its many forms should be considered one of the most serious problems of our time (see paragraph 19). One may say that the council relates the problem of faith in our time largely to this change of culture and, more specifically, a modern historical consciousness. A good analysis of modern historical consciousness is found in Langdon Gilkey, *Reaping the Whirlwind. A Christian Interpretation of History* (New York: Seabury, 1976) ch. 8, "Modern Historical Consciousness," 188–208.

ness that in some takes the form of a *naturalistic historical con-sciousness.* We can describe this condition as follows. While our ancestors lived in societies that were in great part traditional, we now live in non-traditional cultures. Largely through the rapid changes (technological, scientific, political, economic, cultural) that have occurred in recent history through men and women's creative making of their personal and social histories, people of our time realize that the outcome of their lives will depend on their own values, interests, choices, knowledge, actions, opportunities, etc. What they and their societies make of life depends upon them. At times this is interpreted in an individualistic sense,[3] at times in a way that incorporates the individual more within the larger world. Such historical consciousness is naturalistic when *the possibilities of life are thought to be those that are found here and now in history, and the meaning of life is exclusively what occurs now in history.* For many practically, and for some theoretically as well, *human beings are the total agents of their history, and life in history is the total horizon of meaning.* It is important then that one live with openness to options that enhance possibilities for oneself or one's society and that one seek to control one's own future or that of one's society rather than live with the sense that one's way of life is predetermined by some code imposed from elsewhere, such as tradition or religion. What one turns to for meaning in life is not traditional religion but the resources of the present. Other resources have taken over much of religion's traditional function, and the turn to them entails for many a certain religious indifference.[4] The fact of

[3]See R. Bellah, R. Madsen, W. Sullivan, A. Swidler, and S. Tipton, *Habits of the Heart. Individualism and Commitment in American Life* (Berkeley: Univ. of California Press, 1985) 75–81.

[4]See the statistics found in a survey conducted by CARA, the Center for Applied Research in the Apostolate (Washington, D.C.), in 1983. There has been a decline of adherence to institutional religion in the West. In practice, for example, there is just a small proportion of people in Western Europe who regularly attend Church (about 15%); there is a much larger percentage in the United States (about 40%; among Catholics, about 54%). There has been a decline in the global acceptance of the Church's teaching both in reference to morality (especially sexual morality and marriage) and beliefs. See John Coleman, "The Situation for Modern Faith," *Theological Studies* 39 (1978) 604, and Anton Weiler, "Theories about the Causes of Religious Indifference," in J.-P. Jossua and C. Geffré, eds., *Indifference to Religion* (*Concilium,* vol. 165, 1983) 26–37. While Coleman is nuanced on this issue, he ac-

evils in life also shows the urgency of depending upon human agency, initiative, intelligence, and response, rather than accepting evils as something that will be made good in another life. The modern history of discoveries in medicine and all areas of technology show us how this approach can significantly contribute to life. As mentioned earlier, however, in recent decades the hope of progress in history has been eroded for many, even in the United States; in fact, many are haunted by the dark possibilities of the future.[5] Thus one of the main pillars of modern culture, the theory or myth of progress, has collapsed.

This naturalistic understanding of what it means to be a person is itself dependent upon or expressed in a self-appropriation of what is of value to human beings and what is available to human knowledge. People pick up from their environment and their interpretation of their own experiences their views of what is of value to them and their society. What interests them, what answers specific needs are unquestionably their values. A consumerist society and a democracy that is constantly adjudicating conflicts of interest center the question of values around peoples' interests and specifically those that human agencies have it in their power to satisfy. We live in

knowledges that because of modern pluralism, people are less likely to accept as a whole what the Church understands as Christian belief in God or religion. Weiler suggests that a root of religious indifference is in part the fact that those who speak for religion are not succeeding in presenting conceptions of a general order of existence that seem sufficiently related to people's experience and interpretation of reality to be plausible and to result in motivation that supports religious attitudes. When, as in our time, a concept of reality is modeled on what is objective, scientific, and rationalistic, "universal metaphysical and religious concepts no longer have any value as reality" (p. 33). Also, religious functions are taken over by other agencies, and the Christian message is often regarded as irrelevant to our practical activity, which has a context so radically different from that of an earlier age (e.g., with modern technology, and problems of an international order). Also, "man appears to have lost control in the task of building up society . . . [and] people are asking [new questions] today because they are unsure of their own existence and are individually indifferent, believing that it 'simply does not matter'" (35–36).

[5]See *Redemptor Hominis* March 4, 1979 (Washington, D.C., USCC Publication Office) par. 15, where Pope John Paul II expresses his view that "The main chapter of the drama of present-day human existence in its broadest and universal dimensions" lies in the fact that men and women of our time are deeply afraid that what they produce (their technologies, their political, economic and social systems) can turn against them and destroy them. Thus there is now a sense of menace widespread in the world.

a society where patterns, goals, and values have become more rationalized than in traditional societies. Periodically, as in the 1960's, there is a reaction to these rationalized purposes and more attention is given to psychological needs; that is, there is a more widely held view that for the good life one needs enhancing human experiences as well as the external signs of success. This style of life fashioned from instrumental and expressive values has a feedback effect on the way men and women understand themselves, the horizon of their lives, the knowledge important and available to them, and God and religion. This tends to induce in many a fragmentation of life, a religious indifference and relativism. As we said, this widespread current approach to life does not leave everyone with greater confidence and optimism about the future. For some it has resulted in their taking religion seriously once more, at times in a rather fundamentalist sense. But in others, a deep source and effect of this discouragement about the present state of themselves and the world is a sense that little matters in the long run anyway.

Similarly, many people today appropriate what they mean by knowledge from their experience of knowledge in the physical and human sciences and the technologies that such knowledge has led to. Science today is the paradigm of knowledge; its methods and criteria are evident and universally accepted; its benefits are obvious. It merits trust; but the same cannot be said of some premodern forms of knowledge, such as religious symbols or myths and metaphysics. Religious symbols and myths are perhaps open to interpretations that can be adjusted to our present sense of self, but metaphysics seems to be empty knowledge when compared with science, and pretentious. Moreover, it has failed to gain acceptance; in fact, it has always been a cause of contention, and has been effectively critiqued by major modern philosophers, such as Immanuel Kant. Some philosophers have radicalized the modern critique of knowledge and objective human values to the extent that they consider knowledge to be only assertions within a particular historical context, and base human choices wholly on pragmatism. This viewpoint is called at times "post-modernism."[6]

[6]See William Dean, *History Making History. The New Historicism in American*

These attitudes common today in the areas of human values and human knowledge mutually corroborate and support one another, and the views of philosophers that justify them have spread to large numbers of people who have never read the philosophers.[7] *Thus an effective theological mediation of Christian belief in God must evaluate whether our contemporary historical consciousness justifies such a naturalistic sense of self, human values and human knowledge, or rather manifests a self, human values and human knowledge that are transcendent though frequently obscured and even denied.*
A second root of the present widespread disbelief sketched earlier is the image many people have of God. It seems to many that the Christian God has been presented as a judge, a transcendent personal being modeled on the male of the human species who is somewhat deterministic and has perhaps written the text of history beforehand, who is arbitrary and interferes with human autonomy. To these same people this seems at best to be a God whom people have constructed as a myth

*Religious Thought* (Albany: State Univ. of New York Press, 1988) 6. According to him post-modernism is an accentuation of an earlier naturalism; it means a cultural sensibility that is based on the view that "One experiences only what can be experienced within historical time and space: (1) not foundations beyond history; (2) not realities that can be known, without bias, as objective correlatives; and (3) not universal subjective characteristics, inherent in all persons." In this perspective one interprets history in the past and, by creative imagination, projects one's own or society's future with the guidance of pragmatism.
Some see post-modernism in a more positive vein, namely as a period when the negative fruits of the course of the modern history of philosophy have been revealed in the loss of the object and the loss of the subject, when the confidence of the man of the Enlightenment has been overturned, when we are living in a larger world in which European culture is recognized as simply one culture, and so in a period that calls us to discover norms for judgment and behavior in a world more complex than before. See Emerich Coreth, "Metaphysik am Ende der Neuzeit?", an address delivered at an International Symposium on Metaphysics, Culture and Morality in Taiwan, December 1988, and also found in *The Asian Journal of Philosophy* 2 (1989). Also see *Communio* 17 (1990) Summer Issue, devoted to "Christianity and the Question of Postmodernity."

[7] For studies of the erosion of belief in God in modern times, see, e.g., H. De Lubac, *The Drama of Atheist Humanism* (New York: Sheed and Ward, 1950); James Collins, *God in Modern Philosophy* (Chicago: Regnery, 1959); C. Fabro, *God in Exile: Modern Atheism* (Westminster, Md.: Newman, 1968); H. Kung, *Does God Exist? An Answer for Today* (New York: Doubleday, 1980); Michael Buckley, *At the Origins of Modern Atheism* (New Haven: Yale Univ. Press, 1987); and Michael Buckley, "Experience and Culture: A Point of Departure for American Atheism," *Theological Studies* 50 (1989) 443–465.

appropriate to a previous culture; at worst it may be a way that religious leaders have of manipulating people through their fears. God as interpreted by theology influenced by classical metaphysics was said to be immutable and impassible. It was said that while creatures have a real relation to God, God does not have a real relation to them, and is not affected by what they do or do not do. In this view, God does not seem to have much interest in what interests human beings; thus, it is thought that belief in God tends to detract from the value of this world and divert people from the genuine possibilities and problems of life. Also, there have been so many images of God in history—many people are now aware of those in Eastern religions—that the Christian view of God's love and presence loses authority. Moreover, God seems to many, as we stated earlier, to be absent from modern life; people do not experience him or if they do, it is in many cases as a threat and negative principle. The experiences in the twentieth century of massive evils have contributed to the erosion of many people's belief in God's beneficent action in history. The classical Christian understanding of God does not seem to accord with people's experience in our time. Thus there have been philosophers, theologians, novelists, and dramatists in our time who have proclaimed the death of God.[8] From this we see another issue that it is very important to address in a critical evaluation of the meaning and grounds of Christian belief in God: *What is the Christian understanding of God, and how does that relate to the modern experience of history and to views of the Ultimate found in world religions? How does what Christians believe God offers us through Jesus Christ relate to the modern search for meaning in history?* There is a certain correlation between anthropology and our understanding of God and Jesus Christ.

[8]On Nietzsche and the death of God, see K. Löwith, *From Hegel to Nietzsche. The Revolution in Nineteenth-Century Thought* (New York: Doubleday, 1964) 188f, 322, 333, 355f; and W. Kasper, *The God of Jesus Christ* (New York: Crossroad, 1984) 39–46. On images of chaos, absurdity, and waiting for God in modern drama, see Nelvin Vos, *The Great Pendulum of Becoming. Images in Modern Drama* (Grand Rapids: Eerdmans, 1980). See Walker Percy's novels for a perspective on how a contemporary sense of meaninglessness can lead to a religious awakening. For a recent study of religious themes in contemporary literature, see Robert Detweiler, *Breaking the Fall. Religious Readings of Contemporary Fiction* (San Francisco, Harper & Row, 1989).

Where this correlation is denied, there is an erosion of belief. Our understanding of humanity is critiqued by the Christian understanding of God and Jesus, and this understanding of God and Jesus must not be articulated only in terms of the cultural resources of a previous age.

## II. The Task of Foundational Theology

From this analysis of the present situation of disbelief, we conclude that we must critically reflect on whether from our modern historical consciousness we can validly appropriate our own transcendence in values and knowledge as essential to us as human beings, and whether the Christian understanding of God and Jesus Christ is indeed part of a valid appropriation of ourselves in our time and necessary for our living in accord with who we are, or belief in God and Jesus Christ is opposed to human reason and experience.

But more specifically, what does a theological mediation of belief in God through Jesus Christ involve? "Mediation" commonly means a process of bringing initially opposed parties to an agreement. It is a word used in Scripture for the action of Jesus reconciling humanity to God through his suffering, death and resurrection (see 1 Tim 2:5; Heb 9:15; 12:24). He was particularly able to do this because as both man and God he was identified with both parties. He was God's love for human beings, and he was humanity's representative in loving obedience to God.

What is theological mediation in foundational theology? A fuller analysis of this is properly found in a later section in foundational theology—the section that reflects critically on what theology is, and comes after a treatment of the norm of Christian faith. But in a preliminary manner, we must indicate some of the characteristics of such mediation here. In this mediation, we identify ourselves both with Christian faith and the contemporary world. We recognize that in our time there is for many people a radical opposition between their interpretation of experience and Christianity. Theologians are optimally those who are both fully Christian and fully contemporary. Thus they can identify with each party in this dispute, for they experience and value both within themselves. We distinguish our approach then from a fundamentalist reassertion of Christianity as it was articulated in some past period of the Church, as though that is fully sufficient for our own time. We similarly distinguish our approach from one that accepts uncritically an interpretation of our contemporary historical consciousness that is naturalistic or that is found to be incompatible with the full Christian message about God and Christ.

There are many forms of mediation of belief in our time. The proclamation of the gospel fulfills this function in many forms, e.g., in the liturgy, art, a Christian life, political and professional life, action for justice and peace, works of mercy, etc. Mediation of belief can also take place in many different academic studies, such as philosophy of religion, psychology of religion, anthropology, or sociology, when these studies seek to disengage their field from unjustified anti-Christian bias and examine religion and Christianity without such presuppositions.

What then is a specifically theological mediation of belief? Its function, as I understand it, is to reflect critically on the meaning of and grounds for belief in God through Jesus Christ in our time. It uses specifically Christian norms of faith to identify what it is evaluating—namely faith in God through Jesus Christ. That is, it takes Scripture and tradition as normative when it indicates what faith is, and who God is, and what the relevance of faith in God is to human life. We take this in foundational theology not as sufficient evidence that faith in God is true, but as an identification of what we are critically evaluating when we are evaluating the adequacy of the grounds we have for such faith and its meaning, and as an answer to some distorted interpretations of belief in God and its implications for practical life. Thus foundational theology has to be faithful to the Christian proclamation or message, though this fidelity does not prevent us from reinterpreting the Christian message for our time.

Also, such mediation takes the difficulties experienced with this faith seriously, and dialogues with them in an honest way on their own level. This involves using disciplines other than theology in a way that is genuinely faithful to their intrinsic demands, but within a critical theological reflection. We will

clarify what this effort involves when in the next chapter we examine and evaluate prominent twentieth-century theological
ways of mediating the faith.

The word "theology" has been traditionally defined as "faith
seeking understanding" (*fides quaerens intellectum*), and the
theologian has traditionally been a believer. Thus I think that
foundational theology is more properly the function of a believer who reflects critically on this belief than of a non-
believer. This is not to say that the nonbeliever cannot
fruitfully reflect on such belief (e.g., in religious studies, in philosophy of religion), or that the believer's reflection is auto-
matically critical and adequate. But it is to say that a genuine
theological mediation of belief in our time must be an adequate expression of both Christian belief and the modern
situation.[9]

Such a task can be endless, and so we have to restrict it to
some aspects of Christian faith and contemporary difficulties
with faith that we understand as central. As we will indicate
and defend in the next chapter from the perspective of the varied models of theological mediation of faith prominent in our
time, we believe that this task involves a hermeneutical retrieval of the Christian belief, a critical reappropriation of our
human transcendence and need, and a critical evaluation of
grounds of faith and the relevance or transformative implications of faith. We believe that this task should have two stages:
first (the task of the bulk of this book) a critical evaluation of
our belief in God, and then (the task of what we have called the
second part of foundational theology) a critical evaluation of
belief in God through Jesus Christ. Neither of these involves a
treatment of the Trinity as such, since this is found in another
section of theology. However, the theologian engages in the
task of foundational theology from an acceptance of the whole
of Christian faith. A hermeneutical retrieval of faith in God
means that we interpret it in a way that is faithful to Christian
understanding and yet critical of certain presentations of it

---

[9]We should note that our understanding of foundational theology as mediation of
faith is not to be identified with the particular understanding of the nineteenth- and
twentieth-century liberal tradition, as studied, for example, in John P. Clayton, *The
Concept of Correlation. Paul Tillich and the Possibility of a Mediating Theology*
(New York: Walter de Gruyter, 1980).

that identify it unnecessarily with an interpretation of a past age and thus distance it from the present. We first ask whether such belief is counter to what is authentically part of modern historical consciousness. Second, we ask whether a critical evaluation of our human self, human values, and human knowledge in our present age shows a transcendence that can be denied only at the expense of being dishonest to ourselves and our societies. In other words, we ask whether our modern experience of human agency and creativity in history and human knowledge manifest our transcendence or show that such transcendence was proper to the conditions of a pre-modern age, and whether this experience reveals sufficiently our need for a salvation from outside ourselves. Third, we ask whether faith in God is critically grounded so that it is a reasonable human act, and whether it is transformative for individual and society in our shrinking world so that it liberates men and women to seek their genuine human fulfillment. Is it reasonable and fulfilling and liberating for us as human beings to believe in God as a personal being who is deeply concerned for human beings and their history? Is Christian language about God to this effect vindicated? The above description includes what we understand both the first and second parts of foundational theology to treat. What we call the first part is by no means an adequate expression of Christian belief and its relevance; but an adequate expression of such belief, we contend, is not possible without this. If we do not accept the lesser dimensions of God's revelation of himself, it is unlikely indeed that we can accept and understand the greater revelation of himself that he has offered us (see John 3:12).

# 2

# Models for Theological Mediation of Christian Belief in God

Our purpose in this chapter is to specify more fully the approach to mediating faith in God through Jesus Christ in our time that we sketched in the last chapter, compare it with some other models currently used, and thereby evaluate it as a theological model. Our conclusion will be that our approach is similar to a model implicit in the teaching of Vatican II and that it is more adequate than alternative models prominent in the twentieth century. The later chapters of this work will critically evaluate the meaning and foundations of faith in God in accord with this model.

We will (1) recall briefly an opposition between models that are dialogical, that is, which give emphasis to reason and experience, and a model that is dialectical, that is, which gives emphasis to Scripture and hermeneutics; (2) present a model that is implicit in the approach of Vatican II in its reflection on the meaning and grounds of faith for our time—a model that, we will suggest, integrates the major concerns of the earlier models; and (3) recall some models that agree with one another against earlier models in emphasizing process or history, but are mutually opposed in their preference for mediating faith by appealing either to rational objectivity or the transformative power of Christian belief in practical concerns of the social, economic, and political order. Here we will also give brief attention to certain attempts to rearticulate who God is in view of modern feminist concerns, our ecological crisis, and world religions. A full identification and use of the model we propose can only be found in the chapters that follow.

Our treatment of models in this chapter is introductory; we treat individual theologians only as examples of models; our study is no substitute for an adequate analysis of these theologies that may be found elsewhere. We do not propose that these are the only models available, but that they are prominent models in our century. We are attempting no more than a sketch of the theologians' orientations as these relate to our theme. Our analyses may be brief because they are rather commonly accepted interpretations of these theologians; and whether one accepts our sketch of a theologian or even of Vatican II as faithful or not, one can perhaps accept it as a possible model. We acknowledge that because of our brevity, we may appear in some instances to oversimplify. We apologize for this beforehand, but ask forbearance because of the help this gives us to situate our own approach.

# I. Dialogical Versus Dialectical Models

During the first half of the twentieth century there was a rather clear distinction between Catholic and Protestant approaches to the question of the theological mediation of belief in God. Each of these views was in conversation with earlier views proposed in its own tradition. The major issue that divided prominent theologians during this period concerning the way to mediate theologically the Christian faith was how specifically Christian revelation on the one hand and knowledge of God from elsewhere on the other (e.g., natural theology or a general revelation or religious experience) were related to one another. The Catholics tended to give emphasis to problems of philosophy in their efforts, and the Protestant models we shall look at tended to focus on interpretation of Scripture.

## 1. Dialogical Models, the Use of Reason and Experience.

The Catholic attempts to mediate Christian faith in God during this period followed Vatican I and the conflict between Catholic Modernists and the Church.

The First Vatican Council (1869–1870) had as part of its task to examine the relation between faith and reason in the context of theological tendencies to exalt faith at the expense of reason or reason at the expense of faith. Among its responses to this problem, the Church taught on the powers and limits of reason, the primacy of faith, the compatibility between the two, and the service each could give to the other. It is faith in God's supernatural revelation that is the beginning of salvation; but there are foundations for accepting this faith, since the existence of God "can be known with certainty from created things by the natural light of human reason."[1] Moreover, while faith is a gift of grace and a virtue by which, with the help of the Holy Spirit, we freely give full obedience of mind and will to God through believing what he has revealed, this faith is reasonable since God has offered us external evidence for his revelation, such as miracles and prophecies and indeed the sign of the Church itself, constituted through its holiness and fruitfulness in good works.

A couple of decades after Vatican I, some Catholics attempted to reinterpret the origins of Christian faith to accord with the findings of the historical-critical method as understood at the time or with a pragmatic interpretation of religious truth. In his encyclical *Pascendi* (1907), Pope Pius X condemned this position, called Modernism, as resting on a subjectivist interpretation of the origins of Christian revelation and thus as in opposition to Vatican I.[2] Modernism was stamped out in the Church, but not without dampening the creative theological and biblical research necessary to face the genuine difficulties that modernity posed to Christian faith. We will examine two models of foundational theology current among Catholic theologians in the twentieth century prior to

[1]Denzinger, H. and A. Schönmetzer, eds., *Enchiridion Symbolorum* (35th ed., Freiburg: Herder, 1973) 3004 (henceforward referred to as Denzinger). Also see H.-J. Pottmeyer, *Der Glaube vor dem Anspruch der Wissenshaft* (Vienna: Herder, 1968); G. McCool, *Catholic Theology in the Nineteenth Century. The Question for a Unitary Method* (New York: Seabury, 1977), ch. 10, "*Dei Filius* and *Aeterni Patris*," 216 ff.

[2]See for *Pascendi,* Denzinger 3475 ff. On the modernists see John Ratte, *Three Modernists* (New York: Sheed and Ward, 1967), and Gabriel Daly, *Transcendence and Immanence. A Study in Catholic Modernism and Integralism* (Oxford: Clarendon Press, 1980).

Vatican II, and then briefly evaluate them as foundational theologies.

The position dominant among Catholic theologians before Vatican II, Neo-Scholasticism, was one that was in strict continuity with Vatican I and the anti-Modernist documents of the Church. The concern of this theology was to defend the *objectivity* of the grounds for faith. Most manuals of theology for Catholic seminaries at this time were written from this perspective; they made great use of the philosophy of Thomas Aquinas, though they interpreted it in differing ways. If we look to these authors (e.g., R. Garrigou-Lagrange, O.P., and M. Nicolau, S.J.[3] ), we find them treating the question of the existence of God in the tract on "the One and Triune God" and the question of religion and revelation in apologetics. They show that, as Vatican I asserted, the existence of God can be known from creation; and for this they depend primarily on Thomas' five ways and developments of them. The understanding of God that emerges is similarly in continuity with that of Thomas. Humanity has a responsibility to render religious honor and service to God. God has in fact revealed himself through Jesus Christ in a definitive way, as can be shown by arguments available to reason, such as those that are based on the historical character of the Gospel texts; the testimonies that God has given to the validity of Jesus' claims through the miracles that he performed, particularly the resurrection; his personality and fulfillment of prophesies; and the fruitfulness in sanctity and good works found in the Church he established. Thus we have an obligation to believe in what he taught and in him. The problem primarily addressed here is the modern philosophical contention that we cannot know the existence of God or the fact of his revelation through Jesus Christ. Conse-

[3]See, for example, R. Garrigou-Lagrange, O.P., *The One God,* trans. Bede Rose, O.S.B. (St. Louis: Herder, 1943), and *God. His Existence and His Nature. A Thomistic Solution of Certain Agnostic Antinomies.* 2 volumes, trans. from the fifth French edition, Bede Rose, O.S.B. (St. Louis: Herder, 1934–1936). Also see M. Nicolau, I. Salaverri, and others, *Sacrae theologiae summa.* 4 volumes (Madrid: Biblioteca de Autores Cristianos, 1952–1953). Also see Francis Schüssler Fiorenza, *Foundational Theology. Jesus and the Church* (New York: Crossroad, 1984) chapter 1 for an analysis of manualist theology and Rahner on the resurrection in foundational theology.

quently, the understanding of faith in God emphasizes faith as intellectual acceptance of what God has revealed.

There were Catholic theologians who reacted against what they viewed as the excessively intellectual and objective character of this approach. This alternative model emphasized the *intrinsic meaning of Christian revelation and human subjectivity.* We shall recall Karl Rahner's (1904–1984) position to exemplify this model, although there were many others who contributed to this approach (e.g., M. Blondel, R. Maréchal, A. Gardeil, M. D. Chenu, P. Rousselot, H. de Lubac, H. Bouillard, J. Daniélou, and, more parallel to Rahner's efforts, B. Lonergan).[4]

Rahner broke with the emphasis on the objective grounds for faith and centered his attention on developing an anthropology that shows human beings to be "spirit in the world," dynamically oriented toward the Absolute or God. This allowed him to show the intrinsic meaning of God's revelation to us as human. He wanted to answer the questions the Modernists posed and for this purpose analysed human subjectivity by a reinterpretation of Thomas Aquinas' view on the human knowledge of being. This reinterpretation fit his larger purpose, for it offered him a way to show that we are oriented to God and to manifest how God reveals himself to all human beings.

In his book, *Spirit in the World,*[5] Rahner argues for the possibility of metaphysics by a transcendental method. That is, he begins with the fact of our knowledge and shows that the condition of the possibility of our knowledge is an implicit knowledge of the Absolute, and thus that metaphysics is possible. More specifically, he begins (in a way that reflects some dependence on Martin Heidegger) with the fact that the human person questions and indeed must question about being, "if he wants *to be* at all."[6] What are the conditions under which the question of being occurs to us? Of course, it depends in part on sense and in-

---

[4]For a brief treatment of many of these men, see Avery Dulles, *Revelation Theology. A History* (New York: Herder and Herder, 1969). Also see, on Rousselot, B. Pottier, S.J., "Les Yeux de la foi après Vatican II," *NRT* 106 (1984) 177–203.

[5]See K. Rahner, *Spirit in the World,* trans. W. Dych from the second edition (New York: Herder and Herder, 1968); the first edition was published in 1939.

[6]Ibid., 57–58.

tellectual knowledge of the world mediated through the senses, for all knowledge involves a turn to the physical world through the phantasm. But furthermore, this question is grounded on the fact that being is accessible to us as something questionable and that we ourselves exist as a question about being.[7] Indeed, the question presupposes that "man is already at the goal when he begins, since he must already know of being in its totality if he asks about it."[8] We are not the goal of our own drive, however, for we question. Nor can this knowledge of being derive properly from what is delivered through sense, imagination, and abstraction since that is limited to the world of space and time. Rather, being is present to us through our self-presence: "Knowing is the being present-to-self of being, and this being-present-to-self is the being of the existent. . . . If being is primarily presence-to-self, then the real and original object of a knowing being is that with which it originally is, itself."[9] The preapprehension of being or the Absolute mediated by self-presence is, we should note, not an intuition of absolute being, nor conceptual knowledge, nor knowledge of absolute being as an object. Rather it is knowledge that is implicit and co-given with our knowledge of the world. Metaphysics treats being as an object, but this primordial knowledge of being is non-conceptual and apophatic.

In his later book, *Hearers of the Word,* Rahner elaborated further on our dynamic orientation to the Absolute. This self-affirmation that mediates our knowledge of God is an affirmation of our own contingency, and indeed a free affirmation of our contingency. God is, then, known as the condition for the possibility of our affirmation of our contingency. Since this is a free human act, God is himself known as the free subject who is the ground of our contingency.[10] Thus we stand before a God who is free.

[7]See ibid.

[8]Ibid., 61.

[9]Ibid., 69, 75.

[10]K. Rahner, *Hearers of the Word,* trans. M. Richards (New York: Herder and Herder, 1969) 77–78. This is a translation of the second edition of this work; the first edition was published in 1941; the second edition was, at Rahner's request, prepared by J. Metz and published in 1963.

This allows Rahner to explain how God reveals himself to all human beings. That God does so is implied in the Christian message that God wants all to be saved. Since salvation depends upon our response to God's revelation through faith, God must then reveal himself to all men and women. In the present dispensation God orients all of us to a supernatural destiny through what Rahner calls the "supernatural existential," and he gives us all a transcendental revelation of himself that evokes the human being's dynamic movement toward God—a revelation that is non-conceptual, apophatic, and non-objective. All are called to give themselves in response to this by a faith that is a surrender and commitment. Those who present the historical Christian revelation to people for acceptance should assume that those to whom they are speaking have already received this transcendental revelation and even believed it. What is needed is to bring people to an acceptance of categorical revelation through categorical faith—i.e., revelation expressed in an historical mediation. Perhaps the greatest difficulty with this for modern men and women is the "scandal of particularity," that is, that God has offered his definitive salvation and revelation through Jesus, who lived at a particular time and in a particular place. We can mediate this revelation appropriately by showing that men and women have implicitly accepted categorical revelation in accepting transcendental revelation. The problem then is to present the Christian mystery in its relation to human experience and the quest for being; this is the context of its meaning and relevance.[11]

We can see opposition between the "manualists" and Rahner on the question of how we theologically mediate Christian belief in God. Both agree that dialogue is important so that the faith can be presented in a way that will call forth a response of faith that is free and reasonable. Both agree that God's manifestation of himself in the world in a way not formally identified with Christian revelation allows this dialogue, for through this manifestation we can have some knowledge of

[11]See K. Rahner, *Foundations of Christian Faith,* trans. W. V. Dych (New York: Crossroad, 1978) 19 ff., 31 ff., 51 ff. I should note here that Rahner also accepts an historical mediation of the faith, e.g., that Jesus founded Church, though this is not central for him. See Fiorenza, *Foundational Theology, 18.*

God. Both agree that the philosophy of Thomas Aquinas helps
to articulate this manifestation of God and our response. But
they differ on how God manifests himself—the manualists
emphasizing the physical world that reflects God, its maker,
and Rahner emphasizing the human dynamic orientation toward the Absolute as mediating knowledge of God. And they
differ on how they mediate Christian faith—the manualists
emphasizing the objective evidence for the existence of God
and the fact of revelation, and Rahner emphasizing God and
the Christian message as the fulfillment of the dynamism that
constitutes us as spirit in the world. Moreover, the manualists
understand human knowledge as more rational in character
and Rahner understands it as more experiential and dependent on love. We will suggest later that the approach offered by
Vatican II tends to overcome this dichotomy by including it
within a more integrative way of mediating Christian faith.
But here we will limit ourselves to noting that neither of these
approaches seems adequately to address the central difficulties
our contemporaries have with faith in God. As we saw in the
first chapter, men and women today are in search for meaning
within a dramatically changing culture and society. The predominantly objective approach of the manualists is not adequately in touch with this concern, and it results in a rather
extrinsicist defense of Christian faith; also, it does not sufficiently accept modern critical studies of the Gospels. Rahner's
approach is helpful here insofar as he places the question of
meaning first, but it does seem that his view—and particularly
his early view—is more in contact with an existentialist understanding of the individual than with people formed by modern
historical consciousness.

## 2. Dialectical Model, Scripture and Hermeneutics

The early and mid-twentieth-century Protestant theologians
took their positions on the issues of foundational theology
largely through the way they reacted to Karl Barth. The tradition in which Barth is to be understood takes its point of departure, in a sense, in Friedrich Schleiermacher (1768–1834),
whom Barth called the father of modern theology. Without at-

tempting here to do justice to Schleiermacher, we should at least say that he attempted to develop an apologetic addressed to the cultured despisers of Christianity. Accepting Kant's strictures against the validity of speculative arguments for the existence of God, he began his apologetic with an interpretation of religion as a feeling that emerges from an immediate self-consciousness: "The sum total of religion is to feel that, in its highest unity, all that moves us in feeling is one . . . to feel, that is to say, that our being and living is a being and living in and through God."[12] This feeling is a part of being human, and Schleiermacher urged those who would be fully human to recognize that religion is preeminently necessary for this. Within this approach he argued for monotheism over polytheism and for Christianity over other forms of monotheism, for on the model and through the agency of Jesus we are brought from a sense of alienation or distance from God to a sense of communion with him. In Jesus this sense of communion was brought to a higher degree than in any other human being. Thus God, for Schleiermacher, is made known to humankind basically through this sense of total dependence, and is revealed through this experience not primarily as the maker of the physical world but as the object and source of this inner religious experience. This approach was articulated in differing ways and with differing degrees of importance ascribed to the historical Scriptures by Protestant liberalism in the nineteenth and early twentieth century.

It was Karl Barth (1886–1968) above all who broke the hold that this liberalism had on much of Protestant theology. Initially, he too was a liberal; but the difficulty he had in preaching this liberal message from the pulpit, the experience of human beings' inhumanity in the First World War, and the evidence biblical scholars (especially Johannes Weiss and Albert Schweitzer) gave of how distant the historical Jesus was from his liberal interpreters led him to react forcefully against liberalism, beginning especially with the second edition of his commentary on Paul's Epistle to the Romans, published in 1922. His major reaction to liberalism and to Catholicism (largely

---

[12]F. Schleiermacher, *On Religion: Speeches to Its Cultured Despisers,* trans. J. Oman (New York: Harper Torchbooks, 1958) 49–50.

under the influence of Sören Kierkegaard initially) was his emphasis on God as the Totally Other and his view that their approaches subordinated Christian revelation to "religion" and its criteria. There is no way to knowledge of God through the physical world or from human experience; the only knowledge we have of God is that which he reveals through Jesus Christ. Even here, God is not seen directly in the earthly Jesus; rather God reveals himself through his act beyond history in raising Jesus from the dead: "Jesus has been . . . declared to be the Son of God with power, according to the Holy Spirit, through the resurrection from the dead. . . . The Resurrection is the revelation: the disclosing of Jesus as the Christ, the appearing of God, and the apprehending of God in Jesus. . . In the resurrection the new world of the Holy Spirit touches the old world of the flesh, but touches it as a tangent touches a circle, that is, without touching it."[13] We are shown to be sinners by Christ's death, and by Christ's death and resurrection we are offered justification. Revelation seeks to evoke faith or trust in the salvation offered us.

Barth proclaims this by a dialectical theology, i.e., one that witnesses to God as wholly other through its affirmations and denials. In Christ God reveals but also veils himself, and our response is not to possess revelation as an object but to believe through the miracle of grace. Barth accepts the Bible as radically human and fallible; the Bible is a human word and the Word of God only so far as God lets it be his Word, and this latter can be perceived only through grace.

The only source of knowledge of God is then his revelation through Jesus Christ. What is necessary to evoke people's faith is not an apologetic, but rather their decision, in response to God's revelation through Christ, to acknowledge themselves as sinners and as saved. There is no natural theology even as a preparation for revelation and its acceptance. God's revelation "comes to us as a *Novum* which, when it becomes an object for us, we cannot incorporate in the series of our other objects,

[13]K. Barth, *A Shorter Commentary on Romans* (Richmond: John Knox, 1959) 29–30. Also see James Livingston, *Modern Christian Thought. From the Enlightenment to Vatican II* (New York: Macmillan, 1971) 324–342, and Hans Urs von Balthasar, *The Theology of Karl Barth* (New York: Anchor Books, 1972).

cannot compare with them, cannot deduce from their context, cannot regard as analogous with them. It comes to us as a datum with no point of connexion *(Anknupfungspunkt)* with any other previous datum."[14]

Thus Barth rejects the analogy of being because he holds that it subsumes God and creatures under some larger category. Also it involves a "splitting up of the concept of God and hand and hand with it the abstraction from the real work and activity of God in favour of a general being of God . . . which means the introduction of a foreign god into the sphere of the Church."[15] Natural theology results in religion, which is human pride, for it is an attempt to know God and attain salvation by human efforts. There is an opposition between revelation and religion. We can speak of Christianity as "true religion" only as we speak of a person as a "justified sinner"; that is, religion is here turned to its opposite through the grace of Jesus Christ.

Later, Barth did accept a kind of analogy, but an analogy of faith. There is such a corruption in our intellects and words as a result of sin that our human words can apply to God only when God takes them in our profession of faith and restores them as part of his creation and reestablishes their relation to him. Because the Word becomes man in time, all creation is thereby made good. Jesus Christ is the real ground of creation. As von Balthasar writes:

> For Barth, human nature derives from that primeval grace: it can be understood and appreciated only in the light of that grace. So too, reason derives from God's self-revelation in Jesus Christ; if it is viewed apart from its origin there, it cannot be understood correctly. That is why Barth rejects the position of Catholic theology regarding reason. To preserve the notion of grace in all its purity, Catholic theology maintains that reason can exist and be understood even without faith. Barth regards this as an absurd position because it overlooks real beings to examine nonexistent possibilities. It

[14]Barth, *Church Dogmatics,* ed. G. W. Bromily and T. F. Torrance, trans. G. W. Bromily and others (Edinburgh, T. & T. Clark, 1959–1969) I, 2, 172.

[15]Barth, *Church Dogmatics* II, 1, 84.

is also a shameless position because it tries to prove that something has meaning apart from grace, when in fact it only has meaning within the framework of grace. . . .

Man's understanding of truth derives wholly from God's gratuitous self-revelation in his Word. . . . What he [Barth] does deny, unfortunately, is that God's revelation in nature is truly *natural,* that it is an inherent property of nature rather than a supernatural gift.[16]

A number of Protestant theologians who basically agreed with Barth reasserted the need for an apologetics (not a natural theology) and even the existence of what can be called a general revelation, of which Christian revelation was a fulfillment. For example, Rudolf Bultmann (1884–1974), though primarily a biblical scholar, had a long debate with Barth on this question. He acknowledged that revelation was God's act and initiative and that it occurred through Christian proclamation and was known only in faith. However, the presentation of this message to people supposes some *preunderstanding* on their part if it is to have any hope of entering into their lives. There must be a question in their lives to which the Christian proclamation is an answer, if they are to accept it. Bultmann thought that this question was articulated with a particular appropriateness in the twentieth century by Martin Heidegger in his book *Being and Time,* because this book showed human beings as oriented toward authenticity in living and it showed what stands in the way of this orientation. The Christian proclamation in effect gives those who believe in what it says about God's love the possibility of living authentically according to their possibilities—something that outside belief they cannot do. Bultmann thought that revelation occurs through the actual Christian proclamation rather than through the life of Jesus himself, of which we can, in any case, know virtually

---

[16]Von Balthasar, 123–124. Barth did qualify (*CD,* I, 2, p. 82) his earlier rejection of analogy of being, on the condition that it be considered totally subordinate to an analogy of faith. And later (*CD,* IV, 3, 69), he acknowledged there were lights other than Christ (e.g., in creation). It is only *after* believing in Christ that we can claim this and use these lights. His defense of the uniqueness of God, that is, as he who is revealed by Jesus Christ, made him very hesitant to allow any degree of autonomy to human reason or to religions other than Christianity.

nothing with assurance because of the character of the Gospels.

Bultmann also thought that to get to the core of the Christian proclamation we needed a process of demythologizing. The Christian message was presented in an ancient mythology that was cosmic (i.e., spoke of a three-storied universe, physical miracles, resurrection as an historical act) and that we can no longer accept. But this is not essential to the scriptural message:

> The real purpose of myth is not to present an objective picture of the world as it is, but to express man's understanding of himself in the world in which he lives. Myth should be interpreted not cosmologically, but anthropologically, or better still, existentially. . . . Myth is an expression of man's conviction that the origin and purpose of the world in which he lives are to be sought not within it but beyond it—that is, beyond the realm of known and tangible reality—and that this realm is perpetually dominated and menaced by those mysterious powers which are its source and limit. Myth is also an expression of man's awareness that he is not lord of his own being. It expresses his sense of dependence not only within the visible world, but more especially on those forces which hold sway beyond the confines of the known. Finally, myth expresses man's belief that in this state of dependence he can be delivered from the forces within the visible world.[17]

This demythologizing is legitimate and necessary because religious language is the "objectification of understanding,"[18] as poetic language is. The human spirit objectifies itself in language, and thus the process of demythologizing enables one to discover the kernel of the saving message without the husks that are non-essential and, in our time, obstacles to belief.

In conclusion of this brief summary of dialogical and dialectical models for mediating faith in God, we can first note that

[17]R. Bultmann, "New Testament and Mythology," in *Kerygma and Myth* (London: SPCK, 1960) 10–11.

[18]James Robinson, "Hermeneutic since Barth", in J. Robinson and John Cobb, Jr., eds., *The New Hermeneutic* (New York: Harper and Row, 1964) 37.

Barth's and Bultmann's ways of mediating the Christian faith begin with Scripture (though not uninfluenced by philosophies) and the question between them is a hermeneutical one, that is, the question of how one interprets Scripture. The Neo-Scholastics' and Rahner's ways of mediating faith begin with philosophy (though within a Christian context of faith) and the question between them is largely how one knows God. Barth and Bultmann both accept the fact that the modern world is largely naturalistic. From this common position, Barth simply dialectically presents the Christian faith as proclamation, asserting that its acceptance is a matter of conversion and decision rather than of an apologetic. Counter to this, Neo-liberal Protestant theologians like Bultmann and Paul Tillich seek to mediate faith through a dialogue with modern men and women on bases they can accept antecedent to their acceptance of Christian faith; but, I submit, they tend to accept only what is revealed by common human experience and not what is revealed through historical acts and words that are specifically Christian. We shall suggest that dialectic has no meaning if it does not occur in the context of dialogue, whereas dialogue without dialectic, as in Bultmann's model, does become reductionistic.

A second hermeneutical issue emerges here; it is present in the conflict between Barth and Bultmann, but also between Bultmann and the more objective speech about God found in Neo-Scholastic theology and much interpretation of Scripture. Is religious talk and specifically scriptural language to be taken objectively or non-objectively? That is, is it to be taken as directly saying something about God as agent or as expressive of an internal religious experience and only indirectly and metaphorically about God? On this issue depends our understanding of God and the whole Christian message. In this respect, we shall argue later that Bultmann's model, while in part recapturing the poetic character of much scriptural language, loses the distinctively Judaeo-Christian character of Scripture in that he does not relate this language to God's words and deeds through Jesus Christ.

Another issue is contained in the contrast between the way that Catholic apologetics used the Gospels as historical documents and Barth's and Bultmann's mediating faith without such reliance, because of the problems that the historical-critical approach to Scripture raised and because they both tended to bypass conflicts with the modern scientific view of the world, and to seek a way that was not vulnerable to the historical-critical method. We may add that neither Barth's nor Bultmann's model seem sufficiently aware of the main difficulties with faith posed by men and women in our time as we analysed them above: namely, those that derive from their fundamental need—whether optimistic or pessimistic—to make a future for themselves and their societies in history in a culture dominated by technology and science. Both of them seem to have retreated from history; the early Barth considered history the area of meaninglessness, and Bultmann isolated the human person's encounter with God from history and history's future. Some interpreters of twentieth-century theology have held that the remoteness and irrelevance in Barth's God and the lack of transcendence in Bultmann's God both contributed to the short-lived "Death of God" theology in the 1960's.

Vatican II, we shall suggest, presents a model of mediating faith that preserves the primacy of Scripture's view of God, dialogues with modern men and women on their own level, seeks to integrate reason and experience, and defends the historical value of the Gospels while accepting an understanding of them as proclamations of faith.


## II. Vatican II and Mediation of Belief in God

How did Vatican II go about offering meaning and grounds for our belief in God appropriate for our time, and specifically for our belief in God through Jesus Christ? Both the Catholic and the non-Catholic have an interest in this question. It is primarily the Church's views on these issues that the theological student would like to know and evaluate, and so it is these views we shall try to identify here, though we shall do this very summarily because the texts are so widely available.

The council presented elements of the meaning of and grounds for belief in God through Jesus Christ in a way appropriate for a council: as part of its proclamation of the Christian message for our time in accord with its goal of *aggiornamento.* In seeking to identify these particular elements, we are abstracting a part of its teaching from the whole. Indeed, the problem of belief and unbelief in the world today affected everything that the council did. All of the rearticulations of the Church's message and reforms of its life were elements of its attempt to present the meaning of and grounds for Christian faith in God, for the best apologetic for today is found in a truly Christian life and theological articulation of the Christian message appropriate for our time. But most of the council's work must be viewed as context rather than text for our present interest. The one aspect of this context we recall is that it presented the Eucharist as the privileged center of our encounter with God. Thus it taught that God encounters us and we encounter God and know him primarily through symbolic mediation. God is personal mystery and in faith we encounter and know him as such.

Before proceeding with analysis, I would like to say why I think Vatican II's way of giving meaning and grounds for faith in God and specifically faith in Jesus is superior to those methods we have seen so far. In the first place, it seems to address more directly what we have found to be the most serious difficulties with faith in our time, namely, a naturalistic historical consciousness, or contemporary people's sense of themselves as deeply involved in history and the sense many of them have that a relation to God is not relevant to their concerns for history. Vatican II did analyze contemporary difficulties with faith, especially in the Preface to *Gaudium et Spes* (Pastoral Constitution on the Church in the Modern World), and located these in large part in the change from a static to a more dynamic culture, the inequities, growing pains and tensions in this new culture, the impact on it of the physical and human sciences and of technology, etc. Thus the council was aware of and addressed difficulties that come from modern historical consciousness; it tried to integrate the meaning and grounds it gave for faith in God with peoples' efforts to renew their societies; and it corrected distortions in the understanding of God and of Christ's work so that these could be seen in their relation to these efforts. Neither the earlier Catholic nor Protestant ways of mediating faith did this as effectively, since they tended to deal with individuals in their search for truth or meaning or need for salvation in a way that was abstracted from their search with others for a better future for themselves and their world. In the second place, whereas Barth and Bultmann began with Scripture and our need for salvation, and Catholics began with philosophical knowledge of the world or the human being, Vatican II tended to integrate Scripture and human reason and experience in its model for mediating faith in our time. It presented the Christian message in a way related to contemporary human concerns and it dialogued with people on the basis of human reason and experience. While neo-Scholastic theology emphasized our capacity to know the facts of the existence of God and of revelation, and Rahner emphasized the meaning of God and revelation for the human being, Vatican II gave primacy to the meaning of God and Jesus Christ but also insisted that reason, common human experience, and the historical value of the Gospel's support our faith in the existence of God and his revelation through Jesus Christ. Thus Vatican II tended to integrate approaches that these earlier theologians had thought to be mutually opposed, as we will try to show below. In that part of its teaching specifically related to our question we can distinguish without separating (1) its teaching on the meaning of and grounds for belief in God and (2) its teaching on the meaning of and grounds for belief in God specifically through Jesus Christ.

## 1. Vatican II's Mediation of Belief in God

The council's direct response to difficulties with belief in God in the present world is *to carry on a dialogue with the modern world by rearticulating the Christian message in relation to our current search for meaning, by showing us the full scope of this search and by offering us aid in constructing a more humane world.* This is appropriate for our time, since, as the Fathers write in *Gaudium et Spes,* "We are witnessing . . . the birth of a new humanism, where man is defined before all else by his responsibilities to his brothers and at the court of history."[19] The question of who the human person is is one evoked in many people's minds when they try to reflect more deeply on the meaning of their activity, their life, and their suffering. Bishop Guano stated in explaining the text of *Gaudium et Spes* to the Fathers, "In this central question of man which still remains of the greatest importance, all the human problems of our time converge."[20] The council wants to help people understand and accept themselves at a level of their being that for many today is hidden or blocked. On this depends their dignity and their recognition of the central importance for them of their relationship to God and the relevance of Jesus Christ. The reason why God seems irrelevant to many in our time is that they understand themselves so superficially. Thus the council proclaims that its mission "will show itself to be supremely human by the very fact of being religious" (11).

We will present in three points the council's way of mediating belief in God in our time. In the first place, it recalls both Scripture and human reason and experience to propose to people an understanding of themselves in relation to God that can do justice to their experience and that has a basis in reason. It recalls the Judaeo-Christian story of the creation of human beings, their sin and need for God; it recalls this as an understanding with which people can identify and in which they can find illumination of their complex experience—their deeper aspirations and their failures to live up to them. The human being "was created 'to the image of God,' as able to know and love his creator, and as set by him over all earthly creatures that he might rule them" (12). However, he sinned against God "and sought to attain his goal apart from him" (13), with the result that he not only upset his relationship with God but "is divided in himself. As a result, the whole life of men, both individual and social, shows itself to be a struggle, and a dramatic one, between good and evil, between light and darkness" (13). Also, the council affirms that there is a dignity proper to

---

[19]*Gaudium et Spes,* 55. This and other Vatican II documents will be cited by use of the translations in Austin Flannery, O.P., ed., *Vatican Council II. The Conciliar and Post Conciliar Documents* (Northport, N.Y.: Costello Publishing Co., 1975). Numbers in the texts will indicate paragraphs of the document cited.

[20]See H. Vorgrimler, ed., *Commentary on the Documents of Vatican II,* (New York: Herder and Herder, 1969) 5:118.

human beings at every level of their being—their bodies, their talents shown in progresses in scientific knowledge and in technology as well as in the liberal arts, their capacity for wisdom, their consciences where they discover "a law which he has not laid upon himself" (16), their observance of this law, and the freedom by which they respond to God. Since this freedom has been weakened by sin, "it is only by the help of God's grace that man can give his actions their full and proper relationship to God" (17). It is in facing death that the human condition is most shrouded in doubt and anxieties which technology cannot relieve. The Church, enlightened by God's revelation, declares that "God has created man in view of a blessed destiny that lies beyond the limits of his sad state on earth"; it is Christ who has "won this victory when he rose to life, for by his death he freed man from death" (18). One might say that the council proposes a paradigm by which people might understand and accept themselves better than by one that rejects God or the Christian message.

It adds: "The dignity of man rests above all on the fact that he is called to communion with God" (19), though many in our time "either do not at all perceive, or else explicitly reject, this intimate and vital bond of man to God" (19). Thus atheism must be considered as "one of the most serious problems of our time" (19) because it represents and spreads "harmful teachings and ways of acting which are *in conflict with reason and with common human experience,* and which cast man down from the noble state to which he is born" (19). The council (in *Dei Verbum,* 6) repeats Vatican I's teaching on the capacity of human reason to know the existence of God and religious truths, and it turns from a simple condemnation of atheism to a call to dialogue with it.

What exactly the relation is between reason and common human experience that the council affirms it does not further specify; but we can accept what one commentator notes on this relation. The council recalls Vatican I's statement that the existence of God can be known by the natural light of human reason, but it puts this in the context of human experience more broadly considered: "The text indicates . . . that the possibilities of reason in regard to knowledge of God should be thought of less in the form of a non-historical syllogism of the perennial

philosophy than simply as the concrete fact that man throughout his whole history has known himself confronted with God
and consequently in virtue of his own history finds himself in
relation with God as an inescapable feature of his own existence. The background which the text thus adds to Vatican I is
not so much the history of philosophy as the history of
religion."[21]

To acknowledge God is not to oppose human dignity since
this rests on and is brought to perfection in God. Nor does expectation of a life to come "take away from the importance of
the duties of this life on earth but rather adds to it by giving
new motives for fulfilling those duties" (21). Actually, without
God's support and hope for eternal life, human "dignity is
deeply wounded. . . . The problems of life and death, of guilt
and suffering, remain unsolved" (21). The Church knows "full
well that her message is in harmony with the most secret desires of the human heart" for, as Augustine says, "Thou hast
made us for thyself, O Lord, and our heart is restless until it
rests in thee" (21). These truths find their fulfillment in Jesus
Christ who reveals human beings to themselves and in whose
person and mission human dignity is restored and heightened,
for in Christ we are called to relate to God as sons and daugh-
ters. Christ died for all, and thus we should hold that "the Holy
Spirit offers to all the possibility of being made partners, in a
way known to God, in the paschal mystery" (22). In brief, the
Church calls for belief in God because it is essential for human
dignity, it is fully in accord with a deepened historical consciousness, and human reason and experience support it.

We should add that the council regards human persons not
simply as individuals but as members of the human community, and thus reflects on their activity in the world. By
rooting human community and activity in God's creation of
human beings, it affirms that belief in God vindicates much of
our modern historical consciousness. For example, it notes
that there is an "interdependence between personal betterment and the improvement of society" and that in the midst of
excessive economic and social disparity, no one "can allow
himself to close his eyes to the course of events or indifferently

---

[21]J. Ratzinger in Vorgrimler, ibid., 153.

ignore them and wallow in the luxury of a merely individualistic morality" (25, 30). It notes that the modern world's fervent attempts to transform the world in themselves correspond to the plan of God who created us in his image and commanded us "to conquer the earth with all it contains and to rule the world in justice and holiness" (34). It acknowledges a rightful autonomy of human affairs and activity, though not one that in effect denies their relation to the human good and to God. Human activity is meant to transform the world and build up the human person and community; tragically, however, this activity is all too often infected by sin and results therefore in division among individuals and communities. It is Christ who shows by his commandment of love and his revelation of the world to come the true context for human community and human activity. Thus through its reflection in the first part of *Gaudium et Spes* the council attempts to open "up to man the mystery of God, who is the last end of man" and thereby open up to him "the meaning of his own existence, the innermost truth about himself" (41). It does this in a way that integrates the truth found in our modern historical consciousness better than earlier models of theological mediations of faith.

In the second place, the council also corrects distorted understandings of God that militate against belief in him. It emphasizes that Christians understand God to be the source of human dignity, human freedom, human community, and human engagement in history to make the world more an environment of justice and compassion and thus to liberate people from injustice and other forms of evil. God does not compete with human beings as though jealous of their freedom, resisting their rightful autonomy and activity in the world; nor is he unconcerned for human efforts to promote justice. Some aspects of the way traditional popular Christian culture understood God must be revised, since they are inadequate for a fully developed Christian belief; such a critique is necessary if the meaning and grounds we give for belief in God are to be adequate for our time.

In the third place, the council reflects (in the second part of this Constitution) in dialogue with modern men and women on some practical aspects and concerns of modern life, and seeks to contribute what it can by its reflection and its commitment to make the world a more humane place in which to live. Thus it shows that belief in God transforms human existence in our social, economic, political, and cultural lives and not only our individual lives. Its reflection on humanity and God then has not only a theoretical but a practical goal and benefit, since it offers a context, a norm, and a motive for discerning and constructing the humane world we hope and strive for. The basis the Church offers for belief in our time is not only an intellectual foundation but a praxis by which it strives to share the human effort to improve our world and liberate it from the evils that afflict it. Finally, we should note too that Pope Paul VI established a Secretariat for Unbelievers to promote dialogue between Christians and unbelievers.

## 2. Belief in God Specifically through Jesus Christ

The above gives central elements of the council's teaching on the meaning of and grounds for faith in God, a teaching that it presents from the fullness of its Christian belief, but not exclusively on the grounds of Christian belief. What meaning and grounds does the council present for believing in God specifically through Jesus Christ? We shall recall this briefly, because it is more appropriate for the second part of foundational theology, which we will not treat in this book. We include this material here as context for what we do treat in this book. We can summarize the council's teaching on this question through its affirmation of the salvation God offers us through Jesus Christ, the revelation he offers us through him, and the accessibility that the Gospels offer us to what Jesus said and did.

In the first place, belief in God through Jesus Christ has meaning because it is through Jesus Christ that God offers us that communion with himself in which our human dignity and fulfillment consists and liberation from what opposes such communion—gifts signified by Scripture's statements concerning the kingdom of God or salvation. After human beings' initial and later sins, God "did not abandon them, but at all times held out to them the means of salvation, bestowed in consideration of Christ, the Redeemer" (*Lumen Gentium*,

Dogmatic Constitution on the Church, 2). Jesus inaugurated the kingdom of God by his preaching, his healings, his very person, and his death and resurrection. It is through Jesus Christ then that men and women are given access to freedom from sin and freedom for God—communion with God as Father, Son, and Holy Spirit. Christ's mission, however, has implications for the whole of human life: "Christ's redemptive work, while of its nature directed to the salvation of men and women, involves also the renewal of the whole temporal order."[22] That is why the Church in the period since Vatican II has emphatically articulated the transformation of society by the salvation offered us through Jesus Christ and accepted its responsibility to help men and women of our time be freed not only from the oppression of sin but from every oppression. As the Synod of Bishops stated in 1971: "Action on behalf of justice and participation in the transformation of the world fully appear to us as a constitutive dimension of the preaching of the Gospel, or, in other words, of the Church's mission for the redemption of the human race and its liberation from every oppressive situation."[23]

In the second place, the Church proclaims salvation through Jesus Christ because it was this that God revealed through him as the good news, as the council articulates in *Dei Verbum* (Dogmatic Constitution on Divine Revelation): "It pleased God, in his goodness and wisdom, to reveal himself and to make known the mystery of his will (cf. Eph 1:9). His will was that men should have access to the Father, through Christ, the Word made flesh, in the Holy Spirit, and thus become sharers in the divine nature (cf. Eph 2:18; 2 Pet 1:4)" (2). The council understands revelation in a more personal, concrete, historical, and scriptural sense than Vatican I did. It notes stages of this revelation that include the witness that created realities offer to God, the care God takes of the whole human race, and his revelation to the patriarchs, Moses, and the prophets, preparing the Jewish people for the coming of the Messiah. It is Jesus Christ who completed revelation and confirmed it with divine guarantees. To this revelation, and indeed to all the rev-

---

[22]*Apostolicam actuositatem,* Decree on the Apostolate of the Laity, 5.

[23]Synod of Bishops Second General Assembly (1971), *Justice in the World,* 6.

elation that God has offered us, we must give "the obedience of faith" (Rom 16:26), an act by which "man freely commits his entire self to God, making 'the full submission of his intellect and will to God who reveals,' and willingly assenting to the Revelation given him" (5)—a response possible only through the help of God's grace and the Holy Spirit.

In the third place, the council shows that our Christian belief concerning God's definitive revelation and salvation through Jesus Christ is tied to what Jesus did and said during his life and that this is substantially accessible to us through the Gospels. In chapter 5 of the Constitution on Divine Revelation it writes: "Holy Mother Church has firmly and with absolute constancy maintained and continues to maintain, that the four Gospels . . . whose historicity she unhesitatingly affirms, faithfully hand on what Jesus, the Son of God, while he lived among men, really did and taught for their eternal salvation" (19). The council accepts what modern historical critical study has shown us about the unique character of the Gospels as proclamation, as coming from the tradition of the primitive Church, and as expressing the theologies of their various authors, but it continues to affirm with earlier Christianity that the sacred authors "have told us the honest truth about Jesus" (19).

While the council proclaims that God's definitive salvation and revelation came to us through Jesus Christ, it also expresses its belief that God has all human beings in his care. This is found particularly in its document, *Nostra Aetate,* Declaration on the Relation of the Church to Non-Christian Religions, the first of its kind for an ecumenical council. This declaration represents the modest beginnings of a new stage in the relationship between the Church and non-Christian religions, one that has been followed up since then by numerous dialogues, a number of them stimulated by the Secretariat for Non-Christians established by Pope Paul VI. Noting some ways in which pre-literate religions, Hinduism, Buddhism, and other world religions understand salvation and the means to it, the council "rejects nothing of what is true and holy in these religions." Rather, the Church has a high regard for manners of life, precepts, and doctrines which, though differing from its own, "often reflect a ray of that truth which enlightens all men" (2). It still has a duty to proclaim Christ, for "In him, in whom God reconciled all things to himself (2 Cor 5:18-19), men find the fulness of their religious life" (2). The Church finds that it has still more in common with the Moslems, who accept much of the Old Testament, and with the Jewish people to whom was given the covenant, the Law, the prophets, and Jesus Christ according to the flesh. It encourages its members "to enter with prudence and charity into discussion and collaboration with members of other religions" (2).

It seems that the way the council presents God's salvation and revelation through Jesus Christ suggests an approach to the meaning of and grounds for faith in God through Jesus Christ which is appropriate for our time and for the Christian reality, and more integral than the models we recalled earlier. It recalls and rearticulates the biblical message of God's relation to human beings in a way appropriate to our modern historical consciousness and concerns; it seeks to help contemporary men and women understand and accept their search for meaning at a deeper level and acknowledge that their dignity lies mainly in communion with God and that the evils that afflict them derive primarily from rejecting this communion; it asserts that reason and human experience bear testimony to God's existence; and it shows that such belief entails our work for justice in society and the relief of those who suffer injustice. It tends by this to overcome the dichotomies that existed between earlier models of mediating belief in God in our time. In the following chapters, we will critically reflect on foundations and meaning for belief in God in accord with the model we find in Vatican II, and we defer to what we call the second part of foundational theology a critical reflection on grounds specifically for belief in God through Jesus Christ. At the end of the present chapter, we shall indicate more particularly some of the reflections this critical study calls for.

Before we go on to the final section of this chapter, we wish to note that the approach we find in Vatican II to mediation of faith in our time is not exclusively a Catholic approach. The Faith and Order Commission of the World Council of Churches in 1967 issued a document, "God in Nature and History," that attempts in its own way to overcome a dichotomy many people experience today between their view of the world and history and their Christian faith. While the Commission stated that this document "has no pretention of being our contribution to the dialogue of the Church with modern scientific man,"[24] it does speak to the problem of disbelief experienced in our present changed understanding of nature and history. While previously both had been understood statically, now each is understood dynamically. This change may be viewed optimistically, but it also produces a good deal of bewilderment in which the Christian Church shares: "The question must arise whether the God of the Bible has any relation to the modern scientific world-view, or has anything to say to the feelings of either optimism or pessimism which it creates in the hearts of contemporary men" (I, p. 293).

To address this problem the Commission starts with the Bible and what it teaches about God's active presence in nature and history; and it presents its answer as "one way among many others, all of which are complementary to one another" (I, p. 294). It rejects certain "evasive answers": "These answers have either denied the clear facts of science (fundamentalism) or the essentials of the Christian faith (modernism), or else have tried to separate the realms of faith and of science, by limiting God's word to the inner life and to existential decision, and by denying his relations to the visible realities of nature and history (pietism, theological existentialism)" (I, p. 293).

The Israelites knew God first as the God of history and then as the Lord of nature, the creation of which is understood as the opening act of history. "Nature is not so much the realm where God is revealed to man, as the realm in which man, created in God's image, has to realize God's purpose for his creation (Gen. 1:26-30)" (II, 296). The event of Jesus Christ discloses far more than earlier events. In him is found the fulfillment of God's wrath and grace, and the covenant-partner who acts on behalf of his people. "In his resurrection and in the outpouring of his Spirit, the great eschatological future is anticipated" (III, p. 298). Scripture's view of nature, creation, world, the universe,

[24]World Council of Churches Faith and Order Commission, "God in Nature and History," *New Directions in Faith and Order* (Bristol, 1967). I am citing this as it is contained in C. T. McIntire, ed., *God, History, and Historians, Modern Christian Views of History* (New York: Oxford Univ. Press, 1977) 292–328. The following references are to sections of this document.

and history is not static, although the Christian message was later framed in a static world-concept because of the influence of its Greco-Roman scientific heritage. This concept has been attacked since the Enlightenment; and modern science has impelled Christians "to free their faith from elements which, though long supposed to be integral to the Christian message, are now seen not to be so" (V, p. 306). The Commission elaborates on biblical insights related to this matter, rejecting, for example, the opposed views that humanity is an outsider to nature or that humanity is almost exclusively a product of nature. In its study of nature, technology, God and humanity in history, and other themes, it seeks to integrate our modern experience of the physical world, history, and our responsibility in history within a biblical historical view. The emphases here are at times different from those in Vatican II, but they are complementary. The Commission starts from the Bible and shows that it has a view of nature and our relation to nature and history that overcomes many misunderstandings between Christianity and the modern world.[25]

## *III. History and Process: Theory and Practice*

While the differences between divergent approaches to the mediation of faith are not as clear after Vatican II as before it, some of the positions presented earlier in the century continue to be strong options, having been developed since then. For example, both Bernard Lonergan and Karl Rahner developed their earlier views significantly after Vatican II,[26] as Eberhard Jüngel and others developed Barth's position.[27] The problems

---

[25]We may question whether the thoughtful integrative approach of the Commission has always been sustained in later World Council of Churches documents. See George Crespy, "The Image of Man according to Vatican II and Uppsala 1968," in G. Geffré, ed., *Humanism and Christianity* (*Concilium,* vol. 86, 1973) 102–110.

[26]See Rahner, *Foundations,* B. Lonergan, *Method in Theology* (New York: Herder and Herder, 1972), Leo O'Donovan, "Orthopraxis and Theological Method: Rahner," in *Proceedings* of the Catholic Theological Society of America 35 (1980) 47–65, and Matthew Lamb, "Orthopraxis and Theological Method: Lonergan," ibid., 66–87.

[27]See E. Jüngel, *God as the Mystery of the World* (Grand Rapids: Eerdmans, 1983).

of religious language that Bultmann raised continue to affect the interpretation of Scripture and the God of Scripture, and similar problems are raised too by other interpretations of theological language.[28] So arguments between the earlier models on how faith in God is mediated continue to be important.

However, there have been changes in this area of theology since the sixties, and in part these are due to new agreements among theologians. One widespread agreement is the necessity of relating God more positively to the modern experience of history and process. Since the 1960's there have been renewed efforts on the part of theologians to integrate this basic modern experience into the Christian understanding of God. Different models for the understanding of God have resulted from the fact that theologians have turned to different philosophers for this purpose. Some have taken their point of departure in A. N. Whitehead's philosophy (e.g., John Cobb and Schubert Ogden and, to some extent, David Tracy). Some have been influenced by aspects of Hegel's philosophy (W. Pannenberg) or Karl Marx, or a 20th century Marxist, Ernst Bloch (e.g., J. Moltmann and, to some extent, J. Metz, as well as some liberation theologians, though in a different way). While those who use Whitehead tend to speak of God in terms of process, a number of those European theologians who use Hegel or Marx—and a renewed emphasis on apocalyptic—tend to speak of God as the power of the future; both strongly criticize Thomas Aquinas on the immutability of God.

Another issue from which diversity of models has resulted is whether in the theological mediation of faith one should give primacy to theory or practice. In foundational theology's critical mediation of the meaning and foundations of Christian belief in God, should one appeal primarily to rational objectivity or the transformative power of Christian beliefs and symbols in relation to the practical concerns in the social, economic, and political order of men and women of our time?[29] It seems that

---

[28]See, for example, George Lindbeck, *The Nature of Doctrine* (Philadelphia: Westminster Press, 1984).

[29]See Matthew Lamb, "The Theory-Praxis Relationship in Contemporary Christian Theologies," *Proceedings* of the Catholic Theological Society of America 31 (1976) 149–178.

many theological approaches to the mediation of faith over the last several decades do differ on this issue. But there are subdivisions even within the different emphases. We shall note a few models—not necessarily the most important ones—that give primacy to theory and then a few that give primacy to practice, compare them, and suggest that Vatican II's approach continues to be superior to these later models since it, at least in a beginning way, tries to integrate these varied concerns which have become more emphatic since the council. We shall also note several responses to challenges (from feminism, ecology, and world religions) to the Christian understanding of God that seek to revise the view of God, at times in a way that tends to relativize the Christian understanding. These responses add to the diversity among foundational theologies today, even though they are not meant to belong to this area.

Some of those who try to mediate Christian faith primarily on the basis of rational objectivity are the following. In the United States particularly there has been a resurgence of natural theology among Protestant theologians. Some of them think that a prime reason for disbelief in God in our time is the way classical theology was influenced by a pre-modern cosmology in its articulation of who God was. John Cobb, Jr., has shown that major recent Protestant theologies that repudiate a natural theology have assumptions that rightly belong to natural theology; they have assumptions "on the nature of language, of reality, of history or of nature,"[30] many of which militate against an adequate expression of the gospel. It is then necessary for the categories in which the Christian faith is expressed to be rethought in view of an updated natural theology. Unless this is done self-consciously, philosophical assumptions exercise an uncontrolled dominion over theologians. This is true even of the basic categories of God and humanity. The meaning of God has evaporated "as a function of that cosmology which has destroyed the horizon within which early Christian, medieval, and early modern man understood his existence."[31] Thus we need more than an analysis of human exis-

[30]John Cobb, Jr., *A Christian Natural Theology. Based on the Thought of Alfred North Whitehead* (Philadelphia: Westminster Press, 1965) 12.

[31]Ibid., 15.

tence; we need a natural theology where the concept of God and God's relation to the world can be reconstructed in view of modern cosmology and modern views of human life. A. N. Whitehead's philosophy does this, for he reconstructs our understanding of God in accord with a modern interpretation of the world as process and of the value of our aims immanent in the world. This is counter to the quite static notion of God found in Thomas Aquinas, where, Cobb holds, God lacks a real relation to the world and sanctions the status quo. Whitehead shows that God and the world are interdependent and that process is proper not only to the world but to God's relation to it. The issue here is largely that of the kind of power God exercises in the world. Cobb sees a correlation between the Old Testament creator God and the classical theological view of Thomas Aquinas, since for each God is impassible and acts against human autonomy; and he sees a correlation between the New Testament God who calls us into the future by persuasion and Whitehead's understanding of God, since for both God is parent rather than potter and operates through persuasion from the future, thus respecting human autonomy.[32] In his later writings he has also called for transformations of Christianity through the impact of Asian religions and feminism.[33]

Wolfhart Pannenberg is a theologian who is primarily concerned to mediate the New Testament faith in God through Jesus Christ rather than reform our understanding of God in view of modern cosmology and life. The initial thrust of his theology is to react against the arbitrariness of faith and its grounds as proposed by Barth. He interprets Christian revelation as occurring through God's actions in history witnessed to in Scripture, primarily in the action that shows God's power over the whole of history, i.e., the apocalyptic completion of history that is proleptically anticipated in the resurrection of Jesus as an historical event. Against Barth, he denies that Christian revelation is available only through commitment; rather, commitment is grounded in a knowledge of the divine

---

[32]See David Tracy and John Cobb, *Talking about God. Doing Theology in the Context of Modern Pluralism* (New York: Seabury Press, 1983) 39–56.

[33]See ibid., 57–91.

revelatory acts in history that is available to human reason and historical knowledge. Such commitment cannot be grounded solely on our personal experiences nor in some approach to Scripture that is safe from historical-critical questions:

> The history of Israel all the way to the resurrection is a series of very special events. Thus they communicate something that could not be gotten out of other events. The special aspect is the event itself, not the attitude with which one confronts the event. A person does not bring faith with him to the event as though faith were the basis for finding the revelation of God in the history of Israel and of Jesus Christ. Rather, it is through an open appropriation of these events that true faith is sparked.
>
> This is not to say that faith is made superfluous by the knowledge of God's revelation in the events that demonstrate his deity. Faith has to do with the future. This is the essence of trust. . . . Thus a person does not come to faith blindly, but by means of an event that can be appropriated as something that can be considered reliable.[34]

Meaning in history, moreover, depends primarily on the context from which one appropriates it, and final meaning comes only from the apocalyptic context of universal history that we know initially from Scripture. The works of philosophers like H. G. Gadamer are particularly helpful in the hermeneutical task that we face in the study of Scripture. As the context of meaning is the ultimate future, so too God is manifested above all through the kingdom of God to come where he will show his power over all things and events. In fact, God is properly understood only as the power of the future rather than as perfect, omniscient and all powerful from the

---

[34]W. Pannenberg, "Dogmatic Theses on the Doctrine of Revelation," in W. Pannenberg, ed., *Revelation as History* (Toronto: Macmillan, 1969) 135, 137–138. See also, for a model for foundational theology that comes from an important American evangelical, Carl F. H. Henry, *God, Revelation and Authority 1: God Who Speaks and Shows: Preliminary Considerations* and *2: God Who Speaks and Shows: Fifteen Theses. Part One* (Waco, Texas: Word Books, 1976). Also see, Richard Rice's review article on Carl Henry and Donald Bloesch in *Religious Studies Review* 7 (1981) 107–115.

beginning, as the scholastics understood him to be;[35] and the power operative in history comes from the future. For Pannenberg there is no direct access from nature to God, but anthropology raises the religious question (without proving the existence of God) since in human openness to the world and the advent of human freedom, divine reality is manifested as personal power bestowing freedom.[36] This, however, does not legitimate the use of analogy in the way Thomas Aquinas understood it, since to use analogy is to seek to control who God will be in the future rather than commit ourselves to him.

If we compare these views with the model for foundational theology implicit in Vatican II, several things are apparent. In the first place, Cobb's and Pannenberg's models seem to be in tension with one another somewhat as the two poles which Vatican II also seeks to integrate. Cobb gives precedence to a philosophical approach to religion that takes its point of departure in the modern understanding of the world and of secular values, but he seems to give Scripture too little determinative value for his interpretation of God. Pannenberg begins by seeking to mediate faith in Jesus by offering grounds for accepting his resurrection from the dead as an historical fact. Differing in part from these positions (both of which are intellectualist in different ways), Vatican II speaks from the vantage point of what it considers to be God's definitive revelation about his way of salvation and himself (thus giving the New Testament precedence over philosophy), but it seeks to mediate this message to modern men and women and acknowledge their search for an individual and social life in accord with the human dignity that is theirs. It acknowledges a more positive place for human knowledge and philosophy in reference to God than Pannenberg, while at the same time holding that human use of knowledge to reach God depends upon the person's openness to conversion, an openness that is

---

[35]W. Pannenberg, *The Idea of God and Human Freedom* (Philadelphia: Westminster Press, 1973) 93, and W. Pannenberg, *Theology and the Kingdom of God* (Philadelphia: Westminster Press, 1969) 51ff. However, Pannenberg also writes that "This does not mean that God could not be God apart from the existence of finite beings, for God certainly can do without anyone or anything else" (loc. cit.). Whether these views are internally consistent is another question.

[36]Pannenberg, *Idea of God,* 95–96.

made possible by God's grace. Similarly, Vatican II asserts that the historical value of the Gospels, namely the rootedness of their proclamation in what Jesus actually did and said, is still important as a ground for belief in Jesus Christ. The council would agree that the apostolic witness to the resurrection offered a kind of public criterion for the Christian claim that is still important, in spite of the difficulties that contemporary studies of history as science pose to it.[37] Pannenberg tries to give this a place in foundational theology, though the way he does so does not seem to do justice to the relation between this witness and the revelation proclaimed through it or to the dependence of our acceptance of this witness on our subjectivity, which is open to transformation. The council interrelates Scripture and human knowledge differently than these two theologians and its view is in accord with its understanding of the different stages of revelation God offers to humanity and the aid that he makes available to us so that we may accept this transformative knowledge. Both Cobb's and Pannenberg's views call us to critically reevaluate Thomas Aquinas' view on God's relation to history.[38]

[37]For a treatment of the resurrection that seems to me appropriate for foundational theology, see Francis S. Fiorenza, *Foundational Theology. Jesus and The Church* (New York: Crossroad, 1984) 29–55.

[38]David Tracy seeks to integrate the two poles of contemporary experience and Christian texts: what is made known to us in our situated human experiences, especially limit experiences, and the historical Christian experience mediated by Scripture. See David Tracy, *Blessed Rage for Order. The New Pluralism in Theology* (New York: Seabury, 1975) 8. See also David Tracy, *The Analogical Imagination. Christian Theology and the Culture of Pluralism* (New York: Crossroad, 1981) chapter 2, "A Theological Portrait of the Theologian: Fundamental, Systematic and Practical Theologies," 47–98; and *Plurality and Ambiguity: Hermeneutics, Religion, Hope* (San Francisco: Harper and Row, 1987). Two essays that question Tracy's hermeneutics from the perspective of issues in "post-modernism" are the following: Richard Bernstein, "Radical Plurality, Fearful Ambiguity, and Engaged Hope", *Journal of Religion* 69 (1989) 85–91; and Thomas Guarino, "Revelation and Foundationalism: Toward Hermeneutical and Ontological Appropriateness", *Modern Theology* 6 (1990) 221–235. These authors hold that Tracy needs both stronger grounds to legitimate truth claims and an analysis of the human subject that shows it is not dissolved by post-modern critiques. I will deal with these questions in chapters 5 and 6, and I have evaluated some of Heidegger and Gadamer's positions central to these issues in *God's Work in a Changing World* (Washington, D.C., University Press of America, 1985) 194–200, 204–214. Chapters in that work on the human good (chapter 6) and epistemology (chapter 9) are also relevant to this issue.

Among contemporary theologians whose theologies represent or give priority to practice more than to theory, Jürgen Moltmann is prominent. Like Pannenberg, though for significantly different reasons, he reacts against Barth and Bultmann. For Moltmann, it is the question of evil that militates against belief in God; in dialogue with Marxism, particularly as this is represented in the Frankfurt School of critical theory, he seeks to show that Christian belief answers the problem of evil. The answer to modern unbelief is found neither in cosmological nor in existential theology, neither in an argument for the existence of God from the order in the cosmos nor in a discovery of human identity through an existential route. It is found in Christian revelation, as Barth and Bultmann held, although Moltmann interprets revelation quite differently from the way they did. Revelation is not *epiphany*, as those influenced by Greek philosophy interpret it, but rather *promise* as we see in Scripture and particularly in the resurrection of Jesus with its apocalyptic implications. Promise calls for a response, not of theoretical knowledge but rather of *hope*. Such revelation and response give an answer to the problem of evil, not by giving us a new outlook or interpretation of the world but rather by initiating the active transformation of the world by Christian believers. The New Testament is a missionary's manual.[39] Here, as in Pannenberg, God is the power of the future, the one who is to come. But, as distinct from Pannenberg, what is important is not showing reasonable grounds for belief or a universal context of meaning, but rather political action: "If the real predicament underlying the theistic world view was the theodicy question *(Si Deus, unde malum?)*, the Christian initiative for the overcoming of this predicament today, using the possibilities of the modern world, must enter the battle for God's righteousness on earth politically in the battle against human misery. Therefore, cosmological theology must now be replaced by *political theology*."[40] In later writings Moltmann has

---

[39]See Jürgen Moltmann, *The Future of Hope. Theology as Eschatology* (New York: Harper and Row, 1970) 1–50.

[40]Ibid., 47. Johannes Metz develops a similar theme. See, e.g., *Faith in History and Society. Toward a Practical Fundamental Theology* (New York: Seabury, 1980). It is primarily against the privitization of Christianity by the middle-class that Metz's political theology is directed.

given more prominence to the cross. In the cross we see God's liberating love for us and his identification with sinners and the oppressed.[41] Thus God gives the answer to the problem of evil through identifying himself with sinful and oppressed humanity and taking up evil and suffering into his own life—in fact, into his own Trinitarian relations.

Liberation theology in Latin America is also a political theology; and it implies a kind of foundational theology which, appropriately enough, is especially meant for those who already believe and consider themselves Christians while all too frequently supporting economically and politically oppressive structures or being the butt of these, thinking that one should accept oppression patiently because God will make up for it in the next life. Counter to this, liberation theologians insist on the socially transformative character of Christian faith. Their theology basically calls for a reinterpretation of Christian symbols such as God, Church, Christ, and the kingdom to bring out their liberating significance or transformative value for the present human situation, with particular emphasis on the socio-economic situation. Somewhat as Bultmann thought that a *Vorverständnis* or preunderstanding was necessary for the interpretation of the Christian message, so liberation theologians claim that preunderstandings are always present. However, they claim, in modern times Christians have traditionally had a capitalist preunderstanding which justified the status quo and the radical differences in economic conditions that separated the wealthy from the impoverished; many have been comfortable with the Christian message, presented to them as individualistic. Academic theology has not been aware of the capitalist ideology that it represents. A politically neutral theology is an illusion. Liberation theologians wish to justify a hermeneutic that comes from an identification with the oppressed and a search for liberation of their countries in the

[41]See J. Moltmann, *The Crucified God* (New York: Harper and Row, 1974) 192: "(God) took upon himself the unforgivable sin and the guilt for which there is no atonement, together with the rejection and anger that cannot be turned away, so that in Christ we might become his righteousness in the world . . . In the death of the Son, death comes upon God himself, and the Father suffers the death of his Son in his love for forsaken man."

economic and political order.[42] They have found help in Marxist ideology critique and social analysis. Actually, as Juan
Segundo holds, people who come to the interpretation of
Scripture are already concerned with and seeking decisions in
the political area; and they are seeking a basis for such decisions in Scripture and theology.[43] Thus the liberation theologians say that we cannot know the liberating message of the
gospel without a commitment to liberation. Priority is given
here in foundational theology to the transformative power of
the Christian message in social, economic, and political
existence—not to deny the transcendence of the Christian
hope but to show its present impact in human and specifically
economic and political life.

If we compare the approach of these praxis theologians to
that of Vatican II, we can recognize that the council agrees that
Christianity cannot be credible if it is disinterested in men and
women's historical lot and that Christian belief has transformative implications for social as well as individual life. Thus
the Church at the council and since then seeks to cooperate
with men and women in the solution of their political, social,
and economic problems; it sees this cooperation as an integral
part of its proclamation of Christian salvation.[44] The Church's
analysis of the present situation is less influenced by Marxist
sociological analysis than that of some current praxis theolo-

[42]See Juan Luis Segundo, *The Liberation of Theology* (Maryknoll, N.Y.: Orbis,
1976) 39, 69. See Arthur F. McGovern, S.J., *Liberation Theology and its Critics. Toward an Assessment* (Maryknoll, Orbis, 1989); "Liberation Theology is Alive and
Well," *Tablet,* Sept. 15, 1990; and Scott Walter, "The New Face of Liberation Theology. An Interview with Arthur F. McGovern, S.J.," *Crisis* 9 (1991) 34–36.

[43]See ibid., 117, 94, 83.

[44]This is even more marked in the post-Vatican II Second Synod of Bishops document on "Justice in the World" (1971), 6, referred to above, note 32, and later documents of the Church such as the Extraordinary Synod of Bishops Twenty Years
After Vatican II (1985), "The Final Report," *Origins* 15 (Dec. 19, 1985) 444–450;
and Congregation for the Doctrine of the Faith, "Instruction on Christian Freedom
and Liberation," *Origins* 15 (April 17, 1986) 714–728. In this Congregation's earlier
"Instruction on Certain Aspects of Theology of Liberation (*Origins* 14 [1984–1985]
193 ff.), it warns of certain dangers, for example: "One places oneself within the perspective of a temporal messianism which is one of the most radical of the expressions of secularization of the kingdom of God and of its absorption into the
immanence of human history" (10). It warns too against the politization of existence and the way this can distort the transcendence of the person.

gians, and it gives clearer priority to our need for liberation from sin and communion with God over our economic and political needs than some of these theologians do. It also has a more human norm for what constitutes the good of human societies, namely the dignity of the person, than either Moltmann or some liberation theologians. Thus it does seek to answer the problem of evil practically and not simply theoretically, showing by its action its understanding of God's compassion for our human suffering. It does not play off the socially transformative value of the faith against the value it has for individual transformation, for it insists on both. Moreover, the council does not insist on value as the ground and meaning of belief to the exclusion of intellectual grounds in evidence supporting the existence of God and the historical value of the Gospels. For example, it does not dialectically reject the cosmological and existential approaches as grounds for belief in God and intrinsic to the meaning of such belief, but rather integrates with these an insistence upon the socially transformative impact of the proclamation of the Christian message. I see as supportive of the council's approach the statement by cultural anthropologist Clifford Geertz, written in a different context, to the effect that in history human beings move both from theory to practice and from practice to theory in spite of explicit or implicit philosophical censures of such moves: "What all sacred symbols assert is that the good for man is to live realistically; where they differ is in the vision of reality they construct. Probably the overwhelming majority of mankind are continually drawing normative conclusions from factual premises (and factual premises from normative premises, for the relation between ethos and world view is circular) despite refined, and in their own terms impeccable reflections by professional philosophers on the 'naturalistic fallacy.'"[45]

Before concluding this chapter, we should note some movements in our time that seek to answer contemporary challenges to the adequacy of the Christian understanding of God and, in some of their representatives, conclude that one must rela-

---

[45]Clifford Geertz, *The Interpretation of Cultures. Selected Essays* (New York: Basic Books, 1973) 130, 141.

tivize the Christian understanding of God. Though these movements do not present themselves as foundational theologies, they do seek to correct what they perceive to be distortions of the genuine understanding of God in response to modern objections and the larger experience and needs of our time. We should mention several of these, because in their own way they seek to answer problems of unbelief or distorted belief in God. We do this very briefly indeed, but will return to these themes in the course of our study.

One challenge to the traditional Christian understanding of God is that of many feminists. They attack "an almost exclusively male imagery for God as king, lord, master, and especially father in the language of Christian tradition and the Church's practical liturgical life."[46] They claim that such imagery has become an idol that interprets religious metaphors literally, limits God and his way of relating to the world by using a male model for his reality, legitimizes patriarchy, makes women appear inferior and defective, denies them the possibility of religious affirmation of their bodies, sexuality, and power, and supports society's subordination and devaluation of women.

Feminists and others seek to correct such an image of God by speaking of God as mother and by use of the feminine personal pronoun in reference to God. Some feminist theologians almost despair of Christianity and insist on the importance of "the Goddess or Great Mother symbolism as the center of women's religious devotion,"[47] holding that women have a different vision and approach to reality or God than men. Others find it necessary "to move beyond male, female, and parental images entirely or to include but relativize them."[48] For a fuller understanding of God, we must integrate in our images of God the experience of women which includes, but is not limited to, gestation, birth, nurturance, compassion, and power as enable-

---

[46]Ann Carr, *Transforming Grace. Christian Tradition and Women's Experience* (San Francisco: Harper & Row, 1988), ch. 7, "Feminist Reflection on God," 134. There are many feminist theologians who could be cited here. I am relying on Carr's articulation of the main thrust of this movement. References may be found in her book.

[47]Carr, *Transforming Grace,* 141.

[48]Carr, *Transforming Grace,* 142.

ment of others; some Christian mystics support such metaphors of God. Some feminists no longer accept Scripture as
normative for Christian belief; they rather say that we must develop images of God that enhance our life today, whether they
are in accord with or counter to Scripture.

Another challenge to the traditional Christian view of God
is found in modern cosmogony and the need of reversing the
West's destructive exploitation of the physical environment.
Some respondents to this challenge find an answer to this
problem within the context of the Christian view that God definitively revealed himself through Jesus Christ, but others
may appear to realitivize this revelation. For example, the
American Catholic Thomas Berry finds Christianity largely responsible for our destruction of our physical environment
through an interpretation of salvation that severs our connection with the physical world and a myth of creation in which
man is told to dominate the world. He insists that in this "ecological age" we need a mystique of the land opposed to the destructive industrial mystique and a shift from an anthropocentric to a biocentric paradigm. The primary revelation does not
now appear to be that of Jesus, even including his role as cosmic Christ (as in Teilhard de Chardin), but rather the story
given us by modern cosmogony. As Berry writes: "The universe, the solar system, and the planet earth in themselves and
in their evolutionary emergence constitute for the earthly community the primary revelation of that ultimate mystery
whence all things emerge into being."[49] The emerging cosmos
gives human beings a common myth, and this is the context for
the interrelation of religions. Christianity is not the fullness of
what is found less perfectly in other religions. Also, this common myth is essential for "the main human task of the immediate future [which] is to assist in activating the inter-
communion of all the living and non-living components of the

---

[49]Thomas Berry, "Twelve Principles: For Understanding the Universe and the
Role of the Human in the Universe Process," in Anne Lonergan and Caroline
Richards, eds., *Thomas Berry and the New Cosmology* (Mystic, Conn.: Twenty-
Third Publications, 1987) 107. Also see Thomas E. Clarke, "Creational Spiritual-
ity," *The Way. Contemporary Christian Spirituality* 29 (1989) 68–79.

earth community in what can be considered the emerging ecological period of earth development."[50]

A third challenge to the traditional Christian view of God is
found in the almost universal awareness in our time of world
religions and their quite varied understandings of divinity.
Many Christian theologians react to this by claiming that
God's final revelation of himself still occurs through Jesus
Christ and the Spirit he sent. But there are those who react to
this challenge by relativizing the Christian understanding of
God. These assert, for example, "that we must accept the historical relativity of all religious forms and so abandon past
claims of being the 'only' or the 'highest' form of religion."[51]
They may say that the object of religious devotion is infinite
and so must be expressed in many forms; no one religion can
claim to be final. Or, "to hold up Christianity or Christ as the
'norm' for all other religions is just as exploitive as is the attempt of sexism to render male experience the universal norm
for humanity."[52]

Many Christians who reflect on these themes seek to call for
a reform of a traditional Christian understanding of God or a
Western view of our human place in the universe while still
claiming that God's ultimate revelation did take place through
Jesus and the Spirit he sent. Is there room for growth in our
Christian understanding of God and the world that can do justice to these multiple modern experiences that undermine
many people's faith in Christianity? In accepting a model for
foundational theology in accord with Vatican II, I am claiming
that there is. We will return to these themes in later chapters.

---

[50]Berry, "Twelve Principles," 108. Some themes of the New Age movement are in
continuity with those of feminists and ecologists. See, e.g., Marilyn Ferguson, *The
Aquarian Conspiracy: Personal Growth and Social Transformation in the 1980s* (Los
Angeles, J.P. Tarcher, 1980); and David Spangler, *Emergence: The Rebirth of the Sacred* (New York, Dell, 1984).

[51]John Hick and Paul F. Knitter, eds., *The Myth of Christian Uniqueness. Toward
a Pluralistic Theology of Religions* (Maryknoll, N.Y.: Orbis, 1987) ix. For a more
mainline Christian response to this challenge, see, for example, Leslie Newbigin,
"The Christian Faith and the World Religions," in Geoffrey Wainwright, ed., *Keeping the Faith. Essays to Mark the Centenary of Lux Mundi* (Philadelphia: Fortress,
1988) 310–340.

[52]Hick and Knitter, *The Myth of Christian Uniqueness,* xi.

The model we adopt to critically reflect on the adequacy of the meaning and foundations of our Christian belief in God is, as I understand it, the position of Vatican II. This means several things. In the first place, we are evaluating our faith in God and in Jesus Christ as the mediator of God's definitive revelation and salvation. These two processes are not the same, and both are necessary in foundational theology: recall the idea that Jesus came to those who had been prepared to receive him by God's *praeparatio evangelica.* We thus treat mediation of belief in God first, since Jesus' meaning is in his reference to God. We are suggesting that the first part of foundational theology treats the former belief and the second part treats the latter. However, we present the faith in God we are mediating with the understanding that Christ and the Spirit he sent are the fulfillment of the revelation of God.

In reference to the first part, we could start with the human person's self-knowledge and show that this mediates knowledge of God. But religious reflection is culturally situated, and it is our Christian belief in God on which we are reflecting critically. Our belief in God is based primarily on his revelation of himself through Jesus Christ, and not on our knowledge of him through creation. Thus it seems better to ask initially what our Christian identity as seen in Scripture is in reference to the meaning and foundations of our belief in God. We attempt (in chapter 3) to interpret Scripture's teaching on this, but do so in reference to questions and problems that men and women of our time have. Then (in chapter 4) we indicate some major stages of development—and decline—in Christian history of the Christian understanding of belief in God, for these stages in part explain the contemporary Church's belief, difficulties with such belief, and conflicts among diverse Christian understandings of belief in God and ways to mediate it.

To show what Scripture and tradition teach about the grounds and meaning of faith in God is not sufficient. One still may ask whether Scripture is supported by human experience today; after all, many have disengaged from it and many think that the Christian God is just the god of a particular people in antiquity. We cannot say that those experiences which mediated belief to Israel are present in our time, but we can ask whether there are experiences not formally dependent on Scripture that mediate faith in God and whether these can be critically verified. Thus we should ask how people influenced by modern historical consciousness experience conversion to God and whether there is a transcendence in the person today in virtue of which such a turning is a fulfillment rather than an alienation (chapter 5). This leads us to ask also about the scope of human knowledge and whether there are grounds in contemporary human knowledge and experience for believing in the existence of God (chapter 6). Then too we should ask more specifically several critical modern questions about who God is. Is God a transcendent personal being—as shown to us in Scripture but not understood as such by some Christians influenced by certain views on religious language and Eastern religions (chapter 7)? And is God really related to the world and history, even immanent in the world, and changed by history even to the extent of suffering (chapter 8)? Finally, we should reflect critically on the human response to God found in faith, religion and language, and on our need for God's salvation and revelation (chapter 9). The supporting arguments we bring up are not meant to take the place of our Christian faith. Moreover, our treatment of these issues is only an introductory one. In fact, our considerations do not show us that belief in God specifically as he is revealed in Judaeo-Christian revelation is critically validated. But they do help to overcome many objections to the view that belief in God has meaning and foundations and that it is plausible that God should be as Christians understand him to be. This will prepare for the second part of foundational theology.

My primary interest is to give some theological meaning and foundations for our belief in God that take account of some major contemporary difficulties. My secondary interest is to present an approach to this that integrates the concerns of a variety of theologians. It is my view that in making this critical reflection we are critically evaluating an important part of the belief of the Christian community in our time, specifically that articulated by Vatican II.

The task of the second part of foundational theology is to critically evaluate the meaning and foundations of belief in

God specifically through Jesus Christ. Since we will not be engaged in that task in this book, we will not attempt here to spell out the more particular questions that it would deal with. Suffice it to say that here too we understand ourselves as critically evaluating the belief of the Christian community.

# 3

# Scripture and Our Belief in God

In this chapter we ask for the meaning and grounds of faith in God that are offered in Scripture. We are investigating this from the perspective of what we expressed in chapter 1 as central difficulties posed against faith in God in our time. To introduce this study, we will ask first why we turn to Scripture at this point in foundational theology and how we do so, second how from the words that testify to Israel's belief we can evaluate some mutually opposed interpretations of the language of Scripture, and third how from this ancient document with its plurality of doctrines we can answer questions of our time.

In the first place, we turn to Scripture at this point because we are asking critically what we as Christians believe about God's relation to history and who this shows God to be, who human persons are in history and how as such they are related to God, and the meaning and grounds of belief in God in this context. In chapter 1 we indicated that a central difficulty with faith in our time is the view that our human concern is with history, and that many people do not sense the relevance of faith in God to this concern and question the meaning and grounds of belief in God. Thus we must show what Christians actually believe in this matter, for it is this that we are critically evaluating and it is important to correct misunderstandings about it. This effort to retrieve our belief in this matter may make it seem even more alien to many men and women of our time, which means that it still must be shown how this view relates to contemporary experience of history. How, for example, can God act in history?

As Christians we hold that Scripture is normative for our belief.[1] Not all Christians would accept Vatican II's understanding of God and belief in him, but we can find common ground beyond our differences by turning to Scripture for answers. We are not attempting to give a full scriptural theology here, but to concentrate on some central scriptural affirmations relevant to contemporary difficulties with faith in God and to differences among the models of foundational theology that we examined earlier.

Only in later chapters will we face philosophical difficulties that can be raised against the scriptural understanding of God and faith in him. But in our very treatment of Scripture, we are using contemporary studies of Scripture that have in part already addressed many of the difficulties that men and women of our time would find with it. For example, through a recognition of different genres in Scripture, we realize that we should not accept in a fundamentalist sense Genesis' account of creation and the first human beings. Vatican II has a more modest view of the truth of Scripture than fundamentalists do, for it teaches that "the books of Scripture firmly, faithfully and without error teach that truth which God, for the sake of our salvation, wished to see confided to the sacred Scriptures."[2]

We are using Scripture here in a way appropriate to the manner in which it mediates Judaeo-Christian belief and the revelation on which this is based. To be able to enter *medias res* rather than to spend a great deal of time developing concepts at this point, we are using here an understanding that will be developed formally only later in foundational theology:

[1]Foundational theology treats the question of the norm of Christian faith formally in its third part, and thus we will not try to justify here this assertion of the normative character of Scripture, but direct the reader elsewhere. See Vatican II, *Dei Verbum*, ch. 2–6. Also see Avery Dulles, "Scripture: Recent Protestant and Catholic Views," *Theology Today* 37 (1980) 7–26. The view of Vatican II and the present book differ in important respects from that offered by Edward Farley and Peter Hodgson in "Scripture and Tradition," Peter Hodgson and Robert King, eds., *Christian Theology. An Introduction to its Traditions and Tasks* 2nd ed. (Philadelphia: Fortress, 1985) 61–87. And though David Kelsey's analysis of the ways that Scripture is used in recent theology is very illuminating, it does not seem wholly adequate. See David Kelsey, "The Bible and Christian Theology," *Journal of the American Academy of Religion* 48 (1980) 385–402.

[2]*Dei Verbum,* 11.

namely, that Scripture is not claimed by Christians to be of it-self revelation, but to be written by believers for believers to present what God has revealed through words and deeds and done for his people, the grounds in human experience on which this is asserted, and the implications for human life of what he has done. Since it is Scripture as it is understood to mediate God's revelation that we recall, it is the whole course of Scripture that we have to be concerned with, rather than one part of it. Scripture is for Christians an account of a continuing and evolving dialogue between God and his people. As the Epistle to the Hebrews states: "In times past, God spoke in fragmentary and varied ways to our fathers through the proph-ets; in this, the final age, he has spoken to us through his Son" (1:1-2). We are attempting here only an introductory presenta-tion of what is central to our specific questions. We do not re-call specific Scripture texts as "proof-texts" in the way that earlier manuals of theology frequently did, as in and of them-selves ultimate authorities. Rather we recall texts within the context of their mediation of God's dialogue in love with his people and this people's response. We are not attempting here to show that there is a basis in history for Israel's and early Christianity's claim that God has made revelation through definite actions and words. In the second part of foundational theology we will treat the question of history in reference to the ministry of Jesus and his resurrection. Here we simply present the claim that there is such a relationship, because that is es-sential to the Christian identity and belief in God. And it is only that identity and belief that we are critically concerned with at this point.

Second, how can we gain some agreement on the meaning of these texts if, as we have seen (e.g., in Bultmann), there are di-verse interpretations of what the religious meaning is that they mediate to us? In an introductory answer to this, and ap-proaching Scripture from the outside in, we can acknowledge first of all that Scripture is a collection of signs, texts, and dif-ferent forms or genres of literature, such as narrative, poetry, wisdom literature, prophecy, apocalypse, and letters. The au-thors or editors are in different ways testifying to their beliefs and to those of the community of which they are a part. The language they use testifies to what they believe. These books, which were written, edited, and reedited over successive ages, were later recognized by the Jewish and/or Christian community as expressing their beliefs, and as normative for their beliefs. That is, eventually they were put together to constitute a canon. We can look at these books as a whole, together with those who practice "canonical criticism," in addition to using other critical methods. This means that we can interpret a text in its original context, then in the context of its acceptance and "resignification" in later generations, and still later as it is accepted as part of the whole canon.[3]

We can say that as literature or literary forms, these texts depend on the creative imagination of their authors and editors in the context of their communities and circumstances.[4] Poetry shows creative imagination; narrative takes creative imagination to structure a story with beginning, issue, and denouement. Similarly with the other forms of literature represented in Scripture. When we specify imagination as creative, we are distinguishing it from mimetic imagination that simply organizes what is given it. Immanuel Kant articulated the creative function of imagination: its function in synthesizing by giving a metaphor to a concept. What is central then here is *metaphor* (and, analogous to it in narrative, the structuring of a story). As Ricoeur points out, metaphor is a form of enunciation, and not simply a word. It is the whole proposition, such as, "Old age is the evening of life." To use metaphor is to give an unexpected predication of a reality that shifts our view of it and opens up new perspectives on it. Initially this metaphor is destabilizing for our perception, because, for example, old age is obviously not an evening, and the kingdom of God is not a mustard seed. Metaphor is central to the creative imagination and thus to literature and how it means. We find it

---

[3]On canonical criticism, see James A. Sanders, "Hermeneutics in True and False Prophesy," *Canon and Authority: Essays in Old Testament Religion and Theology,* eds. G. Coats and B. Long (Philadelphia: Fortress Press, 1977) 21–24; J. Sanders, *Canon and Community* (Philadelphia: Fortress Press, 1984).

[4]See Paul Ricoeur, *The Rule of Metaphor* (Toronto: University of Toronto Press, 1977); and Paul Ricoeur, "Poétique et symbolique," in B. Lauret and F. Refoulé, eds., *Initiation à la Pratique de la Théologie.* Tome I: *Introduction* (Paris: Cerf, 1982) 37–61. Also see my report on a seminar relevant to this matter, "An Evaluation of Paul Ricoeur's Interpretation of God-Talk in Scripture," *Proceedings,* Catholic Theological Society of America, vol. 42 (1987) 165–167.

throughout Scripture: in the account of the first man and woman, in the epic story of the Exodus, and in the parables of Jesus. These metaphors involve the reader now as they involved the hearer initially, for in them logos and life come to juncture; and they, correlatively, appeal to both logos and life, reason and desire in the hearer or reader.

Scripture is specifically religious literature, and thus has been compared with other religious literature of the ancient Middle East. We shall examine later (chapter 9) a specifically philosophical reflection on theological language, but here we restrict ourselves to the question of scriptural language as Christians believe it to function. Ricoeur joins Eliade in recognizing the reality of religious experience and of language as mediating this experience. In this language the pre-conceptual is primary, though it leads to doxology and confession where conceptual language is evident. It is particularly the pre-conceptual language and rite that is called symbolic. The metaphors in Scripture can often be called symbols—religious symbols. Ricoeur points out an analogical structure in such symbols: "By analogical structure, we signify provisionally the structure of expressions with a double meaning in which a first meaning sends us back to a second meaning which alone is intended, without however it being able to be attained directly, that is, other than through the first meaning."[5] For example, to say that the reign of God is a wedding feast is to speak indirectly of the reign of God through speaking of a wedding feast. To tell the story of Adam and Eve as a "narrative interpretation of the enigma of existence"[6] that confers on humanity the unity of a concrete universal and a direction is to speak indirectly of God and our relation to him. Symbols are not wholly translatable into direct and literal language; by interpretation the plenitude of experience that the myth designates only obscurely will not be restored. The secret of such symbols is metaphor that comes from a creative imagination giving an image to a concept, redescribing reality through a model or reconfiguring reality inaccessible to direct description so that we are enabled to *see it as.*

[5]Ricoeur, "Poétique," 44.
[6]Ibid., 46.

The primary religious language in Scripture thus seems to be not doctrinal but symbolic. It speaks of God not so much directly as indirectly—through stories, poetry, prophecy, apocalyptic, and other literary forms that make central use of symbol. Here, as in metaphor more generally, we have an intersection of logos and life, reason and desire; we have a language that engages the reader or, initially, the hearer. These religious symbols, as Eliade and Ricoeur point out, present the Sacred to the reader or hearer in an almost sacramental manner, making available the power of the Sacred and participation in it, transforming, evoking a knowledge which is participative. This is language that cannot be wholly translated into doctrinal statements. This is as true of Canaanite religious myths and rites as it is of the stories in Scripture. People of antiquity lived in a symbolic universe, a universe the reality and meaning of which was mediated to them largely through religious symbols. One of the problems people in our time have with faith is that many find living in a universe mediated symbolically to them alien; yet, ironically, when they dismiss religious symbols they frequently turn to other and less adequate symbols (e.g., those of a political movement or of popular culture).

However, scriptural language about Yahweh or God cannot be simply equated with that of the Canaanites about their gods, since the acts by which the Sacred is known differ for these different peoples. H. Cazelles calls upon different studies of the religions surrounding the emergence of Israel to understand how Israel's proclamation of God differed from theirs.[7] The Yahwist and Elohist documents of the Pentateuch did use the Semitic designation for god or gods (El) for the God of Israel. To avoid excessive assimilation of Yahweh and the Canaanite El, we have to recall that the modes of action, comportment, and capacities of the gods of the surrounding peoples are shown in their myths and rites. These gods seem, or the symbols and myths by which these peoples speak of their gods seem, to be associated with the powers on which or on

[7]See H. Cazelles, "Le Dieu du Yahviste et de l'Élohiste ou le Dieu du Patriarche et de Moïse et de David avant les Prophètes," in J. Coppens, ed., *La Notion biblique de Dieu. Le Dieu de la Bible et le Dieu des Philosophes* (Louvain: Louvain Univ. Press, 1976) 77–89.

whom these peoples' lives depend. Thus H. Cazelles writes of these surrounding peoples: "Like his neighbors, the Phoenician discerns in the cosmic, political, physiological and even moral or intellectual forces an intelligence and a will more powerful than his own. But when he tries a synthesis by lists or by myths, the inconsistency is apparent. Here we have three Elohim, of whom one is El-father, there we have two; we have seven Baals of whom only one is defined (by the cult of Saphon). The role enjoyed by Mot in one myth is held by Yam in another. Ashtart can replace Anath. . . . The identifications are fluid."[8] The powers shown in the yearly cycle of death and rebirth of vegetation are certainly important in the Canaanite religion, and this is one sense in which their symbols and myths are bonded to the cosmos and not fully translatable into doctrine or the conceptual. In a somewhat similar manner, the God of Israel is known as the power behind the actions ascribed to him. But this God is initially identified, as we shall recall below, through very specific historical actions, such as the call of Abraham and the Exodus. Thus, though God is presented as an "elusive presence," he is known as a definite personality through the initiatives he freely adopts with his people. The world in front of the text into which people are invited by the scriptural message is presented as a revelation initiated by this personal God.

What seems central in Scripture is the witness to the faith of the Jews and then of the Christian community. The message is largely a proclamation of God's offer of salvation and his call for the response of the obedience of faith. This offer and call are reactualized in generation after generation, as is shown by the way that traditions were proclaimed in new ways or reinterpreted to make God's salvation actual for changed circumstances. The prophets proclaimed God's message to the people of succeeding centuries by reflecting on the Exodus event. The New Testament is called the good news ("Gospel" means "the good news"); this is what the apostles proclaimed before it was written. Paul spoke of his gospel which he preached to Jews and Gentiles alike; and this is reactualized as it is proclaimed to succeeding generations, even down to our

[8]Ibid., 79.

own time, e.g., through its use in the liturgy. The proclamation makes this offer of salvation present and calls for the response of faith. Though there are quite different messages given at different times, and a growth and correction with time, God has an identity manifested by these actions, and the one called to believe has identity through the call to believe.

Thus the metaphors and creative imaginations of the human community and of the individual authors and editors are understood to be responses to and mediations of this divine revelation. We can say then that *the ultimate "creative imagination" at work here is understood by these scriptural authors and by the community of believers to be God's.* The action, e.g., of the Exodus, has him as its author. Thus by his words and deeds God performs symbolic actions that give his people access to the Sacred, participation in his saving power, transforming knowledge, etc. Similarly the resurrection and exaltation of Jesus is understood to be God's act by which, as this act is understood through passages of the Old Testament, he vindicates Jesus and declares him to be Lord and Messiah (Acts 2:36). In many different metaphors the authors of Scripture mediate God's saving presence and revelation.

What interpretations of Scripture does this oppose? It opposes those who take Scripture too objectively and too subjectively—e.g., many Neo-Scholastics and Bultmann. It opposes those who diffuse Christian identity excessively by assimilating it to that of the other religions of the Middle East in antiquity, excluding those characteristics that most distinguish it. It opposes those who will not speak of God with the personal pronoun, as though this would be to make an idol of or over-objectify the Sacred. It opposes those who interpret the language of Christian doctrine, also found in Scripture, as stipulating rules for the Christian use of language rather than having ontological reference. We are not here reflecting on the validity of the Jewish or Christian claim concerning the bases for their faith, e.g., God's action in the Exodus or in the resurrection of Jesus. That we will do in the next part of foundational theology. Here we simply assert that their claim should not be diluted, even though modern naturalism and many philosophical interpretations of human knowledge and horizon of values find these claims as such unintelligible or unacceptable. We note also that it is important for a theologian to present the Christian belief in the form Scripture does, and not only in the more conceptual form of theology; to do otherwise does not do justice to the meaning of this belief.

Third, in view of the differing theologies present in Scripture and its antiquity, how can one find an answer to questions we have in our time and a center in Scripture? With many scriptural scholars, we must say that although the critical historical method of studying Scripture is essential to contemporary biblical interpretation, by itself it is not adequate. That approach investigates the origin of the text in such matters as relation to previous themes, the circumstances of the time, the language used, and the intention of the author. But if we restrictedly study the languages that Scripture uses, the history behind the text, or the literary genres used by the author, then, as important as these are, they seem to leave a great gap between what we learn and our present questions. There seems to be such a gap between biblical anthropology or the biblical world and the world of the late twentieth century that we may experience its strangeness rather than its relevance when considering the problems we have with faith or the understanding of God. There are aspects of Scripture that share in the strangeness of other pre-modern religions.

It is here that the whole development of hermeneutics in recent times has been such an aid. Against Adolf von Harnack, Barth and Bultmann showed that the scientific study of Scripture that tried to find out what really happened and was said was not sufficient, and after Bultmann there has been more and more attention given to questions of hermeneutics. Theoretical analyses of what is involved in interpreting ancient texts have been given from the time of Friedrich Schleiermacher (1768–1834), Wilhelm Dilthey (1833–1911), and Martin Heidegger (1889–1976) till our own time with the important contributions of Hans-Georg Gadamer, Paul Ricoeur, and others. Studies of this can be found elsewhere,[9] but at this point we

---

[9]See Richard Palmer, *Hermeneutics. Interpretation Theory in Schleiermacher, Dilthey, Heidegger and Gadamer* (Evanston, Ill.: Northwestern Univ. Press, 1979); David Tracy, *The Analogical Imagination. Christian Theology and the Culture of Pluralism* (New York: 1981); and David Klemm, ed., *Hermeneutical Inquiry.* 2 vols. (Baltimore: Scholars Press, 1986). Also see note 38 in chapter 2 above.

shall simply show something of how we can gain an understanding of the meaning of biblical texts that relates to our present question of the meaning and grounds of faith in God. We cannot achieve this meaning by excluding critical helps that show us what the text meant at the time of its first use or later when it was reedited and included in the context of a larger literary work. However, we primarily want to know the kind of world or universe of meaning that is projected in front of the text. What relationship of God to humankind and of humankind to God does the text project? And what bases for such a relationship does the text offer? The meaning that the text projects can both affirm and challenge us in our understanding of life and the subject matter of the text. For many in our time and in the time when these texts were written, they are counter to the horizon of meaning and the human search; for others they largely affirm their horizon of meaning.

Perhaps the primary basis by which we can understand the meaning of the text in the sense of the kind of world that it projects is to take it as expressing and interpreting actions and words as God's. Using a recent book's analysis of some ways in which this meaning can be conveyed to us through the text, we can list several such ways.[10] The witnesses to faith that Scripture gives us are frequently testimonies to the divine acts by which God offers his saving intervention for his people. These testimonies point not only to the events but to their meaning by giving narrative accounts of such things as how the Israelites came to be a people and how the Christians came to be a people distinct from Judaism of the first century. (Of course, in the process they give accounts of events that transcend our normal expectation. And this raises difficulties for a naturalistic historical consciousness in our time that must be addressed at some point.) Thus meaning is frequently conveyed in Scripture in narrative form. Hence the meaning of an action or statement is not exclusively known through its relation to the intention of the author, but also by its consequences in the nar-

---

[10]See Francis Schüssler Fiorenza, *Foundational Theology. Jesus and the Church* (New York: Crossroad, 1984) 29–33, 108–122; John Farrelly, "Christian Symbols and Cultural Transformation," in George McLean (ed.), *Humanities, The Moral Imagination and Character Development* (Washington, D.C., Council for Research in Values and Philosophy, forthcoming).

rative. Again, the meaning of a statement is known in part through supposing that it conforms to the rules of the language, as human behavior is in part understood through supposing that the agent performed it in accordance with rules of behavior in a certain society (e.g., the meaning of Solomon's building of a temple, Samuel's anointing of David). Both language and action can have a meaning in what they signify and in what they seek to bring about (e.g., commands, admonitions, healings, forgiving). Still further we may have access to the meaning of a document, event, or statement by how it was received at the time and at later times. In some circumstances it goes against the expectations of the period and transforms these expectations or is rejected, but in any case it is always significant. Something similar is true of the way people of a later time may receive the earlier text or statement. Much of the prophetic discourse in the Old Testament shows how the founding event of Israel was interpreted in later times; and this is part of the meaning of the original event for Israel. As this process of resignification took place constantly in the reactualization of the proclamation of God's salvation through the biblical period, so too it has continued to occur through the Christian era. So we in our own time recognize larger meanings in the divine events and words to which the scriptural authors give witness, even to the point of finding there some answers to our questions about the meaning and foundations of belief in God that are proper to the Christian identity.

How can we from the diversity of theologies in Scripture claim to find an answer to our questions that is valid for all Christians? As we wrote earlier, we are not attempting here a biblical theology. That has its own problems in our time, because the difficulty of finding one center in Scripture is more evident now than earlier in our century.[11] And yet we cannot be satisfied with simply a history of the viewpoints of those who formed Israel's traditions and writings in succeeding ages. We

[11]See Gerhard Hasel, "Biblical Theology: Then, Now and Tomorrow," *Horizons in Biblical Theology* 4 (1982) 61–93; Rolf Knierim, "The Task of Old Testament Theology," ibid., 6 (1984) 25–57; and Roland Murphy, "A Response to 'The Task of Old Testament Theology'", ibid., 65–71. We note that our quotations from Scripture follow *The New American Bible* (New York: Catholic Book Publishing Co., 1986).

acknowledge differences of theology, of course, among the writings in the Old Testament and in the New Testament, and we are not attempting to study all these differences. But these writings have been gathered into one canon. This shows that the Christian community has a conviction that there is no basic contradiction between them, even though the parts should be interpreted ultimately within the context of the whole and in view of the development of the dialogue between God and Israel that revelation represents. The theologies had to be different if they were to be appropriate to differing circumstances, and the same is true for our time. But this kind of pluralism is consistent with a common faith. The center of our theology here is found in part in the questions we address to Scripture from the vantage point of our time and circumstances. But the unity of our view of God and of faith, its meaning and foundations, depends upon the basic unity found in Scripture itself. What is central here is the initiative of God through his saving presence and revelation and the response of his people or of individuals to him.

## I. The Old Testament

We want to know what Scripture testifies concerning God's relation to his people in history and who he is thus shown to be, who the human person and community are in relation to history and how this depends on their belief in God, and thus what the meaning and grounds of their belief in God are. We are then asking questions about what we consider the most serious difficulties with faith in our time, not about all the disagreements between theologians noted in the last chapter. We shall return to scriptural teaching concerning some of these issues in later chapters. For the answer to our present questions, we shall recall in succession some central events Scripture relates concerning the early period of Israel through the early monarchy, some relevant aspects of the message of the prophets and apocalyptic, and some central affirmations of the Book of Wisdom. We recognize that this last book is not considered to be part of the canon by most Protestants; but its message is still influential for the New Testament, and its form of dialogue is found in Paul's Areopagus speech in Acts. What we offer here are fragments of the Old Testament, but we trust that they are representative rather than distorting.

## 1. The Mystery of God's Saving Presence and Israel's Response

Does Scripture show Israel testifying that it was addressed with a saving intent in history by Yahweh as a transcendent personal mystery, and that the fulfilment of this saving divine intention depended on their response of faith, that is, belief, trust, and surrender? There is massive evidence that this is the case. We see it in the "cultic credo" that Deuteronomy instructs the Israelites to profess when they offer their firstfruits in thanksgiving before the Lord:

> Then you shall declare before the Lord, your God. "My father was a wandering Aramean who went down to Egypt with a small household and lived there as an alien. But there he became a nation great, strong and numerous. When the Egyptians maltreated and oppressed us, imposing hard labor upon us, we cried to the Lord, the God of our fathers, and he heard our cry and saw our affliction, our toil and our oppression. He brought us out of Egypt with his strong hand and outstretched arm, with terrifying power, with signs and wonders; and bringing us into this country, he gave us this land flowing with milk and honey. Therefore, I have now brought you the first fruits of the products of the soil which you, O Lord, have given me" (Deut 26:5-10).

Here the Israelites identified themselves with their people and its experience in Egypt and the Exodus, confessing God's saving acts on their behalf. Most of the people in the history of Israel did not experience these great saving acts of God firsthand, but his saving action was reactualized for them in their time by the mediation of their traditions and cult. What they proclaimed in later centuries reflects the ancient song of Miriam after the liberation of Israel from Egypt: "Sing to the Lord, for he is gloriously triumphant; horse and chariot he has cast into the sea" (Exod 15:21). We find this testimony in different ways in the accounts of Abraham, the Exodus, and the early history of Israel.

The Yahwist tradition presents the call of Abraham with great simplicity: "The Lord said to Abram: 'Go forth from the land of your kinsfolk and from your father's house to a land that I will show you. I will make of you a great nation, and I will bless you; I will make your name great, so that you will be a blessing. I will bless those who bless you and curse those who curse you. All the communities of the earth shall find blessing in you.' Abram went as the Lord directed him, and Lot went with him" (Gen 12:1-4a).

The initiative here is ascribed wholly to God. He chooses a man who, we must presume, shared many of the views of the surrounding peoples about God or gods. We can apply here what P. Beauchamp says in another context: "He (God) gives himself not as a totality filling a void, nor as a complement adding itself to an incomplete, but as he who establishes everything, beginning with that which precedes the event. We learn then that revelation implies the necessity of an event, that it is not an event without antecedents and that the antecedents are not the negation of the event."[12]

There is mystery in God's presence to Abraham here as there is in his further communications with him and seeming absences from him, but the mystery is definitely a personal one. Here through the specific historical intervention of the choice and call of Abraham, we find testimony to God's freedom of choice, even his apparent arbitrariness at times, and his unexplained actions.[13] He takes up a relation to this specific man within the context of a promise about his future. Abraham, in turn, believes God and acts faithfully. "Abraham

---

[12]P. Beauchamp, "Théologie biblique," in B. Lauret and F. Refoulé, eds. I, 187.

[13]Among God's unexplained actions that are difficult for people of our time to accept, we must count Scripture's statement that God asked Abraham to sacrifice his son Isaac and that he asked the Israelites to destroy all living beings in the cities they took in the conquest of the Promised Land. A statement of Bishop B. C. Butler in *The Church and the Bible* (London: Helicon, 1960) 71 (quoted in Joseph Jensen, *God's Word to Israel* [Wilmington, Del.: Glazier, 1982] 269) is relevant here. He notes that all revelation of God is "a divine self-disclosure within human experience, and therefore subject to the limitations of the human recipient. . . . If it is a revelation directed toward action, it will take form and shape in the conscience of the recipient and will be to some extent limited by his existing moral stature."

put his faith in the Lord, who credited it to him as an act of righteousness" (Gen 15:6). Abraham is presented as a model for Israel and later for Christians. In explaining his faith, Samuel Terrien comments: "The word he'emîn, 'to have faith,' is used in a theological context. The semantic connotations of the root suggest solidity and firmness not only in the realm of space but also in that of time; hence it indicates durability, reliability, and endurance. Abraham took Yahweh at his word. He believed the truth of the promise made to him. He placed his entire trust in the epiphanic speech. He responded with the entirety of his being to the articulated thrust of the divine presence."[14]

The experience and commitment that was basic to Israel's life was that of the Exodus and covenant and entrance into the Promised Land, and thus they recalled this founding event year after year, particularly during the feast of the Passover. They testified to this event as due to God's initiative through Moses; and thus, to use language we used earlier, they understood this event to be God's symbol of his relation to Israel. The account of the Exodus is in epic form and shows the creative imagination of the tradition, authors, and editors involved in composing it; but the escape from the forces of Egypt was such that it was ascribed to Yahweh's exercise of his saving power on Israel's behalf.

First they testified to God's appearance to Moses in the flaming bush (Exod 3:2). Once more there is an initiative on God's part, an immediacy of presence, an abruptness, a sublimation of presence into dialogue, and a relation God adopts toward a person and a history; note that despite all this, God remains invisible. God announces the mission he gives to Moses. When Moses asks for God's name to give to the people: "God replied, 'I am who am.' Then he added, 'This is what you shall tell the Israelites: the Lord, the God of your fathers, the God of Abraham, the God of Isaac, the God of Jacob, has sent me to you. This is my name forever; this is my title for all generations'" (Exod 3:14-15). Yahweh, translated as "the Lord," the special name of the God of Israel according to this account

---

[14]Samuel Terrien, *The Elusive Presence: Toward a New Biblical Theology* (San Francisco: Harper and Row, 1978) 77.

(E), is the third person singular form of the Hebrew word "I am" ("He is" or "He will be").[15] Whether Yahweh is interpreted as the causative form of the verb (as "He causes to be"), the simple form ("He who is"), or as God's promised presence among his people (as "He will be", i.e., with his people), Yahweh is named through the verb "to be." In this engagement with Moses, testimony is given that Yahweh manifests his being, his power to effect what he wills, and his saving presence for his people. This presence is not as definite as Moses wishes, for he wants more and more assurance (Exod 4:1); but it initiates Moses' call and the mediation he exercises to bring God's revelation and salvation to the Israelites. Through him God liberates the Israelites from slavery in Egypt and delivers them from Pharoah's army in the passage through the Red Sea.

It was at Sinai or Horeb that Israel experienced a theophany and received and ratified its covenant with Yahweh. After preparing for this covenant by which God would be their God and they would be his people, "a kingdom of priests, a holy nation" (Exod 19:4-6), the people experienced a theophany (Exod 19:16-18). They feared and trembled and asked Moses to speak for them. Moses approached the cloud where God was, and God delivered his commandments regarding Israel's relation to him and to one another (Exod 20:3-4, 7a, 8, 12-17a). The people ratified the covenant by a sacred meal (Exod 24:10-11) or, according to another tradition, by a sacrifice at the foot of the mountain (Exod 24:3-8) after Moses had read the terms of the covenant and the people answered: "All that the Lord has said, we will heed and do" (Exod 24:7). This event is so rich that no conceptual analysis can exhaust its implications. The authors of this account, through their creative imagination, testify to God's initiative—in a sense, his symbol—to enter into a covenant with a people so that they would be his people and he would be their God. The event occurs through an historical act that also shows God's power over nature (the theophany by mediation of thunder, cloud, etc.) and use of it to symbolize his presence and his hiddenness, the blessings and

[15]For different interpretations of the meaning of "Yahweh," see Terrien, *The Elusive Presence* 115–119, and Bernhard W. Anderson, *Understanding the Old Testament* 3rd ed. (Prentice-Hall, 1975) 52–56.

dangers of his divine power. It testifies to God as the savior of the nation and thus a God of history and of moral concern. It conveys a kind of knowledge of God that is transformative and a ground for the people's commitment of faith. It looks to the future not only of entrance into the Promised Land but of a people who will share in the holiness of God and mediate his holiness to other nations.

Once the people had entered Canaan, they were tempted to turn to the Baals and Ashtarts, the gods of Canaan associated with the powers of nature, as the problems of their lives became those of an agricultural people. The Deuteronomic history (e.g., Judg 2:6–3:6) recounts the period of the judges as one of recurring lapses of the people into idolatry, God's anger and abandonment of them into the power of their enemies, the people's cry to Yahweh for deliverance, and his answer through their liberation by successive judges.

With the establishment of the monarchy, David's conquest of Jerusalem, the Jebusite fortress and religious center, and Solomon's building of the Temple, there was a more pronounced integration of some aspects of Canaan's high god, El Elyon, God Most High (Gen 14:18, 22), with Yahweh.[16] Perhaps associated with this was the announcement to David by the prophet Nathan of God's choice of him and his offspring as a divinely ordained and hereditary kingship (2 Sam 7:8-16), quite different from God's covenant with the nomadic Israel-

---

[16]See J. Coppens, "La notion vétérotestamentaire de Dieu. Position du problème," in Coppens, *La Notion biblique,* 67: "El presented not a few traits and attributes susceptible of being assumed by the Mosaic religion and carried over to Yahweh. The Mosaic religion thus was enriched without changing as such toward syncretism. Hereafter the God of Israel appeared to his faithful equally and largely in the manner of El, as the God creator and sovereign of the cosmos."

We should note that the conflict in Israel between fidelity to Yahweh and worship of the Canaanite gods was complex and continuing. Israel did assimilate in different ways certain aspects of the cult of goddesses found in Canaan. As Rosemary Reuther writes, "In addition to [the] transformation of the Sacred Marriage from a Goddess-king relation into a patriarchal God-servant wife, Yahwism appropriates female images for God at certain points. The male patriarchal image proves too limited to represent the variety of relationships to Israel that Hebrew thought wished to express. In certain texts Yahweh is described as like a mother or like a woman in travail with the birth of a child" *Sexism and God-Talk. Toward a Feminist Theology* (Boston: Beacon Press, 1983) 56. The patriarchal images of God predominated, however. We will address briefly in chapter 8 the question whether that is adequate for our time.

ites in the desert. Now there was some rather revolutionary development of the earlier understanding of God, namely, "a strongly political aspect, that of a god guaranteeing a temporal power incarnated in a dynasty and centered on David in a capital and then, beginning with Solomon, in a national sanctuary."[17] Solomon's Temple was built in the style of the surrounding peoples, and God's presence was now experienced largely through sacred space, whereas earlier the main emphasis had been on God's presence through sacred time and history (see 2 Sam 7:5-8). Similarly, there was now an emphasis on a theology of God's glory in addition to the earlier theology which was dependent on a revelation by presence and name. While there were efforts to integrate the varied modes of God's presence,[18] there was also a strong and pervasive tendency toward a syncretism that led to decadence. This is shown dramatically when Elijah called upon the people to choose between Baal and Yahweh: "How long will you straddle the issue? If the Lord is God, follow him; if Baal, follow him" (1 Kings 18:21). After a contest between the prophets of Baal and Elijah, the people confessed, "The Lord is God! The Lord is God!" (1 Kings 18:39).

## 2. God's Concern for His People's Future: Prophets and Apocalyptic

One question we are asking in our study of Scripture is whether the God Christians believe in is involved in and concerned for their future in history or is disengaged from this. We also are asking whether our human response of obedience in faith is central to the outcome of this future. What we have seen so far provides an answer to this question; but in the prophets and, in a different way, in the apocalyptic writings we find that this is a constant theme. The prophets do not so much describe God as speak for him in diverse historical situations, trying to bring the people back to fidelity to him and the covenant. At times they ascribe their knowledge of God to an

[17]Coppens, *La Notion biblique,* 67.

[18]See Terrien, *The Elusive Presence* ch. 4, "The Presence in the Temple," 161–226.

inaugural vision by which they receive their mission; and we can see that much of it comes from their reflection on the implications of their Yahwistic faith for the circumstances of their time. Knowledge of God is available to those to whom they proclaim their message on the condition that they transform their lives and accept this message. At times they explicitly relate this to faith. For example, Isaiah tells Ahaz: "Unless your faith is firm, you shall not be firm!" (Isa 7:9), and a century later, Habakkuk warns that "The rash man has no integrity; but the just man, because of his faith, shall live" (Hab 2:4).

One aspect of God that is reflected by the passionate concern of the prophets is God's own pathos. As Abraham Heschel writes: "To the prophet . . . God does not reveal himself in an abstract absoluteness, but in a personal and intimate relation to the world. . . . He is not conceived as judging the world in detachment. . . . Quite obviously in the biblical view, man's deeds may move him, affect him, grieve him or, on the other hand, gladden and please him. This notion that God can be intimately affected, that he possesses not merely intelligence and will but also pathos, basically defines the prophetic consciousness of God."[19]

The message of the individual prophets differs according to the circumstances of the time and the needs of the people to whom they are proclaiming the word of God. Because of changing circumstances within the Israelite community or in their environs, the people's faith in God is called into question again and again. The prophets respond with a word that shows God's action and call in such circumstances. And thus there is growth in Israel's understanding of God. For example, Amos

---

[19]Abraham Heschel, *The Prophets,* vol. 2 (New York: Harper Colophon ed., 1972) 3–4. Also see W. Zimmerli, "Gott in der Verkündigung der Propheten," in Coppens, *La Notion biblique,* 127–143; and Terrien, *The Elusive Presence* ch. 5, "The Prophetic Vision." We must take account of the question of genres here, as John J. Collins notes in "Old Testament Theology," in J. J. Collins and John D. Crossan, eds., *The Biblical Heritage in Modern Catholic Scholarship* (Wilmington, Del.: Glazier, 1986) 29: "What is at issue is a question of genre. Does a passage like Hosea 11, which speaks of God changing his mind so that he will not destroy Israel, give us any metaphysical information? or is it rather an expression of a human conviction that mercy is better than anger? Many prophetic texts which speak of God in anthropomorphic terms are primarily concerned with human social values rather than with metaphysics." We will return to this question in chapter 8.

prophesied in northern Israel that the day of the Lord would be for Israel a day of judgment (Amos 5:18-20) because of their injustice against the poor and the weak and their infidelity and idolatry. Hosea also prophesied against Israel for her infidelity and adulterous conduct, shown in her idolatry and ruthless oppression of the poor, the pain of which Hosea experienced through his own marriage to a harlot, Gomer. This experience allowed him to portray God's love for Israel in such terms of marriage and tenderness as are virtually unique in the Old Testament (Hosea 11). Isaiah had a vision of the holiness of Yahweh in the Temple, as he heard the seraphim chanting "Holy, holy, holy is the Lord of hosts" (Isa 6:3), and in his ministry he had a deep sense of the abyss that separates God's holiness and transcendence from human sinfulness. He saw hope for Judah in God's saving help that would come through a child who would arise from the house of David to rule Judah (Isa 7:14-16; 9:5-6; 11:1-9).[20] A century later, Jeremiah prophesied the destruction of Jerusalem for its idolatry and impenitence, and did so at the cost of great personal suffering and opposition. But he also foretold that a day would come when God would make a new covenant with his people and place his law within them, writing it on their hearts (Jer 31:31-34).

During the early part of the Exile, the prophet Ezekiel received his call through a vision which symbolized God's transcendence (Ezek 1:1-28) and prophesied the destruction of Jerusalem that occurred in 587 B.C. Later when the people experienced God's distance and absence, he comforted them with predictions that God would gather his people together again, and that though the one who sinned would receive retribution, the one who turned from sin would live (Ezek 33:10-20). God would give his people "a new heart and . . . a new spirit" (Ezek 36:26). God promised, "I will put my spirit within you and make you live by my statutes, careful to observe my decrees" (Ezek 36:27). God would have the Temple rebuilt and give his people new life (Ezek 37:1-4), establishing "an everlasting covenant with them" (Ezek 37:26).

---

[20]On God's "plan" in Isaiah, see Joseph Jensen, "Yahweh's Plan in Isaiah and the Rest of the Old Testament," *Catholic Biblical Quarterly* 48 (1986) 443–455.

Second Isaiah, toward the end of the Exile, had a message of comfort for the people who had received double for all their sins. God's transcendence was exalted as by no previous prophet so that the people might know that no matter where they are on earth God has power to save them. "Do you not know? Have you not heard? Was it not foretold you from the beginning? Have you not understood? Since the earth was founded he sits enthroned above the vault of the earth, and its inhabitants are like grasshoppers. . . . The Lord is the eternal God, creator of the ends of the earth" (Isa 40:21-22, 28). All idols are as nothing (Isa 44:6-20). God has power over all nations, and he would send his servant Cyrus to free the Jews from captivity (Isa 45:1-5). Monotheism had not been expressed earlier with the same clarity: "I am the Lord and there is no other; there is no God besides me" (Isa 45:5). As God's transcendence was exalted, his—or rather, her—tenderness was expressed in matchless poetry: "Can a mother forget her infant, be without tenderness for the child of her womb? Even should she forget, I will never forget you" (Isa 49:15). This passage shows us that male imagery of God was found to be inadequate to convey God's relation to Israel, even though—in part due to the patriarchal culture of Israel—God was spoken of primarily through male images and symbols. The salvation that God will effect will somehow come through the mediation of the suffering servant of the Lord, and the result will be that Israel will be restored and nations will come to her, and God will give a salvation that will last forever (Isa 51:6). But with all his revelation of God's transcendence and saving presence to his people, Second Isaiah still spoke (as his predecessors had) of the hiddenness of God (Isa 45:15). This is a dimension of his transcendence, and not evidence of God's non-existence or lack of care for his people.

It was probably during the Exile or shortly thereafter that under the editorship of priests the Pentateuch was shaped into its final form. The Priestly tradition began with its account of creation in Genesis 1, thus showing God's power over all the earth and heavens. It integrated the Yahwist and Elohist traditions in the stages from creation to the flood, and from Noah through whom God established a covenant with all humankind until the new beginnings with Abraham. This shows

God's care for all humanity. However, in Israel's perspective all of creation and history leads up to God's special covenant with his chosen people.

On its return from exile and with the reconstruction of the Temple and the reforms of Ezra the priest, this people became a worshiping community. The priestly community found in the Book of Psalms songs to be sung by the group or individuals, primarily during the Temple festivals. These psalms express every human emotion and testify to Judaism's belief in God as personal, as mystery, and as deeply involved with his people and with individuals. There are psalms of praise for God's wondrous works in Israel's history and in creation (e.g., Ps 136); there are psalms of lament and prayers for forgiveness (e.g., Ps 51). There are prayers for liberation from suffering (e.g., Ps 44), and psalms expressing the psalmist's confusion and distress at the suffering of the innocent (Ps 73). Others call down God's blessings on the anointed of Yahweh, the king (Pss 2 and 20), or exalt God as king of the universe (e.g., Ps 93) and praise the wonders of his law (e.g., Ps 119).

The apocalyptic literature of the Old Testament also has something to tell us about Judaeo-Christian belief about God's relation to history and the importance of faith. Since this theme is more appropriately analysed by the second part of foundational theology than the first because of its importance for understanding the kind of salvation that God is believed to offer us through Jesus Christ, we shall be very brief in our comments on it here. To restrict ourselves to the Book of Daniel, it is clear that it deals with the problem of evil, not primarily in the life of the individual (as in Job), but in the life of the people of God. Israel faced this threat to disbelief as severely as any people in history. As distinct from prophecy, apocalyptic was not a preaching that was later written down but a form of literature from the beginning. Daniel was resistance literature; that is, it was an encouragement (in veiled terms because of the oppressive times) for the people to remain faithful to God and their traditions—to keep faith with God in the midst of oppression from which there seemed to be no human escape. This book was written during the Hellenization program that was imposed on the Jews of Palestine by Antiochus IV about 167–164 B.C., when Jews were losing their lives through their fidelity to their traditions. With its anonymous authorship and ascription to a period long past in history, with its visions, numbers, and symbols (e.g., the beasts symbolizing different kingdoms), this apocalyptic demands special care in its interpretation. But some of its central message, conveyed by symbols, visions, and allegories, is as follows.[21] It gives the people reason to persevere at any cost, even at the cost of their lives. The rationale for this is that God, all appearances to the contrary, controls history and will in the age to come, which is about to break in upon the world, make right all evils that have been inflicted on and endured by the just. In the present age, God allows the powers of evil that fight against him and his holy ones to hold sway, but their time is measured and there will be a reversal. God's kingdom, given to his holy ones, symbolized by one like a Son of Man, will in the new age be established as a universal and eternal kingdom by God's power alone, and the just shall rise from the dead to a new life (Dan 7; 12:1-3). History is one and under the power of God; it will appear as such in the age to come. The kingdom to come is not a maturation of the forces for good that at present are operating in the world, but God's sudden irruption into history.

Through the prophets we have testimony to God's profound concern for his people's historical present and future. Through the priestly contributions to the Pentateuch, we have testimony to God's engagement with all peoples from the beginning of creation and history. Through the apocalyptic Book of Daniel, we have testimony to a future that transcends history and embraces all of humankind. Dialectically, the future of the people and of the individual depends on the people's faithfulness even when this faithfulness leads to death. Israel and humanity are destined for a liberation and fulfillment that transcends the limits of history.

[21]See M. Delcor, "Le Dieu des Apocalypticiens," in Coppens, *La Notion biblique* 209–228; John J. Collins, *The Apocalyptic Imagination* (New York: Crossroad, 1984); and John J. Collins, *Daniel, 1 and 2 Maccabees* (Wilmington, Del.: Glazier, 1981).

## 3. An Apologetic in Dialogue with Hellenistic Humanism

What we have seen so far is that Israel based its faith on
God's initiative in offering an historical salvation and historical revelation, and that its liberation and fulfillment through
history depended on its fidelity to God. We have seen something of how this belief was related to the belief of other peoples (e.g., the Canaanites) who based their relation to deity
largely on their experience of nature. We find a particularly
important witness to how the Jews related another people's religious search to their own in the encounter with Hellenism reflected by the Book of Wisdom. Did the Jews think that the
access God gave them to himself was the only possible access?
We turn to the Book of Wisdom for a partial answer to this
question, even though this book is not accepted as part of the
canon by Protestants. We will later suggest that its message is
found elsewhere, e.g., in Paul's Areopagus speech (Acts 17).

This remarkable book was probably written in Alexandria
toward the middle of the first century before Christ.[22] Studies
have shown that the author was a devout Jew who adhered
fully to the belief of his ancestors and yet knew the Hellenistic
culture of his time and place, particularly its religious, philosophical, and psychological aspects. He wrote largely for Jews
who were tempted by the splendor of Hellenistic culture to
abandon the faith of their fathers. His book shows that he himself accepted much of this culture as having value and validity,
that he in fact integrated it into an apologetic for belief in God,
the source of wisdom and justice, and that he expressed his
Jewish faith in a way that was more universal than most of Jewish Scripture. His apologetic continues to have relevance for
the West of today that is in debt to the Greeks, and in which
this inheritance has been in tension with our inheritance from
Judaism and early Christianity. We shall note the author's es-
teem for human qualities highly appreciated in Hellenism,
such as justice and wisdom, his interpretation of these as gifts

---

[22]See James Reese, *Hellenistic Influence on the Book of Wisdom and its Consequences* (Rome: Biblical Institute Press, 1970); M. Gilbert, "La connaissance de
Dieu selon le livre de la Sagesse," in Coppens, *La Notion biblique,* 191–210.

of God and leading to God, and his reflection on philosophical knowledge of God.

The author wrote at a time when the classical philosophies of Greece had been supplanted by Stoicism, Epicureanism, and a broad search for religious salvation. He appealed to people engaged in this search: "Love justice, you who judge the earth; think of the Lord in goodness, and seek him in integrity of heart" (Wis 1:1). The first condition which will ensure the fruitfulness of this search is that of integrity of heart or sincerity or simplicity, conditions opposed to a spirit of deceit, or one which distrusts or tests God. The just are in God's care and, though the unjust attack and even kill them, "yet is their hope full of immortality" (3:4). In speaking thus of the just, the author showed that God's providential care is not exclusively for Israel but also for those among other peoples who seek justice. To affirm the happiness God has in store for them beyond death, the author used a word from Greek philosophy, "immortality" (*athanasia*), though he meant by this God's gift of abiding with him in love rather than a natural quality of the soul.[23]

This justice is not simply the fruit of human effort and labor, but is rather the result of Wisdom's gift, as the Sage shows in his account of the patriarchs (though he does not name them, thus preserving the universal significance of their experience) who received their justice from Wisdom (ch. 10). (We may note that the personalizing of Wisdom, Word, and Spirit we find here and elsewhere in the late Jewish Scriptures reflects the inner fullness of God's life and was used by the New Testament writers to express the Christian mystery of the Trinity.) Through Wisdom God has a care for the just and personal intimacy with them (9:10-13). Through the author's prayer for Wisdom, he intimates that the justice that brings immortality partakes of grace (ch. 9). He ascribes qualities to Wisdom that he draws in part from the Stoic mystic Cleanthes and from a hymn to Isis,[24] and he uses Hellenistic speculation on the kingly ideal to show the place of Wisdom in God's providential care and in God's teaching of those central virtues es-

[23]See Reese, *Hellenistic Influence*, 62–66.
[24]See ibid., 37–38, 45–50.

teemed by the Greeks—"moderation and prudence, justice and fortitude" (8:7). Thus the human values of justice and wisdom, we may conclude, lead to God and do so because they are God's gifts.

In this context the author discusses the question of philosophical knowledge of God (13:1-9). In this beautiful passage, he accuses Hellenistic theosophy of impiety or ignorance of God because it did not reach the personal and truly transcendent God whom the Jews worshiped. It did not reach him because it did not reach God as the maker of all, including matter, but rather concluded its search by divinizing different elements, or with "Eon," a personified cosmic God.[25] In the context of the book as a whole, where the author ascribes knowledge of God to God's gift of Wisdom, he is opposed to every attempt to approach or know God that *is based on human effort alone.* It is this that he condemns in the Hellenistic religious search.

The author, however, asserts that the personal Creator does reveal himself in his works and can be known by human beings when impiety does not intervene: "For all men were by nature foolish who were in ignorance of God, and who from the good things seen did not succeed in knowing him who is, and from studying the works did not discern the artisan" (13:1). This God or "he who is" (an implied association of Yahweh and "being" of Greek philosophy, though the author understands being in a less restricted way than in this philosophy) or the artisan can be known from his works. God is more excellent than his works, as the original source of beauty; and he is more powerful than the might and energy of the forces of nature. Indeed his greatness and beauty are seen by *analogy* from created things. Thus the author is saying that the fact that the Greeks did not know God is not because the things that are seen do not manifest their maker, or because of a lack of intellectual capacity to understand the implications of God's works, or because of a lack of God's help on which such knowledge depends; it is due to their impiety, though these men are less to blame than those who make animals or the works of their own hands their gods. He accepts the legitimacy of philosophical thought but

[25]See ibid., 58–59.

not its limited achievements nor the spirit of self-sufficiency that led to these limitations. His interest is not, however, in speculation but in human beings' surrender to God—that they "may abandon their wickedness and believe in you, O Lord!" (12:2). We can say then that the Book of Wisdom does support the view that faith in God finds grounds in human values and human knowledge when people, by God's grace, are open to their larger meaning and implications.

## II. The New Testament

In our reflection on the New Testament in the first part of foundational theology we are not attempting to show how Jesus proclaimed the kingdom of God and sought faith as a response to him and his proclamation, nor how the early Church proclaimed the resurrected Jesus as Christ and Lord. That theme belongs, in our understanding, to the second part of foundational theology. Here we are primarily interested in recalling several implications that the proclamation by Jesus and the early Church have for our faith in God, and in showing the primitive Christian contact with Hellenism. Because of the disputes among Christian theologians that we saw in the preceding chapter (particularly the dispute between Barth and Catholics), we will limit ourselves to two main texts that relate to this issue, Paul's Areopagus speech (Acts 17:16-31) and two passages in Romans (Rom 1:18-21; 2:14-16).

Jesus' proclamation of the kingdom of God by his words and deeds has implications for who God is.[26] Jesus did not announce a God different from that of the Old Testament, although he did proclaim God in a new way and by a new revelation. There is no antithesis with the God of the Old Testament; Jesus presupposed this God who must be loved and served with an undivided heart. He accepted God's transcendence and proclaimed his absolute holiness, and thus did not seek to diminish reverence for him. He stressed God's unlim-

---

[26]See R. Schnackenburg, "Image of God in the New Testament," *Sacramentum Verbi,* vol. 1, 309–316; see James Reese, "The Principal Model of God in the New Testament," *Biblical Theology Bulletin* 8 (1978) 126–131.

ited divine power which can bring about salvation for humankind: God is the Lord of history and guides it to the end he has
ordained for it. But Jesus also called God "Father" and, more
specifically, "Abba," a word of such intimacy that it seemed
disrespectful to his contemporaries. In fact, the New Testament use of the word "God" almost always designates the First
Person of the Trinity, the Father. Jesus told his disciples to pray
to God with childlike trust, for we can bring our cares to him.
He proclaimed God's initiative and saving presence through
parables such as that of the Prodigal Son and through his own
initiatives with publicans, sinners, and the outcast. By the metaphors and symbols of his words and deeds, he proclaimed
that God takes the initiative to come and be near the human
person and community, to save, comfort, and heal. This God
has a superabundant promise in store for those who follow
Jesus in faith.

The early Christians also proclaimed God as Jesus did. They
stressed that he had made his love known to us, for he "did not
spare his own Son but handed him over for us all" (Rom 8:32).
Or, as John put it, "God so loved the world that he gave his
only Son, so that everyone who believes in him might not per-
ish but might have eternal life" (John 3:16). John also wrote:
"God is love" (1 John 4:8). Paul praised God's wisdom as well
as his love: "Oh, the depth of the riches and wisdom and
knowledge of God! How inscrutable are his judgments and
how unsearchable his ways!" (Rom 11:33). God's immanence
does not detract from his transcendence; nor does his love detract from the fact that he holds human beings accountable
and will judge them on the last day (Rom 2:5-10). We should
note, though we leave its development for the next part of
foundational theology, that apocalyptic formed a central part
of early Christian interpretation of the kingdom of God, the
risen and exalted Christ, and his present saving impact
through the Spirit and proclamation of the word—an impact
not only within the Church but within the political community. The early Church, we may say, thought that God was so
concerned for history that Christians proclaimed it was those
who accepted and acted on God's definitive revelation of himself who would be the inheritors of history in the world to come
or resurrected life.

As we turn to the question of the early Christian proclamation to the Gentiles, some theologians, primarily Protestant, contest the view, primarily Catholic, that Paul dialogues with the Gentiles on the basis of human reason and values. They hold that Paul's approach is exemplified in Romans 1, and it is one of confrontation rather than dialogue; he accuses people of sin and calls them to conversion. To treat this question, we shall treat successively the Areopagus speech in Acts and then Romans.

## 1. Paul's Areopagus Speech

Luke tells us that on his second missionary journey, Paul arrived in Athens from Beroea and began preaching in the synagogue to the Jews and the God-fearing men and women associated with them. Paul also presented his message daily in the public square to those whom he chanced to meet there, among whom were Epicureans and Stoics (Acts 17:16-18). Some of his listeners took him to the Areopagus and invited him to express his views. The Areopagus referred to here could be the hill that is north-east of the Acropolis, but it could also be the educational commission of the Athenian court called by the same name.[27] This commission of enquiry asked Paul, "May we learn what this new teaching is that you speak of?" (17:19). Paul delivered his speech in answer to this (17:22-31).

There are several questions we may ask of this passage in relation to our theme. First, is this a representative example of early Christian preaching to the Gentiles who had not yet been touched by the synagogue? And does Luke consider it a success or a failure? Many exegetes have interpreted it as a failure and thus a method that Paul soon abandoned. They base this assertion on 1 Corinthians 2:1-5 in which Paul describes his ministry among the Corinthians, to whom he went after Athens. Here Paul says that he did not come "with sublimity of words or of wisdom" (1 Cor 2:1), but rather he spoke only of Jesus Christ and him crucified. Thus their faith rested "not on human wisdom but on the power of God" (1 Cor 2:5).

---

[27]See B. Gärtner, *The Areopagus Speech and Natural Revelation* (Lond: C.W.K. Gleerup, 1955).

In answer to this argument for minimizing the importance of the Areopagus speech, we may recall that Paul's stay in Athens and his First Letter to the Corinthians were separated by 7 years (50–57 A.D.).[28] Paul's mind in the early 50's is shown rather in I and II Thessalonians where, as we will see, there is an approach referred to that is parallel to that of the Areopagus speech. Also, what does Paul mean by "human wisdom"? The reference to "sublimity of words or of wisdom" would more probably refer to the use of rhetoric than to "the genuine *bios theoretikos* pursued by Plato and Aristotle."[29] To take Paul's speech as a failure, moreover, is to interpret Luke's recounting of it as rather anecdotal. But Luke's interest in this speech is that it is an exemplification of early Christian proclamation to the Gentiles. In Acts he presents three speeches of Paul, each addressed to a different audience: Jews (13:16-41), pagans (17:22-31), and a Christian community (20:17-35). Thus Acts 17 is not an exception, but rather an indication of the standard approach of the early Church to the Gentiles, and as such it presents a programme for mission. Luke would not have been concerned to present Paul's words verbatim; he probably used the "widespread type of Christian preaching to the Gentiles that went along the lines of monotheistic Jewish propaganda."[30] Paul's speech is followed by acceptance on the part of a few and rejection on the part of many—not unlike what followed other missionary speeches Paul gave. The speech is not presented by Luke as a failure.

A second question we may ask is the following. Is this speech, as some claim, indicative that Paul was tempted to substitute philosophy for the kerygma in Athens? Some interpreters say that this speech is not Pauline, or if it is, it was an approach later rejected by Paul. Paul's preaching, they say, centered on Christ, while this speech centers on God, with a proclamation of Christ added as an appendix. However, is this a just estimate of the speech? It has a double focus—both theo-

---

[28]See L. Legrand, "The Areopagus Speech: its Theological Kerygma and its Missionary Significance," in Coppens, *La Notion biblique,* 337–350, on which my study here of this speech primarily depends.

[29]Ibid., 340.

[30]Ibid., 341.

logical and Christological—similar to what is indicated in 1
Thessalonians 1:9-10 where Paul recalls that at his preaching,
the Thessalonians "turned to God from idols, to serve the living and true God and to await his Son from heaven, whom he
raised from the dead, Jesus, who delivers us from the coming
wrath." The Christological focus is marginal neither in Paul's
preaching at Thessalonica nor in his preaching at Athens. Similarly, in neither case is the teaching about God a "mere preparation, pre-kerygma or pre-catechesis, as a preliminary of faith
rather than the object of faith."[31] The theological part of the
Athens speech is introduced by a word belonging to the
kerygmatic vocabulary—"make known to you," "announce"
(*katangelō*)—having God as its object. Kerygma cannot be reduced to the Christological fact. "The three elements, God,
Christ and conversion are inseparable parts of the kerygma."[32]
This preaching is not a case of philosophy substituting for the
kerygma.

Our third question asks what stand Paul takes to Hellenistic
religion. Some see this speech as radically contrasted to Paul's
authentic theology which, they say, was one of confrontation.
Others interpret it as a "fulfillment" model of theology, as
though Paul were saying that the Greeks worshiped the true
God implicitly in their worship. However, this is a misinterpretation. Paul is not taking one of the Greek gods—Zeus or
Athene, for example—and saying that in worshiping such a
god, the Athenians are worshiping the true God. He does not
tie in what he proclaims to any known god they worship, but
rather to the altar he found dedicated "To a God Unknown."
Theodore of Mopsuestia interpreted this by a story he had
heard. The Athenians at one time were defeated in war, and a
certain demon appeared and said that it happened because
they had not honored him. To placate an unknown—and thus
foreign—god, the Greeks erected this altar. Thus the point is
"not that the Greeks worshiped the true God implicitly but
that, on their own admission, the one true God was unknown
to them." Paul attacks their false notions of God, and thus he is

[31]Ibid., 345.

[32]Ibid., 345. See also Acts 14:15 and John 17:3 for inclusion of teaching on God
in the kerygma.

not presenting a faith that is a "blossoming of Greek religiosity."[33] He is calling them to conversion—to turn away from idols.

But Paul (or the speech) does take a positive stand toward these Athenians. He does not argue or present bases for a better understanding of God and thus for a truer worship simply from Judaeo-Christian revelation, and condemn the Athenians on this basis. Rather he argues from the world and the human experience by which God had revealed himself to them. There were two basic sources from which the understanding of deity was derived in the Mediterannean world outside of Judaism: natural phenomena and the state.[34] It is from these bases that Paul develops his explanation of God and people's relation to him, and thus too his critique of idolatry and call for repentance and turning to God. He begins with the fact that natural phenomena are caused by a divine being, which many of his listeners would accept without difficulty. The natural phenomena he uses are not some restricted part of the world but the world as an ordered whole, the cosmos. Since it is recognized that individual natural phenomena need deity as their source, a fortiori the whole does. From this common beginning, Paul proceeds to show something of God and to criticize false conceptions and religious cult. He who made the world and all in it is Lord and ruler of heaven and earth. Being so transcendent, he is not restricted to temples built by human hands, nor does he depend on human beings; in fact, it follows that all things humans have, including life, are his gift. And in reference to the common supposition of the time that deity is associated with a state or society, Paul avoids taking a particular social organization, but raises his audience's vision to God as the maker of the whole human race from one source, and as governing them and alloting the various times and boundaries that constitute the kingdoms of the world. He shows that the goal of God's governance is that all should seek God, and he

[33]Ibid., 348.

[34]See, e.g., A. Hus, "Greek and Roman Religion," in *Twentieth Century Encyclopedia of Catholicism,* vol. 142 (New York: Hawthorn, 1962) 75 ff.; and R. Bultmann, *Primitive Christianity in its Contemporary Setting* (Edinburgh: Collins, 1960) 124ff. for earlier Greece, and 161ff. for the Stoics.

underlines the uncertainty of this quest. The reason why this quest is like that of a blind man groping for an object is not the distance by which God is separated from us; he is not far from any of us, for "'in him we live and move and have our being' . . . 'for we too are his offspring'" (17:28). These are probably references to statements by Epimenides of Knossos and Aratus of Soli or Tarsus.[35] All of this is presented in the form of an announcement or kerygma and its bases; it leads to Paul's call for conversion in preparation for the one to whom God has given judgment—the one he raised from the dead.

Thus this speech represents neither fulfillment theology nor simple confrontation and challenge. It is rather dialogue, or as one author says: "the Areopagus speech is the first witness in Christianity to an encounter between biblical faith in the creation and the cosmic piety of the Greeks."[36] It is more than this, because it has the eschatological note of the proclamation of the resurrection of Jesus and the coming judgment, but it is still genuine dialogue or encounter. It shows that, as Catholic and many other theologians have constantly affirmed, Christian proclamation is not adverse to dialogue and to recalling manifestations or revelations that God makes in the physical world or human experience to lead people to conversion and Christ.

*2. Romans 1.*

This text is a classical source on which Barth and others base their view that Acts 17 cannot be authentically Pauline, and therefore it is important for us to examine it briefly. In commenting on this passage, Barth recalls that Paul defines the gospel here as "God's power for the salvation of everyone who has faith" (1:16).[37] That is, the gospel *is* God's omnipotence saving human beings, and in this event God's verdict in and through Christ is revealed. It is through the Cross that God re-

[35]See Richard Dillon and Joseph Fitzmyer, "Acts of the Apostles," in *Jerome Biblical Commentary* (Englewood Cliffs, N.J.: Prentice-Hall, 1968) II:200.

[36]A quotation from W. Eltester, in Legrand, "The Areopagus Speech," 349.

[37]Karl Barth, *A Shorter Commentary on Romans* (Richmond, Va: 1959) 21. This book originated in lectures given by Barth in Basle in 1940–41.

veals himself and his verdict of condemnation (for it shows the sin all are guilty of and the condemnation it merits) and justification (for it shows that he has put upon his Son Jesus Christ the condemnation due to all). The human person's response to this revelation should be belief. That is, one should say, "Yes, it is I. I accept this condemnation," thus recognizing the righteousness of God's condemnation. But since this is a revelation of God's justification, one should also say, "Yes, it is I! So I am allowed to be and I desire to be!"[38] This faith is the faith of Abraham who, when all natural reason contradicted his hope, trusted that God's promise to him would be fulfilled.[39]

In Romans 1, Paul is proclaiming God's wrath, and thus it is scarcely likely that Paul would be asserting that the Gentiles were already in full possession of true knowledge of God:

> He tells the Gentiles . . . that God has in fact for a long time, yea always, since the creation of the world been declaring and revealing himself to them. . . . objectively speaking they have . . . always known him. . . . Paul does not dream of paying the Gentiles anything resembling a compliment and of trying to find in their religions some point of contact for the understanding of the Gospel; on the contrary he is merely and simply recalling them to faith in God's verdict. . . . Human religion, as radically distinguished from belief in God's revelation, always originates and consists in this confusion: in the mistaken confidence in which man wants to decide for himself who and what God is, which can only produce this confusion, i.e. idolatry.[40]

Thus we have here an interpretation of Romans 1:20 that is opposed to that traditionally made by Catholic interpreters. To try to understand what Paul is saying and its implications for Acts 17, we will first speak about the context of the passage, second indicate how Paul's affirmation of human knowledge of God fits into this context, and third compare what is asserted here with the apologetic that we analysed in Acts 17. All

[38]Ibid., 43.
[39]See ibid., 52.
[40]Ibid., 28–29.

of these matters are disputed, and in this introductory analysis we are not presuming to treat this complex passage with the thoroughness it deserves. But we shall show that our interpretation is well founded.

What is the context of Romans 1:18ff.? This is offered by the purpose of the epistle, and there is dispute about this purpose.[41] It is widely agreed that Paul did not know the Roman Church in detail as he did the Churches he founded, that he wrote this letter in preparation for a visit he hoped to make to Rome, and that the purpose of his letter was in accord with the purpose he expressed for his projected visit: "I long to see you, that I may share with you some spiritual gift so that you may be strengthened, that is, that you and I may be mutually encouraged by one another's faith" (Rom 1:11-12). The purpose of the epistle, we may conclude, is to contribute to the strengthening of the faith of the members of the Church of Rome. Though Paul did not know them personally (he did know some of them; see Rom 16:3 ff.), he knew that there were both Gentile Christians and Jewish Christians at Rome, and he had long familiarity with problems that might arise to challenge the faith for either of these groups.

The theme of the epistle is shown in 1:16-17: "I am not ashamed of the gospel. It is the power of God for the salvation of everyone who believes: for Jew first, and then Greek. For in it is revealed the righteousness of God from faith to faith; as it is written, 'The one who is righteous by faith shall live.'" It is the last phrase (here given in the New American Bible translation) that is particularly relevant to our question here. Some exegetes say that Paul is trying to show that we are saved by faith and not by works (and it is this interpretation the above translation seems to follow). For example, A. Feuillet writes that "his purpose is not to establish how the just will live, but rather what kind of justice man must be clothed with to be able to live; is it that of faith or that of works?"[42] Another view ties

---

[41]See Karl Donfried, ed., *The Romans Debate* (Minneapolis: Augsburg, 1977).

[42]A. Feuillet, "La citation d'Habacuc ii.4 et les huit premiers chapitres de l'Epître aux Romains," *New Testament Studies* 5 (1960) 52. One interpreter agreeing with this translation is Ernst Käsemann, *Commentary on Romans* (Grand Rapids: Eerdmans, 1980) 21. Käsemann notes that "In Heb 10:38 and even Gal 3:11, as in the original Hebrew text and the LXX, the phrase *ek pisteos* belongs with the verb.

in the last phrase with Paul's preceding emphasis on "the righteousness of God from faith to faith." A. Viard writes: "'From
faith to faith' would mean then: 'from beginning with faith,
which has permitted the justification already acquired, in virtue of faith, that is, [it is] . . . perseverance in this faith, or fidelity, on which salvation depends.'"[43] This latter interpretation is closer to the original from which Paul quotes, namely,
Habakkuk 2:4 which asserts that "the just man, because of his
faith, shall live"—faith in the sense of fidelity. It is also closer
to the way that Hebrews 10:38 cites Habakkuk 2:4: "My just
one shall live by faith, and if he draws back I take no pleasure
in him." Similarly, it is closer to Galatians 3:11 where the just
one is said to have life through his or her faith. There is no
question that Paul's teaching is that we are justified by faith
rather than by works, but the theme of Romans (1:16) which
verse 17 is defending seems to cover more than this point. It
also covers (as chapters 5 and following show) the gift of salvation or life, and this depends not only on initial faith but on
continuing faith or fidelity that includes the "obedience of
faith" (Rom 1:5). According to this interpretation then, which
we accept here, Paul is writing his epistle to encourage the
Roman Christians who already believe to be faithful till the
end. Thus his theme is that God gives his salvation or life to all
who believe, for as Scripture says, the just one shall have life
through faith or fidelity.

Käsemann's view that the whole epistle is governed by an
apocalyptic background supports this. For example, Paul in all
probability took the phrase "righteousness of God" from Jewish apocalyptic, and thus it refers to God's covenant faithfulness.[44] Also, salvation for Paul "denotes deliverance in the
final judgment [that] . . . already has become a present reality
through Christ in the midst of the world."[45] As Käsemann
sums up his position, "The theme, argument, and outcome of
the whole letter point . . . to the sphere of a uniquely modified

---

Here, however, the context and the apostle's doctrine of justification suggest—
although this is strongly contested—that it is related to the subject" (32).

[43]André Viard, *St. Paul: Épître aux Romains* (Paris: Gabala, 1975) 51.

[44]Käsemann, *Commentary on Romans,* 30.

[45]Ibid., 22.

Jewish-Christian apocalyptic."[46] Similarly, the "wrath of God" that Paul says is even now being revealed against wickedness takes its origin from the apocalyptic notion of the last judgment as the day of wrath (see Dan 8:19).[47] But this wrath is already operative in the world, as eschatological salvation is already operative in the world through the gospel for those who believe. The context of this passage then is not missionary preaching, nor is it Paul's call to the Romans to repentance. Rather its context is apocalyptic, somewhat similar to that of the Book of Daniel which encouraged the Jews of 165 B.C. to remain faithful and not succumb to the ways of the Hellenists.

In continuity with and adapting the apocalyptic tradition, Paul is telling both Gentile and Jewish Christians of Rome to be faithful. God is faithful and gives them justification, salvation, life, and deliverance through the gift of their faith. From his experience elsewhere he knows that both Gentile and Jewish Christians are tempted to revert to their pre-Christian past. Therefore he shows that what in this past may tempt their present Christian fidelity is not a value worth such infidelity, but rather an action that manifests the wrath of God. Thus he tells the Gentile Christians of Rome that the "freedom" of their past Gentile ways, which still applies to many Gentiles, is really evidence of God's "wrath" already reaching those who live in such freedom. When Paul recounts the sins such freedom gave rise to, he introduces each section by the phrase, "God handed them over" (Rom 1:24, 26, 28).

How then does Paul's affirmation of human knowledge of God fit into this context? He is explaining why people who exercise such moral license could be seen as objects of God's wrath. It was because, "While claiming to be wise, they became fools and exchanged the glory of the immortal God for the likeness of an image of mortal man or of birds or of four-legged animals or of snakes. . . . They exchanged the truth of God for a lie and revered and worshiped the creature rather than the creator" (Rom 1:23, 25). By perverting the order between God and creatures in this fashion, they became perverted in their relations to one another and within themselves. This present

---

[46]Ibid., 34.

[47]Ibid., 37.

perversion is the present impact of the apocalyptic wrath of God.

But is there not an excuse for these people, we might ask. Here is the place where Paul's affirmation of God's manifestation of himself to human beings and their knowledge of God has its proper place:

> The wrath of God is indeed being revealed from heaven against every impiety and wickedness of those who suppress the truth by their wickedness. For what can be known about God is evident to them, because God made it evident to them. Ever since the creation of the world, his invisible attributes of eternal power and divinity have been able to be understood and perceived in what he has made. As a result they have no excuse; for although they knew God they did not accord him glory as God or give him thanks. Instead, they became vain in their reasoning, and their senseless minds were darkened (Rom 1:18-21).

The origin of human persons' perverse moral life lies in their exchange of the truth of the creator for a lie; and they did this because they did not glorify or thank God, though they had knowledge of him. The knowledge they had of him was not the historical revelation that the Jews had received. But God did manifest himself to them—his eternal power and divinity by which he transcends all creatures. God manifested himself through the things he made, for these make their invisible maker visible in part. Indeed, he manifested himself since the beginning of creation. While this knowledge was clear to them, they suppressed it through their unwillingness to glorify God or thank him. Rather, they speculated in a way that resulted in a darkening of their minds. Paul has no doubt that God manifests himself (*ephanerosen*) to men and women through the realities of the world in a way sufficient for them to avoid the horrors of idolatry and its consequences. He is of course speaking only of the source of the grossly immoral activity that he recounts, and is not accusing all Gentiles of this immorality or the sin of turning away from God.

In fact, there is a passage later in this epistle that supposes that some Gentiles are not guilty of the behavior Paul mentions in chapter 1, and even that they know God. In Romans 2:14-16, he writes: "For when the Gentiles who do not have the law by nature observe the prescriptions of the law, they are a law for themselves even though they do not have the law. They show that the demands of the law are written in their hearts, while their conscience also bears witness and their conflicting thoughts accuse or even defend them on the day when, according to my gospel, God will judge people's hidden works through Jesus Christ."

This passage is found in chapter 2 where Paul seeks to show the limits of the Law in which the Jews are tempted to glory. As in chapter 1 he showed the true character of Gentile "freedom," so here he shows the limits of the Jewish Law. He takes this approach to wean Gentile and Jewish Christians from those attractions in their distinctive pasts that could be a danger to their continued fidelity to Christ. In this section of chapter 2, Paul is making the point that it is those who keep the Law, not those who hear it, who will be declared just. Thus he presents the example of the Gentiles who do not have the Law and yet keep it "by nature" (*phusei*), which shows that the demands of the Law are written in their hearts; "it is a matter of Gentiles experiencing God's will, not from the Torah as such, but in outline, as it were, from what is written in their hearts."[48] This and their "conscience" (*suneidēseos*) that Paul mentions in the next sentence are relevant to our interests here, because they show us that Paul has no difficulty acknowledging that God manifests himself and even his will to some extent to those who have not been privileged to receive the Jewish revelation and Law. And they have accepted it. As there are Jews who will be judged favorably on the eschatological Day of Judgment, so too there are Gentiles. Paul does not get into the problem of the power through which such people are declared just, nor need we; it is sufficient to say that his view here does not imply Pelagianism. He recognizes that there were Jews who were just by God's gift before Christ, and similarly he has no trouble in acknowledging this about Gentiles.

From what we have seen, Romans 1:18ff. is not at all opposed to the missionary method that Luke presents as typical

[48]Ibid., 65.

for the early Church in its proclamation to the Gentiles. Romans has to be interpreted within its own context, and this context is radically different from Paul's missionary efforts. Paul's approach in Romans does not imply a confrontative approach in his missionary effort. Nor does it imply a judgment against all Gentiles as morally corrupt and without knowledge of God. In fact, we may say that Romans is in accord with Acts 17, for Romans asserts that God does manifest himself to those who do not have Jewish revelation and Law, and it is this that Acts 17 presupposes. Romans supports rather than undercuts or disqualifies Acts 17, for it asserts the basis for dialogue that the Areopagus speech in fact uses. As Paul acknowledges that those who do not have the Torah may live in accord with God's will, so he acknowledges that those who do not have the revelation given through the patriarchs, Moses, and the prophets do have a manifestation from God that they do not necessarily reject. The fact that some Athenians accepted Paul's speech and were converted shows their ability, under God's grace, to accept such manifestations from God and thus the legitimacy of Paul's approach. The Gentiles' acceptance of God's revelation through the world and their moral experience must be judged to be God's gift, and their rejection of it attributed to their responsibility.

In conclusion of our treatment of the meaning and grounds of belief in God that we find in Scripture, we can, I think, say that it addresses modern reasons for disbelief and the divisions among theologians on the issue of how to mediate faith in God. It addresses the former, for it overcomes distorted interpretations of the Christian God. It shows that we as Christians believe in God because we believe he has revealed himself to us through his historical acts and words that make him known as transcendent personal mystery and convey his attitude of love for us and for all men and women. It shows that we believe in God as deeply concerned and involved in our historical present and future, as shown through the prophets and apocalyptic literature. Our assurance of the meaning or fulfillment of history depends upon our fidelity to God—even at the cost of death. And our study shows that this God is manifested, though not finally or definitively, through the cosmos and our moral experience. We must later critically evaluate aspects of this in dialogue with contemporary experience, but this study of Scripture shows something of the God we believe in and something of the meaning and foundations of this belief.

Our study in this chapter addresses the divergent theological models by which theologians mediate faith in our century. While Scripture shows diverse approaches to such mediation, it does not diametrically oppose them to one another. It shows that revelation is indeed God's act and that we are called to believe because of this revelation and because God offers us salvation through our faith, but it also shows that he manifests himself to those who do not yet believe this historical revelation and that he does so in a way that legitimates dialogue on grounds accessible to them. It does not erect a dichotomy between dialogue and dialectic. It shows too that Scripture appeals to the transformative value of faith in history but not in opposition to grounds whereby the one invited to believe has objective intellectual reason to believe that God is and has spoken, or in a way that erects an answer to the problem of evil within the limits of human history into an absolute. Also, the transformative value it appeals to is one that is relevant to both the community of men and women and to the individual person. (We shall see more of this in the next part of foundational theology.) In transcending certain oppositions among varied ways of mediating faith, Scripture supports the model we have found in Vatican II for offering meaning and grounds of belief in God.

# 4

## Soundings in Christian History on the Doctrine of Belief in God

We cannot understand difficulties in our time with Christian belief in God or different theological approaches to this issue unless we know something of how the Church's current belief emerged through the centuries. It would have developed differently if the Church had spread to the East rather than to the West, if the Church had faced other cultures or other problems than those it did. The main development in the Church's understanding of God through the early centuries dealt with God as Triune. To be sure, a central aspect of the current response to atheism and religious indifference is a retrieval and rearticulation of this central Christian mystery. But that is not our task here; and it is not, we propose, the only task in responding to modern atheism and religious indifference. We need to show what faith in God means, what its implications for life are and why we should turn to it. To do this, we have to have some awareness of the varied modes of thought and language used historically by Christians to reflect on the question of faith in God. And we have to have some understanding of why the differing theological approaches to the question of faith in God developed in Christianity, and why Christian faith in God eroded in recent centuries.

In this chapter, we will ask three questions. How did the understanding of God develop in the course of Christianity's interaction with Greco-Roman culture and philosophy? The Patristic period shows us the legitimacy, necessity and limits of an integration of the scriptural message about faith in God with the resources, particularly the philosophical resources, of a culture that had not received Judaeo-Christian revelation. Secondly, how did tensions develop between a reflection on faith in God that was predominantly affective, scriptural, and even mystical, and one that was primarily objective, speculative, and theological? Some examples from the Middle Ages can show us these tensions and the way that they led to the rupture of the Church in the sixteenth century. This also shows us the need for transcending the disruptive potential of the pluralism that exists today. Thirdly, in the modern period how was reflection on God withdrawn from the faith context, and how was faith in God gradually eroded? This will show us some of the major reasons for the present problem of faith. All of this is helpful in setting the stage for our critical reflection on the meaning and grounds of faith in God in view of contemporary experience. Our soundings in Christian history will be brief, as we will refer to works which discuss these issues at greater length. We will divide our study here as follows: (I) the Patristic Age, (II) The High Middle Ages through the Reformation, and (III) the Seventeenth to the early Twentieth Century—thus making contact with what we treated in chapters 1 and 2.

## I. The Patristic Age

At times the early Fathers of the Church have been accused of subverting the Christian message by subordinating it to the categories of Hellenistic philosophy. Our previous chapter showed that dialogue with the Hellenistic world began with the first Christian generation, and indeed had existed even in pre-Christian Jewish writings. Here we will discuss briefly the Apologists and Augustine to show the situations they faced, the ways in which they mediated faith in God in their circumstances, and the use they made of the philosophical resources of their time, while they preserved the transcendence and distinctiveness of the Christian God. There was tension in their use of these resources, and there were aspects of the Christian message that lost some of their earlier prominence; but the

genuine Christian message was presented in a way particularly
appropriate to the Greco-Roman culture.

## 1. The Apologists.

The Apologists of the second and early third century differed significantly among themselves. But there were certain
commonalities about the difficulties they faced and the ways
they mediated faith in God. In differing degrees they contended with four rival conceptions of God and the world. First,
there were the popular polytheistic and official Roman religions. Second, there were the philosophers who, at that time,
were largely Middle Platonists.[1] At that time Platonism was affected by a strong religious sense. As Eric Osborn describes it:

> The ultimate first principle is placed at the upper limit of
> transcendence; a widespread and deep yearning for God is
> linked to a strong rejection of worldly sufficiency. Plato is
> . . . represented . . . as the teacher of that divine knowledge
> which is man's greatest good . . . The one question concerns
> the being of God, who is seen as the first cause of all
> things. . . . (T)he creator becomes more than a craftsman
> when the ideas, which give the pattern of his work, are
> within his own mind. Yet the two steps (making of pattern
> and making of world) are clearly distinguished; the two level
> divinity (visible and intellectual) is the most characteristic
> element of Middle Platonism.[2]

There was some inner coherence in Middle Platonism's concept of God. In a certain continuity with the Pre-Socratics and
the Homeric myths, God was understood as the source of the
normal and the natural in human experience: "The truly divine can be no other than the origin needed to bring about the

---

[1]See Eric Osborn, *The Beginnings of Christian Philosophy* (London: Cambridge
Univ. Press, 1981) 28–29; W. Pannenberg, "The Appropriation of the Philosophical
Concept of God as a Dogmatic Problem of Early Christian Theology," in his *Basic
Questions in Theology,* vol. 2 (Philadelphia: Fortress, 1971) 119–183; Robert Grant,
*Gods and the One God* (Philadelphia: Westminster Press, 1986); and John Dillon,
*The Middle Platonists* (London: 1977).

[2]Osborn, *Christian Philosophy,* 28.

familiar reality."[3] Therefore, the divine can be grasped by means of inference from our human experience. Middle Platonism argued that there could not be a plurality of ultimate principles because there would have to be a ground for their difference, and this itself would be more ultimate. It also held that the ultimate principle is totally different from the everyday world, for it is not visible, mutable, or composed. It—designated by this pronoun, because divinity tended to be viewed as impersonal—is, rather, invisible, immutable, simple, and incomprehensible.

A third group with whom the Apologists contended was the Jews, though as time progressed disputes with them became less important. And fourth, there were the Gnostics who tended to despise the world and elevate the first principle to such transcendence that it could have no immediate contact with the world. The origin of this present world is some defective and lesser principle.[4] Marcion and his followers are an example of Gnosticism, since they made a total dichotomy between the God of the Old Testament and the God of the New Testament, the God of justice and the God of love.

The Apologists thus had a complex of views about deity quite divergent from the biblical view with which to contend. Our purpose here is not to follow the thought of each of these men, but rather to point out that in their arguments for acceptance of the Christian understanding of God they made use of the philosophy of the time while modifying it by the biblical message. Thus we are concerned specifically with their apologetic rather than with their proclamation of the Christian message to their fellow Christians, bearing in mind that the former cannot be equated with the totality of their theology.

Osborn puts their apologetic problem as follows: "The ancient world found it easy to venerate the world or to despise it. Christians believed that pagans and Gnostics were both wrong; the world was good but it was not God. You walked on it; you did not worship it. Fortunately there was enough humanitas in antiquity to see the beauty of the world and Christians could

[3]Pannenberg, "Philosophical Concept of God," 125.

[4]See Pheme Perkins, *The Gnostic Dialogue. The Early Church and the Crisis of Gnosticism* (New York: Paulist Press, 1980).

build on this; but, to the extent that they rejected both idolatry and flight from the world, they were building something new."[5] Looking at this problem from the perspective of the question of God, one could say that the Apologists showed how God both was transcendent and could and did communicate with the world. Specifically, they made use of the philosophy of Middle Platonism to defend the visible world against Gnostic attack and to reject popular, polytheistic religious views of divinity.[6] While they used this philosophy, through their Christian faith "the debate with the philosophical question about the true form of the divine was . . . grounded in the biblical witness to God as the universal God, pertinent not only to Israel but to all peoples."[7] The God of Israel had to be shown to be more than the deity worshipped by a particular group of people in the Roman Empire; rather, he must have given testimony to himself in the larger Gentile world. In fact, what was true in the wisdom of the philosophers was ascribed at times to the Logos sent by God who manifests God through creation and illumines people interiorly.

The Apologists used Middle Platonism to argue to a unitary maker of the world, but they also differed from this philosophy. Justin, for example, agreed with Plato that God was unbegotten, but he restricted the term "god" so that it applied only to the one who is uncreated. He placed Genesis and Plato together in holding that God in his goodness brought all things into existence. Theophilus of Antioch went further than Justin, in that he emphasized God's creation of the world from nothing: "Plato and those of his school acknowledge indeed that God is uncreated, and the Father and Maker of all things; but then they maintain that matter as well as God is uncreated, and aver that it is coeval with God. But if God is uncreated and matter uncreated, God is no longer, according to the Platonists, the Creator of all things, nor, so far as their opinions hold, is the monarchy of God established. . . . [T]he power of God is manifested in this, that out of things that are

[5]Osborn, *Christian Philosophy,* 149.
[6]See ibid., 145; and Pannenberg, "Philosophical Concept of God," 137.
[7]Pannenberg, ibid., 134.

not he makes whatever he pleases."[8] Theophilus understood God's activity as creative in the strict sense and as an act of his good pleasure rather than one of necessity. Similarly, Irenaeus argued against the Gnostics for the unity of God and the freedom of his creative activity. Thus the Christian theologians corrected the philosophical view of the ultimate as impersonal, for from Judaeo-Christian revelation God was understood as personally acting in history. They integrated the personal and impersonal in God as the Greek philosophers and Roman religion had not done.[9] In later reflection on the Trinity, the notion of God as personal was further developed, since the word "persona" was used in the West for what distinguished Father, Son, and Holy Spirit and the word "substantia" for what united them.

In agreement with Middle Platonism, the Apologists spoke of the otherness, the spirituality, and the ineffability of God. Justin agreed "with Plato's Parmenides that the One was only capable of negative description,"[10] though he still spoke of God positively as "the most true God, the father of righteousness, moderation and other virtues, untainted by evil."[11] Moreover, God is the preserver of the good and the giver of immortality.[12] Irenaeus said that God is not to be known by human beings and that they cannot speak properly of God; he denied of God what belongs to the body and human passions. He positively ascribed perfections to God, but added that God did not pos-

---

[8]Theophilus of Antioch, *To Autolycus,* Book II, ch. 4, as translated in Kimball Kehoe, ed., *Theology of God. Sources* (New York: Bruce, 1971) 17–18. Also see Jaroslav Pelikan, *The Christian Tradition. A History of the Development of Doctrine.* Vol. 1. *The Emergence of the Catholic Tradition (100–600)* (Chicago: Univ. of Chicago Press, 1971) 35–37.

[9]See Raniero Cantalamessa, "The Development of the Concept of a Personal God in Christian Spirituality," in Edward Schillebeeckx and Bas van Iersel, eds., *A Personal God? (Concilium,* vol. 103. 1977) 57–66. See pp. 57–58: "The God of Plato—to whom man should aspire, but who cannot 'come down to men'—and the God of Aristotle who 'moves by being loved' (not by loving, and loving 'first') are for contemplation, not history. God in fact is conceived as an *object,* not as an active *subject* who acts on the world and converses with man. In other words, he is not thought of as a person."

[10]Osborn, *Christian Philosophy,* 32.

[11]Justin, *First Apology,* 6 (as in Osborn, ibid., 33).

[12]See Osborn, ibid., 35. For other apologists, see Osborn, ibid., 37–50.

sess these perfections as humans do.[13] Clement of Alexandria pushed the notion of God's unknowability the furthest. He held that human beings must be purified because they project their passions and physical properties onto God. Faith and grace alone can find God. God, as first principle of all things, stands at the summit; he is logically above the categories we use to describe things, and has no proper name, for this would bring him down to the level of particular things. Neither can he be defined in terms of higher principles; and so he remains unknown apart from his gift of grace and the Logos. Yet Clement like the other Fathers spoke of God positively, saying, for example, that God is good, though he is good in a unique way.[14] Like others too, he opposed Marcion's distinction of the good God from the just demiurge. The Apologists—again, with Middle Platonism—spoke of God as immutable, simple, and passionless, thus denying of God what is proper to our material or created world, and what polytheism ascribed to God— mutability, composition, and being subject to passions.[15] We may note that, in contrast to the other Apologists, Tertullian stressed that God's transcendence is found in his becoming man: God is so transcendent that we must expect such surprises.[16] Christ, and specifically Christ crucified, is the way to God's mystery.

For Hellenism generally, the path of human transcendence was through escape from the world rather than through the future. The Apologists were in dialogue with a culture for which history as such had little ultimate meaning.[17] By the Greeks it was understood cyclically, while by the Romans it was frequently understood as linear but terminating at the Roman Empire. Many of the Apologists did integrate to some extent

[13]See ibid., 38–39.

[14]See ibid., 53.

[15]See Pannenberg, "Philosophical Concept of God," 158–177.

[16]See Osborn, *Christian Philosophy*, 40–43. On Tertullian and the question of God's "passions," see Joseph Hallman, "'The Mutability of God'": Tertullian to Lactantius," *Theological Studies* 42 (1981) 373–393. We shall return to this question in a later chapter.

[17]See Christopher Hong, *A History of the Future. A Study of the Four Major Eschatologies* (Washington, D.C.: University Press of America, 1981); and Pelikan, *The Christian Tradition*, I, 37–41.

the scriptural message about the future into their theologies. Thus Justin spoke of the second coming of Jesus; Irenaeus developed a view of God's providence in history and was for at least a time a millenialist who thought that Jesus would rule on earth for a thousand years; Tertullian in some ways made future eschatology the dominant theme of his theology.[18] However, on the whole, this was not a dominant theme in the work of the Apologists.

In conclusion, we can say that the Apologists generally accepted the legitimacy of using causal inference to know something of the maker of all things.[19] In part they found the philosophers' critique of popular religions an ally in their own efforts. However, they did not ascribe what the philosophers learned simply to human wisdom, but rather to God's sending his Logos, who manifests God through creation and illumines human beings interiorly. Some even ascribed those philosophers' views of God which they found acceptable to plagiarism from Moses, the prophets, and the sacred books of the Jews. Though the Apologists accepted much of Middle Platonism, they also corrected it. They argued for these corrections on the basis of both Scripture and philosophical arguments. Above all, they understood that Jesus Christ was God's Logos become incarnate to teach and save all humankind. As one author writes of their view of God: "This was a Christian doctrine of God, though in many ways a very inadequate one. It was, however, designed to attract the intellectuals of the period, who were well acquainted with Greek philosophy, and who would be favourably impressed by the fact that this Christian philosophy solved a problem acutely felt at the time, the problem of how the Absolute, identified with God, could under any circumstances and by any means come into contact with this world of change, of becoming, of decay, of transitoriness which we sublunary beings experience."[20] Its inadequacy is found in its limited Trinitarian doctrine which would be developed more adequately in the following centuries. But it was inade-

---

[18]See Osborn, *Christian Philosophy,* ch. 6, "History," 163–195.

[19]See Osborn, ibid., 56–63; Pannenberg, "Philosophical Concept of God," 158f.

[20]R. P. C. Hanson, "The Doctrine of God in the Early Church," *The Attractiveness of God. Essays in Christian Doctrine* (Richmond: John Knox Press, 1973) 77.

quate too in that it lost, in large part, the centrality that eschatology had for Scripture and the early Church; we shall see this in Augustine as well. However, the Apologists do show the legitimacy and necessity of understanding God through what he reveals of himself by means other than Judaeo-Christian revelation as well as by this revelation. Without this attitude they would not have been faithful to Scripture and would never have contextualized their theology in a way appropriate for the needs of the people of their time and culture.

## 2. *Augustine.*

In Augustine too we see the necessity, the value, and the limits of Christianity's dialogue with a culture, including its philosophy, in an articulation of who God is. The view that the Christian message should be kept pure from interaction with that knowledge of God mediated by experiences and reflection not directly ascribable to Judaeo-Christian revelation is seen in Augustine's life to be a myth and indeed a fraud. Even if such interaction leaves not only wheat but weeds in the field of Christian understanding, it is preferable to the attempt— never valid—to rely exclusively on Christian revelation for our knowledge of God and our interaction with God. We are not thereby condoning any domination that philosophy has over Scripture in Christian interpretation, but we wish to say that the Christian message has to take root as seed in a particular soil that contributes to the growth of the message even if there are alien seeds in the field as well. One cannot appreciate or understand God's final revelation through Christ if one does not hear the less transcendent communications with which God has graced us.

In the first place, Augustine (354–430) would not have been the Christian and theologian he was without his culture, his *cursus vitae,* and the philosophies of his time and place, particularly that of Plotinus. We can see his life almost as a dialogue between Christianity and classical culture in the West in the late fourth and early fifth centuries. To illustrate this, we may recall certain ways in which Plotinus and his disciple Porphyry helped Augustine come to a point where he could hear the Christian message in a receptive manner and how their teaching influenced his understanding of God and the human person's relation to God, and thus his interpretation of Scripture.[21]

Through these philosophers Augustine was able to gain some understanding of the reality of the spiritual or non-material order, and through the preaching of Ambrose in Milan he was able to see that this might not be incompatible with Scripture. More than this, he claimed to find the Christian mystery of the Trinity in Plotinus. There he found the ultimate principle of reality to be the One which by a process of emanations gave rise to all lower beings. The first to emanate from the One was the *Nous* or Understanding, and through this there emanated the World Soul. Lesser beings, even matter, emanated in order from these. Plotinus' philosophy contained a deeply religious spirit, for it showed both the derivation of lesser reality from the One, and a model of human fulfillment through a return to the One by a process of conversion from what is physical and outside of us to what is within us, from what is lower within us to what is higher and spiritual within us, and from this to the One, thus ultimately becoming alone with the Alone. More than once in his life, Plotinus had experienced ecstasy in this return, though he expected the fulfillment of this passage to be found in the immortal life of the soul after death.

Augustine's understanding of the return of the soul to God is influenced by this scheme to such an extent that some scholars have interpreted his conversion as a conversion to Neo-Platonism rather than to Christianity. This is excessive, but it has enough foundation to give it a semblance of truth for some scholars. Augustine's way of interiority can be seen both in his view of our knowledge of truth and in his way of spirituality. In reference to the former, he examines what the soul can do in

---

[21]On Plotinus see, for example, Philip Merlan, "Plotinus," *The Encyclopedia of Philosophy,* ed. P. Edwards, (New York: Macmillan, 1967) 6:351–359; Andrew Louth, *The Origins of the Christian Mystical Tradition. From Plato to Denys* (Oxford: The Clarendon Press, 1981) 36–51. On Augustine and a controversy about the way and extent Plotinus influenced him, see Eugene TeSelle, *Augustine The Theologian* (New York: Herder and Herder, 1970). In what follows, we will follow TeSelle's view in this dispute.

the body, in itself and before God, thus going from the exterior to the interior and hence to God. He examines this process in stages. Without attempting here to examine these stages in detail, we may note how he accounts for the fact that we mutable creatures make judgments of truth that are immutable.

> In looking for this source of my judgments, when I did judge in this way, I had discovered the immutable and true eternity of Truth, above my mutable mind.
>
> Thus, by a gradual process, from bodies to the soul which senses through the body, and thence to its interior power to which bodily sensation takes messages about exterior things (and this is as far as brutes can go), and then further to the reasoning power, to which what is taken by the bodily senses is brought for judgment. And this power, also finding itself mutable in me, lifted itself to its understanding and withdrew the thinking process from the customary level, taking itself away from the contradictory crowds of phantasms, so that it might discover by what light it was besprinkled when it cried out without any hesitation that the immutable is to be preferred to the mutable; that it might know from this the immutable itself (for, unless it could know it in some way, it would not put it above the mutable with certainty). And, in the flash of a trembling glance (*in ictu trepidantis aspectus*), it reached up to THAT WHICH IS.[22]

Augustine's reflection on the spiritual ascent of the soul to God is similar to this. His reflection on the mystical experience he and his mother had at Ostia shortly before her death is, in mystical terms, basically a way of ascent, passing beyond material things to our own interiority, from our knowledge in the order of sense to our deeper knowledge in the depth of our soul, and hence to God:

> Rising as our love flamed upward towards that Self-same, we passed in review the various levels of bodily things, up to the heavens themselves, whence sun and moon and stars shine upon this earth. And higher still we soared, thinking in our

---

[22]Augustine, *Confessions,* 7:17, 23.

> minds and speaking and marvelling at Your works. And so
> we came to our own souls, and went beyond them to come at
> last to that region of richness unending, where You feed Is-
> rael forever with the food of truth; and there life is that Wis-
> dom by which all things are made. . . . And while we were
> thus talking of His Wisdom and panting for it, with all the ef-
> fort of our heart we did for one instant attain to touch
> it. . . .[23]

This is a way of access to God that Augustine speaks of frequently, and in it he sees a harmony between the Platonists and
Christianity, though he holds that Christianity alone offers the
means by which this may be effected. He claims that the philosophers can know the things of eternity, but they cannot
know God's dispensations in time, and particularly that the
Word became flesh. This is an area of faith.[24]

Ascent to God then occurs by turning from enslavement by
the bonds of flesh and time to the light within and through this
to God. Like the Platonic tradition, Augustine makes a radical
distinction between the realm of mutability and change and
the realm of immutability: "Only the essence of God, or the essence which God is, is unchangeable. Being is in the highest
and truest sense of the term proper to him from whom being
derives its name."[25] All other things are mutable, for they are
all composed of matter, either corporeal or spiritual, and form.
With this philosophical background, Augustine tends to scorn
the things of change and time, for these are matters of opinion
rather than of certain knowledge.

Augustine later corrected a number of Platonic elements in
his theology which were not compatible with Scripture. This
was due partly to his engagement in theology in the context of
his pastoral work as a bishop in North Africa and of his conflicts with the Pelagians and Donatists.[26] We could mention his
rejection of an hypothesis he had previously held, namely that

[23]Ibid., 9:10, 24.

[24]See TeSelle, *Augustine The Theologian,* 129–131.

[25]Augustine, *De Trinitate,* 5:2, 3. And see Pelikan, *The Christian Tradition,* I,
269–270.

[26]See TeSelle, *Augustine The Theologian,* 259, 266.

of the preexistence of souls, and his increasing emphasis on grace. But we will limit ourselves here to the fact that history and eschatology became more important for him, as seen in his *De Civitate Dei*. He contested the classical cyclical view of history and the ultimacy of the Roman Empire. He came to see positive elements in time, interpreting the span of biblical history "as a kind of education of the human race analogous to the life of an individual, so that it is gradually transformed from the old Adam into the new."[27] He viewed human beings as living in time for a short period, the importance of which is due to the fact that it determines whether they are to share in the blessedness of those who will enjoy the vision of God or in the suffering of those excluded from God.[28] He divided the ages of the world into six epochs, the last of which extends from Christ's first coming till his second. Throughout the whole of history there are two cities, one the city of God and the other the earthly city, the former beginning with Abel and the latter with Cain. Abel and his descendents live in this world as on a pilgrimage toward a nonearthly goal. The *Civitas Terrena* is dominated by pride, ambition, and expediency, while the *Civitas Dei* is being built by love for God that leads to the loss of self in obedience, self-sacrifice, and humility. The events of profane history are not of great intrinsic meaning; it means little to a Christian what rule he lives under, so long as it preserves a peace that allows the gospel to be preached and spread. Augustine emphasized the transcendence of the Christian's destiny over that of an earthly state such as the Roman Empire, showing that it is not the ultimate evil for even so great an earthly state to pass away. This was the message that was needed at the time of the decline of Rome, but the way Augustine proclaimed it perhaps lost something of the intrinsic meaning of human social existence and the message of Scripture on how the gospel is meant to transform our earthly condition.

[27]Ibid., 130.

[28]We may note that Augustine's view of God's predestination of some and lack of such a decree for others was, unfortunately, very influential in later Christian history. It was in part a misinterpretation of Romans 9. See John Farrelly, *Predestination, Grace and Free Will* (Westminster: Newman Press, 1964) 79–96.

In conclusion, we can see that Augustine's reading of Scripture was indeed influenced by the philosophy of his time, and particularly by Neo-Platonism. Thus he was able to present a reading that was related to the problems and resources of his time, forming a dialogue between Christianity and classical culture. In part this helped him understand the Christian proclamation, in part it limited what he understood. Perhaps more than anything else, he lacked a certain understanding of the positive influence of the apocalyptic kingdom on history. However, he did not reduce Christianity to classical culture. Against Plotinus, he understood God as indeed personal, as fully transcending all other things, as Triune, and as interacting with us through providence, prayer, and the sending of his Son to be mediator between God and human beings. Augustine also largely overcame the classical understanding of fate or necessity, though perhaps this is part of the source of his rather fatalistic teaching on predestination.[29]

## II. The High Middle Ages Through the Reformation

We have seen in the Patristic age genuine inculturations of the Christian message that presented the message to the Hellenistic and Roman world in a way that was mostly faithful to the Christian revelation of God, integrative of the resources of the culture, though not without critiques and tensions, and transformative for the Mediterranean world of that time. We find these tensions in later Western theology as well; in fact, they erupted into ecclesial divisions in the sixteenth century. We will recall instances of such tension in the period of thirteenth century Scholasticism and then in the sixteenth century, with antecedents for each period. The Reformation can be understood as initially a reassertion of the primacy of Scripture and its view of God—though read from the experience of Luther in the sixteenth century—to the exclusion of what the Greco-Roman world and its philosophy had to offer, particularly in the form it took in late Scholasticism.

[29]See Charles Cochrane, "Divine Necessity and Human History," *Christianity and Classical Culture* (New York: Oxford Univ. Press, 1957) 456 ff.

## 1. Thirteenth Century Scholasticism

Some major dissociations among Christian theologians in our time in the understanding of God and in the mediation of belief in God are present in germ in the Middle Ages, though still within the bounds of a single Church, and erupt into bases for splitting the Church in the sixteenth century. Here we shall recall some achievements and tensions of the thirteenth century on this issue, but before that we will recall the tension in the preceding century between an emerging Scholasticism and monastic theology in the persons of St. Anselm and St. Bernard.

Anselm of Canterbury (1033–1109) has been called the "father of Scholasticism" with some merit. His own teacher in theology, Lanfranc, was still of the old school that was content with recovering the doctrine of the Fathers of the Church. Anselm had an excellent knowledge of Augustine, but he thought that he should strive to do more than repeat the Fathers; if they had lived longer, they would have said more about the faith. He insisted that theology begins with and rests on faith, meaning by this the Christian's faith in the whole of what God has revealed. Thus he took as his ideal "faith seeking understanding" (*fides quaerens intellectum*). Not to start from faith is to be presumptuous; not to seek understanding is to be negligent. He used reason, meaning by that the dialectics available at the time (largely dependent on the dialectics of Aristotle, the only part of his philosophy available then). We see this in his reflections on God and the reason for the incarnation. In reference to the former, his *Monologium* and *Proslogion* are searches by a man of faith in a spirit of prayer for what reason can offer in support for what he believes about God's existence and nature. What is most famous here is his ontological argument, an argument for the existence of God on the basis that we have an idea of something greater than which nothing can be thought—what we in faith understand God to be. But that which exists in reality as well as in the mind is greater than that which exists only in the mind; and so it would be contradictory if that which is conceived existed only in thought; it must exist in reality as well. From his arguments for the existence of God, Anselm also derived attributes of God, such as his totally perfect being, his distinction from creation, his indivisibility, life, wisdom, omnipotence, justice, eternity, and blessedness. Anselm also used reason to show why the incarnation was necessary, namely, so that the Son of God become man could give adequate satisfaction for the dishonor that the sins of humanity offer to God.[30]

As an example of monastic theology, we mention Bernard of Clairvaux (1091–1153), a man famous as the second founder of the Cistercian Order, an advisor of popes, and preacher of the second Crusade, but also as a mystic and a mystical theologian.[31] His theology was a reflection in faith on the Christian mystery that was meant to lead the monk and the Christian to deeper knowledge of God in prayer. He thought that the knowledge of profane sciences was of small value compared to that of the sacred sciences, and he was suspicious of the dialecticians of his time, as shown in his conflicts with Abelard. The way that leads to truth is Christ, and it is through humility that we gain this truth. There are degrees of humility and of truth, and the culminating point of human knowledge is found in ecstasy in which the person seems to be dissolved into God—though this is a union of charity rather than of substance. This is all explained within a Christian context: God created human beings in his image, but the first man sinned by willing himself for himself rather than for God and so lost his divine resemblance. The purpose and effect of the redemption is to restore us to the divine resemblance, and the Christian life is a re-education in love. Bernard is rightly called the "last of the Fathers" and the "Doctor of Love."

Thomas Aquinas, the greatest representative of the Scholastics, and Bonaventure manifest in the thirteenth century the tension that began to be evident even between Anselm and Bernard. In the prevailing Augustinianism of the time, the new availability of all the works of Aristotle was both a challenge and a seed of discord. The university context of Aquinas' and Bonaventure's theology, as distinct from that of Anselm and

---

[30]See Jaroslav Pelikan, *The Christian Tradition.* vol. 3. *The Growth of Medieval Theology (600–1300)* (Chicago: Univ. of Chicago Press, 1978) 259–262, 139–144.

[31]See Jean Leclercq, *Bernard of Clairvaux and the Cistercian Spirit* (Kalamazoo, Mich.: Cistercian Publications, 1976).

Bernard, had itself a great influence. Aquinas understood theology to be a science,[32] but—as distinct from sciences that proceed from principles known by the natural light of reason—a science that proceeds from principles known by the light of a superior knowledge, namely that of God and the blessed. This is available to us through revelation and the faith by which we accept it. This science is principally a speculative science, since it deals with God and other things as they are related to God rather than with our human works or acts. This science is also a wisdom. It is not the wisdom which is shown in our judgments guided by the Holy Spirit (wisdom as one of the seven gifts of the Holy Spirit), but a wisdom that judges through principles derived from revelation and learned by study. As science, this study uses arguments. For example, it argues from some articles of faith to others, though it does not use reason to establish the articles of faith. If someone accepts part of the faith but denies other articles, as heretics do, then one can argue from what such a person accepts. If someone denies all the articles of faith, one cannot prove them through reason but can through reason dissolve arguments raised against them.

Thomas, like Anselm, understood theology to be *fides quaerens intellectum,* but he had vastly more knowledge through which to understand the whole order of being and to use as an *ancilla theologiae.* We see this in part in his reflection on God. He constructed "ways" by which to prove that God exists—though it is important to see this in the context of theology as we have outlined it above (*ST* I, 2). He argued from the physical world and the movement, causality, contingency, grades of perfection, and finality found there to the conclusion that there exists a first unmoved mover, a first cause, a necessary being, a cause of the perfection of all other beings, and an intelligent being by whom natural realities are directed to their goal—and this is what we call God. From these findings Thomas argued to the attributes of God. He discoursed on the simplicity of God, above all that simplicity found in the identity in God of essence and existence, his perfection, his supreme goodness, infinity, immanence in all things, immutabil-

---

[32]See Thomas Aquinas, *Summa theologiae,* I, 1 (referred to in text as *ST*).

ity, unity, knowledge, love, justice, mercy, providence, omnipotence, and happiness.

This whole study of God implies, of course, an epistemology
and an interpretation of language used of both creatures and
God (an issue we will return to in a later chapter). In brief (see
*ST* I, 12–13), many words we use for the attributes of God are
used in a way that is neither simply equivocal nor simply
univocal with the use of these words in reference to creatures.
We form our words from our knowledge of what is proportionate to our intellects, i.e., the material beings about us, and so
such words do not have the same meaning when applied to
God. However, since God is the author of every created perfection, and these are found eminently and indeed infinitely in
God (e.g., wisdom, power, love, being itself), what we signify
by the word is found in God eminently. By our words and concepts we affirm truly a perfection of God, but a word like wisdom "leaves the reality signified as uncomprehended and
exceeding the meaning of the word" (*ST* I, 13, 5). Since our
knowledge of God is through his effects, and these effects of his
creative activity are not equal to the divine power, by this
knowledge we do not have a proper knowledge of God, i.e., a
knowledge of what is distinctively divine in what we affirm of
him. In fact, our highest knowledge of God is rather of what he
is not than of what he is.

The center of theological knowledge is of God as Triune, as
he has revealed himself to be through Christ; theology studies
other matters as they are related to this revelation. Thus
Thomas studies the world and humanity as proceeding from
God's creative activity, and the condition of humanity as
shown us by Scripture's and tradition's account of the original
state, the fall, and the promise made by God to our first parents. He includes a study of the way we return to God (e.g., of
the supernatural and natural virtues, grace and conversion),
and of Christ, the Church, and the sacraments which God has
given us as means of grace to enable us to return to him. Thus
Thomas integrates theology on an "exitus-reditus" model, that
we have seen articulated differently in Augustine. What we
know by natural knowledge is used by theology as an aid to understanding what we have received by faith from revelation; its
use in theology is subordinate to and controlled by revelation.

This is so true that while Thomas' view of God's knowledge and will is that they impose no necessity on human beings, still because of Augustine's interpretation of Paul's doctrine of predestination, Thomas considers this to be an absolute decree on God's part.[33]

This theology is a magnificent architectonic achievement that relates the mysteries of faith to one another, to our human goal, and to what was known naturally with the help of Greek philosophy in the thirteenth century.[34] Thomas recognized that this knowledge of God was quite different from mystical knowledge of God; theology did not aspire to that, for its knowledge was objective and integrative and the result of human study applied in faith to what God revealed. In this we also see spelled out Thomas' understanding of how grace perfects as well as heals nature, and revelation completes reason as well as preserves it from error in what it in principle can know of God by the natural light of reason (*ST* I, 1).

That this was not the only way that Scholasticism could integrate the Christian mysteries is evident in the theology of the Franciscan School as found in Bonaventure.[35] He was first and foremost a theologian. Thus he integrated philosophy into theology, and made use of Aristotle (though his language belonged more to an Augustinian context than Aristotle's philosophical psychology) for the purpose of rendering the content of belief understandable by reason. The context of his doctrine is the Trinity, with the procession of all things from the Trinity and their return to it. As he writes: "This is our whole metaphysics: emanation, exemplarity and consummation, that is, to be illumined by spiritual rays and to be led back to the highest reality."[36] The Father as "fontalis plenitudo" produces the Son and with the Son the Holy Spirit as the return to the Father. Through the Son too, the Father produces creation as the good

---

[33]See Farrelly, *Predestination,* 115–121.

[34]See Pelikan, *The Christian Tradition,* III, 284 ff.

[35]See Ewert Cousins, "God as Dynamic in Bonaventure and Contemporary Thought," *Proceedings* American Catholic Philosophical Association, vol. 48, *Thomas and Bonaventure: A Septicentenary Commemoration* (Washington, D.C.: Catholic Univ. of America, 1974) 136–148.

[36]Bonaventure, *In Hexaemeron,* coll. I, n. 17 (V, 332), as cited in Cousins, "God as Dynamic," 146.

communicating itself, based on the exemplarity of the Son; and thus the world reflects God as "a stained glass window in which the divine light is reflected in various colors."[37] Through the Holy Spirit God communicates to creation and particularly to us a dynamic return to himself. Human beings then find in all things and particularly in themselves reflections of God. The human soul manifests God's presence so clearly that there is need not so much for proofs for the existence of God as for purification. Bonaventure notes the stages of the ascension of the soul to God. His acceptance of an Augustinian illumination theory shows him both that we understand immutable truths only through God's help and that we find God directly each time we go deeply enough into ourselves. "God is most present to the soul and by that very fact knowable."[38] His view of the world as well as of the human person is Trinitarian, and his view of Christ and the Church is in the context of the soul's ascension to God through love.

We do see tensions among theologies in the thirteenth century as in the previous century regarding the way that theology is related to the Christian's life and to a philosophical understanding of humanity and of God. Thomas' approach to God was more through the cosmos and humanity understood objectively, while Bonaventure's was more through the self that is experienced. The language about God in the one tends to be more analogical, and in the other more symbolic. While for both philosophy is contained within a theological context, and both accept an *exitus-reditus* way of relating God and creation within a Ptolemaic universe, they have somewhat differing views of God, and the theology of one is more oriented to *theoria* and the other to *praxis*. But these differences—which are still found among theologies of our own time—were contained within one faith and Church. In the sixteenth century, on the contrary, Luther's theology led to a rupture of faith and of Church. The central issues on which that rupture developed were not those we treat in this study, but they had implications

---

[37]Cousins, "God as Dynamic," 144.

[38]E. Gilson, *History of Christian Philosophy in the Middle Ages* (New York: Random House, 1955) 334.

for and perhaps derived from serious divergences in the understanding of belief in God and its bases.

## 2. *Luther on Belief in God*

To shift from Thomas and Bonaventure in the thirteenth century to Martin Luther in the sixteenth is to enter a different world. We cannot here explain how those differences came about. But we should at least mention several theological factors that were operative in the intervening years to so change the theological problems posed and stances accepted. Even in the late thirteenth century, there was a dramatic event that changed the direction of theology from that of Thomas and Bonaventure. There were at the University of Paris philosophers who seemed to accept or at least repeat without criticism statements of Aristotle and Averroës that were incompatible with the Christian faith. Men like Siger of Brabant and Boethius of Sweden were philosophers who taught these things in a way that resulted in a growing reaction. The theologians opposed these philosophers; but what gave more importance to their views was the condemnation issued against them by the Bishop of Paris, Etienne Tempier in 1270, and his more extensive condemnation of their teachings in 1277. As Etienne Gilson summarizes some psychological and metaphysical theses condemned at the later date:

> Those already condemned in 1270 reappeared: the eternity of the world, unity of the agent intellect in the human species, mortality of the soul, rejection of free will, and refusal to extend divine providence beyond the species to the individual; but the doctrinal act of 1277 traced all these errors to their very root, namely, the Aristotelian identification of reality, intelligibility and necessity, not only in things, but first and above all in God. . . . [T]he Primary Principle can be the cause of different effects here below only through the medium of other causes, because nothing which transmutes can effect transmutations of several sorts, without itself being transmuted. To maintain this principle was radically to deny the liberty and omnipotence of the Christian God.[39]

[39]Ibid., 407.

This marked the end of the spirit of theological construction by the use of reason that was found earlier in the thirteenth century. In the theological construction of Duns Scotus (d. 1308), and even more markedly in later theologians, there was a reaction against Greek naturalism and more emphasis on the degree of God's freedom. For example, Scotus emphasized that God is infinite and thus a necessary being and that all else is contingent and due to God's will for its creation and its nature.[40] William of Ockham (d. 1350) made much use of the distinction of what God does by his "ordained power" (*potentia ordinata*) in the actual order and what he could do by his "absolute power" (*potentia absoluta*). This is tied up with his epistemology which, while it may have contributed to the beginnings of modern logic, involved a nominalism too. In reaction against the earlier moderate realism of many scholastics, he taught that universals in the mind were no more than common images formed from similar things. Thus he suppressed exemplary ideas in God's mind as sources of the natures of created things; these ideas were no more than the things producible by God. With this, theology is no longer faith seeking understanding, for if there are no created natures there is no support for Thomas' and others' attempt to use reason's knowledge of the world to help us understand what we believe. For Ockham, probability was on the side of faith, but he did not have much concern for the increasing chasm he promoted between reason and faith.[41] Without considering intervening theologians, we can note that Gabriel Biel (d. 1495) also was a nominalist. He also made much use of the distinction of God's absolute power and ordained power. Using this distinction he could teach simultaneously a justification by grace alone and a justification by works alone.[42] Biel accepted predestination as an absolute decree (as theologians generally did at that time, and Luther did later), explaining it as a free eternal decision of God that has no cause outside himself, but also

[40]See ibid., 461.

[41]See Ernest Moody, "William of Ockham," in *The Encyclopedia of Philosophy,* 8:306–317; and Gilson, *History of Christian Philosophy,* 489–498.

[42]See H. A. Oberman, *The Harvest of Medieval Theology. Gabriel Biel and Late Medieval Nominalism.* 3rd edition (Durham: The Labyrinth Press, 1983).

as one which for the normal wayfarer takes place after his merits have been foreseen. For regularly, God does not grant salvation without merits. Biel's view is essentially a Pelagian position, as Ockham's was before him.

Finally, we should note that along with the theological approaches to knowledge of God in the late Middle Ages, there was a remarkable resurgence of mysticism in Meister Eckhart, Henry Suso, Tauler (for whom Luther had a deep respect), the author of *The Cloud of Unknowing,* and others. The influence of Pseudo-Dionysius on some of these mystics is evident. They stressed the knowledge of God that comes through faith, love, and prayer, a knowledge that derives from affectivity rather than study and is largely apophatic, i.e., an acknowledgement of God in darkness, a knowledge that goes beyond conceptual knowledge, and a knowledge of God by what he is not rather than by what he is.[43]

In the late Middle Ages, there was a chasm between much theology and much spirituality. The former had lost its moorings in Christian experience and had degenerated into logic and studies of possibilities. On the other hand, much spirituality was, as in the case of *The Imitation of Christ,* based on Scripture and devotion; it considered theology to be more of a liability than an enlightenment and guide.

In the sixteenth century, we find in Martin Luther an understanding of belief in God and its implications that was no longer a manifestation of a pluralism within the unity of one faith and one Church. It is important for our effort to recall very briefly, and so inadequately, what this difference was and why it emerged. Luther's interpretation of belief in God was related to and largely dependent on the understanding he came to concerning justification by faith. He stated frequently that he had been an anxious man, never assured that his sins were forgiven or that he was justified before God, but that this trial was dissolved by his coming to understand, through the influence of the Holy Spirit, Paul's teaching that "the just man lives

[43]See Jaroslav Pelikan, *The Christian Tradition.* Vol. 4. *Reformation of Church and Dogma (1300–1700)* (Chicago: Univ. of Chicago Press, 1984) 63–68. And see Kenneth Leech, *Experiencing God. Theology as Spirituality* (San Francisco: Harper and Row, 1985).

because of his faith" (Rom 1:17). Against the Pelagians of his time who thought that they could be justified by their works, and against this attitude in his own younger self, Luther now realized that God's justice manifest in the gospel was God's own justice whereby he justifies sinners gratuitously when they believe, in the sense of trusting completely that God does forgive their sins because of Jesus Christ. Justice is passively received rather than the effect of human efforts.

Luther interpreted this, one meaning of which could be seen as congruent with the teaching of Thomas himself, in a way that stressed discontinuities with the faith of his time. This may be understandable given the corruption in the Church, the externalism of much religious practice, the separation of devotion from theology, and the disintegration of theology at the time; but what concerns us is that it still poses a task for us in theology in our time. In his interpretation of belief in God, one discontinuity Luther stressed was that between the understanding that comes through attention to the text of Scripture, particularly when guided by the Holy Spirit, and that which is found in Scholastic theology: "Luther ridiculed the scholastics for investigating the relation between the two natures of Christ and branded such investigation as 'sophistic'. 'What difference does that make to me?' He continued: 'That he is man and God by nature, that he has for his own self; but that he has exercised his office and poured out his love, become my Savior and Redeemer—that happens for my consolation and benefit.'"[44]

The kind of knowledge of God that Luther sought was that mediated to him by his experience of conversion due to the mercy of God and his redemption by Jesus. He opposed this to a kind of objective knowledge of God presented by Thomas' theology. Some of his statements against Scholasticism, which he knew in its late Medieval decadent state, were strong; he opposed the use of Aristotle in the interpretation of the Christian mystery that comes to us through the Bible. His understanding of faith was similarly different from that of Thomas. While Thomas understood by faith primarily a belief in God and what he revealed, based on divine authority, Luther understood it primarily as a trust or "fiducia" that God has forgiven

[44]Pelikan, ibid., 4:156.

his sins, based on Scripture's promise and his experience under the Holy Spirit of the consolation that comes from this trust.

Luther understood God then primarily through his wrath and his mercy—the one experienced by the terrified sinner and the other by the one who came to trust in him. The sinner is so corrupt because of personal and original sin that he is incapable of moral good. "Luther . . . was not afraid to maintain in his polemic against Erasmus that 'we do everything by necessity and nothing by our free will, since the power of the free will is nothing and neither does the good nor is capable of it in the absence of grace,' and he confined free will to 'natural matters, such as eating, drinking, procreating, governing' and the like."[45] This and Luther's nominalism and frequent opposition to philosophy tend to discredit the ability of nature and human nature to mediate knowledge of God. Luther contrasts the law and grace, works and faith, the sinner and the one to whom God imputes justification—existential differences in his own experience that became his basic categories in theology—and this dialectic becomes central for his theology. God for Luther is both revealed and hidden. For example, by his manifest will he wants to save all humanity, but by his hidden will he predestines only some. Predestination is an absolute divine decree that is due solely to the divine will, which itself has no cause. The transcendence and voluntarism of Luther's God is complete. There is no intellectual way of dissolving these dichotomies; theology itself, for Luther, seems to exult in these dichotomies because his theology of the cross gives greater glory to God than the Scholastics' theology, which, in his view, ascribes glory to human beings.

If we seek in the sixteenth century a contrasting viewpoint to Luther's on the Christian God, we can perhaps find it best in the Council of Trent's Decree on Justification.[46] Here, our conversion from sin to justice begins with God's gift of grace and is completely dependent upon God's grace in the process; but our freedom is enabled by this grace to respond to God.

---

[45]Ibid., 4:143. See Farrelly, *Predestination,* 132–138.

[46]See *The Teaching of the Catholic Church,* eds. J. Neuner, Heinrich Roos, and Karl Rahner (New York: Alba House, 1966) 382–402.

Grace is not a substitute for our freedom, nor is there an opposition between ascribing the glory of our justification to God and acknowledging the reality of our free cooperation with God in that process. One may see in this and the whole of Trent a certain integration of the scriptural understanding of God and the best of the Scholastic achievement and indeed of Renaissance humanism and its concerns.

The difference between Luther's understanding of God and Thomas', or between Luther and the Council of Trent on the doctrine of justification of the sinner, is an important source of divisions in theology in our own time, for example, between Jüngel and Moltmann on the one hand and Rahner and other Catholic—and indeed, a number of Protestant—theologians who would still accept the place of metaphysics in theology. Two of these differences we can note. In the first place, in continuity with Augustine and later monastic theology and in exaggeration of it, Luther was almost solely interested in a knowledge of God that fed devotion and was based on Scripture mediated by a kind of religious experience. Here we have an emphasis on the opposition between an objective knowledge of God and one that involves the believer's subjectivity. Second, Luther's emphasis on Scripture as mediating knowledge of God and his resistance to and, at times, rejection of philosophy contributes to the perception of a dichotomy between these two sources of knowledge of God. In that way, too, it tends to dissolve the integration between the scriptural and the Greek philosophical contributions to such knowledge that had been a great fruit of the Patristic as well as the Scholastic period. Counter to this, we have supported the view in our treatment of Scripture and the Patristic period that this dichotomy does not exist. The revelation of God through Christ transcends philosophical knowledge. And there is a dialectical moment in Christian belief and conversion (as we shall see more fully in the next part of foundational theology, e.g., in Peter's development of faith). But this is different from the total opposition proposed by Luther. Perhaps we should say that Luther and Scholasticism used basically different forms of language to speak of God, the one religious, dialectical, and symbolic, and the other theological, analogical, and objective. Perhaps if we interpreted Luther more from the context of a spirituality, as using metaphor and other figures of speech, we would do him more justice and acknowledge that we cannot judge his writings by the same standards we use in judging a theological work such as that of Thomas.

Disciples of Luther and later Lutheran confessional statements at times spoke on these issues in a much more measured way than Luther himself. Indeed, in the century following Luther and the Protestant Reformation, there developed in Protestantism itself a Scholasticism and even an apologetic as theologians tried to systematize the Reformation expression of belief. Some of these theologians took up Aristotle again and used him positively, even investigating evidence for the existence of God in the physical world.[47]

## III. From the Seventeenth to the Early Twentieth Century

It was during this period that the contemporary difficulties with faith in God developed, and we wish to take some soundings in it for the purpose of understanding and dialoguing with these difficulties. We are supposing a certain knowledge of modern intellectual history and specifically of philosophy, so we shall not analyse these difficulties but rather recall representative views that contributed to the decline of Christian faith in God. Analysis may be found elsewhere.[48] We will divide our treatment into two parts, first the seventeenth and eighteenth centuries, and second the nineteenth and early twentieth centuries.

[47]See Pelikan, *The Christian Tradition,* 4:332 ff., ch. 7, "Confessional Dogmatics in a Divided Christendom."

[48]For some analyses of growing modern difficulties with belief in God, see, e.g., James Collins, *God in Modern Philosophy* (Chicago: Regnery, 1959); Cornelio Fabro, *God in Exile: Modern Atheism* (Westminster, Md.: Newman Press, 1968); Michael Buckley, *At the Origins of Modern Atheism* (New Haven: Yale Univ. Press, 1987). I treat some of these philosophical difficulties in "Religious Reflection and Human Transcendence," in *God's Work in a Changing World* (University Press of America, 1985) 161–227. For some analyses of these difficulties and theological responses, I have been particularly helped by James C. Livingston, *Modern Christian Thought. From the Enlightenment to Vatican II* (New York: Macmillan, 1971); and James Turner, *Without God, without Creed. The Origins of Unbelief in America* (Baltimore: Johns Hopkins Press, 1985).

## 1. The Seventeenth and Eighteenth Centuries.

As we stated in the first chapter, we consider the basic difficulties with belief in God in our time to derive from both a misunderstanding of the Christian God and a modern historical consciousness that involves a restriction of the scope of human knowledge and values or interests, dependent upon the experience of knowledge in modern science and values in modern secular life. We can see these difficulties emerging in this first period of the modern era. An example of distortion of the understanding of the Christian God is found in the widespread interpretation of predestination. It was widely thought that Christian belief held that God absolutely predestined some to eternal happiness and withheld such predestination from others antecedent to any consideration of how they lived their lives. Some, like Luther, held that this was inconsistent with human freedom, and so they rejected this freedom; while others, like the Dominican Banez and many Catholic theologians, held that it was consistent with human freedom.[49] But even so, one can appreciate how such an understanding could give rise in some Christians to an erosion of faith in God. In many ways God seemed to be interpreted as basically a limit to human freedom. The division of the Churches, the alignment of both Catholic and much Protestant Scholasticism with Aristotelian philosophy to the point of opposition to early modern scientific advances, the discoveries of new peoples and ancient civilizations untouched by Christian religion, and the wars of religion—all contributed in practice and theory to a disenchantment on the part of many with the understanding of God fostered by the Churches.

There was, in any case, in the early modern period, for good reasons and bad, a flight by many from the control that the Church seemed to exercise on human life. This was part of the context for the widespread acceptance of the Protestant Reformation, the English establishment of a national Church, and the resistance to the Papacy by rulers who remained Catholic. A greater autonomy was sought in many areas of life—government, business, culture, personal mores—at least by the

[49]I have treated this question in *Predestination.*

privileged classes, who, however, did not often seek the same for the less privileged classes.

More than one treatment of the period from the Treaty of Westphalia to the French Revolution refers to it as "The Age of Reason." This designation shows one of the major sources of erosion of Christian belief in God during this period, though it should not be considered separately from the sources of erosion found in a distorted understanding of belief in God or in a search for the values of the time freed from the constraints of religious belief as represented by the Christian Churches. Aside from some resurrection of an earlier scepticism (e.g., in Michel de Montaigne and Pierre Gassendi), much of the growing view of reason as opposed to the full Christian faith in God came from philosophical reflections which depended on the development of early modern science. Francis Bacon (1561–1626) encouraged a scientific method that made use of hypotheses and experiments, and that was free from the deductive style of thought associated with late Scholasticism and dedicated to what was useful. Galileo (1564–1642) developed such experiments effectively, analysed motion mathematically and supported Copernicus' overturning of the Ptolemaic universe. There were important continuities between his thought and earlier Scholastic studies of projectile motion that have been brought to light recently.[50] But he emphasized the opposition of his method to that of the Scholastics; and the Church came publicly to oppose certain of his views, thus fostering a disengagement between the development of modern science and faith in God as understood by the Church and Scholastic theology and philosophy.

Descartes (1596–1650) contributed greatly to the disengagement of modern philosophy from the context of Christian belief and theology, even though he personally continued to be a believing Catholic. To counteract the attack on the value of sense knowledge by the sceptics, he began his philosophy with a universal doubt, and concluded that even in doubting he was thinking and that this was a solid base from which to begin his development of philosophy: "Cogito, ergo sum." He inter-

---

[50]William Wallace, *Galileo and His Sources: The Heritage of the Collegio Romano in Galileo's Science* (Princeton: Princeton Univ. Press, 1984).

preted reason on the model of geometry, and even argued for the existence of God on this basis. His idea that existence pertains to the essence of God, he wrote in one argument, is as clear and distinct as his idea that having three angles equal to two right angles pertains to the essence of a triangle.[51]

The idea of God developed here and in the later rationalist tradition by such philosophers as Leibniz and Christian Wolf is radically disengaged from the richness and vitality of the scriptural understanding of God, and yet it deeply influenced Christian theology. Likewise, the rationalists' arguments for the existence of God were built on conceptual analysis rather than realistic bases, and so were subject to Kant's later attacks. So we see that many who accepted the new ways associated with modern science and mathematics defended belief in God in ways that in the long run both disengaged the understanding of God from Scripture because of the dominance in their thought of philosophy over theology and Scripture, and even promoted unbelief because they assimilated too easily to the new way. There were opponents of this way, perhaps the greatest of whom in the seventeenth century was Blaise Pascal (1623–1662). He showed that reason could be used for evil as well as for good ends, that we are divided creatures, that we depend on grace for good, that faith answers questions central to life that reason cannot, and that there is a risk factor in faith, though it is a gamble well worth the risk. Pascal showed far greater awareness of the human condition than the rationalists, but he had greater influence on a later age than on his own.

We find a growing dominance of reason over faith in the empiricist tradition in England, even to a more marked degree.[52] In answer to the religious divisions within England at the time between the established Church and popular Puritanism, a group of prominent Churchmen later called Latitudinarians took a very "reasonable" approach to religion. They tended to have a great interest in the developments in science emerging

[51]See René Descartes, *Meditations on First Philosophy,* trans. E. Haldane and G. Ross, vol. 31 of *Great Books of the Western World* (Chicago: Encyclopedia Britannica, Inc., 1952) 94.

[52]See Gerald Cragg, *The Church and the Age of Reason: 1648–1789* (Baltimore: Penguin Books, 1966), chs. 5, "The Watershed in English Thought, 1660–1714," and 11, "England: The Rise and Fall of the Cult of Reason."

at the time, to adopt a common sense interpretation of reason, stress the agreement with reason found in revelation, show concern primarily for moral questions, and reduce in revelation what transcended reason. Isaac Newton's work in physics showed an age the presence of order in the physical world; and he himself used such order to argue to the existence of God as its source, even to the extent of making God a function in his physics. John Locke (1632–1704) similarly defended belief in God by a rational proof, and wrote a book on *The Reasonableness of Christianity* (1695) in which he sought to show to his age how few the beliefs are that Christianity calls for, how simple they are, and how they accord with "natural revelation." John Toland, in *Christianity not Mysterious* (1696), sought to show that religion must be reasonable and intelligible and that these conditions are fulfilled in Christianity. Revelation was still necessary, but he defined it in a way that kept reason as the central reality. Revelation cannot contain what is opposed to reason or above it, and thus mystery is removed from Christianity. As one author writes: "[Here] we have the essentials of Deism already developed: the primacy of reason, the supplementary and subordinate role of revelation, the elimination of wonder, the curtailment of the supernatural, and the equivocal position assigned to Scripture."[53] Later proponents of Deism, like Matthew Tindal in *Christianity as old as Creation* (1730), appealed so forcefully to the laws of nature and nature's God that they found revelation supremely manifest in creation and felt no need of any further divine revelation. Natural religion was sufficient. The God so honored was for many the one who established the Newtonian universe, but was impersonal and remote from individual human life.

There were arguments against such Deism, the greatest of which was the *The Analogy of Religion, Natural and Revealed, to the Constitution and Course of Nature* (1736) written by the Anglican Bishop Joseph Butler. Butler attacked the presuppositions of Deism that the course of nature is clear, its evidence for God is certain, and such knowledge is sufficient for us. He showed the ambiguities and darkness in nature and so in our natural knowledge, and thus argued that there is a need for re-

[53]Ibid., 78.

vealed religion, that we can suppose revealed religion has ambiguity and uncertainty also and that it should not be rejected because of that fact. We do not have certainty, but rather probability, and in religion as in other practical matters we are held to act by what seems the right path of action even without certainty. Butler's attack upon the excessive confidence in reason of his time was pushed further and for other purposes by David Hume (1711–1776). Hume developed an empiricist epistemology that he thought accorded with the experimental method of Newton's physics.[54] What we know are impressions, not reality, and we argue to matters of fact through the principles of cause and effect that are, at base, induced in us by custom and experience rather than by knowledge of the natures of material things and their powers. Thus he undercut the basis on which philosophers argued for the existence of God. He concluded that belief in God is more a matter of sentiment and practical inclination than of reason. There is an imperfect order in the world, and this may well testify to a God as a limited intelligence that orders the world. This knowledge is, however, without practical import for the way we lead our lives. Life is governed by more immediate factors such as approbation of our society and one's likes and dislikes. Thus from the seventeenth to the eighteenth century, we see that in England there was a surge of confidence in reason to the point where it became preeminent over Christian revelation for many, resulted in a Deistic religion, and then was subject to a diminishing confidence to the point where scepticism held sway over revealed religion and indeed any belief in God.

On the continent in the eighteenth century, we also see a great confidence in reason to the exclusion of revelation, much of this under the influence of English thought. In G. E. Lessing (1729–1781), perhaps the most representative figure of the German Enlightenment, it was the rationalist school rather than the English empiricist tradition that was most important. He used this rationalism to support criticism of Scripture and revelation. He edited H. S. Reimarus' critique of the miraculous in Scripture and held that contingent truths of history cannot establish the necessary truths of reason (e.g. doctrines

[54]See Livingston, *Modern Christian Thought,* 52–62.

of the faith such as the Trinity). The proof of religion for Lessing "rests not in the historical events as such but through the personal experience of the inner truth mediated through these concrete historical events."[55] Lessing had a respect for historical religion, but he had a rational faith that the positive religions would be superceded by the true gospel of reason. The positive religions are stages in the development of the human race from infancy to maturity. Revelation does not give anything that human beings could not gain on their own, but it does contribute to the progressive education of the race in its infancy. Thus along with his religion of reason, we find in Lessing a new historical consciousness that will become much more marked in the following century.

In France, it was perhaps Voltaire (1694–1778) who was the most influential promoter of a religion of reason and critic of Christianity in the eighteenth century. His philosophy was deeply influenced by his study of Locke and Newton during his extended stay in England.[56] He was convinced that the Newtonian universe justified rational belief in the existence of a divine intelligence. He offered arguments from design and final causality to support this, using the analogy of a watchmaker that William Paley would later make famous in his *Natural Theology* (1802). It was not until after 1750 that Voltaire began to attack Christianity with bitterness and caustic wit. He attacked the miraculous in Scripture and Scripture's inconsistencies. He sought to crush Christianity largely because of the influence of the Church in France, its actions against religious freedom of thought and its support of privilege and traditional customs that seemed to shackle the social changes needed at the time. What he sought in place of Christianity was a vague Deism in which God would be served by the practice of virtue and worship would be simple praise and adoration of God. Voltaire, like Lessing, manifested an historical consciousness. He rejected a traditional theology of history and wrote instead a philosophy of history (a term he coined) in which he used the West's new knowledge of China. His principle of unity was a

[55]Ibid., 33.

[56]See Norman Torrey, "Voltaire, Francois-Marie Arouet de," *The Encyclopedia of Philosophy,* 8:262–270.

view of history as progressing toward increasing degrees of culture and civilization, though he ridiculed optimistic views of history or belief in God's providence.[57]

As so often in history, so too in the eighteenth century, an emphasis on the rational or intellectual dimension of our being as the root of our beliefs and life generated an opposing philosophy that sought to root these beliefs and life more in our feelings, or at least in our knowledge as it is associated with feelings and the access to reality that feelings provide. Jean Jacques Rousseau (1712–1778) exemplifies this resistance to excessive confidence in reason in France as Butler and Hume did in their varied ways in England. Rousseau's way of defending faith in God is associated with his project for a restoration of human nature that is damaged by the corruption of society and yet is essentially social. In the form of a novel he presents "The Profession of Faith of the Savoyard Vicar" (1762). He attacks the evidential claims of special revelation as in Scripture, and claims that for us to hear what God has spoken, we have to hear God himself. And where can we hear God? Not in the claims and counterclaims of positive religions, but: "There is one book which is open to every one—the book of nature. In this good and great volume I learn to serve and adore its Author. If I use my reason, if I cultivate it, if I employ rightly the innate faculties which God bestows upon me, I shall learn by myself to know and love him, to love his works, to will what he wills and to fulfill all my duties upon earth. . . . What more can all human learning teach me?"[58] Rousseau's Vicar develops a religion that is basically Deistic. He finds reason in his experience of himself and of his freedom to believe in a will that moves the universe and animates nature, and to understand this first cause as intelligent. But he differs from some other Deists of the time because of the way he bases his religion on feeling and on conscience, and the way that this religion is colored by his reliance on moral experience.

The Enlightenment or Age of Reason came to its end in

[57]See Karl Löwith, *Meaning in History* (Chicago: Univ. of Chicago Press, 1949), ch. 5, "Voltaire," 104–114.

[58]Jean Jacques Rousseau, *Emile* (London: Everyman, 1961) 270. See Ronald Grimsley, "Rousseau, Jean-Jacques," *Encyclopedia of Philosophy* 7:218–225.

Immanuel Kant (1724–1804). Kant's early experience of the moral seriousness of the Pietists, his acceptance for years of the Leibnizian-Wolffian rationalism, and his later acceptance of Hume's critique on empiricist grounds of our knowledge of causality were all factors in his synthesis.[59] We recall here the bases he gave for rejecting metaphysical knowledge, for accepting rational faith in God, and for limiting religion to the bounds of reason.

Kant accepted Hume's critique of causality and thus his critique of objectively based knowledge of reality. He also accepted the fact that we do indeed have knowledge of reality that is universal and necessary, for this is shown in Newtonian physics. And he accepted from the rationalist tradition that we do not have to go outside reason itself to understand the truths of judgments which he called analytic (i.e., judgments in which the predicate is contained in the subject, e.g., bodies are extended). By a Copernican revolution, he posed the hypothesis that we know reality because we construct it according to forms and categories of our mind. The Newtonian application of mathematics to the physical world manifests this. The condition for the possibility of our knowledge of the world in physics is our possession of forms of sensuous intuition (space and time) and categories of human understanding. By this we know phenomena, or reality as it is constructed by the forms and categories of the mind. We do indeed have ideas of things in themselves, such as the world, the soul, and God. It is the character of the mind to move toward unification of knowledge, and these ideas serve such a function. However, *knowledge* of these realities, or metaphysics, is impossible, because this is an attempt to apply the categories or forms of the mind beyond the limits of experience. Proofs for the existence of God end up being concealed ontological arguments—arguments from ideas to existence. We cannot infer "the properties and the existence of an Author of the world from the constitution, the order and unity, exhibited in the world."[60]

---

[59]On Kant, see Collins, *God in Modern Philosophy,* "Kant on God," 6:162–200; and Livingston, *Modern Christian Thought,* 63–78.

[60]Immanuel Kant, *Critique of Pure Reason,* (trans. N. K. Smith, 2nd edition, (London: Macmillan, 1958) 526.

However, the idea of God is of value. Though we cannot on speculative bases have *knowledge* of God, we can on the basis of a postulate of practical reason have rational *belief* in God. Our practical life is ruled by an a priori form of practical reason, namely the categorical imperative, an oughtness or imperative that "I am never to act otherwise than so that I could also will that my maxim should become a universal law."[61] The moral life is our autonomous application of this imperative to our practical activity, and our supreme good is good will. The highest good, however, includes not only such a good will but a direct proportion between happiness and morality. Our moral reason tells us that this correlation *ought* to exist. Yet we human beings cannot ensure that this will happen:

> The *summum bonum* is possible in the world only on the supposition of a Supreme Being having a causality corresponding to moral character. . . . Now it was seen to be a duty for us to promote the *summum bonum;* consequently it is not merely allowable, but it is a necessity connected with duty as a requisite, that we should presuppose the possibility of this *summum bonum;* and as this is possible only on condition of the existence of God, it inseparably connects the supposition of this with duty; that is, it is morally necessary to assume the existence of God.[62]

Thus morality leads us to postulate the existence of God as a rational belief. This does not give us speculative knowledge of God, but conviction of the existence of God *for me.*

In his *Religion within the Limits of Reason Alone* (1793), Kant interpreted Christianity within his understanding of religion as morality—a way of considering our moral duties as though they were divine commands. He did not admit of a distinctive supernatural revelation, but saw in Christian dogmas

---

[61]Immanuel Kant, *Fundamental Principles of the Metaphysic of Morals,* in Maynard Hutchins, ed., *Great Books of the Western World* (Chicago: Encyclopaedia Britannica, Inc., 1952) 41:260.

[62]Immanuel Kant, *The Critique of Practical Reason,* ibid., 345.

moving symbols or myths that encourage the moral agent to hope that happiness can be realized.[63]

The tendency of the most influential philosophers in Europe in the seventeenth and eighteenth centuries to reflect on the question of God from the perspective of reason—understood rationalistically or empirically—derived largely from the loss of the synthesis or unity, imperfect as it was, achieved by the Fathers of the Church and the best of the Scholastic theologians between God as made known through Scripture and Christian tradition and God as reflected on by the culture and philosophers of the Greco-Roman world. One can say that as Luther went to one extreme to emphasize the God of Scripture to the exclusion of philosophy, the philosophers of the Age of Reason went to the other extreme to emphasize the God of nature or moral experience to the exclusion of Scripture. This tendency also derived from the failure of early modern Scholastic theology to integrate adequately the epistemological and physical discoveries of science as well as the historical and social concerns of some philosophers of the eighteenth century; thus by default it left the field to others. Eighteenth century religious revivals such as Pietism, for all the good they did, failed to stem the tide, since they did not engage the intellectual factors present in the erosion of faith. And always present was a growing sense of the autonomy of the human person in moral decision and in knowledge and the desire to limit the influence of the Christian Churches on personal and social life. Religious leaders at times fostered this through their picture of the Christian God and their opposition to a proper human autonomy.

## 2. The Nineteenth and Early Twentieth Centuries

This period contributed more immediately to the erosion of faith in our time than the preceding centuries, and similarly to the variety of models for mediating faith offered by Christian theologians. Much in this period contributed to an increasingly naturalistic historical consciousness. It was a period of bourgeois revolutions, many of them directed against the

[63]See Collins, *God in Modern Philosophy,* 195–196.

Church as well as against earlier political, economic, and social forms of society. It was a period of reflection on the meaning of history. There was a widespread supposition that history would inevitably progress, a view supported by the discovery of evolution later in the century. If men and women shaped history, what implications did this have for religious beliefs? Philosophers like Hegel, Marx, and Dewey reflected on these questions, as did many Christian theologians. Theologians in the twentieth century can be understood frequently as continuing responses of the previous century or reacting to them. Here we shall simply note some representative orientations of the time, namely those of Schleiermacher, Hegel, left-wing Hegelianism and "masters of suspicion," Protestant liberalism, and the Catholic response.

At the beginning of the nineteenth century, there was in Romanticism a reaction against rationalism as an amputation of an important dimension of the human person. It is not only objective reason that gives us access to reality, but feeling, will, and aesthetic appreciation. Moreover, in reaction against the French Revolution, the past, tradition, and community came to be more positively evaluated than in the Enlightenment. "Attacking the past now appeared childish, since every age, every culture has its own unique individuality and contribution to make to the richness and progress of history."[64] Also, counter to Newtonian science, nature was regarded as possessing a dynamic energy and qualitative dimension that cannot be reduced to mathematics, an "insatiably creative process of increasing diversification."[65]

Both Friedrich Schleiermacher (1768–1834) and Georg Wilhelm Friedrich Hegel (1770–1831) were influenced by this Romanticism in their reflections on culture and religion. We mentioned Schleiermacher's approach briefly in chapter 2. Here we can restrict ourselves to citing a part of James Livingston's evaluation of him:

[64]Livingston, *Modern Christian Thought,* 83.
[65]Ibid., 81.

With Schleiermacher, theology undergoes a radical transformation in its notion of theological authority. It is erroneous to say that for Schleiermacher the Bible and the Church no longer are theologically normative, for we know that Schleiermacher conceived of doctrine as the true expression of Christian consciousness *in the Church* at a given time, and that such a consciousness must be a genuine expression of that piety which appears in the New Testament. Nevertheless, for Schleiermacher the real locus of authority does lie in the religious experience, for the religious man has his own consciousness as the ultimate court of appeal. All external evidences and authorities are finally of no account if they are not confirmed experientially in the religious consciousness of the individual.[66]

Hegel too was influenced by Romanticism, but the continuing influence of rationalism upon him is shown in the fact that, counter to Schleiermacher, he understood religion to be not feeling but knowledge. He sought to unite the poles of experience, and made many unsuccessful attempts before he found a result that was satisfactory to him. He finally came to see that the synthesis of subjective immediacy—as found in feeling—and objective form—as found, e.g., in religion—could be developed by a dialectical process in which Christianity could be taken up (*aufgehoben*) into a final philosophical form. This was to view Christianity more positively than he had been able to in some of his earlier attempts. To show Christianity's positive meaning: "One would have to deduce this now repudiated dogmatics out of what we now consider the needs of human nature and thus show its naturalness and its necessity. Such an attempt would presuppose the faith that the convictions of many centuries . . . were not bare nonsense or immorality."[67] Christianity had grasped the truth in representational form, but it is the function of philosophy to grasp the truth in its rational necessity; this latter function is not possible before the

[66]Ibid., 101.

[67]Hegel, in comments he wrote regarding his plans to rewrite his "The Positivity of Christianity," cited in Livingston, ibid., 149.

truth has been presented to human beings in feeling and representation, which is accomplished above all by Christianity.

Humanity's condition is one of longing to overcome self-alienation and the contradictions of life. Judaism brought to consciousness this sense of history as self-alienation, particularly in the myth of the fall of Adam and Eve. The state of initial innocence was lost by the human desire for knowledge; this knowledge brought separation, and yet it was necessary for human maturity. This sense of separation itself was overcome by God becoming human in the incarnation, a profound symbolic truth though one not available to historical study. God became human to such an extreme extent that he died on the cross: "*With Jesus Christ the history of both God and man has actually changed.* God has passed from abstract idea into historical individuality and *only in so doing attains full reality.* The history of Jesus Christ is the history of *both* God and man."[68] Through the death of Jesus, finitude is destroyed. It is necessary that Absolute Spirit lose its life before it can fully realize itself. What dies is only the Absolute Spirit as standing over and against us—what has traditionally been understood as the personal transcendent God of theism. But this death is a transitional state that leads to the emergence of the Absolute as Spirit or the Spiritual Community or the Kingdom of the Spirit, the goal of the entire process of history. "God is Spirit, but to Hegel this means something very different from what most Christians mean by the term. For him Spirit is *the process of life itself,* 'it is life, movement' whose nature it is 'to differentiate itself, to give itself a definite character, to determine itself.'"[69] Thus God comes to full actualization through the world and humankind; human knowledge of God is God's coming to full self-consciousness.

In sum, Hegel achieved his justification of Christianity by translating its representational forms into a philosophical knowledge devoted to enabling human beings to transcend the

[68]Ibid., 153

[69]Ibid., 155. The enclosed quotation is from Hegel, *Lectures on the Philosophy of Religion,* (trans. E.B. Spiers and J.B. Sanderson, (London: Kegan Paul, 1895) III, 10.

contradictions of life into a fulfillment of consciousness characterized by wholeness and freedom.

The "masters of suspicion," largely deriving from left-wing Hegelianism, and Protestant Liberalism of the nineteenth and early twentieth centuries contributed much to the erosion of faith of our time—the former by undermining faith in God and proclaiming a humanistic faith, the latter by compromising Christian faith in God in order to correlate it with the culture of the period.

Among masters of suspicion we include disciples of Hegel such as Ludwig Feuerbach (1804–1872), Karl Marx (1818–1883), John Dewey (1859–1952), and other critics of Christianity like Friedrich Nietzsche (1844–1900) and Sigmund Freud (1856–1939). These gave psychogenetic explanations of belief in God, understanding this belief to derive from human suffering or weakness, and proposed naturalistic humanisms that would address the human condition more honestly within the limits of history itself. The first three began as disciples of Hegel in seeing nature as an objectification of Spirit, but came to see God as a projection of human beings.[70] Feuerbach was the first to give a psychogenetic explanation of the origin of our belief in God. He rejected idealism on the basis that we do not generate objects from thought but rather thought from objects of the senses. He called himself a realist or materialist to mark his difference from idealism. His first principle was humanity, and he interpreted belief in God as a projection of our being onto an Absolute distinct from our being in time because of the evils of existence. This leads to a depreciation of the self. We should react against this by recognizing that the true Absolute is humanity itself and centering our religious devotion on the human community.

Marx became a materialist through the mediation of Feuerbach. Human beings make religion; religion does not make human beings. Religion is an expression of humanity's real distress and protest against the evils of existence.

[70]See Livingston, *Modern Christian Thought*, ch. 7, "The Post Hegelian Critique of Christianity in Germany," 180–194; James Collins, *God in Modern Philosophy*, ch. 8, "The Emergence of Atheism," 239–284; and H. de Lubac, *The Drama of Atheist Humanism* (New York: Sheed and Ward, 1950).

Feuerbach did not recognize that the distress that is the source of religion is a social evil—the oppression men and women suffer from unjust economic relationships. Religion's projection of human happiness into the next life is an ideological consciousness that reconciles the oppressed to conditions of injustice in this life. If these conditions are overturned, then religion will wither away. The true focus then of human efforts should be to establish the future communist society that will overcome human alienation.

Like Marx, Dewey considered human beings primarily as practical beings dedicated to improving their physical and social environment. He became a naturalist through the influence of Darwin's discovery of evolution. Dewey interpreted this as a discovery of a general law of life and a generalization of the scientific method. Also, he interpreted human being and knowledge in the context of an organism's interaction with its environment. Religion diverts one from the human task which is a practical improvement of the human condition here and now by exploration, experimentation, and creativity.

Nietzsche proclaimed the "death of God" as a cultural fact, meaning by that the death of any ultimate grounds for traditional values.[71] He critiqued Christian belief in God as no longer worthy of support, since this belief represented "the declaration of war against life, against nature, against the will to live! . . . the deification of nothingness, the will to nothingness pronounced holy!"[72] Nietzsche thought that this belief derived from the resentment that the weak masses had against their aristocratic superiors. All human action comes from what is most basic in reality—*the will to power.* Christianity has inculcated a kind of herd or slave mentality, which Nietzsche sought to replace by a master mentality in which we would recognize that the source of all values was our own will to power—a will to power that others, but not Nietzsche himself, interpreted in a way that justified Nazism.

Freud also presented a psychogenetic interpretation of the

[71]On Nietzsche, see Livingston, *Modern Christian Thought,* 194–205; and Collins, *God in Modern Philosophy,* 257–268.

[72]Nietzsche, *The Antichrist,* 18, in W. Kaufmann, ed., *The Portable Nietzsche* (New York: Viking Press, 1968) 585–586.

source of belief in God. He accepted science as the only access to truth, and thus could not give credence to the bases that religion offers for itself. He considered religion an obsessional neurosis, "an outgrowth of infantile impotence in the adult personality who in front of a dangerous world projects the ever-ready protecting help of a father as experienced in childhood upon an illusionary father-God beyond the clouds."[73]

The erosion of belief in God and specifically the God of Jesus Christ resulted not simply from these and other vigorous attacks upon such belief and promotions of varied forms of naturalistic humanisms, but also from the way that the defenders of Christianity responded to the changes in thought and life in the nineteenth and early twentieth centuries. One prominent type of response was to ally Christianity to the life and thought of the past. For example, in France many in the Church sought a restoration of the pre-revolutionary political order and resisted the development of a republican form of government. Many Christians failed to take leadership in fighting for the rights of the oppressed laborers in the emerging industrial revolution. There were Christian theologians who rejected scientific findings, e.g., of the age of the world and the evolution of humanity, to defend Scripture's account of these matters, thereby identifying acceptance of Scripture (which they thought taught science as well as what God revealed for our salvation) with resistance to modern scientific advances.

There was, on the other hand, an overidentification with modernity on the part of many theologians and Church leaders that led to the erosion of belief. The view of James Turner, an historian of the emergence of unbelief in America, is that by the end of the last century unbelief was a fully available option in American culture, and belief was reduced to a subculture in the sense that it no longer functioned as a unifying and defining element of the entire culture or provided a common heritage as it had in the past. He ascribes a great deal of responsibility for this to the way influential Church leaders dealt with modernity by excessively accommodating to it:

[73]Marius Schneider, "Sigmund Freud and the Development of Psychoanalysis," in John K. Ryan, *Twentieth Century Thinkers: Studies in the Work of Seventeen Modern Philosophers* (New York: Alba House, 1964) 253.

Reconciling belief with the standards of science, attending more to the immediate moral relevance of religion than to its incomprehensible mysteries, were ways of keeping belief meaningful in a radically changing environment.

In tailoring belief more closely to human understanding and aspirations, however, many religious leaders made a fatal slip. They were not wrong to think that any significant faith would have to express itself in moral practice. But they often forgot that their God's purposes were not supposed to be man's. They were not mistaken in believing that any resilient belief must ground itself in human thought and experience. But they frequently forgot the tension that, by definition, must exist between an incomprehensible God and the human effort to know Him. Put slightly differently, unbelief emerged because church leaders too often forgot the transcendence essential to any worthwhile God.[74]

This approach was characteristic of Protestant Liberalism toward the end of the last century and the beginning of this. For example, many lives of Jesus were written that pictured Jesus as a moral and religious ideal, but discounted or reinterpreted the miraculous acts, pre-existence and resurrection that are ascribed to him in Scripture.[75] Liberal theologians, like Albrecht Ritschl (1822–1889) built their theologies on an understanding of Christianity as practical, that is, centered on the kingdom of God as a universal ethical kingdom and the supreme end of Jesus and of God. Ritschl sought to base theology on the historical Jesus, but only on certain strata of the tradition to which he thought that such things as the virgin birth, miracles, and the resurrection were not integral. Livingston comments that Ritschlian Liberalism's "formulation of the Christian message was well suited to meet the metaphysical agnosticism, historicism, and moral optimism of the pre-World War I period. But the question that must be asked is . . . were

[74]James Turner, *Without God, without Creed. The Origins of Unbelief in America* (Baltimore: Johns Hopkins Press, 1985) 266–267.

[75]See Albert Schweitzer, *The Quest of the Historical Jesus. A Critical Study of Its Progress from Reimarus to Wrede* (New York: Macmillan, 1968. First published, 1906).

they . . . seeing only an image of their own bourgeois Protestant faces?"[76]

Finally, we should examine some responses from Catholic theology to rising disbelief. To do this adequately would be a book itself, but we shall confine ourselves to recalling the approaches of Vatican I (which we mentioned briefly in chapter 2), which was in part a fruit of and in part a stimulus to a Neo-Thomist revival, and John Henry Newman who, together with the Tübingen school, was more influenced than Neo-Scholasticism was by modern currents of philosophy.[77]

The First Vatican Council (1869–1870) was the first in Christian history to reflect at length on the question of faith and reason. The council found it necessary to speak extensively concerning human knowledge of God through creation and supernatural revelation because faith at that time was threatened by misjudgments concerning the limits of human reason. On the one hand, there were Catholic theologians who, under the influence of Hegelian rationalism, exaggerated the competence of reason to the extent of teaching that it could prove the mysteries of faith once these were revealed (semirationalism). On the other hand, there were Catholics who, unable to answer Kantian agnosticism on its own grounds, taught that though human beings could not come to a knowledge of primary religious and moral truths through reason, they could gain such knowledge through the tradition of the society of which they were a part or through Christian revelation (traditionalism and fideism). Against these mutually opposed views on the relation between reason and faith, the Church taught on the powers and limits of reason, the primacy of faith, the compatibility between the two and the service each could give to the other. It did not make of our human capacity for knowledge a substitute for Christian faith and grace, but affirmed the power of reason to defend faith as an act worthy of human beings who are free and intelligent.

---

[76]Livingston, *Modern Christian Thought,* 268. See ch. 9, "The Ritschlian Theology and Protestant Liberalism," 245–270.

[77]On nineteenth-century Catholic theology, see Gerald A. McCool, *Catholic Theology in the Nineteenth Century. The Quest for a Unitary Method* (New York: Seabury, 1977). Specifically on the Tübingen school, see 67ff.

In its *Dogmatic Constitution on the Catholic Faith* (*Dei Filius*), Vatican I reaffirmed against such errors as atheism, pantheism, and materialism the Church's teaching on the existence, perfection, and creative activity of God.[78] The council used rather abstract and philosophical terms because of the errors it was countering. In reference to our human ability to know God, it taught "that God, the source and end of all things, can be known with certainty from created things by the natural light of human reason, 'for since the creation of the world, his invisible attributes are clearly seen, being understood through the things that are made' (Rom 1:20)."[79]

In this statement the council Fathers had in mind the traditionalists and those who taught, as Kant did, that God's existence could not be known by inference from created things. God here means the creator and author of Christian revelation, and he is explicitly called the "source and end of all things" to indicate that he could be known by human reason as the principle and end of our moral duties and not simply as an abstract principle. It is, however, a limited knowledge of God that the council was speaking about; it did not teach that all the attributes classically ascribed to God could be so known. The medium by which God's existence can be known is "the natural light of human reason, through created things." The council took reason as that power to which some attributed this capacity and of which others denied it. When, in the general congregation on the second draft of the document, it was suggested that this power be more definitely attributed to human reason "as it is now," this suggestion was rejected since, as Bishop Ganser said, "Those things that are taught here must be held to be true generally, whether man is considered in the state of pure nature or in the state of fallen nature."[80] Another bishop suggested that the text should state that God's existence could be known not "by man," as it was worded in the second draft, but "by the natural light of human reason," to avoid defining

---

[78]See H. Denzinger and A. Schönmetzer, *Enchiridion Symbolorum, Definitionum et Declarationum de rebus fidei et morum,* 35th edition (Freiburg: Herder, 1973), D 3001–3002. References are to paragraph numbers.

[79]Ibid., D 3004.

[80]*Collectio Lacensis* VII (Freiburg: 1890) 131.

that there could be no adults who are invincibly ignorant of God; and this emendation was accepted. By the phrase, "from created things" the council was not excluding a basis other than material creation, nor was it excluding the ontological proof of God's existence; rather it was simply asserting the adequacy of creation to show God's existence, and of human reason to rise to this knowledge from God's effects. When it stated that by this natural light of human reason, God "can be known with certainty (*certo cognosci potest*)," what it directly defined was the power of human reason to know the existence of God; it did not treat the question of the exercise of this power. By this teaching, the necessity of any positive revelation or of faith is excluded as an essential condition for human knowledge of God's existence; absolutely speaking, it is within the scope of our natural reason to rise from knowledge of creatures to a certain knowledge of God.

For the First Vatican Council, as for the early Church, it was God's historical revelation and our faith that was the foundation for the Christian's religious adherence to God. Thus the council asserted that it had pleased God's wisdom and goodness to reveal himself and the decrees of his will by another and supernatural way. It is by this revelation that what can be known naturally of God "can be known by all quickly, with firm certitude and with no admixture of error."[81] Without this revelation, such religious truths would at best be known only by a few and even then only through great effort and time, with much anxiety about the truth and with admixture of error. Also, revelation is absolutely necessary since God has called humanity to a supernatural goal or relation to him. Our faith response to God revealing is the "beginning of our salvation."[82] This faith is a gift of grace and a supernatural virtue by which we give full obedience of mind and will to God through believing what he has revealed on the authority of his revealing. That this faith may be reasonable, God has offered us external evidence for his revelation such as miracles and prophesies and indeed the sign of the Church in its holiness and fruitfulness in all good works. This faith is a free act which

[81]Denzinger, *Enchiridion Symbolorum*, D 3005.

[82]Ibid., D 3008.

we offer in cooperation with God under the illumination and inspiration of the Holy Spirit "who gives to all an ease (*suavitatem*) in consenting and believing the truth."[83] While there is a distinction between faith and reason in object and principle, there can be no opposition between them since both come from the same God who cannot contradict himself. In fact they can be of mutual benefit "since right reason demonstrates the foundations of faith and illumined by the light of faith cultivates a knowledge of the divine mysteries [while] faith frees and protects reason from errors and provides it with much knowledge."[84]

John Henry Cardinal Newman (1801–1890) had an abiding interest in responding to the disbelief in God that was present in England in the nineteenth century, but he did not associate himself with Paley's argument from design nor with the Neo-Scholasticism emerging among Catholic theologians. He wanted to show that belief in God is reasonable, but to do so with an understanding of the person as having to make moral decisions. There is difficulty in coming to belief in God. For one thing, reason cannot compel assent. People can always find reasons to question a line of argument, so that it does not compel them to infer the conclusion. They can, for example, disagree about the rules of evidence. This is particularly true with arguments for the existence of God that are based on design in the physical world. In part, Newman was influenced by the epistemology of Locke and Hume, so that he accepted their distinction between reason's function in arguing from one idea to another and its function in seeking to argue from idea to fact. He thought that Paley's argument led to a conclusion that was only an intellectual idea, and, though he did not really dispute some of the Scholastic arguments for the existence of God from the cosmos, he did not think that such arguments led to an assent to the existence of God as personal and as motivating conversion or appropriate action in the life of the believer. He was only interested in bringing people to a belief in the existence of God that would change their lives. One must realize that most people's basis for belief in God is not formal syllogis-

[83]Ibid., D 3010.
[84]Ibid., D 3019.

tic reasoning, but an informal process of reasoning; and God is more hidden in the physical world and in history than some forms of the design argument imply. "If I looked into a mirror, and did not see my face, I should have the sort of feeling which actually comes upon me, when I look into this living busy world, and see no reflection of its Creator."[85] The material world and the historical world both reveal and conceal God. Thus the search for him involves personal effort, and it is entirely possible not to see the evidence for his existence: "Newman's chief theological criticism, then, was that a design-centered theism generates a deistic outlook and even a species of finitism. The only way to break the hold of Enlightenment deism and empiricist finitism upon the European mind was to dislodge the proof from design as the primary approach to God and to show that the God who made the heavens is also the God of our hearts."[86]

Newman argued that our experience of conscience provides a basis for belief in God. He accepted that we do have an experience of conscience within ourselves, as well as an experience of the physical world outside ourselves, and he took conscience here primarily in the sense of its sanctioning our actions—commanding and forbidding, praising or condemning—rather than as simply a rule for right conduct. Without attempting to develop a technical proof, he said that as our experiences of the physical world help us build up a picture of that world, "so from the perceptive power which identifies the intimations of conscience with the reverberations or echoes (so to say) of an external admonition, we proceed on to the notion of a Supreme Ruler and Judge, and then again we image Him and His attributes in those recurring intimations, out of which, as mental phenomena, our recognition of His existence was originally gained."[87] He recognized that there are reductive interpretations of conscience, that people could not find God through

[85]John Henry Newman, *Apologia pro Vita Sua* (New York: Longmans, Green, 1947) 219. Also see Collins, *God in Modern Philosophy,* "Newman and the Assent to God," 348–370.

[86]Collins, *God in Modern Philosophy,* 358.

[87]See Newman, *An Essay in Aid of a Grammar of Assent* (New York: Doubleday, 1953) 97.

this path unless they were sensitive to conscience, and that some people with apparently good will were still not convinced by this evidence for the existence of God. The existence of evil in history and God's apparent silence and hiddenness do give rise to doubts, but in reality they point to the transcendent mystery of God and to human sin. If our God were one we could completely understand, he would not be God. Newman concluded that "In religious inquiry each of us can speak only for himself, and for himself he has a right to speak. His own experiences are enough for himself, but he cannot speak for others."[88]

He recognized that in "natural religion" there were three main channels to knowledge of God—conscience (or morality), the course of history, and the physical world. He sought by his investigation to help others toward a moral certainty of God's existence—moral, not in the sense of meriting only partial assent, but rather in the sense that it rests upon and brings about moral and religious change. Even though evidences for the existence of God merely point toward one explanation, and inference simply on its own level is a matter of probability, still this way does give rise to an assent that is unconditional. The person assents with a certainty of mind to belief in God as the only belief that is coherent with his experience of personal life as involving decisions, the freedom to decide for or against belief, responsibility for one's actions, and a distinction between good and evil.

We cannot do justice to the richness of Newman's thought in this brief account, but we propose it as a response to the problem of unbelief particularly appropriate to his time—and of continuing importance for our time—superior to the accomodations of Protestant liberals or the fideism of Kierkegaard, and complementary to the teaching of Vatican I. It has some of the limits of the Victorian age, e.g., the view of God primarily as Judge in relation to personal morality. Also, in our time there is more need to relate God to questions of social injustice and to our greater consciousness of world religions. But it is appropriate that more than one commentator

[88]Ibid., 300.

sees Vatican II as influenced by Newman in its teaching on belief and its foundations.

In conclusion, in this chapter, we have given some major views in Christian history on the meaning of and foundations for belief in God. We have paid special attention to the use of the Western philosophical tradition from Greece and Rome to articulate this Christian belief and the tensions in it between the scriptural and philosophical dimensions, showing by this the need to integrate these in a way that preserves the primacy of Christian revelation. We have also shown major reasons for the emergence of the unbelief of our time that we analysed briefly in chapter 1, and given important background for the emergence of the varied Christian theological responses to such unbelief that we analysed in chapter 2. This prepares us to address directly in the following chapters the question of unbelief in our time.

# 5

# Conversion and Human Transcendence

The problem we face in the remaining section of the first part of foundational theology is to reflect critically on those dimensions of the meaning and grounds of our faith in God which are particularly relevant to the major modern difficulties that we analysed in the first chapter. We found that many men and women of our time seek fulfillment in their lives in a way appropriate to our historical circumstances, technological culture, and a modern historical consciousness that is more or less naturalistic, at least in practice; that they have a somewhat distorted understanding of the Christian view of God, imagining him as remote and disinterested if not worse; and that they understand themselves through their secular experience and the human and natural sciences. As a result, the Christian view of faith in God seems alien to them. In reaction to this, there are also those who abstract from a modern historical consciousness, as though that abstraction were the condition for belief in God, Christian or other.

How then in the modern world should we attempt to mediate belief in God? I suggest that in the rest of the book it would be appropriate to show first that in fact people do turn to belief in God in our time through conversion, and then reflect on how we can critically understand and validate such conversion, noting some elements of a relation to God that distinguish our age from previous ones, thus leaving belief in God specifically through Jesus Christ for part two. In the present chapter we shall (1) recall that many people in our time do not accept the supposed contradiction between modern identity and Christian faith by giving an example of conversion in Thomas Merton and a brief reflection on how belief in God is mediated in such conversion, (2) answer those who think that for the twentieth-century person to so orient himself or herself is counter to rather than in accord with what it means to be a modern person (i.e., we shall defend a basic value transcendence in the human person from twentieth-century experience), and (3) show similarly that our social existence is also characterized properly by transcendence. An understanding of the human person and human society within a restrictedly naturalistic or historical context is a distortion of the human person and social existence. In later chapters we shall critically reflect on other aspects of belief in God, and shall dialogue where appropriate with some other models for theological mediation of belief in God in our time.

## I. *Christian Conversion in the Twentieth Century*

We have seen through Scripture and soundings in Christian history that people of past ages have again and again found such sufficient meaning and grounds of belief in God that they have turned to belief away from unbelief, persevered in belief in an unbelieving age, and again and again found that God is relevant to every age and its problems, although the ways in which they achieved this have at times compromised full Christian belief in God. The same is true in our own period of history. There is massive evidence in our time that many millions of Christians in every circumstance, in every field of human study and endeavor have continued to believe in God and that very many people have turned to belief from unbelief. A look at some instances of this experience may help us to reflect on why people in our time still find sufficient meaning and grounds for belief in God, and then later to reflect critically on important dimensions of the meaning and grounds of belief available to us in our age. We will choose instances of turning to belief in the Christian God, because that is what we are seeking to ground critically. We are not denying that there are grounds for one to believe, e.g., as a Buddhist, though we shall later suggest that there are ways to transcend seeming dichotomies between Christian and Buddhist belief. We are not asserting that the only people who are genuinely committed to what is true and good are those who explicitly believe in God, though we shall suggest that a full openness to what is true and good is an openness to such belief. Nor are we saying that those who believe in God are necessarily fully open to what is true and good, for we know all too well how believers themselves at times promote unbelief in others through being closed to justice and truth in the world around them. The only kind of belief in God that we are interested in critically grounding is one that comes from an openness to what is true and good wherever it is found, though even such openness will remain all too imperfect throughout this life, and the world around us will similarly remain all too marred by injustice and inhumanity.

Conversion happens in those who are not yet believers so that they come to believe; it happens in believers, so that they come to commit themselves more deeply to belief and to turn away from what is evil in their lives; it happens among those who do not believe explicitly in God so that they are more open to the human good and true. We are concerned specifically with conversion from disbelief in God to belief in the Christian God, because foundational theology critically seeks to ground such belief. We will briefly recall one such example here, the religious conversion of Thomas Merton (1915–1968), and then mention several other examples to show how faith emerges through the interaction between testimonies to God and twentieth-century people's responses to these testimonies. I take Thomas Merton because I know something about him, and because I find in him something of a parable of the modern person. There are studies of many converts in our century that would be equally useful, though we could not positively evaluate all the aspects of their conversion. Indeed, I do not seek to do so much with Merton. There are many ways of studying conversion in our century.[1] The way we do this is in

[1]See, e.g., V. Bailey Gillespie, *Religious Conversion and Personal Identity: How and Why People Change* (Birmingham: Religious Education Press, 1979); William James, *The Varieties of Religious Experience. A Study in Human Nature* (London: Collins, 1960; first published 1902); Walter Conn, ed., *Conversion. Perspectives on Personal and Social Transformation* (New York: Alba House, 1978); Walter Conn, *Christian Conversion: A Developmental Interpretation of Autonomy and Surrender*

view of major problems posed against belief in our time and mutually opposed theological mediations of faith used by Christian theologians, which we treated in the first two chapters. We wish to show that these dichotomies between the present age and belief and between mutually opposed reasons offered for believing are transcended experientially in some instances of conversion in our time.

Thomas Merton's early life and conversion to Catholicism are recounted from a later perspective in his book, *Seven Story Mountain.*[2] The following cannot do justice to the process of his conversion, but what it says is true of this process. He was born to artistic parents who were not particularly religious; his mother's parents believed a vague Protestantism. His mother died when he was six years old, and his father moved from place to place to paint. Merton thus spent some time in southern France, getting acquainted with a medieval village, St. Antonin, and staying at one point with a family that had a very strong faith. He attended a preparatory school in England where he heard a muscular type of Christianity preached, but was not much touched by religion, though he was somewhat impressed by one master's use of Descartes' proof for the existence of God; he also read widely, and tried to develop his own writing skills. His father died, after suffering with a brain tumor in a hospital for over a year, when Merton was about sixteen. Merton really could not face this in any way that would enable him to find any meaning in it that could sustain him.

Living with sophisticated, worldly-wise guardians in London, he revolted against the middle class values of the time.

(New York: Paulist, 1986); Stephen Happel and James J. Walter, *Conversion and Discipleship: A Christian Foundation for Ethics and Doctrine* (Philadelphia: Fortress, 1986); Bernard Lonergan, *Method in Theology* (New York: Herder and Herder, 1972); James Loder, *The Transforming Moment. Understanding Convictional Experiences* (San Francisco: Harper and Row, 1981); Emilie Griffin, *Turning. Reflections on the Experience of Conversion* (New York: Doubleday, 1980); Hugh Kerr and John Mulder, *Conversions. The Christian Experience* (Grand Rapids: Eerdmans, 1983).

[2]Thomas Merton, *Seven Story Mountain* (New York: Harcourt Brace, 1948). Also see Monica Furlong, *Merton. A Biography* (New York: Harper and Row; 1980); and Michael Mott, *The Seven Mountains of Thomas Merton* (Boston: Houghton Mifflin, 1984). Numbers in the following paragraphs refer to pages in *Seven Story Mountain*.

When he was eighteen, he took a trip to Rome where one evening he had an experience of the presence of his father that gave him a sense of the sin in his life, moved him deeply, brought him to pray in the churches he visited and even to visualize himself briefly as a monk. This religious fervor seems to have worn off by the time he entered Cambridge the following fall. There he wasted a good part of his year, trying to take all he could out of life—drinking, becoming sexually involved with a girl (he fathered a child that year), and doing badly in his studies. He seemed to be a rootless young man thrashing around to gain some center, some meaning, some assurance of his worth, looking for this in developing his creative ability and in drink, sex, and the facade of a man of the world. His guardian suggested that he complete his college education in the United States—another blow for the young man.

When he returned to the United States and entered Columbia University in New York (spring semester, 1935), he felt an abhorrence for the life that he had led, and flirted with communism for a while as a way to get beyond his selfishness; but he quickly recognized the unreality of this association. He became deeply involved in his studies and a multiplicity of activities at the university. Courses in literature from one professor, Mark van Doren, interested him most because the professor treated the material directly for its content and the rich perspectives it gave on human life rather than simply for its form. In the midst of all these activities, and after the death of his grandfather and grandmother, he experienced a mysterious collapse (fall of 1936) that involved dizzy spells, a kind of depression, and a loss of interest in what he had previously been frantically involved with. He now had difficulty finding reason to go to his classes. It was as though he had expected too much from all his activities and the frantic search for meaning and fulfillment in them, and now experienced their emptiness— their inability to give him what he was looking for.

It was in these circumstances that he gradually moved toward a change of perspective and of life. He was helped by friends at the University, with whom he could be crazy and also talk about many things—people with whom he felt at home, an enormously important matter for one who had suffered so much from homelessness and the death of many who were close to him. He was helped by van Doren's classes. Then in February, 1937, he picked up Etienne Gilson's book, *The Spirit of Medieval Philosophy,* where he found a concept of God that, unlike the hodgepodge of inconsistent ideas about God he thought he found in Scripture, seemed to make sense to him. God was *aseitas:*

> In this one word, which can be applied to God alone, and which expresses His most characteristic attribute, I discovered an entirely new concept of God—a concept which showed me at once that the belief of Catholics was by no means the vague and rather superstitious hangover from an unscientific age that I had believed it to be. . . . Aseity—simply means the power of a being to exist absolutely in virtue of itself, not as caused by itself, but as requiring no cause, no other justification for its existence except that its very nature is to exist. There can be only one such Being: That is God. And to say that God exists *a se,* of and by reason of Himself, is merely to say that God is Being Itself. *Ego sum qui sum.* . . . Pure act: therefore excluding all imperfection in the order of existing. . . . Beyond all sensible images, and all conceptual determinations. (172–173)

One may see in his being attracted by this aspect of God a recognition of where true fullness exists and a need for something objective and outside himself, acknowledging that it was not enough to follow his interests, impulses, and ideas alone. He regarded freedom and creativity, if left to themselves and separate from the reality of the world, the human person, and God, as self-destructive. He did not have an incontestable proof of the existence of God at this point, but he sensed that the basis on which he had been living his life was false and illusory. Thus he sensed what Gilson wrote about God as in tune with his more basic needs.

At the same time he was exposed to Aldous Huxley's writing on mysticism (*Ends and Means*) and his affirmation of the reality of the "supernatural," its accessibility to experience, its necessity as a source of moral vitality, and the need of prayer, faith, detachment, and love if one is to experience it. Merton graduated in February, 1938, and began working on a Master's degree, reading Blake in preparation for his thesis (*Nature and Art in William Blake*). Through this study, he wrote: "I became more and more conscious of the necessity of a vital faith, and the total unreality and unsubstantiality of the dead, selfish rationalism which had been freezing my mind and will for the last seven years. By the time the summer [1938] was over, I was to become conscious of the fact that the only way to live was to live in a world that was charged with the presence and reality of God" (190–191). He was introduced by his friends to a Hindu monk, Bramachari, who impressed Merton by his simplicity, spirituality, and evaluation of American life. Bramachari told Merton that it was in Catholic churches that he experienced prayer as a reality, and he encouraged Merton to read Augustine's *Confessions* and *The Imitation of Christ.* Jacques Maritain's *Art and Scholasticism* helped him to interrelate artistic creativity with the whole dimension of being human and with religion. This taught him that: "the artistic experience, at its highest, was actually a natural analogue of mystical experience. It produced a kind of intuitive perception of reality through a sort of affective identification with the object contemplated—the kind of perception that the Thomists call 'connatural'" (202).

In the course of the summer of 1938 he stayed in New York one weekend (which he called his first sober weekend in New York) to go to Mass and was amazed to discover many people who were more conscious of God than of one another (208). He heard a homily that struck him with its solid and clear doctrine, backed by the vital, scriptural tradition about Jesus as the Son of God. He came in the following fall close to conversion. He changed in little more than a year and a half (from the time of reading Gilson) "from an 'atheist'—as I considered myself—to one who accepted all the full range and possibilities of religious experience right up to the highest degree of glory. I not only accepted all this intellectually, but now I began to desire it" (204). He took a course in philosophy from Dan Walsh, who lectured on Thomas Aquinas and Scotus at Columbia University. He began reading more Catholic authors, e.g., Gerard Manley Hopkins and James Joyce. While reading of Hopkins thinking of becoming a Catholic, he himself felt "something began to stir within me, something began to push me, to prompt me. It was a movement that spoke like a voice. What are you waiting for? it said. Why are you sitting here? Why do you still hesitate? You know what you ought to do. Why don't you do it?" (215). After some hesitation, he went to a Catholic church nearby, spoke to a priest, and began a more regular study of the Church and its teachings. He was baptized in November, 1938.

We will not follow the continuing conversion he went through that brought him in the next three years to praying more, simplifying his life, giving up drinking and smoking, developing an interest in being a priest, being accepted by the Franciscans and later experiencing in a shattering way their rejection, teaching at a Franciscan college in northern New York, having a retreat at the Cistercian Abbey of Gethsemani in Kentucky at Easter 1941, meeting Baronness de Hueck and helping her with her work for the poor blacks in Harlem, thinking again of a vocation to the religious life, and entering into Gethsemani in December, 1941. We simply want to note that we find in this experience of Thomas Merton evidence that there is still in our age meaning and grounds sufficient for belief in God for many people who are quite modern in their search for meaning. Merton was brought to belief through a search for meaning and identity, through a collapse of his autonomous approach and the focus that he had in this search. The experience of death and of the inadequacy of his goals prepared him to be open to a deeper reality. The search for meaning that was radically important for him was the "golden thread" throughout this process, but there were intellectual criteria to be met and problems to be faced. This is shown, for example, in the fact that he was helped by the self-consistency and profound intellectual meaning contained in the philosophical understanding of God presented by some medieval philosopher-theologians. Also, Blake helped him to realize that a rationalistic and positivistic interpretation of reason is a distortion and an unwarranted reductionist interpretation of the scope and nature of human intelligence. It was important too that he had received an objective presentation of the Christian mystery. His rationale for believing depended on both the transformation that Christian belief offered in his search for meaning and the truth value that the view of humanity, God, and the Christian mystery in such a belief inherently contained. At the initial stage of his conversion he does not seem to have been much concerned for the transformative value Christian belief could have on society in combatting injustice. Indeed, in his monastic life he initially cut himself off from life in the world, but he later came to recognize and affirm his identity with this world and to have a genuine concern for issues of justice and peace. Thus his initial conversion was the beginning of a process that involved later conversions. Similarly, the implications for Christian belief contained in a Buddhist attitude toward life later became important for him. Thus we find in Merton an instance of the adequacy of the meaning and grounds of Christian belief in God in our time, and an instance where Christian belief emerges from an interaction between Christian proclamation and a human search for meaning that faces intellectual difficulties and pays its debts to reason.

We are not saying that Merton's passage to belief is wholly representative. Some people seem to become believers rather immediately, through one experience. But we want to reflect critically only on meaning and grounds for belief that do not shirk the intellectual difficulties people in our time pose to them. Many people do not have to face these difficulties explicitly and at length. An individual experience—perhaps prepared for over a long period of time—may include implicit answers to such difficulties. But there is also danger that such an immediate belief may be shallow, like seed that falls on rocky ground and springs up quickly only to die in the heat of day.

We would now like to reflect briefly on the process of conversion to suggest that the experience of Merton and many other converts shows a mediation of Christian faith and a process of coming to accept this faith that is more integral than some twentieth-century theologies will allow. There has been much reflection on the process of conversion from many perspectives in recent years;[3] we are interested in how Christian faith in God is mediated and responded to in the process of conver-

[3]See footnote 1. Numbers in the following paragraphs refer to pages in Emilie Griffin, *Turning.*

sion. I suggest that Merton's experience shows stages that are found in many others as well, and I find these stages well analysed in the four stages studied by Emilie Griffin in her book, *Turning*—stages which she finds present in her own conversion and that of such twentieth-century Christian converts as Thomas Merton, C. S. Lewis, Bede Griffiths, Avery Dulles, and Dorothy Day.

The first stage is that of *desire.* We see in Merton an exuberant love of life and then sharp experiences of loss through deaths in his family and a sense of how the projects he threw himself into at the university were really so inadequate that he could scarcely summon the energy to continue them. It was after this that he was struck by the medieval theologians' view of God as Perfect Act. There was a desire in him for much more than his projects offered him. In other people this shows itself differently. Both Griffiths and Lewis, for example, seemed to have had an intense experience of nature in childhood that offered an experience of transcendence; Dorothy Day had such an experience as a young adult, even though it seemed opposed to the Marxism she embraced at the time. As Griffin writes, "There is a desire in us for something greater than ourselves, a hunger which we ourselves can never satisfy" (46). C. S. Lewis seems to have deliberately experimented to see whether any form of earthly pleasure or affection could satisfy the desire he felt in himself, and he found that desire itself contained a corrective that showed the falsity of objects from which too much was expected (47).

A second stage may be called *dialectic* in the sense of dialogue with oneself and others (not in Barth's sense). This is a stage of inquiry, investigation, reasoning, and argumentation; not every convert goes through this. It involves a dialogue within oneself between the poles of doubt and affirmation. For example, Merton read Gilson's book, and then too Huxley, Blake, Maritain, the *Imitation of Christ,* Augustine, and others. One of his problems was that the view of God previously given him did not seem intellectually coherent, and another was the tension between the knowledge that his time and place assumed was possible for us—scientific knowledge—and that which is present in the religiously committed, in poets and artists. For Dulles as a student at Harvard, God seemed inconsistent with modern enlightenment and intellectual freedom. His study of Aristotle and Plato helped him to conceive of the reality of the spiritual and of final causes and the objectivity of the moral order, and to trust in the use of his own reason as a way of discovering reality (54); and through a study of Maritain, Gilson, and Thomas he began to move intellectually toward a belief in God. Griffin was troubled by the miraculous in Scripture. The sense of the reality of God she had had as a child passed as she grew older; in college she came to have doubts and to question whether religion was only a myth. Her experience was that religious people were not people of thought and people of thought were not people of religion (68). She had to confront the question of the reliability of Scripture—the historical question. She learned that in this whole dialogical process there is an exercise not only of the mind and heart but of a creative imagination: "A number of ideas and arguments are collected from various sources; the mind works away at them; then, sometimes in a sudden burst of energy, a sorting and ordering occurs not sequentially, but all at once. Things fall into patterns. . . . the puzzle, or riddle, to be solved is not one that can be guessed immediately but one that has to be . . . looked at from every angle, before a solution suggests itself" (63).[4] She began to see that she would never have more scholarship than she presently had. She found C. S. Lewis' argument for the existence of God from conscience most helpful to her. And she acknowledged that: "I think I *identified* with Lewis because I had had the same experience of mythology and legend which he had. I experienced God not only in the Christian myths but in the pagan ones; and I was beginning to trust, because of his experience, something that I had not until then trusted in my own experience: human powers of invention and imagination, not as forms of self-deception, but as ways to truth" (86). It seems then that many who are in the process of coming to faith face real intellectual obstacles. But there comes a point when the tension between the poles of doubt and the beginnings of faith undergoes a change, so that the way to faith opens up.

For many, however, after this there is still another stage, one

---

[4]On creative imagination, see also Matthias Neuman, "Towards an Integrated Theory of Imagination, *International Philosophical Quarterly* 18 (1978).

that can be called *struggle*. A deliberate action of will has been taken and the person has got beyond vacillation at least to the point of some "tiny seed of faith" (89). The person has glimpsed some other sort of possible life—different from the life lived till then. "To have that life, the convert must choose it, must reach out for it with both hands" (90). It can be then that the person experiences the greatest difficulties of all: "one begins to find oneself in a sea of bewilderment, assayed by doubts and difficulties of every sort; and these sometimes quite beyond the powers of the intellect to set aside" (91). An example is the way Dorothy Day faced opposition from her common law husband and was disappointed in how little the Catholic Church seemed to be involved in the struggle for social justice. Griffin realized that religious experience was in part psychological. This led to her greatest difficulty, namely, whether it was all psychological—emotional wish-fulfillment. With the passage of time she came to see these doubts as obstacles to God in her life, as self-centeredness; she began to look away from own inner conflicts to others and to God. The sense of sin plays a part here; the person experiences his or her own sinfulness and accepts it. Merton had a sense of inner division and undecidedness followed by the need to reach or risk beyond this at successive stages of his conversion, and this called for a move beyond ambivalence and an inner transformation.

The final stage is that of *surrender*. Here something fundamental happens; there is a crossing over made in utter faith: "a step into the darkness, an encounter with the unknown, for which the only resource is trust" (130). "Struggle is a rising to the climax, and the surrender its resolution" (130). C. S. Lewis spoke of his fear when in 1929 he became the "most dejected and reluctant convert in all of England" (138); it is the fear that attaches to all irrevocable decisions in which we give up control of ourselves. The fact that it happens without compulsion or without the kind of security perfect knowledge could give leaves room for the freedom of love. It is a solitary moment, and there may well be a sense of "now or never." It is a trust in the dark. Only after does the convert sense the arms of God's love about her or him. It is a letting go and a remaking of the self, or allowing oneself to be remade, because it is a moment of ultimate yielding. The convert is not carried away by some great emotion; indeed, it is more likely that he or she feels beyond wanting.[5] It is a death of sorts that is the condition of new life. It may be experienced at the point a convert begins to believe in God, or at the point of commitment to a specifically Christian belief or denomination, or, perhaps, even later. Perhaps we see this in Merton particularly when his application to the Franciscans was rejected; at that point his sense of self was shattered, and the remaking began at a deeper level. The conflict within oneself is not totally transcended by religious conversion. The problem of a degree of inner division remains, and thus there is need for further conversions, though perhaps not as radical: a basic change has taken place in the person's life.

A theological interpretation of such conversion would insist that it is an *interaction* between God and the human person who is formed by modern culture to a significant degree and is able to respond to God only under the power of God's grace. Testimonies are given to God through Christian proclamation, other religious traditions, and human experiences that bring persons to acknowledge the inadequacy of their present horizons and interpretations of self and the world. They experience the inadequacies of what our contemporary culture offers as horizon and environment and the inadequacies of the selves they have formed through this context. This dissatisfaction reflects that the human spirit is larger than our culture acknowledges; in fact, central elements of this culture reject or deny the deeper dimensions of the human spirit. These persons explore other views of life, some specifically connected to the Christian vision and some not, but all of which acknowledge the religious character of existence explicitly or implicitly. We see that, counter to some modern theologians, there need not be a dichotomy between what other than specifically Christian views of God mediate and what the Christian view itself mediates. And to accept a mediation that is not specifically Christian does not necessarily result in one's view of God or faith being controlled by it; it is a revelation of God but not the final revelation.

[5]Griffin dialogues with William James on some aspects of the "psychology of self-surrender" on 139f.; also see Conn, *Christian Conversion,* 184f.

The search for meaning seems primary in conversion, but the intellectual dimensions in the search for truth cannot be bypassed; it is essential that searchers find reason to realize that their movement to conversion is not simply wish-fulfillment, but has a solid basis on intellectual grounds and that, counter to much modern thought, the human mind has a wider scope than the knowledge found in science. Without this, people have too little reason to believe that their passage is a real interaction with a Transcendent One distinct from themselves. The intellectual grounds for belief are such that they render faith an act in which the person is not denying or rejecting what reason establishes as valid, but they are not so strong that they compel the person or leave no room for freedom. Again, the surrender called for in religious conversion manifests a dimension beyond the search for personal meaning, since by it the person accepts a subordinate position for himself or herself in the order of meaning so that God may have first place.

Thus we can say that the approach to faith that many converts experience tends to support the way that in the meaning and grounds it gives for faith in God Vatican II interrelates the specifically Christian elements and those that are not properly Christian but rather belong to "reason and human experience" or to world religions. We can say also that while the converts we have discussed became Catholics or Christians well before the turmoil of the 1960's, we see in someone like Merton continuing conversions that gradually integrate more contemporary concerns for social justice and the problem raised by Eastern religions. Thus in our age as in previous ages, Christians are asked to continue the conversion process and by this to grow in their understanding of God and of themselves, and accordingly to change their lives. I see in Merton's conversion and Griffin's account of the process of conversion a mediation of faith that transcends the dichotomy between Barth and Catholics before Vatican II (and between different groups of Catholic theologians, e.g., the Neo-Scholastics and Rahner), that integrates the process and pluralism so emphasized after Vatican II, and that overcomes a dichotomy between those who stress the transformative value of faith for society and individual and those who stress the intellectual grounds for faith.

## II. Personal Transcendence

We have examined an instance of conversion and have reflected on some factors in the process. But this manifests a personal identity or self so different from the identity that many assume is consistent with our contemporary culture that it raises the question whether the human person really is perfected by orienting himself or herself toward God—whether human persons are properly characterized by absolute transcendence in the sense of an orientation to constitute themselves freely by their relation to an absolute horizon of being and value. This leads us then to a critical reflection on the experience of conversion. Should we appropriate ourselves in our time and place as subjects with a dynamic orientation toward absolute transcendence? There is obviously a radical difference on this issue between classical Christian thought and much contemporary thought. We will recall this disagreement very briefly and then ask how we can reflect critically and appropriately on this question.

Classical thought had no difficulty with this self-appropriation. For example, Thomas wrote that "the image of God is found in the soul as it is oriented or inclined to be oriented to God. . . . We find the image of God not as the [human] mind is oriented absolutely to itself, but as through this it can be further oriented to God."[6] In accord with earlier Christian tradition, Thomas designated the individual human being as "person." Initially, this word had referred to a mask used by an actor and thus the character that the actor played. Roman law used it to indicate one who had legal rights. Some Fathers of the Church used it in reference to the Father, Son, and Holy Spirit; Tertullian determined the theological vocabulary in the West when he distinguished in God "three persons in one substance."[7] The word thus developed from having a phenomenological meaning to having a metaphysical and theological meaning. In Thomas too we find these different

---

[6]Thomas Aquinas, *Summa theologiae*, I, 93, 8.

[7]See, e.g., Lawrence Porter, "On Keeping 'Persons' in the Trinity," *Theological Studies* 41 (1980) 530–548; Adolf Trendelenburg, "A Contribution to the History of the Word Person," *The Monist* 20 (1910) 336–359.

senses, though the last two predominate. The phenomenological meaning is clear in his explanation that a special
word—person—was formed to designate the "individual substance of a rational nature" (Boethius' analysis of person in the
sixth century), because such individuals, as distinct from lower
animals, "*have mastery over their own acts; they are not only
acted upon, like others, but they act of themselves.*"[8] The person
is characterized by an agency that takes its origin from within
in freedom and reason, as distinct from one that is an auto-
matic response to external stimuli. In this phenomenological
description of the person, he takes the adult as illustrative, for
it is in the adult that an agency that can be called self-
possession is primarily found. The word "person" for Thomas
then means primarily the whole subsisting and acting individual who relates himself or herself to self, to others, and to God.
He understands "person" to signify "that which exists of itself
and not in another" in a rational nature, or that which subsists,
i.e., exists as a substance rather than as a modification of an
existing being (or "accident"), in a rational nature. And he
adds, "person signifies that which is most perfect in the whole
of nature, namely one who subsists in a rational nature."[9] This
calls the philosopher to infer a metaphysical structure that will
account for this agency. What enables the individual human
being to have this agency is the metaphysical structure of the
person—human nature or substance, the act of being (*esse*)
that actualizes it, and the human powers that emerge from this
being. And the actualization (*esse*) of this person (in the sense
of his or her fulfillment) is the intrinsic horizon of this human
agency; through this, persons orient themselves to other
human beings and their actualization and to God. So the
agency of the person has as its metaphysical root this dynamic
structure and as its intrinsic horizon his or her actualization as
a person.

Prominent modern philosophical views of the person have
at times emphasized self-consciousness or freedom in a way
that dissociates these from the one who is self-conscious or free

---

[8]Thomas Aquinas, *ST* I, 29, 1.
[9]Ibid., art. 2 and 3.

or exercises agency.[10] But at this point, we only wish to recall that for classical thought there was no problem asserting the transcendence of the human person, or an orientation to God out of a choice that comes from love and knowledge, as properly characteristic and perfective of the person. (Perhaps we should note that "transcendence" here is a metaphor. It is a verbal noun meaning "going beyond and above." We could as well use the metaphor of going deeper, i.e., beyond the superficial self to the one we more truly are.)

In the nineteenth and twentieth centuries this transcendence is frequently denied, as we have seen. For many social scientists, psychologists, sociologists, and philosophers religion is an alienation of the person rather than his or her perfection. As we noted in the first chapter when we spoke of a widespread contemporary naturalistic historical consciousness, many people in our time appropriate themselves as oriented toward their individual or communal future in history, but not as oriented properly toward God as the fulfillment of their lives. Whether people think that they are their own creation or the product of society or both, many tend to appropriate their fulfillment as located in themselves or in society rather than in their relation to God. They interpret as opposed to classical views such as that of Thomas the fact that individuals and societies construct their own future, that they do so within particular cultures, and that they do so freely.

How can we from contemporary experience critically evaluate whether it is proper to and perfective of the human person and human society (1) to construct themselves in accord with a distinctively human good that is normative for their choices rather than dependent upon them, and (2) to do so in a horizon of an absolute good and absolute transcendence? I suggest that we should turn to a phenomenology that helps us to understand the intentionality present in a growing person as he or she searches for genuine human values in history, and ask

[10]See George McLean, "The Person and Moral Growth," chapter 12 in George McLean, David Schindler, Jesse Mann, and Frederick Ellrod eds., *Act and Agent: Philosophical Foundations for Moral Education and Character Development* (Lanham, Md.: University Press of America, 1986) 361–394 for an analysis of contributions to the philosophical understanding of the person that derive from antiquity through the modern age.

whether this process shows that its meaning is the person's orientation to a properly human good and an absolute dimension of value and meaning, and reflects a potential in the person for such a horizon. We should evaluate this by an articulation of human experience that integrates cultural differentiation, process or history, and the constructive or creative dimension of the way we shape our lives, because these elements of modern experience are thought to undermine a classical view of the person. I suggest that for this phenomenology we turn to developmental psychology's analysis of human growth, which can be broadly accepted by believer and non-believer alike as validly though not adequately representing our human experience. This avoids an interpretation of human behavior in the reductionist manner of the behaviorists; it also avoids an interpretation of this behavior through mind and human ideals in a way that is divorced from the matrix of the body and social environment, as some proponents of the "Human Potential Movement" or of the "Third Force" at times seem to propose.[11] For our purpose here it is helpful to use the social sciences; philosophers who do not use the social sciences in reflecting on human transcendence tend to give us analyses that are too abstract. We note that this phenomenology addresses the question of praxis: we are interpreting the scope and meaning of our action for values.

I suggest that we can appropriate as genuinely honest to our experience of ourselves much of the work of Erik Erikson. Erikson's study addressed the question, "How is the mature personality constructed?" from a particular perspective. His answer was that it is constructed through stages in which the ego interacts with a progressively enlarging social environment and according to the gradual maturation of the individual's human potential. His work—at times supplemented and corrected by the work of others—offers an analysis of the development of the human person that, in its general framework, is widely accepted and shows that persons in their search for

---

[11]See D. Yankelovich and W. Barrett, *Ego and Instinct. The Psychoanalytic View of Human Nature—Revised* (New York: Random House, 1970) 225-226. Also see a critique of the reductionism found in much modern psychology in Bernard Rosenthal, *The Images of Man* (New York: Basic Books, 1971).

meaning reorient themselves in a way that manifests a significant degree of transcendence. This analysis is not a substitute for the concrete history we see in someone like Thomas Merton, but it supports, in a way proper to psychology, the view that the transcendence which classical thought asserts and which we see in Merton and others is basically not counter to but in accord with and demanded by a self-making that accepts the genuine values and insights of our time. This helps us critically evaluate and modify a classical analysis of human transcendence, such as we find in Aquinas.

Erikson's work is readily available and widely known, so we shall be brief in our use of it here. We shall (1) indicate something of the question he seeks to answer, the kind of evidence he uses, and his relation to Freud in his epigenetic analysis of the growth of the person; (2) suggest that a valid though limited phenomeonology of personal growth through adolescence that makes use of developmental psychology supports while it modifies Aquinas' interpretation of the person as oriented toward a good or fulfillment that is properly human, and is opposed to contemporary views that there is no properly human good normative for our actions; and (3) suggest that a phenomenology of our adult stages of personal growth supports the absolute character of human transcendence rather than a naturalistic interpretation of the human venture. All this addresses our critical question, whether we as human persons should appropriate the human transcendence found in religion as proper to us and perfective of us.

## *1. Framework and Evidence for Erikson's Analysis of "Ego" Growth.*

Erikson had a view of what constitutes mature personality, and he sought to analyse the stages and factors through which this mature personality structure evolves. He thought that maturity is not restricted to that of genital sexuality, but is characterized even more by what he called "generativity," namely, care or a concern for the development of the next generation even at significant cost to the adult. This normative adult personality is the evolutionary result of the child's progressive

structuring of self (ego processes) within the stages of its interaction with an enlarging social environment (social processes)
and according to the stages of its maturing human potential
(organic processes). Whereas some contemporary interpretations of human development ascribe it almost wholly to society and some almost wholly to the individual person, Erikson,
with many others, interprets it as occurring through the interaction of these two agencies.

What type of evidence does Erikson offer for his interpretation of the person's growth? Initially he based his interpretation on a clinical method and the evidence it offers; later he
enlarged his insights to include an explicit interpretation of the
normal order of human development. The diagnostic interview exemplifies the clinical method.[12] "The psychoanalytic
method," Erikson notes, "is essentially a historical method.
Even where it focuses on medical data, it interprets them as a
function of past experience."[13] The patient (or the patient's
family) looks back to the onset of the disturbance, and the patient and doctor together try to understand what "world order
(magical, scientific, ethical) was violated and must be restored
before his self-regulation can be reassumed."[14] But therapists
have to interpret the bit of interrupted life presented to them,
and they cannot avoid the involvement this calls for. They have
a model or a variety of models of what it means to be human
and the human processes in their minds (as physicians have in
their own field) that is an essential element in this interpretation. In his own model or models Erikson certainly takes some
elements from Freud, although he dissociates himself from
Freud's mechanistic interpretation of these elements. His full
model of the human person is in debt also to his study of anthropology (specifically his experience with two American
Indian cultures—the Sioux and the Yurok), his evolutionary
viewpoint (he refers to the theorist of evolution, C. Waddington, at times), other psychologists (e.g., he draws on similarities between Piaget's insights and his own in reference to

[12]See Erik Erikson, "The Nature of Clinical Evidence," *Insight and Responsibility*
(New York: Norton, 1964) 47–80.

[13]Erik Erikson, *Childhood and Society* 2nd ed. (New York: Norton 1965) 16.

[14]Erikson, *Insight,* 54.

adolescents), his own experience of life, and his great clinical sensitivity. One factor we should recall is the involvement of his own ethical sentiments:

> The evidence is not "all in" if he [the therapist] does not succeed in using his own emotional responses during a clinical encounter as an evidential source and as a guide in intervention, instead of putting them aside with a spurious claim to unassailable objectivity. . . .
>
> Any psychotherapist, then, who throws out his ethical sentiments with his irrational moral anger, deprives himself of a principal tool of his clinical perception. . . . (W)e somehow harbor a model of man which could serve as a scientific basis for the postulation of an ethical relation of the generations to each other.[15]

This kind of subjectivity is essential if we are to avoid a reductionist interpretation of humanity on the model of the physical sciences. A criterion of the value of the therapist's interpretation is the therapeutic results that occur in the patients. Do they emerge from the encounter more whole and less fragmented than when they entered it? Erikson bases his theory on evidence such as this, and he presents it in part as a heuristic device, as a theory that is subject to supportive or counter evidence.

Erikson accepts elements from Freud but put them in a new context. Freud had studied the neuroses of adult patients and related their illnesses to factors operative in childhood stages of pregenital sexuality that they had not integrated into mature genitality. Erikson's study of somatic processes, social processes, and ego processes in human growth is dependent on but develops Freud's factors of id, super-ego, and ego.

Erikson finds that the child successively centers for satisfaction on different areas of the organism and on activities somewhat correlated with these (*somatic processes*), and we must acknowledge qualitative differences between these stages, rather than consider later stages as hidden searches for the satisfaction proper to the earliest stage. The child at a particular

[15]Ibid., 73–74.

stage seeks satisfaction not simply in the activity of a particular organic zone but in a general organic mode of activity correlated with this zone, and indeed in a modality of life proper to this stage.

Human potential matures beyond the organic and is not reducible to it, and with this maturation the intentional center of the person's search for meaning shifts and enlarges. A distinctive aspect of Erikson's study within the Freudian tradition is the way he integrates the *social processes* as one central positive factor essential for the emergence of the child and the adult. It is the very encounters between the social environment and children at varied stages of maturation of their organic and human potential that present those turning or critical points that provoke children's growth. Societies can fail in offering the experiences and support essential for children's development, but since the welfare of a society depends upon its "maintenance of the human world," it tends to safeguard and encourage the proper rate and sequence of the child's potentialities for interaction.[16] Erikson was aware, however, of failures of societies in this regard. For example, society in the United States did not, at the time of his early writings, give positive encouragement for the growth of blacks, but rather sought to give them a negative identity. Now, some decades after Erikson's initial writings, we unfortunately see much more evidence in our society of disfunctional families that fail children in their developmental needs. For example, there is a smaller proportion of two parent families in the United States; there seems to have been a widespread jettisoning of traditional Judaeo-Christian values in the area of personal and familial life among cultural leaders, the media, and significant portions of our people; there has been an increase in the addiction to drugs and, perhaps, alcohol, an increase of violence and widely prevalent claims to equal moral validity of many alternate lifestyles. In this period of rapid change in our country, the "center has not held." And if we look both in our own country and in many other countries, multitudes of children and adults suffer from great poverty that is accompanied by malnutrition, disease, a lack of education, and an early death. Widespread

---

[16]See Erikson, *Childhood,* 270.

evils such as poverty, loss of freedom, cultural bias, etc., are frequently the result of social systems and are very deepseated and resistant to change.

What implications does this have for Erikson's conclusions? Does it mean that there is not a normative sequence of stages of growth for children and even adults, or does it mean that to acknowledge this and support this in times of rapid—and even cancerous—change demands that we be more counter-cultural? It is obvious to many who are concerned for the next generation that the prevalence of these ills in our society is having a damaging impact upon children. With many others, I suggest that these circumstances make attempts to critically evaluate what the fully human life and the implications of freedom are, work to develop communities that support genuine human values, and efforts to transform society more imperative.

The third factor for Erikson is *ego processes.* For Freud (particularly in the final stages of his thought) the ego was the reality principle whereby the individual, recognizing that the quest for some satisfactions that the id insistently demanded resulted only in greater suffering, defensively adjusted the organization of instinctual impulses to what reality allowed. Disciples of Freud gave the ego more attention, explored its defenses, acknowledged that it had energies independent from the id, and assigned to it functions that were not simply defensive but also adaptive. As Erikson writes:

> The ego was gradually seen to be an organ of active mastery . . . in integrating the individual's adaptive powers with the expanding opportunities of the 'expectable' environment. The ego thus is the guardian of *meaningful experience,* that is, of experience individual enough to guard the unity of the person; and it is adaptable enough to master a significant portion of reality with a sense, in this world of blind and unpredictable forces, of being in an *active state.*
>
> Some of these prerogatives (that the ego must and does guard) are a sense of *wholeness,* a sense of *centrality* in time and space, and a sense of *freedom of choice.* Man cannot tolerate to have these questioned beyond a certain point.[17]

[17]Erikson, *Insight,* 148–149.

In brief, the development of the child's personality depends not only on the encounter between the expanding social environment and his or her maturing human potential, but also on how he or she structures the self within this encounter. It is the three together that are essential to our understanding of an individual's "career." And in the case of a disturbance of this development, the convergence of the three processes "makes the catastrophe retrospectively intelligible, retrospectively probable,"[18] though the factors are not the "cause" of the disturbance in some mechanistic way.

Erikson integrates these factors of human growth in the context of the *epigenetic* principle. The development of the fetus in the womb offers a model for the development of the person in society toward maturity. In the fetus' growth there is a ground plan; and out of this ground plan "parts arise, each part having its time of special ascendancy, until all parts have arisen to form a functioning whole."[19] Similarly, the child interacts with the social environment according to a ground plan based on the gradual maturation of its capacities. As this happens, the enlarging social environment interacts with the growing person to evoke responses appropriate to his or her age and thus helps the person develop toward a maturity that Erikson describes particularly as generativity. It is at least normative that the social environment do so. Failures to do so harm the growing child or deprive it of what is appropriate to its need and its right. There are stages by which the individual approaches maturity (or, in different degrees, fails in this approach), that is, "the *normative sequence* of *psychosocial gains* made as at each stage one more *nuclear conflict* adds a new *ego quality,* a new criterion of accruing human strength."[20] Certain attitudes contribute to the person's growth to this maturity, and others oppose it.

If we ask why growing persons continually restructure their personalities in this sequence of stages, there are two ways in which psychoanalysis has explained this. Freud developed a

[18]Erikson, *Childhood,* 37.

[19]Erik Erikson, "Identity and Life Cycle," *Psychological Issues* (New York: International Universities Press, 1956) 52.

[20]Erikson, *Childhood,* 270.

rather mechanistic explanation based on displaced energies, an explanation that is, perhaps, particularly appropriate for those blockages of growth that he studied so deeply. But he also developed a clinical interpretation of the individual's search for meaning—an interpretation based on the recognition that the individual's actions, symptoms, dreams, and associations are symbols of the person's intentionality. Both of these are found in Erikson, but the former is vestigial and the latter predominant. For him a person changes primarily because "the encounter with some living fellow creature serves as a catalyst that enables the person to transform himself and shape his own self."[21] For example, a child who has just learned to walk repeats this new-found skill again and again out of delight in functioning, but also "under the immediate awareness of the new status and stature of 'one who can walk,' with whatever connotation this happens to have in the coordinates of his culture's space-time."[22] Erikson has great sensitivity to the meanings these new achievements have for the growing child, and he interprets them more by their orientation to future meanings than by their relation to earlier drives or displaced energies.

## 2. Initial Stages of Growth and Human Transcendence

Our question here then is basically whether a contemporary phenomenological approach to the constitution of the mature personality supports what we have found in converts. That is, is it perfective for persons to orient themselves to a value which is both properly human and transcendent? And, does contemporary experience both validate Thomas' interpretation of the transcendence of the human person and modify and enlarge it by relating it to what we now know about the process

[21]Yankelovich and Barrett, *Ego and Instinct,* 152.

[22]Erikson, *Childhood,* 235. We should note that object-relations theory studies these partial representations or images of self and others the child picks up and constructs in the process of growth. The relation between ego psychology such as that of Erikson and object-relations theory is not fully worked out. See Daniel Merkur, "Freud's Atheism, Object Relations, and the Theory of Religion," *Religious Studies Review* 16 (1990) 11–16. Merkur suggests that, "In principle, it should be possible to reconcile the theories of object relations and the superego by recognizing the former as a subset of the latter" (15).

by which the adult person is constituted or evolves? Notice that in our answer we are juxtaposing two views of the person, those of Aquinas and of Erikson. Thomas' question was primarily, "What is it that enables one to have mastery over oneself (*sui dominium*)?", and his answer was on the level of metaphysical principles of being and human powers of intellect and will.[23] The agency of the person has as its metaphysical root this dynamic structure and as its intrinsic horizon the person's actualization.[24] Erikson's question was, "How is the mature personality constituted?", and his answer was on the level of social, organic, and ego processes interacting in an evolutionary fashion. How can we relate these?

We should note also that Erikson's interpretation of the person extends itself beyond the phenomenological toward a sense of "I" that verges on regarding the person as a metaphysical agent. While the ego for Erikson is an unconscious dynamism, the "I" is conscious and reflects on the various selves in the composite self.[25] Perhaps we should point out that Erikson's distinction between the ego and the self has been found to be a contradiction by some critics.[26] Without attempting to resolve the particulars of Erikson's vocabulary, we can note that he finds a need in human experience to acknowledge a basic "I" in the human agent.[27] The phenomenological and the meta-

---

[23]See Karol Wojtyla, *The Acting Person* (Dordrecht: Reidal, 1979) and "The Person: Subject and Community," *Review of Metaphysics* 33 (1979–1980) 273–308.

[24]See Farrelly, *God's Work in a Changing World* (Lanham, Md.: University Press of America, 1985) 238–242, 272–273.

[25]See Erik Erikson, *Identity: Youth and Crisis* (New York: Norton, 1978) 216–221; also see Donald Capps, "Erikson's Life-Cycle Theory: Religious Dimensions," *Religious Studies Review* 10 (1984) 120–127. For stages of development that Erikson studies in the infant through adulthood, see *Childhood*, ch. 7, "Eight Ages of Man," 247–274.

[26]See, e.g., Wolfhart Pannenberg, *Anthropology in Theological Perspective* (Philadelphia: Westminster Press, 1985) 198.

[27]See Erik Erikson, *The Life Cycle Completed. A Review* (New York: Norton, 1982) 85f. It seems to me that we can largely resolve these confusions if we use the word "I" for the person or subject in the metaphysical sense of the one who is and acts. We can use the word "self" for this same person considered as an indirect or direct object of consciousness and speech, though of course the self is not fully known. But the "I" acts through a whole series of structured dynamisms that evolve in the course of the child's, adolescent's, and adult's development, as analysed by Erikson and others. Since we are indirectly and directly aware of the self only through our

physical approaches to the person are interrelated since the former raises the question of the latter and the latter is known through the former; we need both.[28]

Erikson helps us to understand how the person, in the sense of the mature personality, is gradually constituted through a series of stages distinguished by successive interactions of the person and society as the capacities of the human organism develop. We will not attempt to give an adequate account of this process, but rather explore whether it is a distinctively human good that is the goal and norm of this development by noting an aspect of each stage from infancy through adolescence. In the first year of life the interaction is between the infant at its most undeveloped stage and the mothering figure through the care she takes of it. By this interaction, it is critical that the child develop a sense of basic trust on balance over distrust. This "sense of" basic trust is what is primarily called for at this stage. At the toddler stage, the interaction is between the child with some increased muscle control and his or her parents. Part of this encounter centers around the question of the child's muscle control, e.g., in toilet training, given great emphasis in our culture. Through this interaction it is critical that the child be encouraged to have a sense of autonomy and achievement on balance rather than be induced to muscle control by shaming tactics. The older pre-school child has a wider social environment, strengthening muscles that allow much more movement and play, and a certain interest in the opposite sex (and specifically in the parent of the opposite sex). In

agency in these structured dynamisms, it is usually limited dimensions of the self of which we are conscious. Much of the self usually escapes us, since we are acting through limited dimensions of it. There is a phenomenological sense in which we have many selves that we try to integrate, and thus these can be considered "partial selves." Yankelovich and Barrett criticize the psychoanalytic tradition as not getting beyond ego, superego and id, for it presumes "that there is no such entity as a human person aside from the sum of these subdivisions of the psychic apparatus" (323). Erikson seeks to get beyond this, but does not achieve clarity. One problem for Erikson is that he wishes to preserve the word "ego" for the unconscious and the word "I" for the conscious. To make this the determinative element in this linguistic distinction seems to create more problems than it is worth. If one wishes to use the word "ego" for an agency within the metaphysical person, then it and the partial selves would be interrelated somewhat as the metaphysical "I" and the metaphysical self are interrelated.

[28]See references in note 23.

interaction at this stage it is critical that the child be brought to integrate these new dimensions with an overriding sense of initiative rather than through a dominant sense of guilt. A resolution of the Oedipus complex or the Electra complex through identification with the parent of the same sex is part of this process that paves the way for the school-age child's interaction with a still larger social environment and the challenge this presents to learn the tools of the culture. The child gets satisfaction and recognition out of task fulfillment, and the specific ego and/or self development at this time is gaining a dominating sense of industry rather than inferiority. The strengths that accrue to the child at a particular stage depend on earlier growth and contribute to later growth; there does seem to be a stage where specific strengths are called forth with special urgency, but these strengths are to be fostered at each stage.

Through all of this one sees that there is a certain relativity proper to the child's development, because it depends upon the culture in which he or she grows and the differentiated conditions of the child (e.g., sex, age, abilities, etc.) and the parenting agents. But this does not deny that there are normative stages and requirements for the child to develop toward a specifically human maturity. We see also the possibilities of failures on the part of parents and others concerned for the child and on the part of the child, with all the damaging effects that these have and the consequent need for healing. These failures are possible for many reasons. Parents and social institutions that care for children may fail the child. Also, progressing to a further stage demands that the child let go of a narrower horizon of human values and a personality structure no longer adequate to the task of being human; while it takes time and the development of structures for the child to appreciate many human values, it can also be threatening to let go of a current structure and focus when this is no longer appropriate for the growing person: and the value that calls for this change can appear to be a counter-value. The very fact that we recognize some actions, attitudes, etc., of parents, institutions, or the child as failures or regressions testifies to there being a specifically human good that is normative for the child's development and the parent figures' care and concern.

Without attempting at all to present adequately an analysis of child personality development, we may recall one significant addition and adjustment to Erikson's analysis. Robert W. White agreed with much of Erikson's correction of Freud and tried, like Erikson, to make the psychoanalytic theory of personality development more adequate to the reality of child development. He was uneasy with the adequacy of Erikson's theory to cover the child's motor and cognitive development, and so he turned to Arnold Gessel's and Jean Piaget's work, because if we are to fully grasp the ego's relation to reality we must "draw into the picture the facts of manipulation, locomotion, language, the mastery of motor skills, the growth of cognition, the emergence of higher thought processes, indeed the whole putting together of man's complex repertory of adaptive behavior."[29] The energy present in these processes cannot be adequately explained by the instinctual energies proposed by Freud (namely, libido and aggressiveness) and broadened by Erikson. Nor can they be explained by some neutralization of such energies over time, or by another instinct such as the instinct for mastery. These activities of adaptation and reality-testing seem to have a pleasure of their own attached to them that is not reducible to that of the instincts. The infant engages in these actions when its organic needs are satisfied, and it does so in a spirit of enjoyment. Thus they do not appear to satisfy libidinous or aggressive instinctual needs, or to have the consummatory aim of feeding or aggression. To account for these aspects of adaptation that Erikson's interpretation seems

[29]Robert White, *Ego and Reality in Psychoanalytic Theory. A Proposal regarding Independent Ego Energies* (New York: International Univ. Press, 1963) 20–21. Also see Susan Harter, "Effectance Motivation Reconsidered. Toward a Developmental Model," *Human Development* 21 (1978) 21–33; Robert Kegan, *The Evolving Self. Problem and Process in Human Development* (Cambridge: Harvard Univ. Press, 1982); and Richard Knowles, chapters 10 and 11 on Erikson and White in Richard Knowles and George McLean, eds., *Psychological Foundations of Moral Education and Character Development. An Integrated Theory of Moral Development* (Lanham, Md.: University Press of America, 1986) 239–292. Also see Margaret Mahler, Fred Pine, and Anni Bergman, *The Psychological Birth of the Human Infant. Symbiosis and Individuation* (New York: Basic Books, 1975). This analyzes the process—somewhat dialectical—by which new-borns, who almost identify with their mothers, grow to emphatically differentiate themselves from them through a negativism at about the age of two and still later come to identify with their parents, but now with their own agency and distinctness.

to leave out, White proposed that there are independent ego energies that are associated with the sensori-motor system. He called this energy "effectance," and the motivation found in this adaptive activity the developing "sense of competence." He saw his proposal not as a substitute for what Erikson proposed, but rather as a complement. I would agree that this addition makes Erikson's analysis more adequate to the reality of child development, and that what White adds to the picture in reference to the young child has its correlates in each stage of the person's development. It leads to a broader view of the ego's engagement with reality and of the ego itself in the sense of that which is operative in our agency and of which we can be indirectly or directly aware through our agency.

In adolescence, of which we are particularly conscious in our non-traditional culture, growing persons' interaction with the social environment is modified by the changes they undergo at puberty, the larger social environment, their increased capacity for what Piaget calls "formal operations" or ability to make hypotheses and test them (a matter we will recall in the next chapter), and their need, particularly in later adolescence, to take more responsibility for themselves and their future, making choices about occupation, lifestyle, marriage, etc. In our period of rapid change young people are challenged to establish some degree of coherent identity that embraces but subsumes earlier achievements and to prepare to take a part in the adult world, rather than to be dominated by an identity diffusion or overidentification with an authority figure, ideology, or goal that blocks out too much of what it means to be human (foreclosed identity). It may be that there is a somewhat different stage sequence for girls and boys at this point. Carol Gilligan has challenged Erikson's sequence here, namely the establishment of identity and then of intimacy in young adulthood, as based specifically on the experience of boys; she suggests that for girls the establishment of a capacity for intimacy may precede the formation of adult identity.[30] Whatever the truth may be, the young person must have, among many other

---

[30]See Carol Gilligan, *In a Different Voice* (Cambridge: Harvard Univ. Press, 1982); and Sharon Parks, *The Critical Years: The Young Adult's Search for a Faith to Live By* (New York: Harper and Row, 1986).

supports, some overall view and acceptance of himself or herself and the world—some framework for choice and values other than simply those of a subculture or unreflected interests.

This phenomenology of the constitution of the self supports the view that there is what we may call a constitutive human good, i.e., a kind of fulfillment that is appropriate to the human person antecedent to his or her free act, and a kind of normative human attitude toward it. One cannot construct oneself or seek to construct those whom one influences by any blueprint whatever. Some goals and attitudes are appropriate for and perfective of the person, and some are regressive or destructive. The modern recognition that we construct our own personalities and make our own choices and do so in differing cultures does not subvert the reality of human nature and its implications for human action, but rather gives us a more profound understanding of it.

But Erikson's analysis of personal growth also modifies an earlier view of what it means to be human. He shows that there is a psychogenesis of the personality through the growing child's restructuring of the self in view of his or her changing interaction with an enlarging social environment and maturing human potential. What may appear in some earlier philosophers as interpretations of human transcendence that are excessively "vertical" and unmodified by cultural diversity, and what may appear in some contemporary philosophers as interpretations of human development that are excessively "horizontal" and do not acknowledge a normative human nature are in a way synthesized in Erikson's framework. Specifically, through the process of growth there is transcendence in the agency of the person, for the adolescent has (or should have) a far more active, free, and conscious agency than the younger child.[31] This dynamic structure of agency develops be-

---

[31]We should note that at times Erikson seems to find in adolescence simply a need for "a system of ideas that provides a convincing world image" and "an ideological simplification of the universe" (*Identity,* 31, 17); but at other times he seems to claim that the growing person needs to know what the world is really like and what being human is really like. We go further than some of Erikson's assertions here, as we do also, later, in arguing for a dimension of reality beyond history that is a part of the human person's horizon. See *God's Work,* 134–138.

cause earlier forms of human agency are no longer sufficient for the interaction between the person and the enlarging environment with the enlarging human potential that is becoming actual at this time; the earlier forms of agency are surpassed and subsumed. The person, in the sense of "one who is," acts through structured dynamisms that evolve through time; these are the objects of developmental psychology studies. It is primarily in virtue of the young person's search for meaning that this development takes place. Similarly there is a kind of deepening that is normative for adolescents, in the sense that they should be in contact with and act from a capacity or a self that is more fully human than the more surface forms of agency found in childhood. We cannot do justice here to the pain this revolution—as well as evolution—in personality may well entail, with all the dislocations experienced at adolescence.

There is a transcendence in the social environment that impinges on the young person compared to that of his childhood. And there is also a transcendence in the horizon of the young person compared to the one he or she had as a younger child; it includes more fully human values (or, once more, it is normative that it do so, if there is not to be regression) such as the acceptance of more responsibility for one's own life and that of others. This does not exclude a continuation of earlier structures nor a kind of "regression in the service of growth." That the change in the growing person's history should lead to such transcendence is normative for both young people and the social environment that is responsible for their development. We know how, sadly and even tragically, this is so often not the

The whole issue here on how to relate contemporary experience and a classical view of what is normative in human life and thus what virtues are appropriate for us has been studied in many different ways. See Lee Yearley, "Recent Work on Virtue," *Religious Studies Review* 16 (1990) 1–9. Also see Don Browning, "Erikson and the Search for a Normative Image of Man," in Peter Homans, ed., *Childhood and Selfhood. Essays on Tradition, Religion and Modernity in the Psychology of Erik Erikson* (Lewisburg: Bucknell U. Press 1978) 264–292. Browning interprets Erikson as bringing together "an Aristotelian essentialism and a more modern evolutionary and adaptive point of view." My approach in this chapter is close to the position of Alasdair MacIntyre, *After Virtue. A Study in Moral Theory* (Univ. of Notre Dame Press, 1981). On the other hand, if one takes a Humean approach to modern psychological data, as Richard Wollheim does in *The Thread of Life* (Cambridge: Harvard Univ. Press, 1984), one's conclusions are radically different. In the following chapter, we will treat the epistemological problem relevant here.

case. But the very tragedy and loss that results when this growth does not occur shows how normative this transcendence is. And we can see in people like Merton that losses, e.g., of parents, can themselves eventually promote human transcendence.

Developmental psychology and specifically Erikson show us that it is part of being human that there be in the person a "tendency for new characteristics to emerge from previous, global characteristics" and "a tendency (for behavior) to become hierarchically organized, . . . for earlier developments to be continuously subsumed under later developments."[32] The stages of increasingly human agency that Erikson and others analyse in the development of the child and adolescent are possibilities of the human person before they are actualities and are oriented toward the fulfillment of the person. Their sequence similarly is a possibility of the human person—a possibility of which Thomas was not aware as we are today, though classical thought was not without a sense of the stages of life. This raises from another perspective the question Thomas faced as to what it is that enables the person to have distinctively personal action and life. Perhaps we must now say that not only the powers to know and to act freely have metaphysical roots, but that the very sequence of the stages of personal growth emerges from the metaphysical roots of the person as the first *intrinsic* principle enabling the child to so act and change, and that this sequence is directed to and evoked by the actualization of the person (*esse*) as the deepest *intrinsic* principle of this process.[33] Earlier dynamic structures are expressions of the possibility of being human, but when they are experienced as no longer adequate for the human fulfillment being evoked by the child's changing relation to its social environment and the maturation of its human potential, they are let go as dominant attitudes, and a more adequate dynamic structure is formed into which the earlier ones are subsumed. They are transcended. The

[32]Richard Lerner, *Concepts and Theories of Human Development* (Reading, Mass.: Additon-Weslen, 1976) 117.

[33]See *God's Work,* 118f., where I relate the constitutive human good to the restructuring of the growing person's moral judgment and action. In the same work (138f.) I defend an understanding of the person as essentially related to an environment, or as essentially a cultural being.

epigenetic principle seems to be not only physical and psychological, but even rooted in the metaphysical principles of the human person. Moreover, Erikson's analysis shows us that the human person is essentially related to a social environment; the person, philosophically considered, is not only an "in-itself" or "*sui dominium*" but a relationship or intentionality to other persons. There is room for this in Thomas' philosophy; in fact, by giving greater emphasis to this on the philosophical level, it is more understandable that he speaks of the three in the Trinity—Father, Son, and Holy Spirit—as *persons.*

We do not pretend to have resolved all the differences between these two approaches to the person. For example, how is Erikson's understanding of the psychic apparatus related to Thomas'? There is only one thing we will note about this here. The full agent of human action is the person or the "I." But the person acts through structured dynamisms whether one considers these to be the "ego" in Erikson's sense or the "appetites" (sensory and intellectual) and their related virtues and vices in Thomas' sense. In this agency there is a dimension of consciousness and a dimension of preconsciousness and even unconsciousness, as shown by repression, transference, and creative imagination in service of growth. The person undergoes the process of transcendence within an environment; it is this person that we should seek to appropriate for ourselves, understand in others, and explain philosophically and theologically.

## 3. Adult Stages of Life and Absolute Transcendence

Does our human experience of the life cycle and Erikson's illumination of it support the view that a transcendence toward an absolute not limited to history is proper to and normative for the human being? We can recall very briefly the three adult stages Erikson proposes, show how this whole process strongly supports our orientation toward ultimacy, and conclude that if this ultimate exists then it is perfective for persons to constitute their personalities through relation to it (or him).

In early adulthood, in both marriage and the work world, the young person is challenged to develop the "capacity to commit himself to concrete affiliations and partnerships and to develop the ethical strength to abide by such commitments, even though they may call for significant sacrifices and compromises."[34] This calls young people to let go gradually of much of the self-concern that was proper to them as adolescents; they may well refuse to adjust to the larger communions in these adult relationships because of fear of ego loss, and consequently experience a deep sense of isolation and self-absorption. Thus young adults turn either more toward intimacy and mutuality or isolation. We should note that some psychologists who have studied adult stages, particularly in men, have given great attention to young adults' formation of a profession or occupation and their growth into it, which is seldom a smooth process.[35] Some men never seem to get beyond exploring and experimenting in the job world. Some make solid commitments early, but without much examination of self or the value system underlying their goals; they may later regret their lack of exploration. Some are over-achievers whose thoughts and plans are almost wholly centered on this achievement; our society induces this attitude by the way it values "success" and money. Some integrate work and family life better than this. We should note too that even when, as now in the United States, women are free to follow most professions, most women opt for the role of wife and mother in the family, even though for economic reasons many of these must work outside the home.[36] Young adults are also called by their environment to take more responsibility in political and social affairs than they were earlier—recognizing the rights of others and of the community and accepting their responsibilities in these areas.

In middle adulthood, men frequently experience a "mid-life crisis," in reference to which the beginning of Dante's *Divine Comedy* is at times quoted:

[34]Erikson, *Childhood,* 263.

[35]See George Vaillant, *Adaptation to Life* (Boston: Little, Brown and Co., 1977) and Daniel Levinson, *The Seasons of a Man's Life* (New York: Alfred Knopf 1978).

[36]See Robert Schell, ed., *Developmental Psychology Today* (New York: CRM/Random House, 1975), chapter 20, "Early Adulthood: Selecting the Options."

> Midway this way of life we're bound upon,
> I woke to find myself in a dark wood,
> Where the right road was wholly lost and gone.[37]

These words were written by Dante in his forty-second year, but they recall a concrete experience he had some five years earlier when he was banished from Florence, his property was confiscated, and his work and hopes for Florence were dashed. Dante's experience is treated at times as a paradigm for a kind of crisis that many men face around this age in our society. For middle-class men it largely involves the question of meaning in work, whether they have been successful or not. A man's work at this point in life frequently appears to have less meaning than earlier, and this sense of loss of meaning may be complicated by difficulties in his marriage, loss of parents, etc. Erikson speaks of the challenge of generativity at this stage— the challenge to have a greater concern for establishing and guiding the next generation, whether this is one's own children or others, to move toward a dominant attitude of care for others rather than continuing to fixate on one's own achievement; if one fails in this, one experiences more and more stagnation and regression to an obsessive need for pseudo-intimacy. Karl Jung found with his own patients that the question of meaning in life comes to the fore much more critically at this stage. He wrote of his patients over thirty-five that "all have been people whose problem in the last resort was that of finding a religious outlook on life."[38] We should note that women's experience at this period of life may again be asynchronous with that of men. Since early adulthood the center of a woman's concern has usually been care-giving. In mid-life, her children need her less, and she may have a sense of a loss of functionality that gave meaning to her earlier life. Her husband and children fill her life less at this time, at least on a functional level, and she may well in her own way have to raise the question of meaning at a deeper level.

---

[37]Trans. Dorothy Sayers. Also see Lillian Troll, *Early and Middle Adulthood* (Monterey: Brooks/Cole, 1975) on mid-life stresses and reassessments, pp. 64ff.

[38]C. G. Jung, *Modern Man in Search of a Soul* (New York: Harcourt Brace Jovanovich, 1933) 264.

In late adulthood, there is at some point a loss of work and physical abilities and a possible loss of spouse. Thus there is a loss of functionality, highly regarded in our society, a loss of self-image if it depends on this, and perhaps more loneliness. Erikson interprets this stage as the deepening of a theme central to earlier stages and the fruit of the seven earlier stages. This stage calls a person to face and accept the meaning of his or her life *as a whole.* Erikson calls this ego integrity. By this he means that even though one recognizes the relativity of one's own life and culture, one accepts it as transcending this relativity, as something of value and an experience that makes one share what is central in the lives of men and women of other ages and cultures. This self-acceptance is possible if the person has faced the challenges of the earlier periods of life: "Only in him who in some way has taken care of things and people and has adapted himself to the triumphs and disappointments adherent to being the originator of others or the generator of products and ideas—only in him may gradually ripen the fruit of the seven stages."[39] "Life-review" seems to be part of the life of the elderly. The self-acceptance of this age is a "post-narcissistic love of the human ego—not of the self—as an experience which conveys some world order and spiritual sense, no matter how dearly paid for."[40] Of course, it may be that a man or woman cannot or will not accept themselves in this way, and so experience in some degree a kind of disgust or even despair, because it is too late to start over. Thus Erikson sees the ego challenge at this stage of life to lie particularly in the call to integrity versus the possibility of despair. The negativity of the experience of death is the final challenge at this stage. In fact, the realization that death is possible for us and for those we love at each stage seems to challenge the meaning of life as a whole and of each stage—unless death too is a passage to a still more transcendent stage of life.

Does this support the view that the human person is characterized by a transcendence to a dimension that is trans-historical and trans-secular? Certainly, these adult stages are themselves characterized by transcendence. As the social envi-

[39]Erikson, *Childhood,* 268.
[40]Ibid.

ronment changes, e.g., through the possibility and then the reality of marriage, family, work life, and involvement in the problems of the larger society, the adult is called to decenter from the self and to be more inclusive of spouse and children, of colleagues in work, and of the larger society. This human capacity for enlargement of concern reflects an enlarging human potential. The fact that we honor those who have such concern and decry those who fail in it shows that it is not simply a matter of self-interest but a part of the constitutive human good that enables men and women to live in society with others and to seek together the common good of society. The fact that men and women who reject this enlargement of horizon experience a constriction of meaning also shows this call to be part of what it means to be human. This supports what Thomas Aquinas writes: "The particular good is ordained to the common good as its goal; for the being (*esse*) of the part is for the being of the whole; hence also the good of the nation (*gentis*) is closer to God (*divinius*) than the good of one man."[41] We gain our being from family and society, and our being is a participation in the larger community; thus it is part of being human for us to be concerned for the good of the community even more than for our own good, to orient ourselves toward it freely, even at a personal cost.[42]

Does not this whole process strongly support the view that we as humans are meant for some dimension of life and meaning larger than the simply secular and historical? The life cycle, we suggest, includes a self-orientation toward an absolute dimension of being, value, and good that is the deepest dimension of what it means to be human. We can see this in elements of the process and in the process as a whole. For example, we admire those who, when the demands of love or justice call them to accept a diminishment of their own life, willingly accept this, and do so even when it means that they must jeopardize their lives. If we admire these men and women as exemplifications of what is best in human beings, we are sup-

---

[41] Thomas Aquinas, *Summa contra Gentiles*, III, 17.

[42] See "The Human Good and Moral Choice," in *God's Work*, chapter 6, 108–160, where I treat the question of human rights in relation to the person's orientation to a constitutive human good.

posing that through this loss they are putting first in their lives a larger dimension of being. They can only do so freely if they are energized by this larger dimension of meaning, and so their acceptance and our admiration suppose that this is not a total loss of being on their part but their entrance into a larger dimension, as religions claim, at the cost of a smaller. Moreover, their view that obligations of justice have an absolute character implies that they take an attitude toward limited goods within a context of an absolute good and their orientation to it. If they only related to others' rights with, for example, a context of history and the contingent, there would not be a sufficient basis for an absolute obligation to acknowledge these rights.

The way that the meaning of one stage depends in part on its contribution to a later stage; the way the change from one stage to another demands a letting go and a recentering that manifests a greater concern for others and a moral order of good; the way a fixation at one stage through, for example, seeking all one's meaning from "achievement" or possessions blocks out true growth—all this shows that through the stages of life we are meant for progressively more meaning, not less, even though this may well be a mystery to us and demand a seeming diminishment of the self.

Death itself, in this process, is not totally without antecedents in earlier stages of life; and the losses one must accept at earlier stages suggest that death itself is not the end but a passageway toward a still larger dimension of life. As each earlier stage presents a challenge proportional to an enlarging social environment and the maturation of human potential, it would seem that death is similarly a challenge due to the fact that in it we face an environment larger than the simply secular or historical and face it with a human potential that is perfected through relating to this environment or horizon even more than to the more limited environments that immediately engage us in earlier stages—and it is not insignificant that throughout our life we are more deeply engaged with this mystery than with what is more apparent and apparently immediate to us. This larger social environment and horizon is engaged with us through the process of our lives. Thus, it would seem that our lives have immeasurably more meaning than is acknowledged by those who fixate on the immediate to the exclusion of this larger environment, human potential, and horizon. Erikson sees the presence of religion in a special way in the earliest stage of life. At that stage, the mother's care reassures the infant that all will be well, and thus evokes in the infant a basic trust and hope. Such assurance is ultimately meaningless if we have no more than human resources and if death is the final end.

If indeed this larger environment, horizon, and human potential exist, then it is perfective for the individual person to constitute himself or herself in a way that centers on this horizon, relates to this environment, and acts from this personal depth. In fact, it would seem that through the whole process of life, it is this "I" that should be aborning. The person is called to assume this center and subsume earlier and lesser dimensions of human life and relationships within this overriding horizon and relationship. The persons who do this are the ones who fully accept themselves. Persons who do not are rejecting themselves in their deepest possibility in order to fixate on a more superficial self whose continuing meaning depends wholly on the larger context. Such fixation is strongly encouraged by much of our present culture and society, so much so that one social scientist finds that suppression of absolute transcendence is the basic illness in our time and the source of much other illness. Acceptance of limits in human life has lost meaning for many modern men and women because there is no longer any horizon of meaning sufficiently transcendent to justify this acceptance to them. Thus they narrow their horizon of meaning in order to escape facing death and other limits. Ernst Becker describes the modern neurosis that results from this: "Neurotic symptoms serve to reduce and narrow—to magically transform the world so that the [the neurotic] may be distracted from his concerns of death, guilt, and meaninglessness. . . . The ironic thing about the narrowing of neurosis is that the person seeks to avoid death, but he does it by killing off so much of himself and so large a spectrum of his action-world that he is actually isolating and diminishing himself and becomes as though dead."[43]

---

[43]Ernest Becker, *The Denial of Death* (New York: Macmillan, 1973) 181. Becker quotes here from Otto Rank.

In conclusion, we hold that it is indeed perfective and proper for us as human to constitute ourselves primarily through relating to this more than human environment and horizon, and that we are more in touch with what is deepest in ourselves and our possibilities when we act out of such a relationship. To reject such a relationship is to reject oneself at one's deepest level; it is to be deeply alienated from oneself, from reality, and from meaning in life. Of course, this depends upon the existence of this larger than human environment and horizon. We shall address this point in the next chapter, when we reflect on the questions of the scope of human knowledge and the existence of God.

## III. Social Life and Transcendence

Similarly we ask here whether in the way we live our lives in the political, economic, and social orders there are "signals of transcendence." It is clear that virtually all societies in the premodern world did live their social lives within some religious context. Religion frequently legitimated the social order, though at times, e.g., in the case of Israel and its prophets, it critiqued the public lives and not only the personal lives of its adherents. In the contemporary world there are many who think that the context for public life is not religion or morality but rather bureaucracy and technological reason. Most of the social sciences in the present century have interpreted political and economic activity within restrictedly secular and amoral frameworks. The social sciences such as political science, sociology, and economics have tended to deny transcendence in public life. All too often they have sought "value-free" and relativistic interpretations. For some this has been an expression of the limits of their sciences, but for many this has been their view of all that is operative in their fields. We ask then whether it is proper for human beings in the contemporary world to live their public lives in a context that includes more than what is contained within history, i.e., within the context of an absolute horizon of meaning and value. We are not asking whether we should live our social lives within a specifically Christian framework, although there are some Christians who think that the only alternatives are a wholly secular society or one that is professedly Judaeo-Christian.

Why do we ask this question? Because if we are looking for "signals of transcendence", we should not look only in our personal lives. To do so can be a distortion of religion. In fact, Christianity has been distorted in the modern world by such privatization, which induces many Christians to live their religion as though it can govern their private lives while in their public lives they can live simply by the "rules of the game" or total autonomy. We do not want to try to critically justify privatized Christianity; in fact, with others (such as Johannes Metz and liberation theologians) we want to critique this as a distortion of religion and Christianity.

We ask then whether public life is and should be led within a context of transcendence. And we do this by asking whether it is led within the context of a morality that accepts certain obligations as absolute. If so, then, as we explained in treating the development of the individual person, it is led within a context of transcendence. We will present a brief phenomenology of an important instance in the public experience of the United States in the twentieth century. We will ask whether those who interpret human social or political action in a naturalistic fashion or those who interpret it within the context of morality and human transcendence can account for the data better. Analogous examples may be found in the experience of other societies, both in the industrialized West and in other countries influenced by the West.

There has been a debate of long duration in the United States about the ethical foundations of democracy. With the rise of totalitarian regimes in the 1930's, the problem of the rational, ethical foundations for democracy became very important. Was there a moral justification for democracy? Edward Purcell writes of the split among American intellectuals on this issue at the beginning of World War II: "The debate demonstrated the depth of a basic split that divided two groups of American intellectuals who, for want of better terms, might be called scientific naturalists and rational absolutists. The realists, inspired by the successes of modern science, believed that truth was wholly dependent on empirically established facts; the absolutists, such as Hutchins, Adler, and the Catholics, believed that human reason could discover certain universal principles of justice by a philosophical analysis of the nature of reality."[44]

The dominant intellectuals in the United States began "in the late thirties to develop the clear outlines of a broadly naturalistic and relativistic theory of democracy" (200). For John Dewey, philosophical absolutism implied political authoritarianism, because someone had to determine what are the absolute truths. Dewey, who was opposed to epistemological dualisms, "left American social theory with one controlling dichotomy: absolutism and authoritarianism versus experimentalism and democracy . . . one of the central *political* assumptions of most American intellectuals" (201). This was the linchpin of the position, "because it provided the one basis on which most American intellectuals could unite. It was grounded on a thorough naturalism; it required the acceptance of no specific ethical theory or philosophical system; and, best of all, it claimed that rational and religious absolutism was the real enemy of democracy" (202).

So what held democracy together? "A common culture was the obvious answer. With its widely and often unconsciously accepted patterns of behavior and perception, a common cultural framework could cement together individuals and groups who disagreed on any number of specific issues" (211). "The assumptions of scientific naturalism . . . shaped American attitudes for the following two decades" (230–231). Pragmatism was blended into this. There were some (e.g., Leo Strauss and John Hallowell) who continued to defend the need in democracy for commitment to absolute values and natural law. But after the war, relativism and naturalism were dominant.

The view that democracy was based on relativism was both a descriptive and a prescriptive theory. Behaviorism in the social sciences supported this approach. "Established social institutions . . . inevitably appeared good. They represented

[44]E. Purcell, Jr., *The Crisis of Democratic Theory. Scientific Naturalism and the Problem of Value* (Lexington: Univ. Press of Kentucky, 1973) 176, 177–178. The page numbers in the following paragraphs are references to this book. Also see Victor Ferkiss, *Technological Man: The Myth and the Reality* (New York: George Braziller, 1969) and *The Future of Technological Civilization* (New York: George Braziller, 1974).

practical compromise, pragmatism, 'market decisions,' intellectual complexity, and structural rationality" (242). Catholics have to acknowledge that some of their own public statements and attitudes may have contributed to the sensed opposition between an objective moral order and democracy. This was before Pope John XXIII and Vatican II and its documents such as the *Declaration on Religious Liberty.*

Later on, many social scientists and intellectuals in the United States recognized that the earlier context of naturalism, relativism, and pragmatism was not sufficient for public life and its interpretation. Practically, in the Second World War technology at times prevailed in the way the war was waged, but later some of these decisions were morally and negatively evaluated (e.g., saturation bombing and dropping the atomic bomb on civilian centers in Japan). The war trials of Nazi leaders at Nuremberg had to have a basis other than American or even international law. The inadmissability of the defense by perpetrators of the Holocaust that they were simply obeying orders points to the preeminence of conscience over civil law. The Universal Declaration of Human Rights approved by the General Assembly of the United Nations in 1948 listed political, social, and economic rights for all people, and presented as the foundation for these the fact that, "All human beings are born free and equal in dignity. They are endowed with reason and conscience and should act towards one another in a spirit of brotherhood" (Article 1). "Rights are thus not simply *claims against* other persons, but *claims on* the community as a whole."[45] In the United States in the late 1950's, it became more obvious that the interpretation of the United States' political system as a balance of procedures in which people could present their interests and have them addressed was an ideology in defense of those in power and in repression of some minority groups. It became evident to many that it did not represent reality, because the system was distorted; the blacks, for example, were systematically repressed. Martin Luther King and others addressed this issue on the

[45]David Hollenbach, *Claims in Conflict. Retrieving and Renewing the Catholic Human Rights Tradition* (New York: Paulist, 1979) 28. See ch. 1, "The Human Rights Debate," 7–40.

basis both of human rights prior to and guaranteed by the U.S. Constitution and of the Christian tradition. Thus it was on the basis of morality that civil rights in the areas of voting rights, education, housing, employment, and the use of public facilities came to be legally guaranteed to blacks as well as to whites. The issue of the Vietnam War was addressed, not always without ideological distortion, on moral grounds. Moral discourse was central too in the public debates on abortion on demand before and after the Supreme Court made it a constitutional right in 1973. Similarly, questions concerning nuclear policy, the environment, the uses of technology in medical practice for genetic engineering, the prolongation of life, etc., and responsibilities to the poor within our own country and abroad are all questions that are now discussed as moral as well as legislative issues. Governmental officials have had to take account of the moral aspects of such issues. Thus it is less likely today that authors can justify a claim to adequately describe public life if they leave out the moral dimension and human transcendence found in it. As T. A. Spragens writes: "It seems fairly clear that the idea of natural rights has had a very profound operational significance in the context of limitation on government power, civil liberties, and so on which American courts have imposed and guaranteed. It also has had operational significance in the nation's political culture. Any empirical theory of democracy which does not incorporate such realities would strike many of us as rather inadequate."[46]

Thus we find that in modern societies, as in premodern societies, social, political, and economic life is lived within a context that is broader than the individual society with its mores or the autonomous rules of political activity; it is lived within a moral context that may be rejected, accepted, or interpreted differently by different people. And thus it is lived within the

[46]T. A. Spragens, *The Dilemma of Contemporary Political Theory: A Post-Behavioral Science of Politics* (New York: Dunellen Publishing Co., 1973) 105–106. Perhaps we should point out that there are other reactions to the behaviorist interpretation in politics and the social sciences in our time. Some, for example, explain social activity by analogy with games, others by analogy with drama, and still others by analogy with the writing of texts. All these approaches reflect on social activity in a symbol context more than the behaviorists, but as such these interpretations do not evaluate this activity in a moral context. See C. Geertz, "Blurred Genres. The Refiguration of Social Thought," *The American Scholar* 49 (1980) 165–179.

context of human transcendence, since the moral life contains obligations and values that are not only conditional or hypothetical but absolute.[47]

The question may remain whether it is proper and perfective for human beings to lead their public lives within the context of transcendence or the moral order. It is, after all, different than personal life. In a very brief answer to this, we shall recall a phenomenology of an experience of decision in reference to discrimination against blacks in the United States in the mid-1960's and the social legislation that institutionalized non-discrimination as the law of the land.[48] If we imagine a white man in the Southern part of the country at that time facing a decision whether to discriminate against blacks in hiring or in voting rights, we can imagine that he might well favor such discrimination because he has experienced the movement toward offering blacks civil rights as against his tradition, as aesthetically repugnant, and as threatening the purity of his stock. Also, if he were to join the movement, he could be considered a traitor by his own people. He may, however, in circumstances

---

[47]Much contemporary thought seeks to critique political activity without acknowledging a dimension of the absolute. This can be very helpful and even necessary, but one contention of this chapter is that it is not enough. J. Habermas' work attempts to offer a basis for social critique based on procedural criteria of communication. In early works he had spoken of a situation of ideal discourse. In later writings he still bases himself on communication and thus language, but speaks of "universal pragmatics" or "formal pragmatics" as the formal condition for communication. See J. Habermas, *Communication and the Evolution of Society* (Boston: Beacon Press, 1979). An objection made against him is that consensus is not an ultimate criterion. He is opposed to natural law and metaphysics as criteria, and he depends on formal criteria of speech discourse, but these by themselves are insufficient and call for some extra-linguistic and indeed metaphysical criteria. Also see Douglas Sturm, "Politics and Divinity: Three Approaches in American Political Science," *Thought* 52 (1977) 336–365, and "On the Meaning of Public Good: An Exploration," *Journal of Religion* 58 (1978) 13–29; and Peter Lawler, "Pragmatism, Existentialism, and the Crisis in American Political Thought," *International Philosophical Quarterly* 20 (1980) 327–338. On the history of political thought, see Charles N. McCoy, *The Structure of Political Thought. A Study in the History of Political Ideas* (New York: McGraw-Hill, 1963); and Pannenberg, *Anthropology,* 444–484.

[48]I depend here on developments of this theme that I have written in "The Human Good and Moral Choice," cited above, note 42, and in "Human Nature Reflected in Human Experience," delivered at a Conference on "Metaphysics, Culture and Nature" sponsored by the International Society of Metaphysics in Kyoto, Japan, August 1987, the proceedings of which are forthcoming.

where he has the physical power to discriminate, decide not to do so because the law is now opposed to it, or because he would lose economically through such discrimination, or because he would be subject to violence in response to his action. He may decide not to because through role-taking, that is, putting himself imaginatively in the place of the other, and through universalizing the resultant judgment, he may opt for a social order that treats all with equity when it comes to such matters; after all, he would not like to be on the receiving end of such discrimination. None of these motives gives rise to an absolute obligation to respect the other's dignity and rights.

However, in addition to these reasons and even as his primary reason he may judge that he ought not to discriminate against others due to their color because he thinks that they have a right to be respected and treated equally in such matters simply by the fact that they are human beings, even though they are not of his own group. As persons they, like him, are masters of their own actions and lives with their own human dignity, the essential worth that goes with this, and their own human fulfillment to which they are moving. This calls for respect that precludes subjecting them to discrimination, with the indignities that this involves. The necessity or prescriptiveness present in a judgment to this effect is not simply physical, economic, aesthetic, conventional, based on civil contract, utilitarian or consequentialist, or a result of role-taking and universalization. It is properly a moral necessity, that is, one that comes from the recognition of the rights of others that they have as human persons and a correlative duty that the moral agent has to respect this. These rights are a constitutive human good of others that must be acknowledged and respected, and it is a constitutive human good of moral agents to accept the claims that others have upon them since they are social beings. This has more than a hypothetical prescriptive force (i.e., it means more than that one should act in a certain way if one wants certain consequences or a certain kind of society).[49]

---

[49]This position differs from a form of liberalism described by Edmund Sullivan as follows: "The essence of liberalism is a vision of society made up of independent autonomous units who cooperate only when the terms of cooperation are such as to

Considerations of this sort were central in changing the consciousness of many people in the United States and in changing the laws so that they came to prohibit discrimination in hiring, in public accomodations, in segregated schooling of children, in voting rights, in housing, etc. That these considerations had this transformative social impact was in accord with the Constitution, because this founding document recognized the existence of human rights antecedent to and normative for the rights and actions of the state. By a long overdue reinterpretation of the Constitution, discrimination was found to be contrary to the constitutional rights of blacks. Similar changes have happened in other countries—and still must happen—from similar reasons.

As we indicated earlier, much contemporary political science has interpreted political activity in the sense of reciprocal human relations, but it has done this in a positivistic vein that has been criticized as leaving out such things as human rights and values that have been operative in political institutions. However, sociologists and political scientists are not always so reductionist. Peter Berger and Thomas Luckmann, for example, provide us with a social science interpretation that is not positivistic, because it relates institutions to the whole order of human behavior and search for meaning.[50]

The most sustained interpretation and critique in the modern world of human activity in the political order which takes into account the whole human being is that offered by the social teachings of the Catholic Church. This has merited for many of them, e.g., Pope John XXIII's *Peace on Earth* (*Pacem in Terris*) in 1963, respect and acceptance by many outside the Catholic Church and, indeed, outside Christianity itself. I propose that we can, from considerations such as those we offered above, appropriate several elements of this teaching as human beings rather than specifically as Christians.

If we engage in political activity as human beings, then our

make it further the ends of each of the parties." See Sullivan, "A Study of Kohlberg's Structural Theory of Moral Development; a Critique of Liberal Social Science Ideology," *Human Development* 20 (1977) 362.

[50]See P. Berger and T. Luckmann, *The Social Construction of Reality* (New York: Anchor Books, 1966). See Pannenberg's analysis, *Anthropology,* 397–412.

political communities should be evaluated by the genuine respect they manifest for human dignity and the service they provide for human needs. As John XXIII wrote: "Any human society, if it is to be well-ordered and productive, must lay down as a foundation this principle, namely, that every human being is a person, that is, his nature is endowed with intelligence and free will. By virtue of this, he has rights and duties of his own, flowing directly and simultaneously from this very nature. These rights are therefore universal, inviolable, and inalienable."[51]

It is only this context that is adequate for an understanding and critique of political, economic, and social institutions. A serious problem in our time is that institutions are interpreted by consequentialist and bureaucratic criteria divorced from the understanding of the institutions' source and purpose in human beings considered as persons. The only adequate critique must understand political communities as existing for the common good or a certain area of the common good that can be called the "public order," since the state is not responsible for all areas of the common good. The members of society then must find ways of regulating the social relations among themselves that are in accord with their human dignity and help individuals, families, and groups achieve their human fulfillment. Thus, Pope John XXIII commends as in accord with human dignity and the common good such aspects of modern political communities as the division of government into legislative, judicial, and executive branches, and the practice of spelling out in a constitution fundamental human rights, procedures for appointment of public officials, and the scope and term of their office. By interpreting political, economic, and social institutions in the context of human persons and the common public good, we are relating these institutions to a moral order. And we have a basis that in part legitimates them and in part critiques them and calls for their reformation and change. As circumstances change, we need to reevaluate these

[51] *Pacem in Terris,* 9. Quoted according to the translation in Joseph Gremillion, ed., *The Gospel of Peace and Justice. Catholic Social Teaching since Pope John* (Maryknoll: Orbis, 1976) 203. For a somewhat longer analysis of this social teaching of the Church and its context, see "The Peace of Christ in the Earthly City" in *God's Work,* 1–33.

institutions to see whether they are failing to respect and serve their citizenry, to relate to the people of the larger world in a way appropriate to our common humanity, and to seek to bring about necessary and appropriate changes. "It is the right and duty of every man and of all men to carry out this discernment between events and the moral good that they know through their consciences," wrote Cardinal Roy on the tenth anniversary of *Pacem in Terris*.[52]

Thus to be fully human involves taking responsibility for our institutions, supporting them and seeking to change them as called for by the dignity and genuine human needs of their members and by the interrelationship this society has to other societies in our shrinking world, where the welfare of one political community cannot be fostered or preserved except through relationships with other communities. Our full human horizon is an ultimacy, absolute and sacred, mediated by our personal fulfillment and the common good of our political community and, indeed, of the larger human community. And if this ultimate environment and horizon exists as personal, he interacts with us by evoking our action for our personal fulfillment and even more for the development of our society and the future of the human family. What works for the future of our communities is not, in this view, only human interests or the common good but God as source and goal of our common humanity.

We may conclude this chapter by noting that living one's life in accord with human transcendence, the constitutive human good, or the moral order cannot be identified with facing the past and accepting the norms of our traditions or our own culture as ultimate. It is rather to face the genuine future of the human individual and community, recognizing these to be historically conditioned, to seek to construct that future and accept the changes it necessitates, and to contribute with others toward the establishment and support of local, national, and world communities in line with our world's demands. In this chapter we have found reason to appropriate such transcendence as proper to us as humans.

---

[52]Cardinal Maurice Roy, "Reflections on the Occasion of the Tenth Anniversary of the Encyclical *Pacem in Terris* of Pope John XXIII," par. 152 (Gremillion, 562).

# 6
## Grounds for Belief in the Existence of God

In this chapter we will continue our critical reflection on the meaning and grounds of belief in God. Here we are not reflecting on belief in God specifically as Christian revelation makes him known to us, but in God as transcendent personal being— believed in as such by Christians, Jews, Moslems, and many others as well. Christians believe that God made himself known as transcendent personal being before making himself known as Father, Son, and Holy Spirit; and in the twentieth century some converts come to believe in him as transcendent personal being before believing in him as Father, Son, and Holy Spirit. As Christians then we are in this chapter treating only a part of our full belief in God. Also, we are reflecting not on the most proper grounds for this belief, because that proper basis is God's historical revelation, but rather on meaning and grounds that are accessible also to those who do not yet accept this historical revelation—grounds which Scripture and tradition affirm and part of the modern world denies.

Scripture states that, "Without faith it is impossible to please [God], for anyone who approaches God must believe that he exists and that he rewards those who seek him" (Heb 11:6). Such faith means more than an intellectual act, for as Scripture also states, "You believe that God is one. You do well. Even the demons believe that and tremble" (Jas 2:19). Without dealing with other questions raised by these texts, we note that by faith we mean a personal knowledge that includes both a belief that God exists and a commitment to him. This faith is a response to God's making himself known and to his grace. Christians believe that God's grace is operative in people's coming to this faith, for they hold that people do not come to faith in God without God acting within them, giving them by the Holy Spirit the desire to turn to God and illuminating their minds so that they will be responsive to his testimonies to himself. This is true of the process by which people come to believe in God as well as the process by which they come to believe in God specifically as Christians believe him to be. Thus we are not in this chapter primarily giving grounds for a philosophical knowledge of God or a constraining demonstration of the existence of God. Rather, we are reflecting critically on the meaning and grounds of faith in God. Is faith a reasonable and free human act? Is this faith without grounds and an abdication of reason, or is it a fidelity to God's manifestation of himself and invitation to us?

While vast multitudes of people in our time accept such belief as consistent with what we should appropriate of modern values and knowledge, many reject it because of what they conceive modern values and knowledge to be. In the preceding chapter we addressed in part the question of true human values; here we shall continue that dialogue but deal more directly with some difficulties that come from current interpretations of human knowledge and the world. We will treat this in three parts. We shall (I) raise an epistemological question relevant to our project of grounding faith, and then critically reflect on intimations many have today as in the past of the existence of God (II) from their moral experience and (III) from their experience of the physical world. Once again, this is only an introductory treatment of these large and critical themes.

## I. Critical Grounding of Faith: An Epistemological Question

We have already examined briefly the process of coming to believe in God as exemplified in some twentieth-century Christian converts. Here we would like to ask whether in principle one can show such faith to be perfective and reasonable. We will (1) reflect briefly on how faith as a personal act supposes a form of knowledge of reality that is mediated by symbols, experience, and creative imagination; (2) defend a larger horizon of our human knowledge than is acknowledged by much modern philosophy; and (3) show how the knowledge involved in the turn to faith in God is related to the epistemology we propose.

## 1. A Form of Knowledge Found in Faith.

Faith in God is indeed a personal act, an act in which the whole person is involved. It is an act of mind and heart by which persons accept a certain interpretation of reality and themselves and commit themselves to live in accord with it. In our world today it is not simply a growth or development from earlier personal acts; rather, it is a paradigm shift in people's values, knowledge, and commitments. It is an acceptance of reality and self that is in part a rejection of a previous acceptance of reality and self, and in part a subordination of an earlier self-acceptance within a more inclusive whole. Through faith one accepts a larger horizon for one's personal life and a larger environment—namely, God and communion with him; and one rejects an earlier fixation on immediately human values and reality to the exclusion of God from one's life. This involves a basic restructuring of the self.

Such faith is a response to God's testimony, and this testimony is mediated for the person through experiences, symbols, and a creative imagination, as we saw in Thomas Merton. Experiences of the inadequacy of life as one is presently living it call into question one's present attitude and viewpoint, and lead one to desire something more out of life. After this, one may, as Merton did with the help of a book by Gilson and people of faith around him, encounter an understanding of God that seems coherent and indeed answers a heart-felt need in one's life. Believers who really express their faith in prayer and action may mediate to the searcher the reality of God and a kind of self that calls into question the way one who still does not believe interprets reality. They and the Church or the community of believers of which they are a part thus mediate God and a kind of indirect experience of or

218  *Grounds for Belief in the Existence of God*

relationship to God. They do so symbolically. We can say of them what Ricoeur says of a linguistic symbol such as myth, namely that there is a double meaning in their action "in which a first meaning points to a second meaning which is alone intended, without however it being able to be reached directly, that is, other than through the first meaning."[1] The non-believer sees the action of the believer, which symbolizes both the believer's belief and, indirectly, the Sacred's or God's presence and reality to him or her. "Logos" and life are both involved in this symbolic mediation. Tradition too mediates the Sacred or God to the person who is searching for belief. Truth and values thus are present to the person not nakedly but by way of mediations such as these.

For many people today, as in the past, experience of the self and of the world also symbolically mediate a possible or real Other. Antoine Vergote summarizes the results of a sociological study:

> The intellectuals interviewed by our research-workers deny religious experience but acknowledge certain personal experiences which we have defined as pre-religious. The direct object of these experiences is not God—neither the divine nor even the sacred in the strict sense of the word. Thus the terms "religious experience" and "experience of the sacred" are inadequate. . . .
>
> These pre-religious experiences refer to the world and to existence—to the world as a totality; to existence seen as something supported and penetrated by a transcendent. Scientific thought is conscious of its natural limitation. It does not explain the existence of the universe. The enquiring mind is led to the ultimate question: why do things exist?
> . . .
>
> Existence is not felt to be in complete possession of the principle of its own being; this is something it has received. . . . Nature has been desacralized. But the universe as a whole, existence as such, have become indices of an

---

[1] Paul Ricoeur, "Poétique et symbolique," in Bernard Lauret and François Refoulé, eds., *Initiation à la pratique de la théologie*, I, *Introduction* (Paris: Cerf, 1982) 44.

Other, which is not just pure negativity, but rather the foundation, giver, perfection, and inspiration of the good.[2]

These experiences stimulate the creative imagination of those who are open to them, so that in a sense these searchers "indwell" the symbols that are presented to them and the symbols have a transformative influence on them. They present an alternative way of be-ing, an alternative world to live in which these people may find more inclusive and healing than the one they presently inhabit. Symbols may reveal to them how much they exclude of reality and of themselves by the way they structure their world and selves and by the criteria they accept for judging what is true and valuable. Thus before accepting this new way of being, one can by creative imagination project oneself into it. This self-projection happens, at least frequently, not so much through a deliberate shaping of the imagination, but through a semi-conscious or even unconscious reconfiguration of the self-in-reality. We see something analogous happening in many areas of life, for example, when young people fall in love and imagine themselves married to the loved one, or when people confront the challenges of a new stage of life, or when people have a sense through literature, an encounter, or a day-dream of a way of being more fully human than their present one. Erikson speaks of this process as occuring through the dynamism of the ego, but the social environment and the individual's human potential are involved as well. Yet this is not wholly unproblematic because for it to be possible, the new way of being has to be seen as integrating what is good and valued in the present self, as Merton was helped by Maritain's writings to see how the artist could be integrated into the fuller human being. Through such experiences, one can creatively imagine oneself in a new way of being, subsuming one's present "selves" into a larger context and no longer accepting one's present horizon or self as all-inclusive. Once more, as we said earlier of symbols, values and truth are not accepted nakedly but through the mediation of creative imagination in which they are integrated. The person responds not

---

[2]Antoine Vergote, *The Religious Man. A Psychological Study of Religious Attitudes* (Dayton: Pflaum, 1969) 76–78.

simply to fact or to value but to these as concreted in persons and community. One does not come to faith by evaluating what is presented as reality without the involvement of one's affectivity, nor does one comes to faith by simple attraction to the values it presents without the question of the validity of the view on which they are based arising in one's mind.[3] People come to faith through accepting that the symbols presented to them as mediating God and a way of relating to him do indeed mediate reality, and through surrendering to this understanding of God, thus restructuring the self within this relationship.

## 2. An Epistemological Question

However, one may say that this supposes an epistemology widely rejected in our time. Intimations of God one may have through other people and one's self and the physical world are a religious reading of the self and world, and are in accord with the epistemology of Thomas Aquinas and other classical philosophers, but not with much epistemology since then. As long as people accept certain modern strictures against metaphysics, they can scarcely have confidence in the objective validity of intimations of God that come to them through experience. I will not give an extended treatment of this matter here because such a study may easily be found elsewhere,[4] but we must deal with it briefly. I will recall an interpretation of Thomas' view on how we know reality as being, and then a few modern difficulties raised against our capacity to know reality metaphysically. Following this I will present a contemporary phenomenology of our human knowledge relevant to this issue, using data from the work of some developmental cognitive psychologists, and ask whether an epistemology that accepts our capacity for metaphysical knowledge or one that rejects it is better able to explain this data.

Thomas Aquinas has a psychology and epistemology to explain our experience of knowledge. In accord with Aristotle

---

[3]See John Henry Newman, *Grammar of Assent* (New York: Doubleday, 1955) passim, and specifically 84–85.

[4]See my more extended treatment of this in *God's Work,* ch. 9, "Developmental Psychology and Knowledge of Being," 287–314.

and others he discusses the senses, such as seeing, hearing, feeling, smelling, tasting. But, also in accord with Aristotle and others, he finds these inadequate to account for our knowledge of reality, since in many cases we know *what things are* and not only their physical or sensible characteristics. For example, we can distinguish a human being from a beast as a "rational animal"; we can distinguish a thing's change in some characteristics (e.g., size) from its change in being (e.g., in death). This is to know something at least of the nature or essence of a thing, what makes it be the kind of thing it is. This we do by intellectual penetration into what is offered us through the senses; besides our senses we also have a power of understanding which we call the intellect.

But more than this, we know the distinction between something be-ing and something as merely possibly be-ing. To be is not identical with being a particular kind of thing. The constitutive principles of a thing at its deepest interior dimension include both one that determines its kind of being (nature or essence) and one that makes it simply to be (*esse*—to be or existence). To know a thing specifically as be-ing then, it is not sufficient to know what *kind of being* it is by direct intellectual apprehension mediated by sense knowledge. In fact, for Thomas, to be is more directly an object of the human will than of the human intellect, because of the way the good, which is the object of the will, is related to the actualization of the being of the one who acts. He writes: "The good is that which all desire . . . but all things desire to be (*esse*) actually according to their manner, which is clear from the fact that each thing according to its nature resists corruption. To be actually then constitutes the nature of the good."[5]

This is reflected in our language, for we say "I want *to be*" or "I want *to eat*," etc., thus expressing in many cases the direct object of desire, love, and will by the infinitive form of the verb. We generally signify the direct object of knowledge by a noun or noun phrase, such as "I know him," or "I know how to swim." If we place an infinitive after a word signifying knowledge, it means not the direct object that is known but the pur-

[5]Thomas Aquinas, *Summa Contra Gentiles,* I, 37, 4. Also see his *De Veritate,* q. 22, a. 1, ad 4; q. 21, 2; *De Potentia,* q. 3, a. 6.

pose of our knowledge, as in "I study to learn." The point of this excursus is that it seems we know being through, in part, the mediation of our desire and action for be-ing—initially for our own be-ing. As we intellectually know color through the mediation of the sense that has color as its direct object, so too we know be-ing through the mediation of the power by which we desire and love to be, namely our will or "rational appetite." Thus our knowledge of being, which is systematically investigated by metaphysics, is mediated both through our direct knowledge of what things are in the world about us and through our desire to be, or our response to our own be-ing through desire, love, etc. This we know more through presence than the intellect, as we know the things about us.

In this classical view, knowledge of God is mediated through both knowledge of self and knowledge of the world, for God is the fullness of being in which our being shares and he is the source of the world. Knowledge of God is mediated not only by objective knowledge but by the presence that comes through a desire and love of being that extends beyond our immediate self and the selves of fellow human beings as such. And, conversely, God can communicate to us through our interiority and the physical world or, more properly, through both within the context of history.

How can we evaluate this view, given the fact that most modern philosophers deny such scope to our knowledge? As John E. Smith writes: "The modern problem of rationality in religion has been set largely by the decline, beginning in the eighteenth century, of the classical philosophical traditions, coupled with the rise of a new conception of rationality which has been determined by three factors; first, the norms operative in experimental science; secondly, a logic which purports to be entirely formal and thus independent of particular philosophical commitments; and, finally, a technical and instrumental as distinct from a reflective and speculative, reason."[6] In our chapter on soundings in the history of reflection on God we recalled some of these difficulties which have influenced

[6]John E. Smith, "Faith, Belief and the Problem of Rationality in Religion," in C. F. Delaney, ed., *Rationality and Religious Belief* (Notre Dame: Univ. of Notre Dame, 1979) 47.

contemporary views of human knowledge. Many people in our time take their understanding of what knowledge is from what is found in the physical and human sciences. Some who reject this position accept one such as that of Heidegger who acknowledges our awareness or knowledge of Being but rejects metaphysics.

Our answer to these difficulties is in continuity with the responses of Karl Rahner and Bernard Lonergan. However, I suggest that certain currents in developmental cognitive psychology can help us to evaluate Thomas' epistemology in regard to our knowledge of being from our contemporary experience and the human sciences' study of this. Very briefly, we shall recall two diverse psychological studies of human knowledge, those of Jean Piaget and of James and Eleanor Gibson, and then suggest that both are needed and together offer us a "phenomenology" of our knowledge that an expansion of Thomas Aquinas' view can account for but that Hume's, Kant's, and Heidegger's cannot.

Jean Piaget's work is recognized as perhaps the preeminent twentieth-century psychological study of the child's cognitive development.[7] He accepts the validity of scientific study of the physical world, identifies the structure of this kind of knowledge, and studies the evolution, through infancy and childhood, of cognitive structures present in the adolescent who has the capacity to engage in simple scientific experiments. Thus he begins with a characteristically modern experience of knowledge, and studies the evolutionary emergence of the cognitive structure that it manifests. Mathematical physics studies the world through assimilating it to quantitative relations and accommodating such relations to it: this is but one example of how fundamental the process of *assimilation* is in knowledge. It is evident in infants' first cognitive interactions with their environment. Infants assimilate objects about them to their sucking reflex used as an action schema; and by accommodating this structure to the variety of objects they suck, they

---

[7]See Jean Piaget, "Piaget's Theory," *Carmichael's Manual of Child Psychology,* 3rd edition, ed. Paul H. Mussen (New York: Wiley; 1970) vol. 1, 703–732; J. Piaget and Bärbel Inhelder, *The Psychology of the Child* (New York: Basic Books, 1969); and my article cited in n. 4.

can differentiate among them. For example, infants suck the breast and know it through this act; but they also suck a coverlet, their thumbs, and toys; and all of these are sucked differently. Notice that infants then organize or construct their world cognitively by assimilating it to an action schema and accommodating this schema to different objects. The schema is developed in the very process of accommodation. Such construction is not opposed to knowledge of the world, but rather is what mediates this knowledge. In mathematical physics also, we construct the world through assimilation and accommodation, though we do so by applying mathematical schemas to the world. Knowledge therefore is mediated by action on the world about us.

We should note that Bernard Lonergan philosophically analysed the structure of knowledge found in mathematical physics and made use of Piaget's work in the process. He argued for the possibility of metaphysics through showing that it is a search for intelligibility and, indeed, absolute or unconditioned intelligibility. However, even if we agree largely with his analysis, we must admit that this is not what Thomas primarily thought human knowledge to be. We can acknowledge the difference between Thomas' understanding of concept formation and that implicit in modern mathematical physics, while—as we shall show below—incorporating both forms of knowledge into a more inclusive analysis of our cognitive capacity.

We shall return to this question below, but here we can add that our cognitively structuring the world about us, as Piaget analyses it, is for the *good*—the actualization—of the person who is seeking knowledge and of others (e.g., scientific knowledge is sought for the benefits of technology). Thus we can see a relationship of this kind of knowledge to one aspect of Thomas' explanation of our knowledge of being. Action is itself dependent on our desire *to be*; and thus at different levels of knowledge mediated by action, there is some cognitive presence to the knower not only of our action but of our desire to be, and thus too of our being itself. This form of knowledge is akin to a dimension of knowledge by presence emphasized by Heidegger and Karl Rahner among others.

Piaget's approach to knowledge should be complemented by

another type of psychological study, namely by the work of those psychologists who analyze perception, or how the person discriminates shapes, colors, etc. Here the work of James Gibson and his wife Eleanor Gibson is particularly helpful. James Gibson reacted against the empiricist view that we initially sense only two-dimensional color (as points or blotches of color), and that perception of three-dimensional distance or depth is basically learned, that is, that this perception is the effect of one's interpretation of two-dimensional cues or clues and is thus a construction by a process of association. On the contrary, Gibson shows that the stimulus considered globally has correlates for one's perception of depth (e.g., in gradients of texture in the ground or setting of our normal perceptions in the visual world) and that three-dimensional physical reality is basically given in perception rather than learned. In continuity with this, Eleanor Gibson reacts against the behaviorist interpretation of perception, which says that learning occurs through association of objects with the behavior or response they evoke. She writes: "Perception, functionally speaking, is the process by which we obtain firsthand information about the world around us. It has a phenomenal aspect, the awareness of events presently occurring in the organism's immediate surroundings. It has also a responsive aspect; it entails discriminative, selective response to the stimuli in the immediate environment."[8] This analysis is based on the fact "that there is a structure in the world and structure in the stimulus, and that it is the structure in the stimulus—considered as a global array, not punctate—that constitutes information about the world. That there is structure in the world is self-evident to the physical scientist who uses elaborate tools and methods to discover it."[9]

Both Piaget and Eleanor Gibson examine growth in knowledge in a developmental framework. While Piaget analyzes the development of structures of knowledge, Gibson studies how

[8]Eleanor J. Gibson, *Principles of Perceptual Learning and Development* (New York: Appleton-Century-Crofts, 1969) 3. Also see James J. Gibson, *The Perception of the Visual World* (Boston: Houghton Mifflin, 1950); and, in reference to the philosophical implications of this, R. Harré and E. H. Madden, *Causal Powers: A Theory of Natural Necessity* (Oxford, 1975).

[9]E. Gibson, *Principles,* 13–14.

discrimination of features of our world moves from the gross features of an object to greater specificity. We wish to note that the differing interpretations of knowledge in these two views correlate with the primacy given in the one to touch and in the other to sight. In the first, motor activity as mediating knowledge of the world is more emphasized, while in the second, emphasis is placed on the stimulus present in the environment. It does seems to be a fact that these two initially unintegrated aspects or forms of knowledge are present in the infant and that both are essential principles of our developing knowledge of the world. D. Elkind judges that Piaget's study of concept formation reflects a mode of concept formation present in Galileo and much modern science while Gibson's reflects one present in Aristotle. He concludes that "taken together . . . these two versions of the concept can provide a comprehensive view of the concept that will account for the modes of conception found in both the individual and science."[10]

Likewise, in knowledge of reality as being, both of these forms of knowledge are involved. We saw that knowledge of being, according to Thomas' understanding, is essentially dependent on two modes of knowledge—a knowledge of the intrinsic intelligibility of physical reality and a knowledge of our be-ing through presence. In the one, mediated by sense knowledge, intellectual abstraction, and insight, we see more of what Gibson emphasizes. But, in light of modern science we must now add that knowledge of the intrinsic intelligibility of the world about us is mediated not only by intellectual penetration of the natures of material things in the way Aristotle and Thomas analysed, but by our cognitive organization of the world about us through assimilating it to action schemas and accommodating such schemas to the world in the way supposed by modern physics and analyzed by Piaget and philosophers such as Lonergan. As for our knowledge of our be-ing (*esse*) by presence, it has more to do with the implications of Piaget's emphasis that knowledge comes through action or, we may say, praxis; namely, that this action is for be-ing and is ac-

---

[10]David Elkind, "Conservation and Concept Formation," in D. Elkind and J. H. Flavell, eds., *Studies in Cognitive Development* (New York: Oxford University Press, 1969) 188.

companied by a consciousness of such be-ing. Thus we find in these two forms of knowledge present even in the infant a point of departure for our explanation of the psychogenesis of being.

Studies can be found elsewhere on how these forms of knowledge exist in the infant, how language develops only secondarily to and dependent upon them, how language and internal symbols such as imagination increase enormously the scope of knowledge, and how the child around age seven develops concepts concerning the conservation of quantity, number, area, space, and volume dependent both upon an interiorized activity on the environment and upon perception of sameness despite change. We wish to note that this involves knowing necessities in the physical world about us, such as the distinction between a quality such as color and quantity, and the conservation of quantity (e.g., when water is poured from one beaker to a differently shaped one) in spite of change of appearance.

The pre-adolescent goes beyond these achievements to be able to engage in simple scientific experiments. Piaget gave such experiments to younger children and pre-adolescents, and studied, for example, how they approach testing which combination of liquids can give rise to a specified color. A younger child immediately tries to attain an empirical correspondence with the experimenter's results. This is connected with the fact that children's organization of the physical world about them proceeds by their development of "more or less separate islets of organization,"[11] which do not yet form the integrated systems found in adolescents. The pre-adolescent, on the other hand, begins a consideration of the problem by a systematic recognition of all the possibilities, and only then proceeds to look for the actual solution by an examination of the different variables. This older child proceeds by a hypothetico-deductive method, systematically trying all the possible solutions. The greater scope and possibilities of the pre-adolescent's knowledge are based on this more advanced structure. Piaget describes this structure and relates it to the

[11]J. H. Flavell, *The Developmental Psychology of Jean Piaget* (Princeton: D. van Nostrand, 1963) 204. Also see B. Inhelder and J. Piaget, *The Growth of Logical Thinking from Childhood to Adolescence* (New York: Basic Books, 1958) 117.

adolescent's growth in affective and social interest in the following passage:

> The subject succeeds in freeing himself from the concrete and in locating *reality* within a group of *possible* transformations. This final fundamental decentering, which occurs at the end of childhood, prepares for adolescence, whose principal characteristic is a similar *liberation from the concrete* in favor of interest oriented toward the *non-present and the future.* This is the age of great ideals and of the beginning of theories, as well as the time of simple present adaptation to reality. This affective and social impulse of adolescence has often been described. But it has not always been understood that this impulse is dependent upon a transformation of thought that permits the handling of hypotheses and reasoning with regard to propositions removed from concrete and present observation.[12]

In both the affective and the cognitive areas, the adolescent, while retaining the operations characteristic of the younger child, is capable of going beyond these by systematically considering what is possible and centering on the actual in its relation to the possible.

It seems that the key to adolescents' advance over younger children, their reflective use of the schema of the distinction between the actual and the possible, is mediated by a process of discrimination as well as by the process of reflective abstraction that Piaget studies. This new structure of knowledge is in part, as Piaget shows, the result of pre-adolescents' adjustment to their environment (including here both physical environment and value horizon), their experience that this environment is larger than that to which they previously cognitively adjusted themselves and thus that the adjustment made in middle childhood is no longer adequate, the feedback of both environment and earlier adjustment to it upon them as cognitive subjects, and the development by reflective abstraction of a new action structure of knowing reality within the context of the actual and the possible. In part too this new knowledge is

---

[12]Piaget and Inhelder, *Psychology,* 130–131.

due to a kind of intellectual discrimination between the actual and the possible, a discrimination not central for the younger child and one made through a negation: the real is distinct from the simply possible. This simple abstraction lies in the area of qualitative knowledge that Piaget does not investigate at length, and it occurs by means of a natural logic that questions why things are the way they are rather than otherwise. Making this discrimination seems to require a higher order of abstraction than the abstraction of one attribute from another (e.g., height from quantity), which underlay the child's grasp of conservation in the earlier period of cognitive growth. While depending genetically on the earlier discrimination of the child, this later growth contributes to the greater scope of the adolescent's knowledge.

What is the relevance of this to our question whether in principle there can be intellectual knowledge of grounds for belief in God? I suggest that this knowledge of adolescents we have briefly analyzed is implicitly metaphysical, because it is a knowledge of being that enables its possessors to interact cognitively with their environment in a new way. Piaget shows that what is basic to this new cognitive interaction is that adolescents have reflective knowledge of the distinction between the actual and the possible. But this is exactly what is meant by a knowledge of reality as being. This knowledge is of *reality* in the environment and not simply of language or concept, for it is only such knowledge that enables these young people to operate as they do in realistically forming and testing hypotheses. Similarly, through their acting for their future, their knowledge does reach a dimension of the actualization of their possibilities. And, as we indicated earlier, this entire achievement is what is meant by the word "being." The major modern opposition to the possibility of our having intellectual grounds for faith in God is the denial of metaphysics. However, implicit in our scientific knowledge and in our planning for the future is our orientation to being and to a knowledge of being. Thus those who deny the possibility of metaphysics, such as Hume, Kant, Heidegger, and their many followers, cannot account for our scientific knowledge and our planning and acting for the future unless they enlarge their view of human knowledge—as, indeed, even Aquinas' view must be enlarged.

## 3.  *Epistemology and Knowledge Found in the Passage to Faith.*

We shall reflect critically in the next section on some grounds for belief in the existence of God, but before that we can ask how this epistemological analysis of human knowledge relates to the knowledge present in those on the way to faith in God, such as Thomas Merton. The answer is that Merton and others had to have a less restrictive understanding of the capabilities of human knowledge than that of many modern philosophers who deny to human beings the capacity to know beyond the limits of science. The above analysis sought to show that we can know reality as being. If we can know it as such, then we can ask what things are as being, what the interrelation among beings is, and what causes are operative in the beings we know; and we can ask what the horizon of our own intentionality is in our action and life. If we cannot know reality on this level, we cannot critically validate the grounds for belief in God that many find in their experience of the world or of conscience.

We recognize that the knowledge on which people come to faith is not normally explicitly metaphysical. It is larger than a metaphysical knowledge, for it is more fully personal—involving affectivity as well as intellectual knowledge, experience as well as intellectual analysis. This occurs in the context not simply of a person's attempt to gain an objective understanding of the world or the human being, but in the midst of a search for meaning and an openness to a restructuring of the self. The knowledge involved here is not so much analysis of the physical world or of inner human experience, as a reading of what is mediated by these experiences as testimonies God gives of his existence and presence. Thus the viewpoint searchers adopt is not so much the question of whether they can infer the existence of God from what they experience, but whether God is really manifesting himself through these experiences. It is a question of discernment of the signs and symbols through which—as the searchers perhaps half believe and half doubt—God is making himself known to them and calling them. What has precedence is not one's own intellectual shrewdness or search for fuller meaning, but rather the question of what the mystery is that encompasses one. Thus it is also a question of creative imagination, of how one will construct a reality and life that are inclusive of oneself—whether as mediating God or not. As in the physical sciences we cognitively construct the world about us, so too in the process of coming to believe we cognitively construct reality and our life in a larger context. Will one see reality and life as limited by the finite or inclusive of the infinite? Is the model for existence and reality that the person will accept one that includes God or not? To recognize that this is the type of knowledge concerned in the process of conversion is to see some kinship between the modern believer and believers in pre-modern cultures who interpreted the experiences of life—e.g., the fruitfulness of the fields and flocks, and the identity and welfare of the people—as mediating God's or the gods' reality, care, and presence.

To assert that a cognitive construction of reality by creative imagination is operative here is not to deny that there are grounds for such construction, but it is to see these grounds as more than simply objective metaphysical knowledge of being and its causes by intellectual insight into that which is. It is a knowledge mediated as well by one's affective orientation toward a fullness of being and by having one's imagination touched by symbols that evoke the possibility of a paradigmatic change in the form of being that one accepts as real and relevant to one's life—a new form that seems more coherent, more inclusive, and more consistent with what one knows from elsewhere.

Another problem we may raise here is the following. Christianity holds that the act of faith must be free to be saving and that it must be reasonable if it is to be fully human. But it may appear that if such faith is free, then it is not reasonable, for to be free means that one is not compelled by reason or anything else. Again, since faith is a real commitment, it may seem unreasonable unless there is enough evidence to support it. On the other hand, if it is reasonable, i.e., if there is fully sufficient reason to believe, then we know rather than believe and the act is not really free.

The answer to this lies in what faith is. The faith we are speaking about is both a belief that God exists and a belief in God—a personal knowledge of God joined with personal commitment. This is, of course, in no way sufficient until it is completed and, in part, corrected by the self-revelation God gives us of himself in Christianity: we are dealing here with only the beginnings of faith, but the later revelation does not simply deny God's earlier revelation of himself. As said above, we look to evidence from the world and from the self not restrictedly as empirical evidence for God's existence, but as means by which God reveals his existence to us, or testimonies that he gives of himself. Considered as God's testimonies, they are understood to be the results of God's action, which manifests something of him and communicates something of him to us—his personal act. On our part, then, our coming to believe in God is coming to interact with a personal being. Seen in this context, evidence is a sign to be discerned, and discernment is a free act—one that involves risks, even when there are sufficient reasons for us to believe that God has given testimony to his existence. Because of the personal character of the interaction between God's revelation and our response of faith, the acceptance of this revelation is not simply an objective analysis of scientific or philosophical evidence for an objective fact. Affectivity is involved in the whole process, and so too is freedom. But freedom here depends on the personal context of this encounter and thus on the dispositions that are brought to it, not on the inadequacy of the testimony that God gives of himself.

Seen in this context, it is well for us that our acceptance is free and involves risks, because otherwise it would not involve the whole of ourselves and call for some transcendence beyond the self toward God. We do have in our culture a tradition that values objective and certain knowledge as essential to human life. Some sceptics say that if one fears or doubts, one should not act. As Karl Rahner wrote, the Greek ideal of man saw "knowledge as simply the absolute measure of man . . . [and] a given piece of ignorance only as a falling short of the perfection to which man is ordained as to his end."[13] Against this, a philosophy of the person finds that:

[13]K. Rahner, "Dogmatic Considerations on Knowledge and Consciousness in Christ," in H. Vorgrimler, ed., *Dogmatic vs. Biblical Theology* (Baltimore: Helicon, 1964) 248.

a risk is of the essence of the self-perfecting of the finite person in the historical freedom of decision. Risk is involved;
coming out into the open is involved; committing oneself to
what is not totally visible, the hidden origin and the veiled
end, a certain manner of not-knowing is essential to the free
act of man. . . . There is therefore undoubtedly an ignorance which, since it renders possible the accomplishment of
the free act of the finite person while the drama of his history
is still being played, is more perfect than a knowledge in the
act of the free will which would abolish the latter.[14]

It is the nature of us as human "to be directed toward the mystery, which is God, *qua* mystery."[15] We are not things but subjects, and God is not a thing but a subject. If we are a mystery
to ourselves, God is even more a mystery to us; and the access
to God that is faith preserves this. We do not control God or
confine him to our own criteria.

One may ask whether we are here defending meaning and
grounds of a specifically supernatural act of faith in God, and
if so, how can supernatural faith result from God's testimonies
in nature and the human person? Agreeing largely with
Rahner's answer to this question, I would say that since this
faith is one to which God leads a person in the present order,
and in the present order he orients all to a communion with
himself and a salvation that is beyond the rights, exigencies,
and capacities of our humanity, then the faith of which we are
speaking is a supernatural faith, even though it leaves very
much to be desired and is oriented toward a fuller faith. The
testimonies God gives of himself in the interiority of the
person and in the physical world are, in Christian understanding, acts of God in his intention for the salvation of humankind—an intention that acts in the interiority of human beings
to make them apt for this destiny. And so, while these acts are
of themselves natural testimonies to God, they come to us
from an intention and context that is more than this. Moreover, they are mediated to the person within a context of a historical tradition such as Christianity, and thus have larger

[14]Ibid., 248–249.
[15]Ibid., 249.

implications than what they explicitly mediate. They are God's personal acts for human salvation, and the faith response of which we are speaking is a personal act for our salvation.

## II. Experience of Conscience as Testimony to God's Existence

What we are attempting here is a critical reflection on experience of self or the world interpreted as revealing the existence and presence of God. Although many deny the possibility of this knowledge, there are vast numbers of men and women in the modern world as well as in the pre-modern world who assert that they have had such experiences and who regard them as valid. We are critically asking whether such experiences on the part of modern men and women may be objectively valid. The conviction of the existence of God, we may add, comes more from the experience than from the critical evaluation we or others may give of it. The latter is secondary and dependent on the former, and because of its abstract character lacks the immediacy and fully human character of the experience itself. Furthermore, the knowledge that these experiences—common human experiences as distinct from specifically Christian experiences—mediate is minimal and preliminary and finds its completion, purification, and preservation only in God's revelation of himself through Christ. We are asking whether it is reasonable to believe in God, whether there are grounds for such belief; we are not presenting constraining proofs of the existence of God. The acceptance of these "ways" is a free act which depends on one's moral dispositions and involves personal risks. We believe too that this acceptance depends on an acceptance of God's moving and illuminating grace. In other words, there are valid reasons for thinking God reveals himself through experiences; grace is not a substitute for the critical evaluation of such intimations of God, but it enables us to perceive and accept such intimations.

We shall briefly elaborate two ways in which modern experience and critical reflection on it give valid grounds for belief in God. The first is our experience of values and particularly that value which is the basis of our sense of moral obligation. The second is an experience and interpretation of the physical world as, in some sense, both a whole and incomplete or unable to explain itself.

Many of us in the present, like so many people in the past, have interpreted the experience of moral values as implying the presence of God or an Ultimate. For example, we find that the profoundly moral and even heroically moral life of another person mediates for us an experience of the Sacred or God. We have been moved by holiness, by self-sacrifice when it has been for reflectively and critically accepted moral values and inspired by love. We have ourselves felt the impact of moral values and the call to respect these even at significant cost to ourselves, and interpreted this as an impact of God upon us. Many of these intimations have of course been colored by our previous religious beliefs. But our question is whether such experiences do validly mediate some knowledge of God in a way that is not formally dependent upon the religious beliefs of Christians, Jews, Moslems, or other believers. The knowledge present in these experiences is frequently of some presence or power or claim upon one that transcends the person or indeed society or humanity generally. What we attempt through our critical reflection is not to replicate those experiences, but to ask whether men and women validly interpret them as mediating the presence of God. Not that by this reflection—and independently of our later chapters—we are attempting to show that the characteristics of God that we know through Christian revelation are exemplified and validated critically through this experience, but rather whether some reality or principle is mediated by this experience that has some of the characteristics of the Christian and Jewish and Moslem God—and indeed of the God or Ultimate believed by many other peoples.

Many theologians have thought that such experiences do indeed mediate knowledge of God. St. Paul himself points to such experiences as signs of God's presence (Rom 2:14–15). Perhaps Aristotle implies a religious awe experienced in the moral order when he writes, "And therefore justice is often thought to be the greatest of virtues, and 'neither evening nor morning star' is so wonderful."[16] For Augustine the itinerary of the soul to God was not necessarily by way of specifically moral experience, but it was by going from the exterior to the interior, from the inferior to the higher.[17] Among the many followers of Augustine, Bonaventure in the thirteenth century emphasized the way of interiority as the privileged way to God, because the soul is God's image. Immanuel Kant based his assertion of God's existence as a rational belief on the experience of the categorical imperative, and John Henry Newman took the experience of conscience as the privileged access to knowledge of God in the religious person.[18] Many twentieth-century Protestant theologians, following Schleiermacher, have understood that God offers a "general revelation" accessible to all through human experience, e.g., of Ultimate Concern or Holy Being, where Being refers more to what concerns human beings than that which is in the physical world. We saw earlier that Thomas Merton considered that an experience similar to an aesthetic experience validly gives one access to what is beyond science, and even to some grounds for belief in God. And there is a family resemblance to this in the way that Karl Rahner and others have articulated our access to God and God's transcendental revelation to us through our preapprehension of being, in virtue of being oriented to the fullness of being. Perhaps we can even see the teaching of some major Eastern religions such as Hinduism and Buddhism as having some resemblances to this approach, because they stress that human access to the Absolute is through the way of interiority. What we are reflecting on is not some isolated individual expe-

---

[16]Aristotle, *Nichomachean Ethics,* 1129ᵇ28.

[17]Augustine, *Enarratio* in Ps. 145, 5 (Migne, *Patrologia Series Latina* 37, 1887). See E. Gilson, *History of Christian Philosophy in the Middle Ages* (New York: Random House, 1955) 70–81.

[18]See Newman, *Grammar,* 95–109. Also see J. H. Walgrave, "La preuve de l'existence de Dieu par la conscience morale et l'expérience des valeurs," in *L'Existence de Dieu* (Tournai: Casterman, 1961) 109–132; Adrian Boekraad and Henry Tristram, *The Argument from Conscience to the Existence of God According to J. H. Newman* (Louvain: Nauwelaerts, 1961); J. L. Mackie's critique from the background of a Humean epistemology of moral arguments for the existence of God in *The Miracle of Theism* (Oxford: Clarendon, 1982) 102–118; and Robert Roth, "Moral Obligation—With or Without God?", *New Scholasticism* 59 (1985) 471–474, and his references to the discussion of which this article is a part.

rience, but rather one that has been widespread throughout the history of humankind and one that has been reflected on critically many times in the past by prominent theologians and philosophers.

In the previous chapter we have already presented something of a phenomenology of modern Western men's and women's experience of value and search for values on many different levels, culminating in a genuine concern for values that are of the moral order and thus of absolute worth. We have also indicated something of how the individual subject experiences, recognizes, and responds to values through a subjective dynamism that has been formed by earlier experiences, and how the person can experience truly human values as antivalues. Now we are reflecting specifically upon the experience of value that enables us to accept loss of pleasure, of the security of moving in a familiar and controllable environment, of money, of power, or of life itself when our conscience, formed in true openness to all relevant data, calls us to accept this loss. When we act in this way, not primarily out of constraint but in freedom, there is a sense that we are acting out of a claim of some value or person or principle higher than ourselves. We are acting by relaxing our control of our lives in favor of something greater than ourselves. Our action is more a response to a value that precedes us and is superior to us than our own choice and manipulation of our lives. There may well be a certain sense of emptiness regarding lower values such as pleasure, money, security, personal power, or even physical life itself. But there is also a sense of the rightness of what we are doing, and we are sustained in an action that seems to be beyond our native ability and inclinations, or at least those inclinations that are more immediately tangible or external. It seems in such circumstances that we are opening ourselves to a larger dimension of value, while accepting closure or threats for some lesser dimension of value; but there seems to be meaning enough in this turning in our lives to enable us to do it without constraint. There can even be a sense of liberation and enlargement of our spirits. What is primary is not a sense of ending but of beginning, not of loss but of gain, not of closure but of opening. And so we sense a reality in this larger dimension of value, for we are sustained by it. Perhaps this experience is similar to that which some mystics describe. At any rate, what sustains us is interpreted by our religious beliefs, but across a variety of beliefs this experience is consistently supposed to reveal a reality totally superior to oneself.

It is such an experience that we are reflecting on here. Of course, there are many ways we could do so. We may simply describe it as it appears. We may attempt to account for it psychologically or sociologically, that is, by the factors for human behavior that these sciences study; for example, I think that honesty is a value because of the family I was raised in, and so I am able to accept the losses that it entails. Or we may explain it by our culture or by the impact of an earlier culture or religion which is still influential for many people. However, these human sciences do not raise all the questions or answer all the questions that this experience or similar experiences give rise to in us. For example, they do not answer the question whether we should obey our conscience or what norms there are for distinguishing a correct from an incorrect conscience. There are then other legitimate questions about such experiences that rise in our minds, and unless these are suppressed they call for different kinds of reflection than simply those offered by psychology, sociology, or cultural anthropology.[19]

If we agree that the social sciences are not adequate as a reflection on or explanation of conscience and moral values, because they do not explain adequately why we interiorize some values offered us by our families or societies and reject others, then we can realize that we need philosophical reflection. We have offered such a reflection in the preceding chapter, giving bases for our acceptance of some values and rejection of others. There we saw that it is natural and proper for us as human to orient ourselves toward an absolute value. This orientation is not simply a fact but an integral part of our being. To fail this is to fail to be fully human.

While in the preceding chapter we examined this phenomenon in regard to the question of human transcendence, that is, from the viewpoint of the intentionality of the person, here we are approaching it from another viewpoint. There we exam-

[19]See John Bowker, *The Sense of God* (Oxford: Clarendon, 1973) for a critique of the adequacy of the social sciences to account for the origins of the idea of God.

ined persons' self-direction toward an actualization of their being and that of others and to an order of value that transcends all human persons. Here we approach the phenomenon with the question of whether this value exists in some sense that is not dependent upon us and our projection of an ideal through imagination. It is clear in our treatment of this process of human development in the preceding chapter that there is a certain potentiality in our affectivity and will, and that as the human intellect does not generate its own object wholly from itself but is activated by an independent reality, so too our human will or human intentionality proceeds from us as we are moved by the good or value that preexists our action. The act involved in our free choice or the mass of choices that make up a community's development at a particular stage of history are not explicable simply by some projection of an ideal through imagination.

Modern psychology has recognized that an analysis of human desire or intentionality based simply on a meaning that the person seeks is insufficient. That is why there have been various theories proposed about where the infant, the child, and the growing person draw their energies from in human motivation or search for meaning. Many answers have been reductionistic, but the question is legitimate and has to be answered. We have previously shown that Thomas Aquinas explained that the good is intentionally present to the affectivity and will of a person through the person's actualization (*esse*), and that the person is metaphysically energized through this mediation.[20] The value the person seeks—his or her actualization—preexists as a lure soliciting the person's engagement and as an actualizing principle to elicit the appropriate activity and self-creation. Of course, the person may simply accept a part of himself or herself as goal and interest and thus be energized or actualized by a part of the human good that is appropriate for him or her at a particular point, even at the expense or cost of turning against the integral human good appropriate at that time. Traditionally, this has been called sin, but at this point we should call it at least alien-

[20]See, e.g., ch. 5, "Conversion and Human Transcendence," 180, 202.

ation from the person's own being and possibilities.[21] This actualization (*esse*) is the first or deepest *intrinsic* principle accounting for the impact of value on us in our process of self-creation, and we have seen that progressive dimensions of it have an effect on one's self-direction only gradually as one goes through successive stages of human development.

However, self-actualization cannot account for the actualization of one's self-orientation to value on all its levels, if it is considered as the *ultimate* principle of actualization or lure attracting us. Individuals seek not only their own good but that of others as well, and they seek this good not simply as a conditional value but, at times, as related to absolute moral values. For example, there are times when one has a sense of moral obligation to respect one's own dignity and that of others that goes beyond the limits of simple hypothetical and pragmatic injunctions. Others have rights that we must respect, even though they are, considered only in themselves, conditioned and limited values. Thus if there must be some pre-existent actualizing principle to account for our actual self-orientation to value, this has to be something larger and more ultimate than simply our own individual existence. Our individual existence must participate in this larger principle if it is to account sufficiently for the way we really act, since we in fact seek conditioned values within the context of an overarching and absolute value. We can, of course, seek these conditioned values in a way that ascribes absolute value to them and turns us away from a larger value, but we have argued previously that the regressive or destructive character of such action for the individual and community manifests indirectly that this is an exclusion of reality rather than an acceptance of it.

Thus we seem to have testimony to the existence of an ultimate and overriding value in which lesser values participate—an existence independent of and antecedent to us, rather than simply in our intentionality as a goal. It is reasonable to believe that there exists some Absolute *Esse* or Actuality in which lesser values or goods participate; lesser values

---

[21]For an account of how persons may still be actualized by their being even in such a defective act or attitude, see Farrelly, *Predestination, Grace and Free Will* (Westminster, Md.: Newman Press, 1964) 197–200.

move us, but they do so ultimately through their relation to this Ultimate Value or Good. Indeed, there seems to be as much reason to affirm the existence of this Ultimate as there is to affirm the existence of more immediate principles actualizing our self-movement. We affirm the latter through recognizing that we move ourselves because of the impact of value upon us, but the impact of these lesser values considered in themselves is not proportional to our human search for meaning and value. The Ultimate Principle that lures the individual to its appropriate self-making and humankind (or segments of it) to the fulfillment appropriate for them as human communities in time must itself *be,* because its effects *are.* It cannot be simply an indefinite good or complex of values such as a conglomerate of human goods that move the individual or community, since these are all limited and so not sufficient to elicit of themselves the sense of ultimacy or ultimate responsibility that is revealed in our moral behavior. It must, in fact, be infinite, since only then will it be truly ultimate, not dependent on another value but rather able to be the ground of all other values. No individual value of this world or complex of them is infinite; thus the Absolute *Esse* must be distinct from and superior to any value or values in this world. That is, it must be absolutely transcendent to our human level of being, while operating in and through lesser values. Thus this Absolute Good has characteristics of the God of Western religions and, in part, of the Ultimate in Hinduism as it is interpreted by many Hindu religious thinkers.

We could go further at this point and try to show that all this implies that this Absolute is personal. But we will defer that to the next chapter and here conclude by raising two possible objections to our analysis. Some may say that the fact that a person is sustained by a goal is no proof of the reality or existence of that goal. A woman may think that a certain man loves her and will in the future return and ask her to marry him; and from this conviction she may be supported emotionally to be active, keep herself in good health and spirits, etc. But the expectation may be illusory. So too, if we are moved to act morally by certain values considered as absolute and overriding, this does not prove the existence of such values outside ourselves. In answer, we can say that there is a radical difference between the justification for each action. While the woman's expectation is illusory, the moral demands on the human person are at times, as we saw in the preceding chapter, critically justified by the very core of what it means to be human. The effect of values in this latter case is not simply a fact like the first case, but it is at the center of human life and what it means to be human; thus it is critically justified. (Even the woman who is subject to illusions is moved by an actualizing value of her being, but she is wrong to identify it with the man's love and return.) Moreover, as much modern psychological study has asserted, we infer the existence of energies to account for the growing person's orientation toward immediate values. Similarly one should assert the existence of energies or actualization proportional to our moral activity for an absolute value that is critically justified to be such.

One may also object that the above critical evaluation of a human intimation of God proves too much, since it is an attempt to prove the grounds of faith, and by that very fact renders faith non-existent. In answer to this, we point out that we are claiming that there is in human experience a certain testimony given to himself by God through the call of the value that he is—a revelation that is mediated to people through a moral experience that has absolute exigency; and we hold that God is mediated by this experience non-objectively. So the intimation of God that people have frequently had through these experiences is some initial response to God's self-revelation—though a revelation that is quite small when compared with Judaeo-Christian revelation. What our critical evaluation of this intimation of God does, however, is not contradictory to the response of faith to God who so reveals himself. It can be looked upon as showing that it is reasonable to believe, or that to believe is not a "*sacrificium intellectus*" or simply arbitrary like a belief in fairies. Belief is a commitment of oneself to God in a personal acceptance of what he reveals; our reflection here cannot take the place of this commitment or elicit it of itself. It may, we hope, help men and women to see that such commitment may be a wholly free and "reasonable" act (in the sense that it is not contrary to the use of reason we are responsible for as humans), indeed, that it may be an acceptance of themselves and their relation to reality that is both profound and justified.

We shall treat the objection that comes from the problem of evil in a later chapter, simply recalling that here in terms of the full Christian faith there is no adequate answer to the problem of evil outside the death and resurrection of Jesus Christ.

## III. Intimations of God Mediated by the Physical World

Vast numbers of people in the modern world as well as in earlier history have had intimations of God or divinity through experience of the physical world and the wonder or awe that its magnitude, its order, its power, its fruitfulness, and its destructiveness have caused in them. One student of African religions, for example, notes: "Over the whole of Africa creation is the most widely acknowledged work of God. This concept is expressed through saying that God created all things, through giving Him the name of Creator (or Moulder, or Maker), and through addressing Him in prayer and invocations as the Creator."[22] The sense of awe is not absent in our own time, even though science has subjected the world to extensive rational analysis. In fact, many scientists themselves have intimations of God through what science brings to light.[23] There have been philosophical and theological critical reflections on the validity of such intimations at least since the time of the first Greek philosophers, the Ionians, Plato and Aristotle and later philosophers of the Hellenistic age continued to find testimonies to the existence of divinity in the physical world[24] —testimonies that St. Paul himself confirmed and interpreted more adequately (see Acts 14:15–17; 17:22–31; Rom 1:18ff.). Many early Christian theologians continued this theme, as did both Muslim and Christian theologians and phi-

[22]John Mbiti, *African Religions and Philosophy* (New York: Anchor Books, 1970) 50. Also see Mircea Eliade, *From Primitives to Zen. A Thematic Sourcebook of the History of Religions* (New York: Harper and Row, 1967), ch. 2, "Myths of Creation and Origin," 83–118.

[23]See for evidence of this Enrico Cantore, *Scientific Man: The Humanistic Significance of Science* (New York: IHS Publishers, 1977).

[24]See, e.g., Plato, *Symposium,* and *Timaeus;* and Aristotle, *Physics* VIII, and *Metaphysics* XII.

losophers of the Middle Ages, particularly Thomas Aquinas. On the other hand, with the rise of modern science and its mathematical and mechanistic approach to the interpretation of the physical world, many prominent philosophers such as David Hume and Immanuel Kant have denied the validity of knowledge of God through the physical world. The continuity between the physical world as studied by modern science and God as acting in this world is by no means as apparent as it was in earlier approaches to the physical world. Much modern Protestant theology has left the physical world to science while it has located God's self-manifestation elsewhere. But more recently this dichotomy has been negatively critiqued. A theology that abandons the effort to relate God to the physical world or, better, to relate the physical world to God, has been found inadequate; and the study of the physical world by the physical sciences has been found lacking in that its method leaves so much of this world (such as qualities and purpose) out of its consideration.[25] The work of Teilhard de Chardin and Alfred North Whitehead and their influence on theologians is evidence of the attempts to get beyond this dichotomy.

We ask then whether, given our reliance on the physical sciences, we can still critically validate intimations of God that people so widely have through the physical world. Does God give testimony to himself through the physical world in a way that does not essentially depend on historical revelation for its validity? To answer this question within the limits of our brief treatment, we shall (a) ask whether the physical sciences' interpretation of evolution is sufficient, (b) show the necessity of a philosophical viewpoint or study of the physical world, and (c) indicate how such an approach does critically support religious intimations mediated through the physical world. Finally we

---

[25]We should refer here to the related question of whether scientific theories are to be interpreted in a non-realist or a realist sense. For the dispute on this, see, e.g., Mary Hesse, "Cosmology as Myth," in David Tracy and Nicholas Lash, eds., *Cosmology and Theology (Concilium,* vol. 166. 1983) 49–54; in part counter to this, William Rottschaefer, "The New Interactionism between Science and Religion," *Religious Studies Review* 14 (1988) 218–224; and specifically Ernan McMullin, "Truth and Explanatory Success," in *Realism. Proceedings,* The American Catholic Philosophical Association 69 (1985) 206–231. I would accept the latter explanation of the truth value of the theories of contemporary physical sciences. Piaget's work supports a realist interpretation of science.

shall answer several objections that can be posed to this position.

(a) Jacques Monod writes that "the cornerstone of the scientific method is . . . the *systematic* denial that 'true' knowledge can be got at by interpreting phenomena in terms of final causes—that is to say, of 'purpose.'"[26] In accord with this, he writes of evolution: "Chance alone is at the source of every innovation, of all creation in the biosphere. Pure chance, absolutely free but blind, is at the very root of the stupendous edifice of evolution: this central concept of modern biology is no longer one among other conceivable hypotheses. It is today the *sole* conceivable hypothesis, the only one that squares with observed and tested fact."[27]

Counter to this, even though such an account *may* be all that biology can achieve by its method, it is becoming more and more apparent that an explanation of evolution simply by chance mutations and the survival of the fittest is totally insufficient. If "fitness" is proposed as the ordering principle or plan for evolution, we have both to note that fitness is not objective and to ask who determines why some attributes are more fit than others. Documentation of this insufficiency may be found elsewhere. We shall simply recall several fragments of it here. Let us recall what science tells us of the evolution of the reptile from some primitive amphibian form. While the amphibians reproduced in the water, the reptiles laid their eggs on dry land. The unborn reptile inside the egg needed water or it would dry up. It needed food too. So these had to be provided by something like yolk for food and albumen for water. Also, it needed a shell to contain this, and a kind of bladder to get rid of its waste products. Finally, it needed a tool to get out of the shell with when the time was ripe—an appropriate form of tooth for reptiles and lizards. It needed all these beneficial changes to occur at the same time and in a coordinated way.[28]

---

[26]Jacques Monod, *Chance and Necessity* (New York: Knopf, 1971) 21.

[27]Ibid., 122.

[28]See Arthur Koestler, *The Ghost in the Machine* (New York: Macmillan, 1967) 128–129; and Koestler, *Janus. A Summing Up* (New York: Random House, 1978) 175–176. See in the latter book, Part III, "Creative Evolution," 165–226. Quotations below from Grassé are from Koestler, *Janus*.

The improbability of this happening by chance mutation and natural selection is so great that it could not have happened in the time span of evolution. Moreover, to hold that it happened by chance "is like suggesting that if we went on throwing bricks together into heaps, we should eventually be able to choose ourselves the most desirable house."[29] Beyond this, chance mutations would also have to account for new types of behavior or instinctual skills that are innate and hereditary—skills that are incredibly complex.

With the discovery in the 1950's of the chemical structure of DNA, the nucleic acid of the chromosomes and carrier of the "hereditary blueprint," it was recognized that the configuration of all the more important features of the organism depended not on single genes but on the totality of genes or the gene complex acting cooperatively. Also, experimental embryology has shown a self-healing in the gene complex as a whole. For example, there is a recessive mutant gene in the fruit-fly that results, when two flies with it are paired, in eyeless offspring. Yet within a few generations flies appear within this stock with eyes that are perfectly normal. Koestler concludes:

> The re-combination of genes to deputize for the missing gene must have been coordinated according to some overall plan, or set of rules, governing the action of the gene-complex as a whole. It is this coordinating activity, originating at the apex of the genetic hierarchy which ensures *both* the genetic stability of species over millions of years, and their evolutionary modifications along biologically acceptable lines. *The central problem of evolutionary theory is how this vital coordinating activity is carried out.* This is where the big question mark comes in. The metaphor has shifted from the croupier at the roulette wheel to the conductor directing his orchestra.[30]

[29]C. H. Waddington, in *The Listener,* 13 February 1952. Also for an extended study of teleology in the physical world and its philosophical implications, see L. Stafford Betty and Bruce Cordell, "God and Modern Science: New Life for the Teleological Argument," *International Philosophical Quarterly* 27 (1987) 409–435.

[30]Koestler, *Janus,* 190.

This perspective seems to resurrect the view of Lamarck that acquired characteristics that correspond to the vital needs of the species are transmitted through the channels of heredity. The main non-ideological reason for which this was rejected was that there was no apparent mechanism by which such characteristics could affect the gene-complex. However, some biologists claim that new evidence shows "that there exists a molecular mechanism which, in certain circumstances, supplies information from outside to the organism and inserts this information into the organism's genetic code."[31] Whether this is the mechanism or not, the environment has an indirect influence on organisms in the evolutionary process.

Many biologists are acknowledging purposefulness in both ontogeny and phylogeny and the whole evolutionary process.[32] It is not human intentionality because it is neither conscious nor free, but it is that which is inherent in the phenomena of life, as opposed to what appears in a reductionist interpretation of life on the model of cybernetics. It "reflects the active striving of living matter towards the optimal realization of the planet's evolutionary potential."[33] This viewpoint is a reintroduction of finality in nature, but more and more biologists are acknowledging that without such a viewpoint their account of evolution is reductionistic. "The purposiveness of all vital processes, the strategy of the genes and the power of the exploratory drive in animal and man, all seem to indicate that the pull of the future is as real as the pressure of the past. Causality and finality are complementary principles in the science of life; if you take out finality and purpose you have taken the life out of biology as well as psychology."[34] This particular expression of a contrast between causality and finality perhaps

[31]P. Grassé, *L'Évolution du Vivant* (Paris: Albin Michel, 1973) 367.

[32]Koestler mentions a half-dozen theories of evolution and sums up their agreement: "What all these theories have in common is that they regard the morphic, or formative, or syntropic tendency, Nature's striving to create order out of disorder, cosmos out of chaos, as ultimate and irreducible principles beyond mechanical causation" *Janus* 269–270.

[33]Ibid., 213.

[34]Ibid., 226. On the quite varied meanings of "causality" in the history of science and the explanations it offers, see William Wallace, *Causality and Scientific Explanation,* 2 vols. (Ann Arbor: University of Michigan, 1972–1974).

depends too much on physical science's identification of causality with the antecedent condition that they call on to account for change. Traditionally, however, finality has been
understood as one of the causes; and modern biologists who
call upon it actually treat it as a cause in this larger sense.

(b) There is then the necessity of an interpretation of the evolutionary process by a way other than the physical sciences,
namely, by a philosophical viewpoint. If teleology is beyond
the methods and tools of biology, for biologists to insist that it
does not exist or that knowledge of it is not "knowledge" is a
philosophical and epistemological assertion; it is not an assertion they make as physical scientists. Human intelligence is
not satisfied with the self-restriction of biologists, even though
this self-restriction may be very fruitful within the limits of
their science. Thus when evidence shows that there are aspects
of nature that cannot be handled by the questions and methods
of the physical or life sciences as practiced today, rather than
deny the evidence, many people will adjust their questions and
methods to be able to deal with this dimension of nature. They
are thus led to the threshold of philosophy. As the French biol-
ogist P. Grassé writes: "The joint efforts of paleontology and of
molecular biology purged of dogmatism, ought to lead eventually to the discovery of the precise mechanism of evolution but
possibly without revealing to us the causes which determine
the direction of evolutionary lineages, and the purposefulness
of structures, functions and vital cycles. It seems possible that
confronted with these problems, biology is reduced to helpless-
ness and must hand over to metaphysics."[35]

The kind of knowledge that a philosophical viewpoint gives
us in reference to evolution does not compete with or substitute for biological science. It is complementary to it. Looking
upon physical reality as physical beings in process, we can examine or explain evolution philosophically from the "within"
of organisms and not only from the "without." We can acknowledge that these organisms are active agents that are seeking the fulfillment or the preservation of their being within an
environment which they adapt to themselves and to which
they adapt themselves by strategies. Here we are considering

[35]Grassé, *L'Évolution,* 401.

the organisms not primarily as either substances or processes but rather as physical beings or agents of particular species that are in process. We must interpret their restructuring of themselves in the process of phylogeny as well as in the course of ontogeny as being for the purpose of the realization of their possibilities. At times this leads to dead ends, to maladaptations, and to parasitical forms of life; but at other times it leads to the evolution of new forms that constitute what we must call an advance or development in the evolutionary process, for they possess an enhanced capacity in physical being. There is a kind of transcendence here, because through this restructuring the physical being or series of physical beings achieve capabilities or dimensions of being that are not found at earlier and lower levels. Whereas a simple mechanical or statistical approach cannot assert that one level is higher than another, a philosophical approach can articulate this obvious reality. A monkey can do more than a virus; it is capable of knowledge, of an emotional life, of a primitive form of social interaction, etc. These are qualitatively different and higher operations or activities or ways of being than those of which a virus is capable.

What can we say about the causal factors of the strategies and transcendence evident in this evolution, so as to give some articulation to what is obvious to us even though it cannot be explained by physical science as such? It is evident that the physical organism or agent is a cause of the evolutionary process by its interaction with its environment over a long period of generations. Also, the end or goal of enhanced or preserved being that restructuring makes possible is a causal factor, since that is what motivates agents in the strategies that lead to their restructuring. We as self-conscious beings experience and affirm the purposiveness of our own activity and thus the influence of the goal or end of such activity in evoking, energizing, and giving direction to our actions. We know this because we do it, and attempts to define knowledge in a way that would exclude this are forms of reductionism. We recognize analogous activity on the part of animals, and the very characteristics of their organic activity manifest this. While we do not have reason to affirm freedom or self-conscious choice in the physical world below human beings, we do have reason to judge that animals, plants, and even inorganic matter[36] are influenced by goals and do adapt themselves to the pursuit of these goals. Thus we find that physical organisms themselves, the environment, and the goal that motivates the strategies of the organisms effect changes in the revolutionary process.

If we ask how the good or the goal sought by the organism can influence or activate it in a way that is appropriate for an agency less than human, diverse philosophies can help to explain this. I have found some aspects of Thomas Aquinas' philosophy helpful in this regard.[37] As we have seen earlier, the good and its influence is associated by Thomas with the *esse* or the actualization of the being or agent. Everything seeks to be, and thus its "to be" is an inner principle that acts as final cause to activate or elicit the agent's actions called for by this goal. It is the agent that acts but it acts in virtue of a goal or good that moves or motivates it. While the immediate good may be eating food or engaging in sexual intercourse or fleeing from a predator, all of these purposes influence the agent in view of their relation to its existence and actualization. This is always the *esse* or "to be" of a *particular kind* of agent or physical being—a physical being structured in a certain way in virtue of which certain actions and interactions are beneficial and possible. The environment and the feedback from the agent's interaction with it are also intrinsic principles of the physical being's process of restructuring itself and so of the transcendence of the evolutionary process. What is true in ontogeny is also true in phylogeny. It is not exclusively the actualization or "to be" of the individual agent that is an activating principle for its actions, but the actualization of the species or the kind of physical being that the agent instantiates. The agent seeks not only the fulfillment or preservation of its own individual

---

[36]Joseph Esposito in "Teleological Causation," *The Philosophical Forum* 12 (1980–1981) suggests that such causation is found when two oppositely charged leptons attract each other, in the phenomena covered by Newton's second law on the influence of two bodies on one another by gravitation, and whenever the object in process "increasingly reveals a systematically developing pattern during the duration (of the process) . . . and increasingly suggests reference to some other object." (124; 123)

[37]See Farrelly, *God's Work*, 242–247.

being but that of its species and indeed of physical reality in its still larger possibilities.

In this view, contrary to some process philosophers, being is so little opposed to process that it is the enhancement of being that is the activating principle of the agent's process. We need neither deny being to assert process nor deny process to assert being; rather, we need to integrate being and process in a way that does justice to the teleology, initiative, spontaneity, creativity, pluralism, and perdurance in being of the individuals and species of the world around us.

(c) How can we by this philosophical interpretation of physical agency critically evaluate the intimations of God that people have through experience of the physical world? Many people continue to have these intimations. In fact, Koestler suggests that in many cases the very denial of purpose by scientists occurs because they feel that such an admission would imply the existence of God![38] However this may be, purpose is evident throughout creation for those who do not restrict what they see there to the limited insights scientific questions and methods allow.

There are many ways in which the physical world has been interpreted as a revelation of God. Some have seen in the purpose and order of the physical world evidence of a directing intelligence on the analogy of a watch pointing to the intelligence of the watchmaker, but without analysing this analogy in any depth. We are not adopting this approach, because while the watch as a mechanism has only that order that is imposed upon it from without, living organisms have of themselves an order and a purpose that is constitutive of their being. Evidence for the existence of God is not to be found through denying that the organism has an order or intentionality proper to itself.

Evolutionary studies have given convincing evidence that humankind did originate from lower anthropoids and that these in turn came from more primitive mammals which developed from amphibians that emerged from aquatic organisms. There is a real sense in which lower organisms caused or brought into existence the higher organisms in the evolution-

---

[38]See Koestler, *Janus*, 212.

ary scale. Here we refer by "cause" not only to antecedent conditions but to the physical agents that actually effect the being of another through conveying to it something of themselves and their own actuality. This other as effect genuinely receives something from the agent and its act. And the agent, as we have said above, operates under the influence of a goal that has a causal influence upon it and its activity. This is present not only in ontogeny but in phylogeny.

It may be that biology will eventually be able to give a detailed account of the antecedent conditions present in the links that led to succeeding stages of evolution. But when we look at this process from the viewpoint of the *being* of the agent and its effect, we must ask whether the organism can be the total cause of its offspring and the higher organisms of the evolutionary scale (admitting that there are indeed qualitatively differing levels of being in this scale). The lower organism cannot be the total cause of what it causes in the evolutionary scale, because this would be to give to the other what it does not have to give. The lower organism would somehow cause more being than it itself possesses; to assert this is to settle for irrationality, and thus wholly to oppose the search for explanation that characterizes science. To act in this way is to adopt a philosophical standpoint that is self-contradictory.

Another way of seeing that the agent is not the total cause is through acknowledging that though living things are "self-starters" they are potential too; that is, they depend on others in their action. They depend on much that is around them, such as air, water, food; and they depend upon being moved by food, sex, safety, etc.—all goods related to their be-ing and its actualization and protection. Living agents then act in a way that is partially dependent upon being moved or supported by a causal influence that can and does move them to act in a way appropriate for living beings.

In terms of final causality, we can see that the activity of a cell in an organism depends not only on what is within that cell but on the goal of the welfare of the organism as a whole. In a way analogous to this, the activity of a particular organism depends not only on its own actualization as a final cause, but on the welfare of the species as a whole. And in an ecological environment, the way individual organisms and species act depends on the whole environment both as a source of their food, etc., and as a determining whole or totality.[39] By another stretch of analogical thinking, we can see that much larger orders of time and space are not without influence upon individual species and agents as supportive, determining, and purposive contexts for their action. Some scientists speak even of an anthropic universe, since the physical world from its earliest stages seems, counter to all chance, to lead toward the evolution of human beings and an environment that will support them. There is an "active striving of living matter towards the optimal realization of the planet's evolutionary potential."[40]

The kind of dependence upon a causal influence that we are asserting is one that is present in the very process of the organism's acting. We are not here referring to the organism's dependence upon its own progenitors, but of a dependence upon a causal influence operative at the very time of its own causal activity or operation. We must infer the existence of a sufficient causality to account for what is happening, and thus a causal influence that can enable an organism to move from not acting to acting and to cause an effect that is disproportionately greater than the physical organism that originates it. This causal influence is similar in some ways to the influence of an artist and his artistic vision on his material in that it works with the intentionality of the physical instruments to bring about something greater than they. It does this through the influence of the larger whole to which the organism's activity is directed, through the environment and through the structures that it designs for these purposes.

If we look at the evolutionary process as a whole, we can infer a causal influence with power proportionate to the effects that we see emerge in the evolutionary process. We can reasonably infer a causal influence that is able to initiate action or aid others to initiate action without being similarly dependent

[39]See David Attenborough, *The Living Planet. A Portrait of the Earth* (Boston: Little, Brown and Co., 1984).

[40]Koestler, *Janus,* 213. For a study of the "anthropic principle" see William Lane Craig's extended review of John Barrow and Frank Tipler, *The Anthropic Cosmological Principle* (Oxford: Clarendon Press, 1986) in *International Philosophical Quarterly* 27 (1987) 437–447, and L. Betty and B. Cordell, "God and Modern Science".

upon being moved to act. There may be intermediate causal influences, but ultimately what is called for is a causal influence and cause that is not itself potential but rather actual and indeed totally actual so that it initiates action in others without itself being dependent on anything outside itself. Nothing less would give a sufficient explanation; no other causal influence is proportioned to the phenomena that face us. We assert then the evolutionary process gives testimony to the existence of such a causal influence operative in the cosmos—a cause possessed of being proportioned to its causal power. That is to say, its being is totally actual or unmixed with potentiality or dependency.

This cause cannot be identified with anything in the cosmos taken singly or together, since all such realities are themselves limited and potential or interdependent. In moving from the limits of each agent in the universe to assert the limits of all taken together, we are arguing as we would in saying that no individual cabbage is intelligent and therefore cabbages are not intelligent. We can argue from essential limitations of a kind of being to a conclusion about that kind taken as a totality. This differs from arguing that since the particular material things that make up a conglomerate are triangular in shape, the whole must be triangular in shape. We cannot conclude this, but we may conclude that the whole is spatial. Similarly the cosmos cannot as a whole be essentially and indeed infinitely higher in being than all its members.

The cause that we infer then is essentially distinct from the cosmos since its causal influence and activity is essentially distinct and superior to that of the cosmos. This cause must be infinite; that is, in its being it must be unlimited and wholly actual. Only such a cause is not dependent in its initiating the activity of others as final and efficient cause. Such an agent that is wholly unlimited in being can only be one, for there would be nothing to distinguish it from another like agent, similarly unlimited in actuality. It would be distinguished from another being by something that the other had and which it itself lacked; but then it would not be unlimited. It could not be distinguished by place, since to be unlimited is to be incorporeal: bodies by their nature are limited in efficacy and being. These characteristics, which we must infer to account for the evolutionary process, are those proper to God as Christians, Jews, Moslems, and many others understand the Ultimate.

In conclusion, we find that there are grounds for believing in God in our evolutionary world as in the pre-modern world. God gives testimony to himself in this world as in previous ages; many have read these signs and come to belief by their help. One can critically conclude that there are sufficient grounds for belief in the existence of God. This understanding of God is, however, only initially adequate, since the Christian God is much beyond what we have asserted. It is only an understanding of God as personal and as related to us that can be consistent with the Christian vision or faith. We will discuss these aspects of God in the following chapters. In the meantime, we will conclude this section by turning to several objections that may be raised against the position we have advanced.

We may briefly recall what Donald Burrill calls "the three most impelling criticisms that are presently brought against the cosmological arguments," the first of which is based on the distinction between "analytic" and "synthetic" propositions. Burrill writes: "I judge . . . that the arguments are regarded as having, in some degree, both the self-evidence of mathematical propositions, and the factual confirmation of empirical experience.

But it is precisely the conditions of analytic necessity and probable occurrence that cannot be fulfilled simultaneously. If we begin with the factual premise that there is a universe, and conclude that this necessarily entails a prior entity as its source, we are advocating a proof—not in any empirically demonstrable sense, but totally on definitional grounds—that not having a 'first cause' is inconceivable."[41]

In answer, we showed earlier in this chapter a scientific analysis of human knowledge that neither Hume nor Kant, on whose viewpoints the above objection is based, can account

---

[41]Donald Burrill, ed., *The Cosmological Argument. A Spectrum of Opinion* (New York: Doubleday, 1967) "Introduction," 14. This and the next objection are basically the arguments that J. L. Mackie offers against Thomas Aquinas' cosmological argument in *The Miracle,* 87–92.

for. Both Piaget and Gibson, we have seen, show that we do reach a necessity in the physical world that grounds some of our judgments and propositions. Otherwise we cannot explain the concrete operatory stage of human knowledge, the formal operatory stage of human knowledge, or science. The necessity that binds events to physical and metaphysical powers and acts that are causes proportioned to these events is not logical necessity; it is a necessity in the reality itself that we can grasp intellectually. To say, for example, that something can come from nothing contradicts the intelligibility we have, through experience and insight, come to expect from our world and renders us incapable of accounting for the kinds of knowledge the child achieves.

Burrill presents another objection: "The second general objection questions the claim that the universe is rationally explicable. The assertion that the universe implies a God because it is ultimately rational is, at the least, a metaphysical assumption open to question. . . . The notion that the universe is ultimately 'rational' rests not on the nature of rational necessity, but on an individual's fundamental belief that it is so—that is, on an act of faith alone."[42]

In answer to this objection we can recall that earlier in this chapter we found that our engagement in science rests on an implicit metaphysics—that is, on our knowledge of the distinction within the world between being and non-being. Thus the metaphysical search for causes of phenomenon rests on the same basis as the similar search by scientists. The difficulty that scientists have with the metaphysical genre of seeking causes comes when they absolutize their own method and are unaware that it depends upon the validity of metaphysical knowledge of reality about us. Neither the scientist's nor the metaphysician's search for knowledge is properly based on faith; it is based on the infant's, child's, and adolescent's growing awareness of the world and its inherent characteristics and intelligibility; the physical world is understood, and thus is capable of being understood.

Finally, we may cite a third difficulty presented by Burrill: "It calls into question the meaningfulness of the arguments by

[42]Burrill, *The Cosmological Argument,* 15.

contending that they seek answers to nonsensical questions
. . . (A) question about origin requires an explanation that
falls outside the sensible boundaries applicable to the term
'universe'. . . . The term 'origin' is no more significant than are
the terms 'location,' 'speed,' and 'direction' (at least in the light
of our present state of physical description).

The upshot is that some questions that are perfectly sensible
within subseries are not applicable to the total series."[43]

In answer, we acknowledge that if our question of the "origin" of the universe were concerned with a physical origin,
then indeed it would be an illegitimate question. Similarly, the
"location" of the universe as a whole demands a physical context; to ask for this or the "speed" or "direction" of the movement of the universe as a whole would be illegitimate.
However, this does not constitute a legitimate objection to a
question concerning whether the universe as a whole has a
cause of its being, because this is a question of another order. It
asks whether there is evidence from the nature of the cosmos
that the cosmos is dependent in its be-ing and, if it is, whether
it depends upon a cause that transcends it in being, not in location. Actually, we did not ask for a temporal beginning or origin of the universe; even Thomas Aquinas acknowledged that
we know that the universe had a temporal beginning only
through historical revelation. What we asked was whether the
movement and change manifest in the evolutionary process
have characteristics that show that physical organisms and
their physical environment are not the total cause of this process, and then whether the ultimate origin of this is a totally actual being. This is asking for a series of causes not temporally
but essentially (or "per se") interrelated. In the very act of developing, is the physical organism dependent upon something
that has a causal influence on it (e.g., the enhancement of its
being as a final cause) and through this on a ultimate causal influence that is totally actual? Moreover, we showed previously
the possibility of metaphysics and thus the legitimacy of asking questions about becoming and being.

Our conclusion is that it is reasonable to believe that the
course of evolution gives testimony to the agency of an ulti-

[43]Ibid., 16–18.

mate and totally actual cause operating through such immediate influences as the impact of the actualization of an organism's being that moves it to act, the structure of organisms, and the structure of their environment.

Finally, we can note that what we have said has implications for ecology. Pre-modern peoples had a sense of the sacredness of the physical world about them, as we see from a letter sent by the leader of the Hopi nation to the President of the United States in 1855 in response to a proposition to buy their land:

> How can one buy or sell the air, the warmth of the land? That is difficult for us to imagine. We do not own the sweet air or the sparkle on the water. How then can you buy them from us? . . .
>
> We are part of the Earth and the Earth is part of us. The fragrant flowers are our sisters. The reindeer, the horse, the great eagle are our brothers. . . . all belong to the same family.
>
> So when the Great Chief in Washington sends word that he wants to buy our land, he asks a great deal of us.
>
> We know that the White Man does not understand our way of life. . . . The Earth is not his friend but his enemy, and when he has conquered it, he moves on. . . . He treats his Mother the Earth and his Brother the Sky like merchandise. His hunger will eat the Earth bare and leave only a desert.
>
> Humankind has not woven the web of life. We are but one thread within it. Whatever we do to the web, we do to ourselves. All things are bound together. All things connect. Whatever befalls the Earth befalls also the children of the Earth.[44]

Modern Western men and women have all too commonly taken an exploitative approach to the earth, in part because modern science has led us to view the earth from a mechanistic viewpoint and in part because of a desire for instant individual or national gratification that blocks from view the long-term

---

[44]Quoted in Anuradha Vittachi, *Earth Conference One. Sharing a Vision for Our Planet* (Boston: New Science Library, 1989) 142–143. Among many other treatments of this issue, see Pope John Paul II, "Peace with God the Creator, Peace with all of Creation," *Origins* 19 (1989) 465–468.

effects of our action. We are now becoming painfully aware of the disastrous results of large-scale industrial pollution, hazardous waste, deforestation, etc. We have mistreated the earth, our environment, to such an extent that the effects of this constitute one of the greatest crises of our time. Part of a solution is a renewed sense of kinship with the earth, which is supported by our acknowledgement that the whole physical world is united by being shot through with purpose and a common finality. There is a continuity between that part of creation lower than the human and human beings themselves that physical sciences and an exploitative approach to nature have made us forget. Also, a religious sense that restores a kind of sacredness to nature and leads us to respect it as we use it can contribute greatly to the conversion necessary in our approach to nature and to a renewed contact in depth with ourselves as part of nature.

# 7

# God as Transcendent Personal Being

The Christian Churches believe in God as a transcendent personal being who is related to human beings in a changing world. This is evident in Vatican II and also in the World Council of Churches' Faith and Order Commission's statement, which we cited in chapter 2. This understanding of God is present in Scripture, and it is very evident in the liturgies of the Churches. In writing of Christian worship, Geoffrey Wainwright notes that "the various moods and attitudes characteristic of Christian worship express the multiple aspects of the *personal* relationship, both dynamic and purposive, between God and humanity which is entailed in the making of humanity in the divine image."[1] Christians have related to God as personal throughout their history, but this belief has been expressed more or less strongly at times, as we indicated in chapters 2 and 4. In our century, many Christians and others have opposed aspects of classical theologies which concern God as transcendent personal being related to humanity in history, on the basis either of modern experience or of their interpretations of Scripture. In chapter 3, we argued that Scripture presents God as a transcendent personal being deeply related to men and women in history. Now, we seek to examine and evaluate certain tensions in theology concerning this Christian belief. In this chapter we shall focus on the question of God as transcendent personal being, and in the next on God's relation to the world and history.

[1]Geoffrey Wainwright, *Doxology, The Praise of God in Worship, Doctrine and Life. A Systematic Theology* (New York: Oxford Univ. Press, 1980) 37. See also 351.

Some important issues relevant to the present chapter are the following. In the first place, reacting against nineteenth- and early twentieth-century Protestant liberalism's tendency to excessively harmonize the Christian view of God with modern culture, Karl Barth in his neo-orthodoxy stressed that our only knowledge of God is that revealed through Jesus Christ, that God is the Totally Other, and that Protestant liberalism and Catholic use of analogy, e.g., in Thomas, introduce alternate and false gods into Christian theology. Agreeing as we do on the primacy of Scripture's understanding of God and on the inadequacy of modern dilutions of God's transcendence, are Barth's and, earlier, Luther's reactions to Thomas' use of philosophical theology in this matter the appropriate ones? In the second place, many people in our time have found much in modern science and life to call into question Scripture's view of God as transcendent personal being (e.g., Deists, some scientists such as Einstein and, in another way, A.N. Whitehead). Others have seen a kind of universal revelation of God in religious experience rather than in the physical world, and have raised questions about God as personal on the basis of their experience of Ultimate Concern or Holy Being. In the third place, in accord with this last view, some have through the influence of Eastern religions questioned whether the Christian view of God belongs only to our culture, and whether some non-personal interpretations of the Ultimate in Eastern religions are equally valid. In view of these difficulties, I propose to treat successively (I) disputes in the West, namely the first two mentioned above, concerning God as transcendent personal being, and (II) some Christian and Buddhist theologians on the nature of the Ultimate. We do this within the severe limits of the first part of foundational theology. Much that is relevant to these themes belongs more properly to other areas of theology.

## I. God as Transcendent Personal Being

In this section, I would like to note briefly something of (1) Thomas' theological view of God as transcendent personal being, and then dialogue with those in the West (2) who call this into question from the primacy of Scripture or (3) who call both Thomas' view and Scripture's into question from experience of the world or self.

## *1. Thomas Aquinas on God as Transcendent Personal Being.*

For Thomas, as we recalled in chapter 4, theology is a knowledge of God that is under the light of revelation and is scientific in the sense that it is knowledge through causes. In the very beginning of his theology, then, Thomas considers God, because "the principal intention of this sacred doctrine is to give knowledge of God not only as he is in himself but also as he is the principle and end of things and particularly of the rational creature."[2] He considers what pertains to the divine being, what pertains to the distinction of persons, and what pertains to the procession of creatures from God. In reference to the first, he asks whether God is, how he is or rather how he is not, and how he operates (questions about God's knowledge, will, and power).

Within the context of theology, Thomas shows that through God's effects in creation we can validly infer the existence of a first mover who is unmoved, a first efficient cause, one who exists necessarily rather than contingently, the greatest and essential good or being, and one who directs nonrational beings toward their goal. From what we know of this first principle through his effects, we may then know not what he is but what he is not. We cannot know properly what he is because his effects do not show the fullness of his being; and since we know him through his effects, we know more what he is not than what he is. For example, from the fact that God is an unmoved mover, we know that he is not a body, for no body moves another without being moved itself. Similarly, we can show that

[2]Thomas Aquinas, *Summa theologica*, I, 2, Introduction, and 1, 6, ad 3. Some recent treatments of God as personal and of divine attributes are the following: E. Schillebeeckx and B. van Iersel, *A Personal God? (Concilium*, vol. 103, 1977); Claude Geffré and J.-P. Jossua, *Monotheism (Concilium*, vol. 177, 1985); Richard Swinburne, *The Coherence of Theism* (Oxford: Clarendon Press, 1977); Ronald Nash, *The Concept of God. An Exploration of Contemporary Difficulties with the Attributes of God* (Grand Rapids, Mich.: Eerdmans, 1983); and Thomas Tracy, *God, Action, and Embodiment* (Grand Rapids, Mich.: Eerdmans, 1984).

God is not composed but rather simple in his being, that he is all perfect or essentially good, infinite, immutable and one. While infinitely transcending all his effects, God is also immanent in them, because he is where he operates, and all things have their being from and in him. We name God in accord with our manner of knowing him. We know him by way of negation, i.e., denying of him what is specific to creatures. But we also know something positive of him, since his creatures do represent him and their perfections preexist in him in a transcendent fashion as their analogical cause. Among all the names of God, "He Who Is," as revealed to Moses (Exodus 3:13) is the most proper, "For it does not signify some form but 'to be' (*esse*) itself. Hence since the to be (or act of be-ing) of God is his very essence, and this is true of no other . . . it is clear that among all names this most properly names God, for each thing is named from its form."[3]

After considering the divine being, Thomas discusses what pertains to God's action or operation. Here he deals first of all with the operations or actions that remain immanent within God—his knowledge and his willing. God's knowledge has as its first object himself, but he knows all things, even future contingents, by an eternal knowledge that is infinite as he himself is. In fact, from his knowledge other beings derive, and he is the ultimate foundation of all truth (*ST* I, 14–17). In God then there is life in its fullness. Similarly there is will in God, who loves himself and all that he brings into being, for his will is the cause of things, not out of any need he has for them but from his own free, overflowing love. He has a providence for those things that he creates, particularly the rational creature—a providence that is under the sign of his justice and mercy, and even more under mercy than under justice. God's power and happiness are themselves infinite, as are all his perfections (*ST* I, 19–26). One can see that Thomas considers God to be transcendent personal being to a degree we cannot comprehend, because he is one who knows and loves and initiates action to an infinite degree. However, it is not until Thomas treats God as triune that he raises the question whether the name "person" should be ascribed to God and

[3]*ST* I, 13, 11.

what it signifies in God. Claiming that "person" "signifies that which is most perfect in the whole of nature, namely one who subsists in a rational nature," he ascribes this perfection to God, but does so in accord with the Christian mystery of the Trinity.[4]

## 2. Primacy of Scripture and Philosophical Theology.

One way in which this viewpoint has been contested for a long time is that which we find in Luther and then revived in the neo-orthodoxy of Barth. As we saw in chapter 4,[5] Luther dialectically opposed the understanding of God he received through his liberating experience of the efficacy of faith and that which was present in Scholastic theology (which he knew primarily in its late medieval form) in its objective talk of God and its use of philosophy. Similarly, Barth dialectically opposed the understanding of God the Christian has through belief in God through Jesus Christ and that which others derive from religious experience or God's effects in the world.[6] This dialectical opposition is asserted also by Pannenberg and Moltmann in their own ways.[7] Pannenberg, for example, denies the capacity of reason to argue for the existence of God and the validity of analogy. Moltmann rejects both a cosmological and an existential approach to giving grounds for faith. Both, too, speak of God as the power of the future in a way that contests the Scholastic view of God as all-perfect personal being from the beginning.

How should we evaluate these positions? As a preliminary note, if I may recall a personal experience, my own monastic tradition gives me a particular appreciation of this difficulty. In fact, I vividly remember how as a young Benedictine I ex-

---

[4]*ST* I, 29, 3. See Johannes B. Metz, *Christliche Anthropozentrik* (Munich: Kösel, 1962) on Thomas' Christian form of thought (*Denkform*) that lay behind his extensive use of the categories of Greek philosophy. This gave his thought more of an anthropocentric than a cosmocentric character.

[5]See above, chapter 4, pp. 137–138. Also see Alister McGrath, *Luther's Theology of the Cross: Martin Luther's Theological Breakthrough* (New York: Basil Blackwell, 1985).

[6]See above, chapter 2, pp. 39–40.

[7]See above, chapter 2, pp. 60–61, 63–64.

perienced the tension between the kind of knowledge of God I was introduced to as a novice through a spirituality fed by liturgy, Scripture, and meditation, and the kind of knowledge of God I was offered in most of the philosophy I was taught in the seminary after my novitiate. My first philosophical efforts were directed toward resolving this difficulty. At least we may all agree that there should be a better integration between Scripture and philosophical theology than is frequently the case, that in principle Scripture and philosophical theology need one another, and that to support a dichotomy between them is to promote the erosion of faith in the Christian God that, as we have seen, took place in the last several centuries.

The God we are reflecting on in theology is the God who has revealed himself definitively through Jesus Christ and the Spirit, and Scripture and Christian prayer and life have a primacy in the systematic and critical reflection on faith that theology is. That God is personal is shown much better by Scripture than by philosophical theology, because persons are manifested by their actions and their stories. And God is known as personal more directly through prayer than by theology, because to know someone as person involves subjectivity as well as objectivity. Since theology is *"fides quaerens intellectum,"* and faith is personal knowledge of God, we should say that theology feeds upon such encounter with God—and thus on the gift of wisdom that comes from the Holy Spirit—as well as on a more intellectual knowledge of God through his effects. Theology is knowledge of God that derives not only from his effects but from that "devotion" to God that comes, as Thomas teaches, both from our sense of our great need and of God's gifts in response to our need and from the thanksgiving that results from meditation or contemplation on both of these.[8] Thus I would in part disagree with Thomas on his division between theology and the wisdom that comes from the Holy Spirit, and I think that in practice Thomas himself differs from this view. Theology derives from the way God reveals himself, and this revelation occurs

---

[8]See *ST* II–II, 82, 3. Vatican I, Denziger, 3016, stresses the importance of piety as well as care and sobriety in the theologian's efforts to gain some understanding of God and his revealed mysteries.

through the mediation of God's acts and words through Jesus and the Spirit. A development of this theme, however, belongs to later parts of foundational theology.

We have not found in Scripture itself the degree of dichotomy between God's revelation through Jesus Christ and his revelation of himself through the Old Testament or through nature and human experience that Luther, Barth, and some other dialectical theologians construct. The relationship between these revelations is not only that the New makes the former revelation Old or surpassed, but that it fulfills and thus affirms what Moses and the prophets and our human experience of self and the world have revealed while it subsumes this into a definitive revelation. We come to know God more fully as he reveals himself more fully, and earlier knowledge is then subsumed under a new and more adequate paradigm. Similarly, we know a human person better if we are aware of his full story rather than simply the earlier parts of it. Specifically, as I seek to show elsewhere, the Christian view of God as the power of the future manifested by the apocalyptic character of the kingdom of God does not contradict but fulfills God's revelation of himself in pre-Christian revelations and corrects what many have falsely associated with these partial revelations.[9] We may also say that theology that is derived from Scripture, prayer, and Christian life has to speak of God objectively and at times abstractly, as the Council of Nicea did in speaking of the Son as *homoousios* with the Father. Without this we have a ghetto God and not one who is related to all that is and all that we are and know. The dichotomy placed between God's successive revelations of himself by some dialectical theologians is thus opposed to both Scripture and tradition, even that of the Patristic period, and so cannot be considered a fully adequate Christian view of God. There is, indeed, in Christian conversion, an experience of a need to reject as partial and misleading insufficient views of self and of God if these have been previously taken as adequate. But a critical reflection cannot justify a total rejection of such earlier views of God, since they are in part ways by which God leads one to a later Christian conversion.

[9]See "Trinity as Salvific Mystery," *Monastic Studies* 17 (1986) 81–100.

Luther's and Barth's negativity toward philosophy (while they were actually influenced by it in important ways) in theology contributes to the modern world's interpretation of human experience of self and the world in ways opposed to the Christian revelation of God. We have seen that modern philosophical reflection on God, divorced from the context of Christian revelation, has contributed substantially to the erosion of Christian faith in God. Many who have been deeply influenced by science have claimed a cosmic religious feeling, but have viewed the Ultimate as an impersonal source of order and dynamism displayed magnificently in the physical world. For example, Einstein said that "I believe in Spinoza's God who reveals himself in the orderly harmony of what exists, not in a God who concerns himself with the fates and actions of human beings."[10] We can answer this by saying that experience of what it means to be human, and not only of the physical world, reveals something of God. So, while it is understandable that a person may interpret the physical world as pointing to an Ultimate as Einstein did, for him to restrict the Ultimate would be to accept only part of the human experience through which he is revealed to us. We can even say that the revelation God makes of himself through the physical world is important and irreplaceable; it is essential to our understanding of God in our time. We must integrate the cosmic with the anthropological, the impersonal with the personal in our knowledge of God, and not simply dismiss the cosmic and impersonal once we relate to God personally. Theologians should not, by the way they articulate who God is, make themselves responsible for such inadequate views of God. People need an integration of the varied elements of their life and knowledge, and if they are told that faith cannot do justice to other dimensions of their knowledge and values that are genuinely human, they may well tend to subordinate Scripture to a simply scientific or humanistic interpretation of themselves and their world. One does not accept God's revelation more fully by rejecting revelations he makes antecedent to the coming of Jesus or through less de-

---

[10]Banish Hoffmann, with the collaboration of Helen Dukas, *Albert Einstein, Creator and Rebel* (New York: Granada Publishing Co, 1972) 95. This is cited in Hans Küng, *Does God Exist? An Answer for Today* (New York: Doubleday, 1980) 628.

finitive mediations. As Jesus said to Nicodemus, "If you do not believe when I tell you about earthly things, how are you to believe when I tell you about those of heaven?" (John 3:12).

## 3. The Objectivity or Non-objectivity of God.

The view of God as personal, whether as in Scripture or in Thomas' theology, is contested in our time also by some theologians who give a primacy to intimations of God they find either in modern experience of the physical world and human agency or in a universal religious experience of Ultimacy. Some theologians who follow the philosopher A. N. Whitehead exemplify the former, and we shall deal with some specific objections they raise to a classical view of God in the next chapter. Some theologians who are influenced by philosophers such as Heidegger exemplify the latter. We may consider Paul Tillich as of this latter company, though perhaps the primary philosophical influence in his work comes from German Idealism. He writes about God as follows:

> "God" is the answer to the question implied in man's finitude; he is the name for that which concerns man ultimately. . . . (U)ltimate concern must transcend every preliminary finite and concrete concern. It must transcend the whole realm of finitude in order to be the answer to the question implied in finitude. But in transcending the finite the religious concern loses the concreteness of a being-to-being relationship.
> The being of God is being-itself. . . . If God is *a* being, he is subject to the categories of finitude, especially of space and substance. . . . The power of being is another way of expressing the same thing in a circumscribing phrase . . . the concept of being as being, or being-itself, points to the power inherent in everything, the power of resisting non-being.[11]

If Thomas' theology of God seems at times too objective, this view seems too non-objective to do justice to what Scrip-

[11]See Paul Tillich, *Systematic Theology* (Chicago: Univ. of Chicago Press, 1967) I, 210, 235–236.

ture says of God, for Scripture uses of God words such as "I,"
"You," or "He," and speaks of him as an agent in history and
creation. If Tillich's position depends upon a more general
revelation of God in light of which he reinterprets Scripture's
assertions, we may note that many religions speak of the revelation of God as personal. We can see this through their
prayers. To take only one example, we can recall a hymn to
Mwari, the God of Mashona (Southern Rodesia, now
Zimbabwe):

> Great Spirit! Piler up of rocks into towering mountains!
> When thou stampest on the stone, the dust rises and fills the
> land. Hardness of the precipice; waters of the pool that turn
> into misty rain when stirred. Vessel overflowing with oil! Fa-
> ther of Runji, who seweth the heavens like cloth. Let him
> knit together that which is below. Caller forth of the branch-
> ing trees: Thou bringest forth the shoots that they stand
> erect. Thou has filled the land with mankind, the dust rises
> on high, O Lord! Wonderful One, thou livest in the midst of
> the sheltering rocks, Thou givest of rain to mankind: We
> pray to thee, hear us, Lord! Show mercy when we beseech
> thee, Lord. Thou art on high with the spirits of the great.
> Thou raisest the grass-covered hills above the earth, and
> createst the rivers, Gracious One.[12]

Such petitionary prayer and ascription to God of creative
agency shows a belief in God as a personal agent who acts and
interacts with human beings. There is much that is anthropomorphic in many religious views of God, but to transcend this
it is not necessary to deny that God is indeed personal. Admit-
tedly, there are some religions that do not call for interaction
with the Ultimate as personal; and we shall say something
of Zen Buddhism below, though some refuse to call this a
religion.

It may be that at the source of Tillich's position on the non-
personal or supra-personal character of God, there lie both a
philosophical view that to be personal is to be limited and a re-

---

[12]Mircea Eliade, *From Primitives to Zen. A Thematic Sourcebook of the History of
Religions* (New York: Harper and Row 1967) 269–270.

liance on a specific mediation of the Ultimate through experience of Ultimate Concern. Since these are widely held viewpoints, it is worth addressing them both briefly.

Is to be personal to be limited? It is true of course that the persons we primarily know, namely ourselves and other human beings, are limited. In a preceding chapter, we used Erikson's work as a kind of phenomenology to evaluate whether transcendence is proper to and perfective of the human person. We proposed that the fully developed human person is one whose agency, horizon, and potentialities have come through intermediate stages to the point where a self-orientation toward God is dominant and overriding in the person's life. Thus the fully developed person, we might say, is one who with heart and mind relates himself or herself in love to God, and to self and others in a way that is integrated within this context. The person then is disclosed particularly in one who is fully active, but this full activity comes about only as a term of a process and history. Thus the persons we know are imperfect and limited. However, this does not necessarily imply that limitation is essential to being a person.

Thomas Tracy argues against such essential limitation in a book[13] in which he seeks to mediate between a classical Thomistic theology and a Whiteheadian theology. We understand person through intentional agency. That is, we know a person through character traits or ways in which the person orients himself or herself to action, to self, to others. This is different from what we know of other things about us; it properly belongs to a person to initiate activity, and thus we know a person not so much by what happens to him or her but by what he or she does and the intentionality which this action expresses. Counter to behaviorism, we claim that personal action is not simply the external event or happening, but this event in relation to intentionality. This does not imply a dualism between mind and body; rather we are psychophysical units in our bodily actions. But need there be a bodily basis for intentional action for all persons? It is not the bodily as such that is most characteristic of persons, but intentional agency. Thus we can-

[13]T. Tracy, *God, Action and Embodiment* (Grand Rapids, Mich.: Eerdmans, 1984).

not stipulate that bodily existence is necessary for intentional action and personal agency; these latter are sufficient to preserve personal identity. Christians believe that in God is found the perfection of personal agency. We find this in the "story" of God in his relation to humanity that the Bible proclaims and recounts, for this story manifests a continuing identity of purpose and action over time, and thus a continuing personal identity.

We are not saying that it is essential to God as personal to have this relationship with creation, though it is by this relationship that we know something of God and, indeed, know God. His actions over time disclose him but do not exhaust his identity. In the next chapter, we shall speak more directly of God's relationship to humanity. While active relation to another seems essential to intentionality and personal agency and identity, Christians believe that Father, Son, and Holy Spirit are subsistent intentional relationships to one another through knowledge and love. In fact, it is from this mystery that the word "person" came to such prominence in the Western world. Relation to another does not of itself imply limitation, though it may do so for a modern understanding of the person as absolutely autonomous. Nor is God limited by being in a process of "self-creation." There is a sense in which this is true of human beings, since they do not have their perfection save through their engagement in action through time. But the need for time and agency to become who they are is part of their finitude and materiality. It would not be true of one who is eternally perfect, as God is.

A second basis for the position of Tillich and some others who stress the non-objectivity of God is the particular mediation by which they find God revealed to them, such as the experience of Ultimate Concern. In his method of correlation, Tillich begins with the question that, he holds, we pose to ourselves in life; our answer comes from Christian revelation, for it is there that the Ground of Being or Ultimate Concern is revealed to us. Tillich seems to take our human question as purely concerned with ultimate value or concern, and he accepts from Christian revelation only what is an answer to this question. Thus he finds in revelation the reality of Ultimate

Value or Ground of Being or Power of Being, but not a personal God.

We agree with Tillich on the legitimacy and great significance of this approach to the Ultimate, and we acknowledge that of itself it does not ground a view of the Ultimate as personal in the full sense. It is relevant to this difficulty to note that with our present-day realization of the plurality of religions in the world, we can assert that it is appropriate that different peoples receive intimations of God that are different from one another, because these intimations are relative to their experiences. So it is the case with religions generally, for there God is normally mediated by particular experiences of the community, for example, for Israel through the liberation from Egypt and the covenant, and for many pre-literate peoples through their own traditions. It is proper for an agricultural people to experience God differently than a nomadic people or a fruit-gathering people. This is of itself not relativism, but simply relativity. God is so transcendent that he is related to all human experiences. Diverse peoples begin with very restricted experiences, since they differ from one another in time, location, culture, traditions, etc. It is appropriate then that they experience God differently, both for their own needs and that the glory of God may be manifested in diversity. But human knowledge enlarges as the context enlarges within which the individual person or culture interacts with the environment or world and values. The more this enlarges the more the world of one people touches that of another and indeed has common ground with the world of another. Then, a people must come to grips with the way another people understands God.

While the knowledge of God is mediated in a way relative to differing experiences of the physical and human world, we must add, from our critical evaluation of intimations of God in the last chapter, that God is legitimately understood to be transcendent being. Religious experience reaches God in this manner, and our philosophical reflection concurs. We reflected on our value experience and our experience of the physical world as mediating knowledge of God, concluding that in both cases we know God—in response to his testimonies to himself—as transcendent being, though these experiences mediate his transcendence somewhat differently. In experiencing the world as made, we know God as transcendent agent—as One Who Acts as agent and cause in the operations of nature. (Correlatively, in experiencing God as acting in history, Israel knew God as transcendent agent in history.) This agent is transcendent in the sense that he is not identified with the physical or human world or any dimension thereof. Since we know this agent in part through the very limitations of the world, we know him as not having the limitations of the world or humanity. Thus, as Thomas teaches, God is manifested as an ultimate principle who is pure act, totally actual and unlimited—who *is* in the fullest sense. Thus we know God not only as relative to us or to the world (though we know him through these relations) but in a way that allows us to speak of him and say that he is not the world and that he is totally perfect, or totally being.

We cannot say that this is an adequate statement of who God is, since it is relative to the experience that mediates this knowledge. We have discussed another basic manner of knowing him, namely, through values. Here too God is reached or known—or revealed—as transcendent being or Being, but not primarily in the sense of one who is. Through this approach, rather, God is known as the *good,* the fullness of value or power—the value or power operative in all lesser values and powers that rightly draw us to the fullness of being, despite being limited and themselves grounded in an ultimate value or power. God is known here as the ultimate issue for us—our Ultimate Concern. Even "knowledge" here is somewhat different from the knowledge of God that we discussed above. For here, knowledge is not properly objective and intellectual, or expressed by concept and judgment. Rather, this knowledge is knowledge of presence mediated by affectivity, and it is frequently expressed symbolically in action and words. This knowledge is therefore in a special sense non-objective. Many religious images (e.g., "God is my fortress") do not express properly what is so known, but express it rather as "pointer-knowledge." (We shall return to this question when we treat religious language in chapter 9.) God is not known to be distinct from the world and humanity in the same way as we saw from knowing him by the mediation of the physical world or historical actions. The relation of limited values to an ultimate value differs from the relation of finite agents to an ultimate agent. If we expressed this metaphysically, we could say that the participation of the creature's *esse* or "to be" in the *Esse* of God differs from the participation of the created agent in the uncreated agent.[14] And so by this access to God through values, many experience and stress a continuity between God and human values or power rather than discontinuity. Thus some think that they have got beyond theism through this approach.

Both the meaning of God that results from value experience and the meaning that results from acknowledgement of the existence of a first cause of the created world are valid. They are not contradictory but rather complementary. They are considered contradictory only if either is thought to be the exclusive way of God's manifestation of himself or the exclusive way we have to know God. If God is understood through ultimate concern it may appear as though the knowledge of God gained through the cosmological approach is a distortion of Being or an objectification of Being that forgets the difference between Being and beings. But if the relativity of the meaning of God in either of these ways to the experience through which he is mediated is kept in mind, it can be recognized that as legitimate as one way and understanding of God is, it is not contradictory to God's meaning as mediated by the other. It can also be recognized that neither way taken by itself and exclusive of the other is adequate. God is both the Being who is totally actual and First Agent or Cause, and he is Being in the sense of the Ultimate Ground of value or Power of Being. There has often, historically, been opposition between these two meanings of God. Some mystics and some of those who have articulated their understanding of God in dependence upon religious experience have condemned those who have identified God with the First Cause or the Agent who liberated the Israelites from Egypt. And many formed through the cosmological approach or the Western experience of God through a specific historical event have condemned some mystics' and Eastern religions' understanding of God as pantheistic. We do not say that such

[14]Several references in Aquinas on participation are *ST* I, 104, 1; II–II, 23, 2, ad 1. I have treated this subject briefly in *Predestination, Grace and Free Will,* 158–162.

an evaluation has never ben justified; we simply note that the meaning of God made manifest by the cosmological approach is not an adequate standpoint from which to make this judgment.

The proper way then to evaluate critically the question of God as personal is to use both of these experiences and approaches—that through the physical world and that through values. Both are given to humanity and both are seen in history, religion, and philosophy; and both are valid. It is through both of them together that we have a human experience of God as personal. Through the cosmological way we do reach God as distinct from us and creation—as one who *is* objectively and supremely. And it is only with one who is distinct from us that we interact as with a person, not with some power that is an extension of us or of which we are an extension. Through the way of values we reach God through action—the impact of the good on us and our response, our engagement in the moral life; and we have a knowledge through presence, or connaturality. This subjectivity is necessary for knowledge that is personal or for knowledge of another as person, but it is not of itself sufficient. Only if this presence of the transcendent is the presence of One Who Is, and is freely and intelligently, is our relation to transcendent Being personal.

What we have presented is a reflexive critical evaluation of our belief in God as personal in view of some overly objective and overly non-objective interpretations of the Ultimate. But, such critical evaluation is really secondary. In ordinary life God is known as personal not so much through the combination of these two avenues we have been discussing, but rather through the child's growth and the way that parents symbolize God in their care for their child.[15] We have seen that Erikson explains the growth of the child, adolescent, and adult through the child's interaction with an enlarging social environment according to the stages of the maturation of his or her human potential. This social environment mediates or should mediate

[15]See A. M. Rizzuto, *The Birth of the Living God: A Psychoanalytic Study* (Chicago: Univ. of Chicago, 1979) and John McDargh, *Psychoanalytic Object Relations Theory and the Study of Religion. On Faith and the Imaging of God* (Lanham, Md.: University Press of America, 1983).

God's personal engagement with the growing person; the horizon of the child's and growing person's concern is not, or at least should not be, only the immediate human values appropriate for its stages of development but the Ultimate Value mediated through these, or of which these are participations, and the Personal Being beyond created personal agents. The human potential of the child and growing person can be satisfied with no less than this engagement with God.

Through giving grounds for a knowledge of God as personal, we have been giving grounds for faith in God, since faith is personal knowledge and knowledge of God as personal depends upon both *theoria* and *praxis.* These grounds, since they are more than intellectual, are not specifically proofs for faith, because faith as a personal acceptance and surrender is not restrictedly an intellectual act. It is a personal relating to the other, in this case, God. Proof is not proportionate to such an act, but there can be a critical validation of faith such that the person's entrusting of self is not arbitrary or a *sacrificium intellectus.*

Objections may well be raised by some theologians and philosophers to the view presented above. For example, one may object that if God is total value, then the things of the world have no value but are simply maya or illusion. On the other hand, one may object that if God is one who is, then he is reduced in reality to being one being among many. Both of these objections would, it seems, be answered through a proper understanding of *participation,* that is, the way that creatures share through the being proper to them in the being of God. It is true that on the above view God is Being or Good itself in the sense that whatever being exists outside of God does not add to the perfection or degree of being that exists. But there are numerically other beings than God who have value or being; their goodness and being is a share or participation in the goodness or being of God although they exist with a "to be" distinct from that of God and are good with a goodness distinct from that of God. There is not a greater intensity of Being when creatures are added to God, but there are more beings. Likewise, as knowledge of God is mediated through experience of his effects, so too growth in goodness or perfection on the part of creatures comes largely through the mediation of the created goods that motivate their action and in which they share through their engagement and action, and not simply by their seeking God in a way divorced from seeking their created good and development. Similarly, to assert that God is One Who Is demeans God no more than to assert that he is Good Itself demeans creatures. If participation is truly understood, then this does not make God one being among others, since he is One Who Is in an unparticipated and infinite way—be-ing with the fullness of being—while all others *are* simply through participation.

From what we have said above it follows that those who claim to have an experience of God as personal, even outside of Judaeo-Christian revelation, are correct; those who deny that God is personal are basically wrong if they understand the personal correctly, rather than simply in an anthropomorphic way. This means then that the ultimate power that sustains us is personal; the ultimate value to which we are oriented is personal; the call that we receive from value is ultimately personal; revelation of God is ultimately personal; our interaction with the Ultimate is most properly personal. Our ultimate environment is personal; the law of life is ultimately personal; our maker and the world's maker is personal; the purpose for which the physical world as well as humanity was made is ultimately personal; and the Ultimate's relation to the world and to men and women taken individually or socially is personal. The relationship to the Ultimate that we are called to is personal. It is in this sense that we say we are called to a religious relation to the Ultimate rather than to one that is simply a relation of knowledge or of the moral order. As Vatican II said, our greatest dignity consists in our call to communion with God. Similarly, our rejection of the Ultimate is also personal—sin; and our loss, if we lose union with the Ultimate, is personal. Similarly, our service inspired by religion is ultimately personal.

## II.  Some Buddhist and Christian Reflections on the Ultimate

The view of God as personal, commonly presented as the Christian view, is markedly different from the view of the Ultimate presented by a number of Asian religions. This poses a challenge in our time to the legitimacy of the Christian view of God beyond Western culture. To many it seems that Christians are provincial if they simply accept their own understanding of God as adequate, and they are imperialist if they act toward others who have different views of God in a way that is complaisant and superior. Since this is a matter that should be treated even in an introductory study such as this, we will contrast and compare an Asian articulation of the Ultimate with a Christian understanding of God as personal in this chapter, and with a Christian understanding of God's relation to the world in the next chapter. We will be limited to taking just a few aspects to reflect upon from a much larger religious whole of life and thought, without properly contextualizing them. And I recognize that I risk making statements where my knowledge is quite limited. Even though I depend on professors of comparative religion who are acknowledged experts, I present my views on this matter as hypotheses subject to refinement and correction.

To consider in this chapter one of these alternative views of the Ultimate, it may be good to accept some representatives of Zen Buddhism, since that differs so markedly from Christianity. We will consider particularly some philosophers of the Kyoto school of philosophy in Japan who have developed their philosophy within a religious context in their lives, a context which is shaped by their acceptance of Buddhism, and (for most of them) Buddhism in the form of Zen Buddhism. Kitarō Nishida (1870–1945), the founder of this school, and others who have continued it, such as Keiji Nishitani (b. 1900) and Masao Abe (b. 1915), interpret the Ultimate in relation to a specific religious tradition, and do so in a philosophical mode that is aware of and in dialogue with philosophers in the West and with Christianity. Thus there can be to some extent a comparison between their interpretation and an interpretation offered by Christian theologians. This may make the differences more understandable than would a comparison of a nonphilosophical statement on the one hand and a philosophical or theological statement on the other. In this matter, we are particularly helped by a recent book in which Hans Waldenfels ably presents the position of the Kyoto school.[16] We shall first present this Buddhist view of the Ultimate and then ask how we would relate it to the view of God as personal which we have articulated. We do this after having presented our reasons for thinking there is something proper to human beings that is transcultural and something that is validly revealed to us of God by God that is accessible to men and women of varied cultures.

To present this Buddhist view, we shall first examine the thought of one of the representatives of the Kyoto school, Nishitani, and then recall something of its relation to earlier Buddhism. For Nishitani and other philosophers of this school, philosophy should serve an emerging world culture that can unify the East and the West, save human beings from the dehumanization and denaturalization that a scientistic and technocratic culture subjects them to, and save them from

---

[16]See Hans Waldenfels, *Absolute Nothingness. Foundations for a Buddhist-Christian Dialogue* (New York: Paulist, 1980). Also see, among many other books, Heinrich Dumoulin, *Christianity Meets Buddhism* (LaSalle, Ill.: Open Court Press, 1974); C. Geffré and M. Dhavamony, eds., *Buddhism and Christianity* (*Concilium*, vol. 116. 1979); and H. Byron Earhart, *Japanese Religion. Unity and Diversity* 3rd edition (Belmont, Calif.: Wadsworth Publishing Co., 1982). Zen, we should note, is simply one sect of Buddhism, and that not the largest, even in Japan. For example, in Japan there are 20 million adherents to Amida Buddhism, and 10 million adherents to Zen Buddhism. The page references in the following paragraphs are to Waldenfel's book. On Nishida's philosophy, see Andrew Feenberg and Yoko Arisaka, "Experiential Ontology: The Origins of the Nishida Philosophy in the Doctrine of Pure Experience," *International Philosophical Quarterly* 30 (1990) 173–206. It is very interesting that Nishida's philosophical approach to reality is from the perspective of the subject acting for the good and in this context conscious. His first philosophical work, *A Study of the Good* (1911) was influenced by the radical empiricism and pragmatism of William James who was, among other things, an early phenomenologist. Nishida later corrected some aspects of his earlier philosophy and put his insights in the context of the "'logic of *basho*,' usually translated as 'Place,' or '*Topos*' by which he means, very roughly, a variety of relational ontology. Contextuality becomes an essential category of being in his theory. As Nishida put it, no being can exist by itself, but all being is an 'In-being.' This view has obvious sources in Hegel and Heidegger, but it is also congruent with deep features of Japanese, a context-dependent language that tends to blur the distinction between inner states of the subject and the objective world" (Feenberg and Arisaka, 185). These authors also note that, "Nishida identifies the common thread that links the existentialist discovery of concrete experience as an unsurpassable absolute and 'a long tradition of Eastern metaphysics which expounds that true reality can be affirmed and lived only through an experiential dialectic of negation'" (192; the quotation is from David Dilworth, "Nishida Kitaro: Nothingness as the Negative Space of Experiential Immediacy," *International Philosophical Quarterly* 13 (1973) 482).

a human-centeredness that alienates them from their own
deepest selves as well as from others and that keeps them
bound to samsara or the endless cycle of rebirths. For this purpose, Nishitani returns again and again to the question of
nothingness. "His entire thought revolves about this nothingness" (64). This is connected with Buddhism itself, for "the
ability of Buddhism to disclose man in his depths resides in its
operational realization of what is called 'absolute nothingness'
or 'emptiness'" (7). Nishitani acknowledges the enormous contributions of the West, for the East "could not give birth to science or technology, nor could it create what we call an
'individual subjective self-consciousness,'—for example, the
human posture upon which democracy is based" (59, a quotation from Nishitani). However, the West's specific religion,
Christianity, cannot of itself present the answer to the problem
of the modern world. For this one would have to go beyond and
in back of Christianity and the West. In fact, exposure to an
alien religion and culture may allow the West to do this.
Nishitani holds that "with the help of Buddhist insights, the
sort of elements that can be brought to light in Christianity are
such as to offer it, too, the possibility of entering meaningfully
into contemporary discussions of nihilism and of permitting
man to achieve the 'breakthrough' to his true being and true
self"(61).

Nishitani's approach to nothingness is through "the Great
Doubt"—a doubt "released in many by the great negative realities of life, by the experience of nihilization and death" (66).
Through this we come face to face with the question of the
meaning of existence, for such experience calls into question
our own existence and that of others, calls us to assume another attitude, and so calls us to transcend in a sense the distinction between doubter and doubted, between subject and
object. "The Great Doubt emerges always as something that
opens up the field of nothingness, which gives place to the
turn-about of the Doubt itself. . . . And, as such, it is called
the Great Death. For example, the sayings: 'Once (when occurs) the Great Death, then the Universe becomes new,' and
'Under the Great Death, there is the Great Enlightenment,'
refer to that turn-about. . . . This Enlightenment . . . must be
the 'falling off' of our mode of existence in which the 'I' is the

agent" (67, quotation from Nishitani). In the West the question of being or existence has been treated for the most part in terms of subject and substance. But is there a mode of being that is neither subjective nor substantial? "The concept of substance as well as that of subject is established after all on the field of subject-object duality; the former is concerned with the 'object' and presupposes the 'subject', and it is the same with the latter, *mutatis mutandis.* This field of duality is broken through by *nihilum (kyomu)* in which . . . the being of things as well as of the self becomes thoroughly questionable by being transported to a region beyond the reach of "logical" thinking" (75, Nishitani). As Waldenfels comments: "His way of treating the question of being leads through the experience of negativity—'nothingness' (*kyomu*)—into unspeakable and unobjectifiable emptiness (*kũ*). It becomes, therefore, a religious question in which the call for a ground ends in the groundlessness wherein man must repudiate every form of attachment" (75).

The locus of nothingness in the West is found by Nishitani to be on the side of God. In this matter Nishitani and others from the Kyoto school find some affinity with Meister Eckhart, the medieval German mystic and Dominican who distinguished God and God's ground or God's godhead. As Nishitani writes, "Godhead means God being in Himself. . . . This essence of God, which transcends every mode of being or every aspect, cannot be expressed except by absolute nothingness" (76). His disciple Ueda comments: "God is nothingness. Not that he is without being; rather he is neither this nor that, nor anything that man can predicate of him—he is a being above all being. He is a modeless being" (76). Thus Eckhart is understood to say what Buddhism tries to express in its understanding of nothingness. The thought of Heidegger also bears similarities to the Buddhist understanding of nothingness, although Nishitani, who studied briefly under Heidegger, questions whether Heidegger's thought does not contain some objectification of nothingness.

Clearly, then, while Nishitani and many others of this school are opposed to the interpretation of God as substance or as subject, they are not without respect for Christianity and its understanding of God. Nishida, the founder of the Kyoto school, writes: "Thus, when the relative confronts the absolute, the relative must die, it must come to nothing. Only through death, in inverse correspondence, can our self touch God and be bound to God. Objective logic may say: 'If the relative dies and comes to nothing, does it not thereby cease to be anything that can be related to?' But death is not simply nothingness. The absolute, of course, goes beyond objects. But what simply goes beyond objects is not anything, is nothing other than simply nothingness" (44).

To understand something of this interpretation of the Ultimate and acknowledge its depth as well as its relativity, we should recognize that it is in continuity with the experience of Siddhartha Gautama of the sixth century B.C. in northern India, about one hundred miles from Benares. From the traditions surrounding the life of Gautama, who became the Enlightened One or Buddha, it is evident that his experience centered on the transience of such individual goods as health, wealth, and life itself and on the deceptiveness of the desire for personal gain that centers our lives on these goods. Thus after he reached enlightenment he preached the Four Noble Truths: life is suffering (*dukkha*); desire (*tanha*—the will to personal fulfillment) is the cause of suffering; the cure of life's dislocations is found in the extirpation of desire; and the way out of our captivity is through the Eightfold Path of right knowledge, aspiration, speech, behavior, livelihood, effort, mindfulness, and absorption.[17] Nirvana is the bliss that is the fulfillment of this whole way of extinguishing the boundary of the finite self:

> Nirvana is the highest destiny of the human spirit and its literal meaning is extinction. But we must be precise as to what is to be extinguished; it is the boundary of the finite self. It does not follow that what is left will be nothing. Negatively Nirvana is the state in which the faggots of private desire have been completely consumed and everything that restricts the boundless life has died. Affirmatively it is that boundless life itself. Buddha parried every request for a positive description of the condition insisting that it was "incom-

[17]See Huston Smith, "Buddhism," in his *The Religions of Man* (New York: Harper and Row, 1964) 80–141.

prehensible, indescribable, inconceivable, unutterable," for after we eliminate every aspect of the only consciousness we now know, how can we speak of what is left?[18]

Buddha would venture only one positive characterization of Nirvana: "Bliss, yes Bliss, my friends is Nirvana."[19]

There was a refusal on the part of Buddha to get involved with metaphysical questions, and this refusal was taken up again by a successor of his, Nāgārjuna, who lived c. 150 A.D. and was an important figure in the ancestry of Mahāyāna Buddhism and Zen Buddhism.[20] Nāgārjuna used the word śūnyatā (emptiness) to articulate what liberation offers people: "'Emptiness' has its true connotations in the process of salvation, and it would be a mistake to regard it as a purely intellectual concept, or to make it into a thing, and give it an ontological meaning. The relative nothing ('this is absent in that') cannot be hypostatized into an absolute nothing, into the nonexistence of everything, or the denial of all reality and of all being. Nor does 'emptiness' mean the complete indeterminate, the purely potential, which can become everything without being anything."[21] Statements by Buddhists about absolute nothingness as preeminent over being should not be interpreted ontologically but existentially. Thomas Merton comments on the teaching of Hui-nĕng (638–713), an important Chinese mediator between Buddhism and Zen Buddhism:

> (T)he "purity of *śūnyatā*" is not purity and void considered as an object of contemplation, but a non-seeing, a non-contemplation, in which precisely it is realized that the "mirror" of the original mind (of *prajñā* and emptiness) is actually a non-mirror, and "no-mind" . . .
> For Hui-nĕng there is no primal "object" on which to stand, there is no stand, the "seeing" of Zen is a non-seeing, and as Suzuki says, describing Hui-nĕng's teaching, "The seeing is

---

[18]Ibid, 111.

[19]Ibid., 112.

[20]See Waldenfels, *Absolute Nothingness*, 15–23.

[21]Edward Conze, *Buddhist Thought in India. Three Phases of Buddhist Philosophy* (London: Allen and Unwin, 1962) 61.

the result of having nothing to stand on." Hence, illumination is not a matter of "seeing purity" or "emptiness" as an object which one contemplates or in which one becomes immersed. It is simple "pure seeing," beyond subject and object, and therefore "no-seeing".[22]

Granted that the Buddhist and specifically the Zen Buddhist way of speaking of the Absolute is so different from the usual way Christians speak of God or the specific way Thomas Aquinas speaks of God, and granted that it is relative to their experience, how can we relate it to what Christianity understands of God? This question cannot be adequately treated outside the context of the mystery of the Trinity, and this goes beyond the bounds of this book, though we shall say a few words about it below. But first we can note that a number of Christians who are dialoguing with Eastern religions suggest that what these Buddhists seem to be speaking of is close to the apophatic tradition in Christian mysticism and theology, i.e., the way of negativity in experiencing and speaking of God.[23] If we interpret Buddhism philosophically, we have to say that it is not a way of knowledge in the primary Western sense, i.e., sense knowledge of what is outside us in the physical world and then intellectual insight into this reality. It seems to be the way of interiority through the human orientation by affectivity and will toward the good; it is a turning away from lesser goods toward that which is the very center of the human person—and thus, in accord with what we have seen earlier in chapter 5, toward the *esse* or "to be" of the person—and to the transcendent good which this mediates. This way then is indeed not a kind of seeing, because affectivity and willing are basically not

[22]Thomas Merton, *Mystics and Zen Masters* (New York: Farrar, Straus, 1967) 23, 32.

[23]See Raimundo Panikkar, *The Trinity and the Religious Experience of Man* (Maryknoll, N.Y.: Orbis, 1973). Panikkar sees three major spiritualities present in world religions, "apophatism, personalism and divine immanence" (55), and he relates apophatism primarily to Buddhism. Also see R. C. Zaehner, *Concordant Discord* (Oxford: Clarendon Press, 1970), who writes of three major forms of mysticism: personal love of God, cosmic consciousness, and "mysticism of isolation." He finds the last of these particularly in Buddhism, though differently in different forms of Buddhism (59–60, 106 f.).

a seeing but an impulse. In terms of seeing, it is indeed an emptiness; it is also, in terms of lesser goods, a kind of emptiness insofar as it is a denial of these as the center of the human thrust or the thrust that constitutes the human self at its deepest level.

Now, we recall that, as Panikkar and others contend, the West has developed its interpretation of the Trinity very much within the context of a Logos theology. This was necessary in Christianity's dialogue with Hellenism. But it is no longer sufficient, because for both an appreciation of the positive value of much Eastern religion and for a representation of Christianity that acknowledges this positive value, dialogue with the East must be carried on in the context of the whole mystery of the Trinity and a Trinitarian spirituality that gives greater prominence to the Father and the Spirit. Neither Buddhism nor Hinduism give primary emphasis to the word, but spiritualities centered on Nirvana on the one hand and immanence of divinity on the other have affinities with the Father and the Holy Spirit that remain hidden to a Christian theology too centered on Logos. We are not by this saying that these Eastern religions have proper knowledge of the Trinity. But Christian theology has recognized affinities between aspects of creation and what is proper to each of the three persons of the Trinity, such that it has developed a teaching on "appropriations." That is, it has ascribed by appropriation certain qualities, acts, or perfections to one person because of a special fittingness, without denying these to the other persons. For example, creation is ascribed to the Father since he is the origin of the Triune life, wisdom and form to the Son or Logos, and love and unity to the Holy Spirit.

Panikkar finds an affinity between Buddhism and the Father, because of the apophatism of Buddhism and the Silence associated with the Father from which the Word comes.[24] From what we have indicated above about Buddhism's spirituality, we can largely agree with Panikkar on this, though we

---

[24]See Pannikkar, *Trinity,* 44–50. Also see Ewert Cousins, "The Trinity and World Religions," *Journal of Ecumenical Studies* 7 (1970) 476–495. Using Panikkar's and Zaehner's work, I briefly treat the issue of how Christians can interpret non-Christian mysticisms in "Notes on Mysticism in Today's World," *Spirituality Today* 43 (1991) 104–118.

must recall also that different forms of Buddhist spirituality are contextualized by myth and ritual, prayer and devotion, and folk religion, and thus contain a devotionalism and personal relationship to transcendence. There is perhaps another and even more striking way in which we may appropriate Buddhist spirituality to the First Person of the Trinity. The First Person is the origin of the Trinity (as Father) but also the end or goal of the Triune relations. The Holy Spirit has been understood in classical Christian theology as Love in Person, or a Person who is most properly personal love. The Spirit has been understood to "come" or proceed from the First Person as love comes from the Good, and from the Son as love comes from knowledge of such good, and thus to be the union between Father and Son. In the way that the good evokes love and is its term, the First Person is the goal or fulfillment of the Trinitarian relations. In this relation the First Person is "unnamed"; the name "Father" is his as the origin of the Trinity, not its goal. Nirvana designates the Ultimate not as the origin of all but as the fulfillment, good, and goal of human aspiration and life. And it is in this sense that we find a cerain connection between Buddhist spirituality and union with the unnamed goal of the Trinitarian relations, which is also the goal of our human life and all creation.[25] Specifically with reference to Zen Buddhism, we must note that it tends to immanentize the Ultimate. Here, "to realize the Buddha-nature means to experience the eternal in oneself and at the same time to see it in and through everything else."[26] The difference between Zen and initial Buddhism in this matter is largely due to the fact that Zen came to Japan through China and a Buddhism there that had been influenced by Taoism, and similarly it was influenced in Japan itself by Shinto. Zen Buddhism gives attention to the

---

[25]See Dominique Dubarle, "Buddhist Spirituality and the Christian Understanding of God," in Geffré and Dhavamony, *Buddhism and Christianity,* 70: "Why cannot *nirvanna* itself be a sort of peaceful and silent union with the energy of the divine goodness, nameless and formless, existing as a withdrawal from all things, but never rejecting anyone who comes to it?" We do not even raise the Christian question of the operation of grace in Buddhism and specifically Zen Buddhism. On this, see Dubarle's article.

[26]Zaehner, *Concordant Discord,* 285. See his whole chapter "What is Zen?", 279–301.

beauties of nature and to experiences like the tea ceremony and flower arranging in which it can find an experience of the sacred. Thus it (and religious or quasi-religious experience more generally) has affinities with aesthetic knowledge. In aesthetic experience, as Louis Lavelle writes, one is interested not so much in the outside phenomenon as in "the within of the thing, that is to say, the interior movement which makes it be and of which it is the manifestation, and the within of ourselves by which precisely we try to seize the within of the thing."[27] Thus in acclaiming the beauty of nature, we mean that "in this nature the spirit finds once again a sort of accord with its own essential aspirations which nature anticipates and prefigures."[28] We can both acknowledge great value in what Buddhism has to tell us about the Ultimate and our turn toward it, and claim that it does not so much undermine the Western view of God as help us rediscover dimensions in it that are larger than theology has usually acknowledged.

In conclusion, we may note that Nishitani, who represents for us a reflection on the Ultimate from the perspective of Zen Buddhism, finds that it is appropriate to ascribe the word "person" to God:

When we encounter His (God's) transcendence and omnipresence in . . . an existential way . . . that encounter can be termed a personal relationship between God and man. But it must be in a very different sense from what is usually meant by "personal." . . . This should be considered, so to speak, as an im-"personally" personal relationship, or as a "personally" impersonal relationship. *Persona* in its original meaning is probably close to what we are speaking of now. In Christianity, what is called the Holy Spirit possesses such characteristics. At the same time that it is thought of as one *persona* in the Trinity of "personal" God, it is no other than God's Love itself, the breath of God; a sort of impersonal

[27]Louis Lavelle, *Traité des Valeurs* Tome Second. *Le Système des différentes Valeurs* (Paris: Presses Universitaires de France, 1955) 301.

[28]Ibid., 310.

person or personal imperson, as it were. But if such a point of view be once introduced, not only the Holy Spirit, but also God Himself with this Spirit, and man himself in his "spiritual" relationship with God, can be seen in the same light.[29]

---

[29]Waldenfels, *Absolute Nothingness,* 141–142. Nishitani wrote also: "There is no doubt that the idea of man as a personal being is the highest idea of man which has thus far appeared. The same may be said as regards the idea of God as personal being" (Ibid., 80).

# 8

# God's Relation to the World and History

In this chapter we will reflect, once more in only an introductory way, on God's relation to the world and history. Classical theology acknowledged that God was not only transcendent but also immanent in the world. Thomas, for example, asserted that God is where he acts; and since he acts in all things, he is present in all things by his essence, presence, and power.[1] However, the adequacy of this view has been contested from a number of perspectives in our time. In the first place, the West has been accused of understanding God too much as a transcendent personal being "up there," quite different from the experience of God in other religions, for example in Hinduism. The immanence of God has also been emphasized by some feminists of our time, for they think that the West has viewed God by predominantly masculine symbols and that this has led to an androcentrism and a denial to women of their full human equality in theory and in practice. Second, this classical view, associated as it is with a doctrine of the immutability of God, has been criticized by some who claim that it is opposed to a modern experience of human autonomy and history and to a Christian belief in reciprocity between God and human beings, and that it encourages the status quo in society rather than social change by human beings. And third, the experience of evil in the world has led many to contest a classical view of God's presence in history as providence. In only an in-

---

[1] See Aquinas, *Summa theologica*, I, q. 8.

troductory fashion, we will reflect on (I) God's Immanence in the World: Symbol and Concept, (II) The Reality of God's Relation to History, and (III) The Mystery of Evil.

## I. God's Immanence in the World: Symbol and Concept

In a manner somewhat similar to our dialogue with Buddhism in the preceding chapter, we will here dialogue with some forms of a religious relating to divinity as immanent in the world, particularly as this is found in India. We will recall briefly some religious symbols and explanations of this immanence and ask how such a view is related to our Western understanding of God in Scripture and philosophical theology. Once more, aware of how complex these issues are, we present the following in dependence on experts in this field and as a hypothesis.

Before turning to some examples from India, we should note that symbols of God as immanent in the world and a religious relating to God as immanent seem to be as old as religion itself. In the remains of the Paleolithic age, where men's occupation was primarily hunting and fishing, there is evidence of different ways of imagining divinity. For example, divinity was worshipped and implored as the "Lord of Wild Beasts." And from the time of the last Ice Age feminine representations have been discovered very widely distributed from southwestern France to Siberia. Statuettes discovered in the Ukraine, for example, seem to be related to domestic religion. Six figurines discovered here "are carved summarily, with an abdomen of exaggerated size and a head without features . . . some of them can be interpreted as female forms reduced to geometric elements."[2] In the Neolithic age the development of villages and agriculture show a much more pronounced presence of religious symbols of immanence. There are many myths explaining the origin of food plants as derived from the bodies of gods,

---

[2]Mircea Eliade, *A History of Religious Ideas.* Vol. 1: *From the Stone Age to the Eleusinian Mysteries* (Chicago: Univ. of Chicago Press, 1978) 20. The following section is dependent on Eliade.

in some cases a divine maiden who was murdered. But, as Eliade writes:

> The first, and perhaps the most important, consequence of the discovery of agriculture precipitates a crisis in the values of the Paleolithic hunters: religious relations with the animal world are supplanted by what may be called *the mystical solidarity between man and vegetation*. . . . woman and feminine sacrality are raised to the first rank. . . .
>
> The fertility of the earth is bound up with feminine fecundity; hence women become responsible for the abundance of harvests, for they know the "mystery" of creation. It is a religious mystery, for it governs the origin of life, the food supply, and death. The soil is assimilated to woman. . . . Born of the Earth, man, when he dies, returns to his mother. "Crawl toward the earth, thy mother," the Vedic poet exclaims (Rig Veda 10. 18. 10).[3]

The development of agriculture gave rise to a *cosmic religion* in which religious activity was centered on the mystery of the periodic renewal of the world—a renewal that occurs each year and is celebrated and fostered by religious rites. Statuettes were discovered in Anatolia (c. 7000 B.C.) showing that the principal divinity was the goddess, represented as a young woman, a mother giving birth to a child, and an old crone. Masculine divinity appeared here also, largely as child or lover of the goddess. The heritage of the Paleolithic hunters continued in many areas, but for millenia the goddess was predominant in areas over which agriculture spread.

Sumerian religious texts, going back to the third millenium and representing earlier myths, show in the triad of their great gods and in the triad of planetary gods representations of transcendence and immanence. The first triad seems to have emerged from the goddess Nammu, "the watery mass . . . identified with the original Mother, who, by parthenogenesis, gave birth to the first couple, the Sky (An) and the Earth (Ki), incarnating the male and female principles. This first couple was united, to the point of merging, in the *hieros gamos*. From

[3]Ibid., 40.

their union was born En-lil, the god of the atmosphere."[4] There is also a triad of planetary gods: Nanna-Suen (the Moon), Utu (the Sun), and Inanna (goddess of the planet Venus and of love). The myth associated with Inanna was particularly significant. In this myth Inanna marries a shepherd, Dumuzi, who thus becomes sovereign with her in the city she rules. Inanna, sovereign of the great above, expresses her great joy. But her joy leads to suffering when she decides to go into the underworld, the Land of the Dead, to supplant her elder sister. In the underworld, Inanna is stripped of her power and killed. En-lil sends emissaries to the underworld who revive her, but they are not allowed to bring her out unless she offers a substitute to stay in the underworld. On coming out Inanna finds Dumuzi enjoying his sovereignty and she sends him to the underworld, but in pity on him the goddess of the underworld keeps him there for only half the year and accepts the substitution of his sister for the other half. "The myth relates *the defeat of the goddess of love* and fertility in her attempt to conquer the kingdom of Ereshkigal, that is, *to abolish death.* In consequence, men, as well as certain gods, have to accept the alternation life/death."[5] This mystery, understood after the emergence of agriculture, governed every aspect of life. And it had many parallels in the later ancient Middle East.

Later in Babylon En-lil was supplanted by Marduk, the national god of Babylon who was raised to the rank of a universal divinity. Marduk's preeminence is explained in a myth that recounts his defeat of the earlier gods, and particularly of Tiamat, the primordial goddess of the sea from which all came. While goddesses remained of great importance in the later Middle East, some see in Babylon a beginning of a preeminence of the deity symbolized by the male over the goddesses.[6]

[4]Ibid., 58.

[5]Ibid., 67.

[6]See ibid., 70 f. Also see Gerde Lerner, *Women and History.* Vol. 1. *The Creation of Patriarchy* (New York: Oxford Univ. Press, 1986), and the critical comments on this by Elizabeth Fox-Genovese in *Journal of the American Academy of Religion* 55 (1987) 608–613. Rosemary R. Ruether, in *Sexism and God-Talk. Toward a Feminist Theology* (Boston: Beacon Press, 1983) recalls both Inanna-Dumuzi and the Marduk-Tiamat myths, and concludes that "the concept of gender complementa-

India is an important example of deity honored in its immanence. The Aryan invasion of much of India is manifested in Vedic religion.[7] In this the cult of the gods—such as Varuna, Indra, Soma, and Agni—was prominent. But the Aryan religion overlay the religion earlier prominent in India, which reasserts itself, as shown in some hymns of the Rig-Veda. The gods seem to lose their primacy for a more primordial, immanent principle that is the source of all that is, even the gods:

> Then neither Being nor Not-being was . . .
> That One breathed, windless, by its own energy:
> Nought else existed then. . . .
>
> In the beginning this [One] evolved,
> Became desire, first seed of mind. . . .
> Beneath was energy, above was impulse.
>
> Who knows truly? Who can here declare it?
> Whence it was born, whence is this emanation.
> By the emanation of this the gods
> Only later [came to be].
> Who then knows whence it has arisen?
>
> Whence this emanation has arisen,
> Whether [God] disposed it, or whether he did not—
> Only he who is its overseer in highest heaven knows.
> [He only knows,] or perhaps he does not know.[8]

rity is absent from the ancient myths. The Goddess and God are equivalent, not complementary, images of the divine" (p. 52). Would it be more exact to say, as Eliade seems to imply, that different experiences of the human and of nature were reflected in these different myths, and that part of this difference in experience was that reflected in sexual differentiation between men and women? On "Mother Earth" in the aboriginal American Indian, see J. Baird Callicott's review of Sam Gill, *Mother Earth: An American Story* (Chicago: Univ. of Chicago Press, 1987) in *Religious Studies Review* 15 (1989) 316–319.

[7] In the following I depend in part on Ninian Smart, *The Religious Experience of Mankind* (4th edition, New York: Macmillan, 1991) chapter 4 "The Indian Experience"; and R. C. Zaehner, *Concordant Discord* (Oxford: Clarendon Press, 1970).

[8] *Rig-Veda* 10:129, cited by Zaehner, *Concordant Discord,* 68–69. Also see Ursula King, "The Divine as Mother," in Anne Carr and E. Schüssler Fiorenza, eds., *Motherhood: Experience, Institution, Theology (Concilium,* vol. 206, 1989), who comments on later Hinduism: "A very powerful Indian idea is that of *Shakti,* the primal divine energy always represented as female and without which no male god can act. *Shakti* is the dynamic power which reverberates through the entire universe and

What is central here is that from an initial chaos associated with water there came forth One that breathed, evolved, became desire, and gave rise to the gods and, seemingly, all that is, though the hymn retains the possibility of the existence of an "overseer in highest heaven."

In the Upanishads this mysterious One also seems central. Brahman, that initially signified the sacrifice, came to signify the power immanent in the sacrifice and then the power immanent in the world as the preeminent principle. There are quite diverse interpretations of ultimate reality and religious experience in India—some dualistic, some nondualistic, and some a qualified dualism. The way that Panikkar expresses the teaching of the Upanishads is as follows:

> The central message of the Upanishads interpreted in their fullness . . . is neither monism, nor dualism, nor the theism that is evidenced in some of them, but *advaita,* i.e. the non-dual character of the Real, the impossibility of adding God to the world or *vice versa.* . . . For the Upanishads therefore, the Absolute is not only transcendent but both transcendent and immanent all in one. . . .
>
> The whole *sruti,* the hindu revelation, leads to this point and to this alone: to bring about the realisation that *atman* is *brahman* . . . that only *I* is.[9]

The spiritual or mystical awareness to which religious practices were to lead one was this "cosmic consciousness." It is a consciousness of union with an Absolute that is immanent, and a consciousness in which there is a sense of the dissolving of the individual self into this ultimate Absolute or Self. It is not a sense of *personal* union in which both the individual self and the Absolute retain their identities.

There is a shift later in the Bhagavad-Gita, for what is central in this myth is a devotion to God as personal. But, as Zaehner writes, "In Christianity it is the Transcendent Lord of

makes everything alive. [*Shakti* is] invoked by many names and represented in many different forms" (131).

9Raimundo Panikkar, *The Trinity and the Religious Experience of Man: Icon—Person—Mystery* (Maryknoll, N.Y.: Orbis, 1973) 36–38.

History who becomes man, in the Bhagavad-Gita it is the immanent principle of the universe."[10] Divinity is worshipped in Hinduism under varied personal symbols, particularly those of Shiva and Vishnu. We should mention that one primary symbol in such worship is Kali, "the fearsome destroyer, . . . the Death that destroys death and the Fearsome that destroys fear. But she is also the Divine Mother, the creator and sustainer of life. . . . [T]he Goddess in her various forms embodies the dynamism of the world, both in its creative and destructive forms. . . . [T]he Divine Mother provides the model for a loving relationship between mother and child."[11]

We will not go on to reflect on the classical schools of Hindu philosophy that interpret differently the underlying reality, or the medieval systems of Vedanta that tend either toward non-dualism, modified non-dualism, or dualism in their interpretation of reality and its relation to the Absolute. We have attempted to illustrate some ways in which divinity was found immanent in the world in religions of antiquity and in Hinduism of today.

We could proceed to show in Taoism, Shintoism and animism more generally something similar to the sense of divinity as immanent that we find in central texts of Hinduism.[12] But at this point we ask rather how this sense of divinity relates to what we have so far articulated in this book. In the first place, we can relate this to what is expressed of the experience of the West in Scripture. As we indicated in chapter 3, there was in Israel a conflict with the religion of the Canaanites that overidentified God with nature, particularly in the fertility of fields and flocks.[13] Against this, Israel proclaimed Yahweh, the Lord of history who is transcendent to nature which he brings into existence. In the process of this conflict, it may be that what was legitimate in the experience of God in nature's life

[10]Zaehner, *Concordant Discord*, 150.

[11]John M. Koller, *The Indian Way* (New York: Macmillan, 1982) 239, 241–242.

[12]See, e.g., Zaehner, *Concordant Discord* 214–236 on Taoism, and H. Byron Earhart, *Japanese Religion. Unity and Diversity* (3rd ed., Belmont, Calif.: Wadsworth Publishing Co., 1982), chs. 3 and 4 on Japan's prehistoric heritage and the formation of Shinto.

[13]See above, chapter 3, 78–79, 89.

and creativity was somewhat lost to view. However, we do find in the Jewish Scripture testimonies to such experience. This is apparent, for example, in Israel's ascribing the breath of living things, in which the life was thought to be lodged, to the Spirit of God. Spirit, *ruah,* initially meant breath or the wind that brought water and sirocco (or life and death) to the fields of Israel. And one may see some affinity between this presence of God as Spirit and what the hymn of Rig-Veda quoted above refers to, when it asserts, "That One breathed, windless, by its own energy." Zaehner comments on this passage:

> We are immediately reminded of the opening words of Genesis: "Now the earth was a formless void, there was darkness over the deep, and God's spirit hovered over the water." The symbolism is the same—water and darkness representing chaos, the spirit, the "breathing" One representing emergent life. In Genesis the spirit is God's spirit; in the Rig-Vedic hymn God is the "overseer in highest heaven" who may be responsible for creation or not. . . . [In the Bhagavad-Gita] the immanent and transcendent God will be one: here they appear to be two—the Father, one might almost say, and the Holy Spirit.[14]

In Scripture there is testimony to the experience of God in life, creativity, the emergence of life, and its manifestations. This is at times ascribed to God's Spirit, under the symbols of wind, breath, life, and extensions of these. As distinct from this, Scripture at times ascribes created realties to God's Word that effects his will in nature (e.g., Genesis 1) and history. Both of these testimonies to God's saving presence in the world and in history were later used by Christians in a new context to express their experience and understanding of God as Triune. Without developing the connection here, we note that much that is found in the religious experience of India has affinity with our Christian belief and experience of the Spirit. We can

[14]Zaehner, *Concordant Discord,* 69–70. See Panikkar, *Trinity,* 63: "There is no doubt that hindu thought is especially well prepared to contribute to the elaboration of a deeper theology of the Spirit." Depending on Zaehner and Panikkar, I reflect on this in "Notes on Mysticism in Today's World," *Spirituality Today* 43 (Summer, 1991).

note too that the presence of God as Spirit reflects an influence of God that leads to God being pictured at times as feminine and specifically mother.[15] This was in the course of time subordinated to images of God that were excessively influenced by a patriarchal culture. It is particularly in our time that these riches of our heritage have been brought once more to light. We can say then that in the dominant religion of the West there are experiences of God that can be correlated with experiences of God as immanent in the East, provided that the latter do not include denials of God's transcendence.

How would we relate this conceptually to the way we have critically reflected on bases for belief in God and on God as transcendent personal being (chapters 6 and 7)? In the first place, we recall that we interrelated experience and critical reflection in these earlier chapters. We reflected on the validity of certain religious beliefs in our Western tradition and a Buddhist tradition, and argued that some aspects of these beliefs have critical grounds validating them. In the present context, we note religious experiences and expressions of divinity as immanent in the emergence and creativity found in nature. For many people these point to God not so much as first cause transcendent to the world or ultimate good, but rather as immanently operative in the life and creativity of nature, in its very emergence through stages: not evoking this as the goal or good does, but as present in the deepest human desire or, as it were, the deepest desire and response of nature that brings it to emerge into greater possibilities. Here the experience is of the very dynamism of nature and its agency. The first religious response to this experience is, therefore, not critical evaluation, but rather entrance into this very dynamism to cohere with it—invited to this by a "connatural knowledge" or an experience that has some characteristics of an aesthetic experience that mediates nature's testimony to the divine. On a visit I was privileged to take to Ise, the main Shinto shrine in Japan, I could well understand why the remarkable natural surround-

---

[15]See my chapter, "Feminine Symbols and the Holy Spirit," in *God's Work in a Changing World.* Also see, e.g., Ruether, 55 ff.; Helen Schüngel-Straumann, "God as Mother in Hosea 11," *Theology Digest* 34 (Spring, 1987) 3–8; and Othmar Keel, "Yahweh as Mother Goddess," *Theology Digest* 36 (Fall, 1989) 233–236.

ings of such a shrine could evoke in many men and women an unarticulated religious response, a response also expressed in myth and ritual.

From what we have seen so far in this book, we can conclude that people legitimately experience the divine in the creativity of nature, an experience they express in cosmic myths. Even Thomas asserts that God is where he acts. And, as we sought to show in chapter 6, he acts by causing the actions of created things, e.g., in the process of evolution. What we stressed there was God as efficient cause and God as final cause—as transcendent agent and transcendent good. But to restrict ourselves to these forms of agency would be inadequate. God effects an action of a created agent with it, not only as first efficient cause or ultimate final cause, but also as concurring cause, with the creature responding to the good and to the agency of God operating through the good and environment. Thus God acts not only in what evokes the creature's action, but in and with the creature's response. The creature's spontaneity, creativity, and dynamism are participations in God's spontaneity, creativity, and dynamism. Creatures, and particularly human beings, can be called co-creators with God. Thus the fruitfulness of the creature's act and its resulting emergence toward a new way of being are rightly ascribed to God and not only or even primarily to the creature.[16] People rightly sense that more is operating here than nature, or that the creativity of nature and human beings—e.g., in begetting children, creating works of art, and performing deeds beneficial to many people—gives testimony to their being possessed by a power beyond themselves. Access to this realization is open not primarily to a process of reasoning but to an appreciation of the Sacred. The way we would critically evaluate this is similar to the process we used in chapter 6 in evaluating grounds for faith in God. And since the process by which people discern the divine in the spontaneity and fruitfulness of nature and human beings is more by affective or dispositional identification and appreciation than rational analysis, let this suffice here.

[16]For a classical articulation of participation and God's concurrence with creatures' actions, see Farrelly, *Predestination, Grace and Free Will* (Westminster: Newman Press, 1964) 158 ff., 192 ff.

How does this relate to what we have said of God as transcendent personal being in chapter 7? The main implication of
our present reflections is that what we have said in the previous chapter needs to be supplemented. This is related to certain objections that are being made today by those who say we
have imagined God too much through the lens of the male of
the human species. The agency of a carpenter who builds a
house differs from the agency of a woman who conceives,
bears, and gives birth to a child, and who then nourishes, protects, and raises that child. Many peoples of the world have
found that this latter form of agency and other expressions of
such agency give testimony to God. They understand God and
relate to God as witnessed to by such agency. Thus we must say
that God is witnessed to by diverse agencies operative in the
world of nature and human activity. To use one of these to dis-
count another would distort our understanding of God and our
discernment of where God is present to us.

## II. God's Relation to Change in History

In much of our Western world, as we indicated in the first
chapter, history is understood naturalistically. That is, it is
thought to be solely the creation of human beings and to have
them alone as its goal. This view has been growing since early
modern times and the beginnings of modern science. As one
theologian accounts for this, the notion of process central to
history in modern consciousness involves an understanding of
the "relation of the forms of life to the process of time and of
change"[17] different from that of Aristotle and of medieval theology. For Aristotle there was growth in the individual, but specific forms were changeless. Both antiquity and Christian
thought found in such changeless forms a basis for "natural
law." In early modern science, however, with its "call to useful
knowledge, knowledge that would effect changes in man's life

---

[17]Langdon Gilkey, *Reaping the Whirlwind. A Christian Interpretation of History*
(New York: Seaway, 1976) 188. The experiences of modernity need not lead to
irreligiousness and do not in vast numbers of people, as Andrew Greeley notes in
"Sociology and Theology: Some Methodological Questions", *Proceedings* of the
Catholic Theological Society of America, vol. 32 (1977) 31–54.

for his own welfare,"[18] there was implicit a sense of new possibilities and an open historical future. In this view, forms of life and culture seemed relative to their space and time rather than absolute and normative. There are successive forms in history, and the meaning of this succession came to be interpreted by the theory of progress. The meaning of history, in this view, is "the perfection of the humanum, a concrete, historical community of justice, peace, freedom and communion."[19] Time is the passage toward this.

The development of modern historical consciousness occurred in part through the influence of science upon human life, through the Enlightenment, the French Revolution, and nineteenth-century philosophers such as Hegel and disciples who reacted against him, as we saw in chapter 4.[20] Two of these exemplify naturalistic forms of historical consciousness current today—Karl Marx and John Dewey.[21] These philosophers rejected religion largely because, in their estimation, it was an ideology in defense of the status quo and an obstacle to the transformation of individual and social life in accord with modern experience.

Some theologians in our century have, as we indicated in the second chapter,[22] attempted to rearticulate the Christian understanding of God to do justice to this new sense of our relation to history; and for this purpose they have made use of philosophical analyses of natural and historical processes. Many have been opposed to a classical view of natural law as an implication of belief in God, and have presented substitutes which integrate our human practical life with belief in God. They have frequently proposed their views of God in opposition to classical views of God, such as that of Thomas Aquinas. Process theologians make use of A. N. Whitehead's process

[18]Ibid. 190.

[19]Ibid. 222.

[20]See chapter 4, 151–155.

[21]I reflect briefly on difficulties with human transcendence found in Hegel, Dewey, and Marx in *God's Work*, 176–183. Also see Michael Buckley, "Experience and Culture: A Point of Departure for American Culture," *Theological Studies* 50 (1989) 443–465.

[22]See chapter 2, 57f.

philosophy to present a view of God as really related to the world in process and human creativity (so valued in our non-traditional culture), and as really changing through the impact upon him of values achieved in the process of time. Some German theologians have been influenced by Hegel and have interpreted God's being, primarily through a renewed biblical hermeneutics, as being in becoming, not only within the Trinity but in reference to the world and humanity. E. Jüngel understands God as love, and concludes, in opposition to Rahner and Thomas Aquinas, that "Before all 'self-having,' all 'self-possession,' God is self-communication in the most original form . . . the being of God [is] a Going-Out-Of-Himself into nothingness."[23] And some liberation theologians have found parts of Marx's social analysis of the causes of poverty and the path to change in economic and political structures (e.g., class conflict) helpful, and have rediscovered in the Christian understanding of salvation implications showing God's desire to overcome all that oppresses humanity even in the economic and political orders within history.[24] All of these have reinterpreted God as positively related to changes in nature and history and to our efforts to bring about our historical future. Many base their theologies in large part on the praxis they find in contemporary life, whether secular or Christian, or on reflection on human efforts in our time to change life for the individual or society so that it may be more fulfilling and liberated from the evils that afflict us.

In this context, our reflection will be very modest. We have previously shown in Scripture that God is understood, e.g., by the prophets, to be very much concerned for the history of his chosen people and specifically for justice to the oppressed. Genesis asserts that God initially gave human beings dominion over the world (Gen 1:26-29), and this implies that God gives human beings responsibility to change the world—as co-

[23]E. Jüngel, *God as the Mystery of the World: On the Foundation of the Theology of the Crucified One in the Dispute between Theism and Atheism* (Grand Rapids, Mich.: Eerdmans, 1983) 222–223.

[24]See, e.g., Gustavo Gutierrez, *A Theology of Liberation* (Maryknoll:Orbis, 1973); Rebecca Chopp, *The Praxis of Suffering: An Interpretation of Liberation and Political Theologies* (Maryknoll: Orbis, 1986); and Arthur McGovern, *Liberation Theology and its Critics. Toward an Assessment* (Maryknoll: Orbis, 1989).

302    *God's Relation to the World and History*

creators with God, we may say, but not in opposition to God. We will not repeat this "narrative" theology here. Nor will we deal specifically with God's entry into history through the incarnation, life, death, and resurrection of his Son, Jesus Christ. The order of redemption or the "kingdom of God" belongs to another area of theology (partly to the second part of foundational theology). Yet this order is very relevant to this question, since naturalists such as Marx in a sense immanentized Christian eschatology, seeking the kingdom of God within history and as a purely human achievement. And the only adequate response to such naturalisms is found, as political and liberation theologians of our time rightly point out, in a reinterpretation of Christian eschatology to deal more positively with our concerns for our historical future than much classical theology did: the order of the kingdom of God or redemption is related to the order of creation or history in that it exists for the salvation of human beings who have diverted creation and history from the fulfillment God meant for them.

Scriptural assertions of God's concern for history call us to ask whether our philosophical reflections on human experience can support this. And a study of the meaning of redemption demands not only a scriptural hermeneutics but a study of the intrinsic meaning of nature and history, and the relation of this to God or, rather, God's relation to this. For this we depend on a reflection on the praxis that we analysed in previous chapters in reference to the questions of human conversion and transcendence (chapter 5) and the testimony conscience—in individual and social life—gives to the existence of God (chapter 6). Our agreements with and differences from theologians working out of Whitehead's, Hegel's, or Marx's philosophies are found in our reflections in these earlier chapters.

What we restrict ourselves to in the second part of this chapter are the questions of (1) how God is related to history as this is implied in our previous analysis of the human search for the integral human good in history, and (2) whether and how change is found in God. We seek to give only an introductory answer to these questions; they call for much more treatment than we are giving here. What we present here is incomplete too because it does not deal with God's liberation and redemption of the individual or of history through Jesus Christ, though we say what we do in full acceptance of this larger picture.[25] As we said earlier, theology is inadequate if it simply accepts the revelation God makes to us specifically through Jesus Christ. We cannot claim to accept God's revelation of himself through Jesus Christ if we reject God's lesser revelations of himself, nor is it Christian to use God's greater revelation of himself to deny his less ultimate revelations.

## *1. Some Reflections on God's Relation to Change in History.*

We will reflect both on God's relation to the life of the individual person and his relation to the life of a human community.

"Natural law" and the implications of God's actions in history need not be interpreted within the confines of a pre-modern agricultural society. To reject natural law and to find a norm for moral action in consequences alone or the universalizability of a moral prescription when these are divorced from human nature and the integral human good is, we propose, counter to human fulfillment. We examined earlier the individual's orientation to an integral human good and through this to God, and God's impact on the individual through this good. We argued (chapter 5) that it is normative for the individual to seek such a good, that that good is historically conditioned by the environment of the person, that the individual is oriented to that good only through a series of stages of development proportioned to his or her maturation and an enlarging social environment, and that the individual is oriented to it in a way that depends upon his or her freedom and creativity. The search for the integral human good in this fashion is a search for fulfillment through a historical process. In chapter 6, we found that this experience mediates intimations of God that can be critically validated. Belief in God that this reflection critically justifies is in God as Transcendent Personal Being who calls the person toward fulfillment or draws the person to his or her completion through history.

---

[25]For a brief study of the relation between creation and redemption see *God's Work,* ch. 1, "The Peace of Christ in the Earthly city," 1–33.

Thus a faith commitment to God entails an understanding of God as calling the person to a fulfillment within the context of the integral human good. We may briefly note several implications this has.

First, since God is acting through such a good as is appropriate for the growing person in his or her circumstances and stages of life, this faith entails an understanding of God as calling growing persons to restructure themselves as their human potential develops and as society around them challenges them to new stages of growth appropriate to their human maturation. God is acting here as a lure through the attraction and energy by which this fulfillment motivates the person (I would explain this metaphysically through the part that *esse* plays as actualizing persons in eliciting their actions, as mediating the attraction of the good that is appropriate to them, and as participating in God's goodness and creative, conserving, and concurring action.[26]) Process theologians also stress the lure that God offers in the creature's initial aim and the possibilities derived from God's primordial being. But, perhaps due to their stress on creativity as an ultimate value seemingly divorced from an understanding of the integral human good, they do not sufficiently relate God's lure to a good that specifically constitutes us as human beings. Creativity is destructive of self and of society if it does not serve a genuinely human good, and it is only creativity of this sort that we can say God evokes and faith in God calls us to.

Second, since the person's development toward human fulfillment depends largely on the social environment promoting this growth, our earlier reflections point to God as one who has given caring agents and institutions in the child's life a share in his own creative activity and responsibility in history; and their faith in God entails that they accept their parenthood or other responsibilities as a divine mission and fulfill them faithfully. This calls them at times to change the institutions on which children's development depends (e.g., educational), when these are not furthering their proper purpose, because

---

[26]For a study of this question see Farrelly, *Predestination,* 174 ff.; and Owen Thomas, ed., *God's Activity in the World. The Contemporary Problem* (Chico, Calif.: Scholars Press, 1983).

God seeks to draw persons to fulfillment through this very environment. This also entails that as children become adults and take their place in adult life, they accept their responsibilities for themselves, spouse, family, and society as sharers in God's concern and action in history for the welfare of others as well as for themselves. Far from there being opposition between our creation of history and God's creation of history, God gives human beings responsibility for history.

Third, since the growing person moves toward his or her fulfillment through the mediation of choice or self-creation, particularly as he or she becomes more adult, our faith is in God as one who has called the human person to a life that is free, and thus to be a co-creator with him of who the individual will be. There would be an opposition between God's action here and the individual's freedom if God operated in us through force, but he operates through the attraction of the human good and through the human potential we have that allows us to grow to be free persons and that itself is a gift from God through use of which we grow. In claiming this we share a concern that process theologians have to explain God's relation to human beings in a way that is in accord with their creativity. But we do this in a way that also preserves the human person as an enduring subject—though one who is restructured through his or her own actions.

Of course, both the growing person and caring agents fail and all too often fail seriously in this cooperation with God's creative activity. They subvert human values, so that the more central values are rejected to achieve something more immediate. Such persons are rejecting themselves at a deeper level to support a sense of self at a more superficial level. These rejections harm others in the family and society as well as the subjects themselves. Thus evil—that is, the rejection, not the person—multiplies itself like a cancer or an alien body in the individual, in the family, and in society. It saps many people's trust that God is really operative in their individual lives or in history.

This shows the need of conversion in our lives. The call to conversion can come to individuals in part through their experiences of ultimacy mediated by either positive experiences, such as those of giftedness, unmerited love, the beauty and power of the physical world, joy and trust, or negative experiences, such as sickness, the danger of death, guilt, the inadequacy of the things that "fill" our lives, anxiety, and need for some ultimate norm by which we exercise our freedom. By these experiences we can be disclosed to ourselves at a deeper level and God can be disclosed to us through their limits. By these experiences too, we are invited to live our lives more in the context of their ultimate meaning—more in communion with God and in an orientation to a communion with God, in which the dignity of the person primarily consists. Christians believe that acceptance of such disclosure and the conversions it calls for is possible only through God's special help, traditionally called grace. We have seen something of how these experiences can contribute to human conversion in the case of Thomas Merton, but religious literature provides many examples of this. Gautama Buddha, for example, has shown how the negative experiences of life disclose reality and invite one to turn to the Ultimate. And the religious rites by which peoples of the world have throughout history marked birth, puberty, the coming of spring, and the fruits of the harvest have testified to the fact that positive experiences can turn people to God.

What understanding of God in relation to changes in societies and specifically in states does this belief in God entail? We earlier showed that we are engaged in social life as moral beings and not simply in a naturalistic, pragmatic, and relativistic manner. Major developments in modern history have occurred through the acceptance of the moral context of political life. An instance of this is found in the establishment of the Constitution of the United States, because the form of government thus instituted was one that took as its basic principle the responsibility of government to further the God-given rights of its citizens. Acceptance of the natural law was basic to the writing of the Constitution.[27] It is important that we recall this because many people have believed in God as related only to their personal lives, not those they lead in society, politics, and economic activity. They have privatized religion and Chris-

---

[27]See, e.g., Andrew Reck, "Natural Law and the Constitution," *Review of Metaphysics* 42 (1989) 483–511.

tianity, and this has led to the public arena being guided in large areas by simply pragmatic considerations or by the overriding influence of conflicting interest groups. We used a phenomenology of the acknowledgement of human rights in the civil rights movement in the United States to show both that human transcendence includes the social dimension and that the impact of Ultimate Value, or God, upon our lives is present in our social lives as well as in our individual lives. Human beings are by their very nature social beings, whose fulfillment in part consists in their promotion of the welfare of others and of a society that furthers the welfare of all within it. Moreover, our fulfillment depends not simply on our own virtue but on the impact of social structures on us. Thus our adult responsibilities call us to seek change in political, economic, social, and cultural structures when these inflict injustice on people, particularly the poor and others who are not able to defend themselves. And God is as operative in calling us to action in this area of life as he is in calling us to action in our individual lives.

Faith in God on the bases we have presented as justifying this belief entails an understanding of God as calling for those initiatives and institutions that are necessary for human fulfillment. Thus, since civil societies are necessary for human fulfillment, they have not only human beings as their source but God himself, who both gives us being and orients us to what is necessary for the fulfillment of this being. God works in the community in a way analogous to the way he works in the individual. He calls a community through what is demanded of it for the common good. The exigency that such a good has for a human community is a moral exigency and thus it is not only a pragmatic value but a good sanctioned by God. The lure it constitutes is a participation in the lure God exercises in human affairs. God is operative in the call to change that the common good of our societies demands if human rights are to be respected. On those who have special responsibility for a political community through their engagement in public office, God places a moral responsibility to act beyond their individual interests or those of a special group for the good of the community as a whole. As agents of the formation and guidance of the political community toward what is necessary for it, they are called to cooperate with God, who operates here by what has classically been called divine providence and divine govern-ance.[28] He has given the future of the human community into human hands, but not in a way that makes them totally auton-omous. He rather calls them to be co-creators of history with himself.

Also, through changing conditions it often happens that there must be changes in the policies and structures of the state—and of the economy, the culture, and social relation-ships—if the common good is to be furthered, for the existing structures were, at best, originally established for other condi-tions and would be ineffective unless modified to accord with new circumstances. Thus God calls societies and states to change as the common good calls for these changes. When these social structures inflict injustice on people, as they did on the blacks in the United States or as they do on the poor of the world, particularly the extremely poor in the southern hemisphere, to the extent of killing them or stunting their physical and personal development and depriving them of a life in accord with human dignity, it is the responsibility of all to seek changes in these structures to rectify these injustices. Priority should be given to correcting the worst evils in society. In other words, there should be a preferential love for the poor and oppressed.

Among these changes, when the welfare of one state depends in part on its relationships with other states, it is a moral exi-gency and thus an exigency from God that these relationships be established. And if because of closer communication and mutual dependence among the states of the world their welfare calls them to establish interrelationships among all countries of the world, whether in reference to some particular issues (e.g., an international economic order) or in more general terms, this too is a moral exigency and thus a call from God in these changed conditions.

Thus God calls for changes in history, but he does not bring about these changes save through the agency of human beings. Faith in God is not fully genuine if it is viewed as entailing only a private relationship with God or with one's immediate

---

[28]For a study of God's providence see Farrelly, *Predestination*, 277–289.

neighbors. It entails as well the need to work for the establishment and change of social institutions—political, economic, and cultural—in a way that progressively recognizes more adequately the dignity of the human persons within them and furthers their human development, particularly that of the poor and oppressed. This is radically different from a collectivism that sacrifices individuals with their God-given dignity and rights to the whole, and from a society in which individuals commit themselves to the common welfare only insofar as it serves their private interests.

We believe then in a God who calls for those changes that are necessary to assure human dignity for all. As an example of what this implies about God as Transcendent Personal Being engaged in history to promote human fulfillment, we can recall the six principles based on the dignity of the human person that were affirmed by the Catholic bishops of the United States in their *Pastoral Message: Economic Justice for All.* We quote from their summary of this document without giving the intermediate analyses that justify these specific principles:

> Every economic decision and institution must be judged in light of whether it protects or undermines the dignity of the human person.
>
> Human dignity can be realized and protected only in community.
>
> All people have a right to participate in the economic life of society.
>
> All members of society have a special obligation to the poor and vulnerable.
>
> Human rights are the minimum conditions for life in community. . . . This means that when people are without a chance to earn a living, and must go hungry and homeless, they are being denied basic rights. Society must ensure that these rights are respected.
>
> Society as a whole, acting through public and private institu-

tions, has the moral responsibility to enhance human dignity and protect human rights.[29]

This interpretation of the implications of belief in God is of course opposed in part to interpretations of religion given by naturalisms of both the capitalist and the Marxist varieties.[30] But it also differs in part from a view of God proffered by some recent theologies. For example, it differs from some fundamentalist and evangelical political theologies that do not give sufficient attention to analysis of the human good as this can be discerned by all people of good will without dependence on specifically Christian revelation. It is neither practically helpful or intellectually possible to understand how God operates in history by the use of Scripture alone. We have been defending the view that God reveals something of his will, or the good he seeks to lead us to, through what it means to be a human person and a human community in our changing world. Our view also differs in part from some political theologies that may be called more "dispositional" than normative in the sense that they understand God as calling for certain dispositions in men and women engaged in political activity but do not sufficiently analyze the norms that derive from the common good of society.[31] It differs in part from the understanding of God found in political theories excessively marked by an individualist view of the human person—a widespread phenom-

---

[29]*Economic Justice for All. Pastoral Letter on Catholic Social Teaching and the U.S. Economy* (National Conference of Catholic Bishops, Washington, D.C., 1986), "A Pastoral Message: Economic Justice for All," 13–18, pp. ix–xi.

[30]The approach we have been taking is in accord with the social teaching of the Catholic Church. See Joseph Gremillion, ed., *The Gospel of Peace and Justice. Catholic Social Teaching Since Pope John* (Maryknoll: Orbis, 1976), and John Paul II, *On Social Concern.* Encyclical letter (Dec. 30, 1987) (Washington, D.C.: U.S. Catholic Conference, 1988).

[31]See Dennis P. McCann, *Christian Realism and Liberation Theology. Practical Theologies in Conflict* (Maryknoll: Orbis, 1981), who characterizes Reinhold Niebuhr's practical theology as a "dispositional ethic" (127).

In a somewhat parallel manner, our treatment differs in part from that of J. Habermas who seeks to critically evaluate and promote society's maintenance of the social-cultural life world, but does this on procedural criteria of communicative rationality (as distinct from technical rationality) rather than on the basis of metaphysics or religion. We basically affirm much that he states, but also think that more is needed.

enon in the United States—or that do not recognize human rights that are proper to persons and the correlative duties of others and of the political community itself to respect these rights. And it differs from any political theology that would embrace the Marxist view that the dynamism of history is class struggle or that the overriding goal of history is achieved by establishing a justice of equality in the economic order, to the neglect of human freedom. Freedom too is a human value, and thus the common good as a whole constitutes a moral exigency and an invitation and action of God in history; subversion of other human values to those of the economic order is counter to rather than in accord with God's action to bring about justice in human communities and history. Liberation theologians in general cannot be accused of this distortion, though some people engaged in defense of the poor can be understandably tempted to this position by the enormity of the injustice wealthy individuals and countries inflict on the poor.

We conclude by saying that as a Christian community, we celebrate God's concern for us and the least of our brothers and sisters in history through the proclamation of Scripture, liturgy, prayer, and communal reflection among believers. But we do not derive our awareness of God's action in history wholly from Scripture; an analysis of the moral character of individual and communal human life manifests this to us. Through this we see that God calls human beings to be agents in history, but that this role is not wholly autonomous, for there is a moral good that God calls these agents to respect, and this moral good depends upon what genuinely promotes human well-being individually and communally. In this sense, we may say that this position interprets our relation to God neither as autonomous nor as heteronomous but, to use Tillich's term, as theonomous.

This analysis may seem overly optimistic or idealistic. But we want to note that it points to some areas in which God is positively acting in history and calls human beings to act in history. We fully acknowledge the all too frequent failures of political communities in our time—as well as in past times—to act in accord with the moral order and thus with God's direction. For example, economic individualism has been rampant in the United States in recent years in such instances as the short-term horizons of leaders in business and government, and has contributed to the worsening economic condition of the country and a greater income disparity between the rich and the poor. And in Eastern Europe and the Soviet Union, the long-term repression of individual initiative and freedom has borne fruit in massive destruction of human life and growth and in stagnant economies in the presence of abundant natural and human resources, and more recently in widespread repudiation of Marxism. The next part of foundational theology reflects critically on the Christian belief that it is only through Jesus Christ that salvation comes to humankind in its straits. But the fulfillment and liberation that God gives us through Jesus Christ must be related to what seems central to our present sense of foreboding and anxiety—namely, that the future of our individual and communal history is in our hands, and that through our decisions we may well destroy this future. What we have said so far supports a degree of transcendence in our individual and communal life so that its horizon is not restrictedly secular. And what we shall reflect on in the next part will support the view that God through the kingdom mediated by Jesus offers a fulfillment and liberation relevant both to the ultimate and to the earthly future of the human person and the human community. This offers us communion with God and with one another, to be fully achieved in a life beyond this one, but already operative here to transform us in history.

## 2. God's Real Relation to Human Beings, and Change in God.

If we grant that God created a changing world and acts in it, the question arises whether God is affected by changes in the world so that he himself changes. We have shown earlier that Scripture seems to uphold both change in God's relation with human beings and total perfection in God so that human beings can neither add to his perfection nor detract from it. Scripture proclaims God as personal. For example, God freely chooses one people with whom he enters a covenant to which he attaches moral requirements, and his reaction to his people depends on their response to his initiatives. As one author writes: "Through anthropomorphic description the living personality of Yahweh is constantly emphasized. . . . The election of Israel, the formation of the covenant, and the saving acts by which Yahweh made Israel a people are acts of favor arising from personal benevolence. . . . The response of Yahweh to love or to disobedience is a personal response of love or anger."[32] God is deeply involved with his people, and his people's response makes a difference to him. Yet Scripture forcefully expresses the transcendence of God: "Behold, the nations count as a drop of the bucket, as dust on the scales; the coastlands weigh no more than powder. Lebanon would not suffice for fuel, nor its animals be enough for holocausts. Before him all the nations are as nought, as nothing and void he accounts them" (Isa 40:15-17). God is so transcendent that nothing can diminish his life, even sin: "Though I have sinned, what can I do to you, O watcher of men?" (Job 7:20; see 35:6). Neither can anything increase his life—not human justice, purity, fasting, or sacrifice (see Job 35:7; 22:2f.; Zech 7:5; Isa 1:11f.). James writes of "the Father of lights, with whom there is no alteration or shadow caused by change" (Jas 1:17); yet God seems to change his disposition toward people in answer to their prayers and to rejoice at the good and be saddened and angry at his people's opposition to him.

When the Christian message was preached in the Hellenistic world, it met a culture that in its philosophy, particularly in Middle Platonism, stressed the immutability of God, because it associated any change with loss or gain of perfection— impossible in an all-perfect being. There was a tension between expressing the transcendence of God in Christian and in philosophical terms. Tertullian manifested this tension. He argued that immutability is a property of eternity and so of God: "what is eternal does not change; obviously it would lose what it had been by becoming what it was not."[33] But Tertullian also ascribed change to God. For God to be wholly good, he must

[32]John L. McKenzie, "Aspects of Old Testament Thought," *JBC* II, 740.

[33]Tertullian, *Adversus Hermogenem,* 12, 3, trans. H. H. Waszink, *Ancient Christian Writers,* vol. 24 (Westminster, Md.: Newman, 1956) 42. Also see for a history of the question of change in God, Thomas Weinandy, *Does God Change? The Word's Becoming in the Incarnation* (Still River, Mass.: St. Bede's Publications, 1985).

be able to condemn evil; if he is not able to condemn he is not able to be responsive to different situations in history. As Joseph Hallman summarizes a part of Tertullian's argument: "We have seen two instances of divine mutability in Tertullian, and they are related. Although God is eternally good and just, He becomes a judge vis à vis human sinfulness; and He begins to feel the emotions of a judge, such as offense and anger. Essentially, however, because He is eternal, He cannot become less or more, or in any basic sense be affected by time."[34] There is a tension in Tertullian between his view of God as personal and deeply involved in salvific history and his view of God as supremely perfect.

In Augustine we do not experience the same tension as we do in Tertullian, because the weight of his emphasis is more on the immutability of God. This is in part due to the influence of Neoplatonism in Augustine's thought, though his thought cannot be equated with that of the Neoplatonists. Pelikan writes in reference to this:

> When he came to speak of the divine essence, it was usually defined in relation to absoluteness and impassibility rather than on the basis of the active involvement of God in creation and redemption. Biblical language that spoke about this involvement, as, for example, Exodus 20:5, "I the Lord your God am a jealous God," was an analogy and an accommodation to the childish understanding of men; "but Scripture rarely uses terms which are spoken unmetaphorically (*proprie*) about God and which are not found in any creature" (*De Trin.* 1.1,2) . . . [Augustine's constant refrain was that] "he who is God is the only unchangeable substance or essence, to whom certainly being itself (*ipsum esse*), from which the noun 'essence' comes, most especially and truly belongs" (*De Trin.* 5,2,3). . . . Neoplatonic elements were unmistakably present in this definition, but in setting it forth Augustine believed himself to be—and he was—expressing the catholic creed.[35]

[34]Joseph Hallman, "The Mutability of God: Tertullian to Lactantius," *Theological Studies* 42 (1981) 379.

[35]Jaroslav Pelikan, *The Christian Tradition.* Vol. 1. *The Emergence of the Catholic Tradition (100–600)* (Chicago: Univ. of Chicago, 1971) 196–197.

Thomas similarly stressed the immutability of God, and that for three reasons. In the first place, God is pure act without the admixture of any potentiality, but whatever changes is in potency in some way—toward gaining what it does not now have or losing what it does now have. Second, everything that changes is composed of parts, because while it changes there is something in which it remains the same and something in which it changes. But God is completely simple, without composition. And third, everything that changes gains something by its change and reaches or extends itself to something to which it had not previously extended itself. But God as infinite "including in himself the full plenitude of the perfection of the whole of being cannot acquire anything or extend himself to something to which he had not earlier reached,"[36] and so cannot change. Also, while Thomas asserted that the relations that creatures have to God are real, he held that those which God has toward creatures are "relations of reason" and not real, for "God is outside the whole order of creation, and all creatures are ordained toward him, but the converse is not true."[37] It seems that this denial that God has a real relation to creatures has a technical meaning for Thomas, since he also affirms that "God is really Lord and not according to reason alone."[38]

Many theologians and philosophers over the last few centuries have contested the adequacy of this language to express the Christian mystery.[39] Unfortunately, many of them, like Hegel and Whitehead, end up making God essentially dependent upon creation and increasing in perfection through it; and thus they express God's intimacy with the world at the expense of his transcendence. But the problem remains and is gaining more and more attention, due in large part to the persistent attacks by theologians influenced by Whitehead and Hegel on Thomistic theology in this matter. Christians, and not only Christians, believe that there is mutuality between God and us

[36]*ST* I, 9, 1.

[37]*ST* I, 13, 7.

[38]*ST* I, 13, 7, ad 5.

[39]For surveys of kenotic theology and other recent questioning of the immutability of God, see Weinandy, 101 ff., and Walter Kasper, *The God of Jesus Christ* (New York: Crossroad, 1984) 189 ff.

as human beings, that God is intimately involved in our lives and concerned for us, and that our lives make a difference to God. We must acknowledge that if our theological expression defends God as the Absolute in such a way that it weakens emphasis on his love, then this theology distorts our understanding of the Christian God. Some modification of Thomistic language and philosophical theology is necessary here. We are, however, not giving a full treatment of this issue, since this is simply an introductory treatment and we are not dealing with the question of Jesus Christ's suffering and death, the ultimate expression of God's love and concern for us.

Our use of philosophy here is within a Christian tradition. Does philosophy demand that we deny change in God, or does it wrongly associate change and loss or gain of perfection so that we cannot ascribe it to God? Part of our answer to this question will come in our next chapter where we will examine religious language. Our primary religious language seems to be symbolic; and thus part of the problem we find with Thomas' philosophical and theological language may be due to its objective, intellectual character. On the other hand, to point out the variety of religious languages is not a sufficient answer, because that leaves unanswered the question whether scriptural language about God changing is used properly of God or improperly. In our understanding of God we give primacy to Scripture and Christian experience (e.g., in prayer). Because both of these seem to imply God's involvement in human concerns, we ask whether we can properly ascribe change to God in a way consistent with his transcendence. I write hesitantly about this, but somewhat less hesitantly because of recent writings of Catholic theologians and philosophers who do ascribe change to God (e.g., Jean Galot and W. Norris Clarke).[40]

What is central to an answer here is that our paradigm for understanding God is transcendent *personal* being, as we indi-

---

[40]See particularly W. Norris Clarke, *The Philosophical Approach to God. A Neo-Thomist Perspective* (Winston-Salem, N.C.: Wake Forest Univ. 1979), ch. 3, "Christian Theism and Whiteheadian Process Philosophy: Are They Compatible?," 66–109. Also see W. Hill, "Does the World Make a Difference to God?" *The Thomist* 38 (1974) 146–164; and J. H. Wright, "Divine Knowledge and Human Freedom: The God Who Dialogues," *Theological Studies* 38 (1977) 450–477, and "The Method of Process Theology: An Evaluation," *Communio* 6 (1980) 39–55.

cated in the last chapter. In creating and interacting with his creatures, particularly with personal beings, God's action involves his intelligence and his freedom. Thus this action should be referred to God as personal more directly than to God's nature, for it is the agent who acts, knows and chooses, not the nature; the agent acts through his nature. Through God's action, then, creatures are intentional objects of his knowledge and freely given love. Thus we should say that God has a personal relation to these creatures, particularly human beings. Moreover, this relation is real, not in the sense of it being a transcendental relation whereby God is essentially oriented to creatures, nor a predicamental relation whereby something is added to or detracted from the divine being, but rather in the sense that God freely orients his intentional consciousness to objects and persons he would not have been oriented to if he had not created them and did not interact with them. A clarification of the notion of the freedom of God's creative activity brings this out. God's freedom in creating means not only that he could create or not as he wished. On analogy with the distinction between a free person and a slave, it means too that God's action comes from inner desire and choice rather than from external coercion. God's freedom in creation points to the fact that he brings us into being and interacts with us out of a full inner desire or love. The source of God's real relation to us is God's own choice and love.

God really adopts an attitude of love toward us to such an extent that we make a difference to him. God's knowledge and love or his personal intentionality bear upon subjects he would not have known or loved if he had not created. He is in a sense distinct from himself considered as not creating, distinct in virtue of the personal relations he now has. Does this mean then that there is change in God through his relationships with us—through, for example, his knowing our free acts and through his call to us and response to us in accord with our response to him? After all, since men and women are free, God has not determined everything from eternity, as a play written before it is acted out.

Traditional theology has given an explanation of God's knowledge of our free acts that leaves this freedom intact and yet is consistent with God's immutability.[41] God knows our acts by a kind of causal knowledge, as an artist knows his creations. Thus God knows our free acts through his evoking them and in accord with the manner of his evoking them. He evokes them as first cause through the good to which he calls us, and he does so through our genuinely free cooperation with him or our rejection of his call. Thus he knows them in a way that is not independent of what the creature freely chooses to do. However, God's knowledge is related to free human acts differently than ours is. We are within the order of time in which there are past, present, and future, interrelated to one another. We can be said to foreknow future free acts; but since they are free, our knowledge cannot be certain. But God's knowledge is not in the order of time, and thus is not related to a free act which is future to us by a relationship that can properly be called foreknowledge. God's mode of duration, eternity, is related to history in the sense that God in one act (*tota simul perfecta possessio vitae*) is present to all acts in history, somewhat as Thomas taught that the human soul is present to all the parts of the body. Thus God knows free acts in time both in virtue of his causal influence and the causal influence of the free person, and in virtue of his presence to all creatures by the "now" not of time but of eternity. God knows free acts which are future to us as present, not future, to him. Similarly, it was said that in his interaction with free creatures, God does not really change his will if we change our dispositions, so that he would want one thing and then another. Rather, in the same act of his divine will he wants one thing after another. For example, by the same divine act of will, God wills that grace be offered to us and that on our acceptance we grow and on our rejection of it we lose a dimension of his grace.

We are not contesting here the adequacy of this account of God's knowledge of free human acts in time. But we are suggesting that neither of the two basic reasons why traditional theology did not ascribe change to God—the view that God is totally perfect in a way that can be neither increased nor diminished, and the view that God is totally simple and change

---

[41]This is treated in Farrelly, *Predestination,* 243–270, and articles referred to in the preceding note.

involves multiplicity—seems conclusive. First, it would seem that God's intentional consciousness, such as his knowledge of free acts and his interaction with free agents in love, can change without this implying that God's perfection is increased or diminished. Previously, we noted that by creation itself there are more who are or have being, but there is not a qualitatively greater degree of being, since God's being is infinite. Similarly, through creation God knows, loves, and rejoices in beings he would not otherwise have known, loved, or rejoiced in. But they do not bring God to a higher degree of perfection in knowledge, love, or joy. Moreover, we have been speaking of a *relationship* God has to these creatures and, in particular, human beings. To predicate a relationship is not of itself to predicate a perfection to a being, for a relationship is a reference to another rather than—directly—a perfection in the being. To take an example here from theology, God the Father is said to have a relationship to the Son that is distinct from that which the Son has to the Father, but one does not have a *perfection* that the other does not. Thus God can change in his relationships with us so that we make a difference to him, without this increasing or diminishing his perfection. The traditional view acknowledged that the modality of God's relationship to the rational creature was changed by whether the human person accepted his grace or did not. There is not much difference, if any, in saying that God's relationship changes.

  Neither does the above view seem to deny the divine simplicity. While Thomas ascribed absolute simplicity to the divine nature, he, along with the whole of the Christian tradition, acknowledged a real distinction of persons in God. This distinction was compatible with the simplicity of the divine being since the distinction was in the order of the relation the Father had to the Son and both had to the Holy Spirit, not in the order of being. Similarly, the kind of "multiplicity" that we are acknowledging to exist in God is not in the divine being but rather in the order of personal relations God has to finite selves or creatures more widely, or in the order of intentional consciousness. Thomas acknowledged that there is a kind of change that does not involve potency, namely that by which the intellect derives conclusions from its knowledge of premises and we by our will move toward means in virtue of our desire of an end or goal.[42] God can have the complexity that is appropriate to him as personal being who truly loves and knows and interacts with a multiplicity of changing creatures, without this involving potency or imperfection. In fact, it is distinctive of God to be related to all creatures rather than a few. It seems to us that we are called to acknowledge this by Christian faith and a broader religious consciousness that ascribes mutual relations of love between God and created persons. God can receive love from human beings as well as give it; counter to Aristotle, there can be friendship between God and human beings.

Someone may argue against the above that it makes a division between the divine being and the divine intentional consciousness that traditional theology does not. Thomas, for example, denies a distinction between act and being in God; God's knowledge and love are his being (*ipsum esse*). And it is because of this lack of division that he denies change and multiplicity in God. In answer to this, we must note that our prime analogue for God must be person rather than being, and we must interpret "being itself" or pure act in accord with this. Human beings become fulfilled persons, perfected persons, only by passage through the stages of life in a way that results in the person acting from a far deeper agency than the infant and child do. But God, as pure act or being itself, does not go through such stages to reach the fullness of his possibilities; he is the fullness of personal agency and action or operation from the beginning. In fact, Christians believe that God has a full personal life in the Trinity. Far from there being a division between being and consciousness in God, his being should rather be understood as the infinite fullness of personal love and knowledge and thus consciousness. We make a distinction between God's love of himself and his love of creation, ascribing a freedom and non-necessity to the latter that we do not to the former. It is in reference to this free, loving, personal relation to creatures and particularly to human beings that we affirm that God has real relations to us, relations that make a difference to him, that are multiple, and that change. Philosophy has

---

[42]See *ST* I–II, 9, 3, and Farrelly, *Predestination,* 180–183 and 187–191 on Thomas' analysis of acts of the human intellect and will as *actus perfecti.*

no reason to reduce to an improper analogy the basic thrust of Scripture in ascribing such relationships to God.

We have to acknowledge that it is largely through the persistent critiques by disciples of Hegel and Whitehead against Scholastic theology that such modifications of traditional language about God and theological understanding of God have been incorporated into more and more Catholic theological and philosophical writing. But process thought itself needs serious modifications if it is to do justice to the personal, infinite, and freely loving God who exercises a causal influence in the creation and salvation of humankind.[43]

## III. The Mystery of Evil

Many would say that an awareness of the massiveness of evil in our world is the greatest challenge to belief in God. Looking at the number of people killed in this century in wars, concentration camps, the Holocaust, genocide in such places as Cambodia, terrorist attacks, natural disasters, the many diseases and malnutrition that ravage the world, particularly the poor, and innumerable senseless accidents, it is difficult for many people to think that God is active in history. If one adds to this the number of people in our world suffering from injustices because of distorted political and economic systems, broken families, etc., an assertion of God's care for humankind may seem a mockery. Thus we must address this question of evil and what implications it has for belief in God. We do so briefly, because the whole of theology addresses this from different perspectives. Our present treatment then is incomplete. Specifically, Christians believe that there is no adequate answer to the question of suffering and evil save in the death and resurrection of Jesus, which are treated in the next section of foundational theology. And a theological or philosophical re-

---

[43]For critiques of Whitehead on the basis that his philosophy does not do justice to God as enduring and acting personal subject, see above, chapter 7, part I; Thomas Tracy, *God, Action, and Embodiment;* and Frank Kirkpatrick, "Process or Agent: Models for Self and God," *Thought* 48 (1973) 33–60.

sponse to the mystery of evil is inevitably incomplete, since there is no adequate response to it save in life itself.

Our basic answer to the experience of evil, whether the evils that afflict the individual or those that afflict the larger society is that this is a call for conversion to belief or further conversion. We have already seen this in the case of Thomas Merton, Dorothy Day, and other converts of our century, and we reflected on aspects of it when we discussed Buddhism's approach to the Ultimate and what we can learn from it. We argued that the human person is one who through stages of human change is oriented toward a good that transcends the world and what it offers, namely God. This good is incommensurable with the goods that one loses in the process of this pilgrimage. In spite of the suffering it entails, an experience of the contingency and uncertainty of the goods of this life gives a "limit experience" without which most, perhaps, would not turn either to God or to their own deeper selves. Buddhism and Christianity agree in large part on this understanding of human beings. In the pages that follow, we shall reflect on aspects of such conversion or continuing conversion, namely on it as intellectually responsible, as entailing action to change the world, and on the legitimacy and place of lament. In reference to this latter theme we shall raise the question of whether God himself suffers.

It is not only our own age that has experienced a discrepancy between belief in God and his care for us on the one hand and the experience of evil on the other. This sense of discrepancy has been present since the beginning of religious history, and there have been many answers given to it in the course of history. Paul Ricoeur recalls some of these reflections on suffering and guilt. There were levels of discourse on evil antecedent to theodicies. Myth incorporated the dark and luminous sides of the human condition and placed "our fragmentary experience of evil into those great narratives of origin, as Mircea Eliade has emphasized throughout his many works on the topic."[44] There was a profusion of these explanatory schemes; no con-

---

[44]See Paul Ricoeur, "Evil, A Challenge to Philosophy and Theology," *Journal of the American Academy of Religion* 53 (1985) 637. Page references in the following paragraphs are to this article, on which I particularly depend for what follows.

ceivable solution to the order of the universe and the enigma of evil seems to have been overlooked. Constantly new answers were essayed to the question, "From whence comes evil?"[45] The story of Adam and the Fall was important in the reflection of Israel as a partial explanation of how the goodness of God and the evils human beings suffer can be thought of together. This form of discourse, however, did not sufficiently answer the expectations of acting and suffering human beings, for it did not answer such questions as, "How long?" and, "Why me?" Wisdom literature called upon God, in long human laments, to account for suffering. Much of this literature gave the explanation of retribution; but the response in the Book of Job is that God's designs are unfathomable and thus the answer must be deferred to the eschaton, or the human question is displaced as inappropriate, or the experience of suffering is interpreted as purificatory. In a very different vein, the Gnostics later explained evil by a kind of gigantomachy "where the forces of good are engaged in a merciless struggle with the armies of evil, in order to bring about a final deliverance of all the particles of light held captive by the shadows of evil" (639).

The anti-Gnostic views of Augustine have influenced the West enormously. In the first place, Augustine used philosophical categories to show that evil was not a substance but a lack of being, and that the very deficiency characteristic of the creature makes sin a possibility and probability. (This combination of ontology and theology is considered by Ricoeur to be an onto-theo-logy that has now been disqualified by Heidegger's work. Since, however, we have earlier in this book critically justified metaphysical knowledge as a legitimate articulation of our knowledge of being, we do not find this aspect of Augstine's work invalid.[46]) Second, Augustine shifted the problem of evil to that of free will, so that evil as a privation of being came to be through sin. This has the result of moralizing the answer to the problem of evil, so that all evil is either sin or punishment, and this was extended to the whole of history by

---

[45]See P. Ricoeur's treatment of this in *The Symbolism of Evil* (New York: 1967).

[46]See above, chapter 6, part I. Also see *God's Work,* 194–200, for an evaluation of Heidegger's understanding of being.

Augustine's teaching on original sin. It does take up the enigma of evil as already present before our free decision; but, in Ricoeur's view, with which we in part concur, it explains it "within the false clarity of an apparently rational explanation" (640) in a rationalized myth, and it "leaves unanswered the protest of unjust suffering, by condemning it to silence in the name of a massive indictment of the whole of humanity" (640).

We can speak of a stage of reflection as theodicy when the goal is clearly apologetic, when the principle of coherence and the focus on the totality of reality are present, and when the propositions used are intended in a univocal sense (e.g., God is all-powerful). This is found above all in Leibniz who justified evil by God's opting for the best of possible worlds and the fact that evil can contribute to this. Here too, "it is the lament, the complaint of the suffering righteous persons or people that overthrows the notion of a compensation for evil by good" (641).

Also, we can note a mode of thought used in reference to the problem of evil that can be called dialectical. Hegel is one example of this. For him, on every level the positive is negated by its opposite, and both are sublated by a new synthesis. The cunning of history brings it about that all conflict in this process is reconciled. However, Hegel's system contains intellectual hubris since he extends this scheme beyond the human to include God; and, once more, the lament of those who suffer unjustly is marginalized and excluded. Another form of dialectic, here a "broken dialectic," is found in Karl Barth. Barth sees in evil "a nothingness hostile to God, not just a nothingness of deficiency and privation, but one of corruption and destruction" (643). This viewpoint gives voice to the cry of lament on the part of suffering humanity, and we are called to confess that Christ has conquered nothingness by "'nihilating' himself on the Cross"; God has fought nothingness in Jesus Christ. This Christological turn has much to commend it, but one difficulty with Barth's viewpoint is that he "relates the reality of nothingness to the 'left hand of God,' the one which rejects when the right hand elects: 'As God is Lord on the left hand as well, He is the basis and Lord of nothingness too'" (644). Is this ascribing evil to God? If so, it is a failed dialectic.

The intellectual dimension of the response to the mystery of evil continues to be important. We must note that it does not make more sense of evil to deny the existence of God. Previous attempts to explain how evil and the goodness and omnipotence of God can be thought together continue to have value, even if we must reject in part Augustine's and others' explanation of the sufferings of the innocent.[47] If God creates, he does create beings that are limited. If he creates human beings with freedom, then there is the possibility and probability that they will use this to oppose God in his desire for what genuinely promotes human fulfillment. This is relevant to a philosophical and theological theodicy for which we still have need. One very important implication is that the major disasters of our century, such as war and genocide, have come from human beings' rejection of God's guidance toward the moral good, and particularly toward respect for the dignity of the human person. The widespread modern claim to total autonomy and a naturalistic historical consciousness have led to attempts to establish a "final solution" to the problems of history within history,[48] an idolatry of history itself, the disastrous consequences of which show its falsity more effectively than any apologetic could.

One may rightly say that this does not answer the problem of the suffering of the innocent. This difficulty is exacerbated in our time of rampant individualism, when people are not as aware as in earlier cultures that they are members of a community. Such membership means that they not only benefit from the good things that happen to a community, but suffer from the evil that afflicts a community, at times as a result of what we must call communal sin rather than the personal sins of all

[47]For a treatment of Augustine's approach to the question of evil see Farrelly, *Predestination,* 79–96. For a brief contemporary study of the question of original sin, see G. Vandervelde, *Original Sin: Two Major Trends in Contemporary Roman Catholic Reinterpretation* (Amsterdam: Rodopi N.V., 1975), and a review article I wrote on it in *The Thomist* 43 (1979) 482–488. For a collection of patristic passages on the question of evil, see James Walsh and P.G. Walsh, eds., *Divine Providence and Human Suffering (Message of the Fathers of the Church.* Vol. 17. (Wilmington, Del.: Glazier, 1985).

[48]See Karl Löwith, *Meaning in History* (Chicago: Univ. of Chicago, 1949) 159. Also see John Pawlikowski, "Christian Ethics and the Holocaust: A Dialogue with Post-Auschwitz Judaism," *Theological Studies* 49 (1988) 649–699.

the members. This is not to say that the individual is sacrificed to the community. The prophets of Israel, particularly Ezekiel and those who followed him, proclaimed that the one who keeps faith with God receives life.

A fuller treatment of God's providence would include the whole of the Christian mystery, and this is beyond our present project. It would show, as of central significance here, that God has chosen to use means leading us to our fulfillment and liberation that he allows us to resist, at least in the short run, thus respecting the freedom with which we are endowed and which is a condition for the possibility of our response in love to God, but that God will gain his larger purposes through human co-operation and in spite of what efforts we may make to frustrate his purposes.[49] And this would need to be supplemented by a treatment of the apocalyptic nature of the kingdom, an issue that is appropriate for the next part of foundational theology.

The answer to the problem of evil does indeed essentially include our response in action, though this is not—as some philosophers and theologians have thought—evidence that an attempt to understand the world and God, to the extent that we are able, is either invalid or unnecessary. The prophets and Jesus himself certainly called for action in response to the evils that afflicted Israel. Christians at times have forgotten this message; and people like Marx and Dewey, imbued with a naturalistic historical consciousness, have taken up this theme in an atheistic context, with great consequent suffering. In our

---

[49]This is a central theme in Farrelly, *Predestination*. On the question of evil: Much mystery remains . . . , but this much seems to be true, namely, that one cannot say that the physical evils an individual suffers involve the sacrifice of his essential personal good without culpability on his own part, or that the personal good does not more than compensate for the physical evils the individual endures. Moreover, there is a greater good than that of the individual, the good of creation as a whole and the uncreated divine good, that adds further light to this mystery of suffering. And by faith we know that God would not allow an evil from which he could not draw a greater good.

. . . The fact that some men will make a sinful use of created goods is, of course, in no way a reason for God not to create; for if it were, evil would overcome good through preventing the existence of the great good realized in the creation of the free creature and the glory God thereby gains. In fact, it is an indication of the transcendence of God and his mercy that he has created the world in the midst of the possibility of this evil, as the measure of the evils a man is willing to suffer for love of God and service of him is a sign of the measure of his sanctity (242–243).

own time, political theology and liberation theology have emphasized the transformative impact on society of genuine faith
in God. God has given history into our hands so that we as co-
creators with him may and will answer the problems of evil
that afflict us, within the limits possible in this life. He will not
normally intervene to deliver us from such evils save through
our cooperation with him in this process. The social teachings
of the Church have similarly emphasized this. God is source
and goal of the moral order; and the dignity of the human person, with the moral rights and duties this entails, shows that
God has given to us as individuals and as community the task
to construct our history in cooperation with his purposes. This
frequently entails the need to change social structures, since
conditions in society are all too often oppressive and dehu-
manizing, particularly for the poor and weak who are not able
to defend their rights. Moreover, in our contemporary world,
science and technology have dramatically modified the way
human beings interact with one another; and this calls for
changes in society that assure that the use of science and technology will promote human welfare rather than detract from
it. Action to change the world is not a substitute for the primacy of our relation to God but an entailment of this relationship. Understanding the meaning of the kingdom of God
teaches the Christian that human action to change not only the
self but the structures of society is integral to our response to
God. But even antecedent to this study, our very humanity
shows God's call to justice and so to conversion of self and society. Many religions have recognized and proclaimed this call.

Yet neither is action enough. "The arbitrary and indiscrimi-
nate way in which suffering is apportioned" (646), including
violence and such afflictions as illness, weaknesses of age and
death, continually raise the question of why and "Why me?"
Thus there is also necessary a response of feeling—"a catharsis
of the emotions that nourish the lament and that transform it
into complaint" (646). A process of mourning that enables us
to let go of old attachments and to be free for new affective
attachments is a part of this. So too is the approach that we see
in Wisdom literature. It allows us to develop a complaint
against God that we find in the "cry of the psalmist, 'How long,
O Lord?'" (647). Job cries out: "I will speak in the anguish of

my spirit; I will complain in the bitterness of my soul" (Job 7:11).[50] This may lead us to acknowledge our ignorance of God's ways, so that victims do not become self-accusatory. Beyond this, some go as far as letting go of lament because they discern some educative and purgative value in suffering. The experience in history of unjust suffering led, for example, in the apocalyptic literature of the Old Testament, to the deep sense that God's justice and goodness and promises would be contradicted if oppressive powers and suffering had the last word in history, no matter how much this seemed to be the case. And this deep wisdom was understood to be a revelation by God. Some degree of revelation of the triumph of God's justice over the injustice that oppresses so much human existence is found in many religions. This includes intimations of a life after death itself, a personal life of communion with God and with others.

Some find consolation in the fact that, as some Jews and Christians believe, God suffers too, though this does not have meaning save for those whose lament undergoes a transformation that comes from "a renouncement of those very desires the wounding of which engenders our complaint" (647), above all the desire to be spared suffering. This is a wisdom shown perhaps at the end of the Book of Job, "when it is said that Job came to love God for nought, thus making Satan lose his bet" (647). This approach of wisdom is not to be separated, however, "from the ethical and political struggle against evil that may bring together all people of good will" (648).

We wish to reflect briefly here on the question of whether God himself suffers, as Scripture seems to assert in its portrayal of God in the Old Testament and particularly in the New Testament. There are theologians in our time who assert that God suffers in such a way that his transcendence is compromised, because they do not consider creation to be a totally free act that God need not have chosen. On the other hand, classical Christian theologians, for example Thomas Aquinas, considered God impassible, i.e., incapable of suffering. Of course, Thomas believed with Christian tradition that the in-

---

[50]See Christian Duquoc and Casiano Floristan, *Job and the Silence of God* (*Concilium*, vol. 169, 1983).

carnate Son of God suffered through his passion in his humanity. But to ascribe suffering to God in a way other than this
would, he thought, detract from the divine being and divine
happiness or beatitude. Thus, for example, he ascribed mercy
to God in that aspect of it which is included in one's relieving
another's suffering, but not in that aspect which involves being
saddened by another's suffering.[51] Similarly, he held that when
a person sins he cannot effectively harm God in any way, but
can only show contempt for his commands and harm one who
is under God's care.[52]

We can wonder whether this is sufficient as an interpretation
of Scripture that considers sin a genuine offense against God
(e.g., calling it Israel's adultery) and describes God's mercy in
the Old Testament as well as in the New by images that show
God to be deeply moved. "Can a mother forget her infant, be
without tenderness for the child of her womb? Even should she
forget, I will never forget you" (Isa 49:15). It is difficult to say
that the many scriptural statements concerning the way God
bears his people's burdens, his mercy for them, and the pain
that their sin against his love causes him should be taken metaphorically, as not properly signifying what they assert.[53] It
seems that it is philosophical principles rather than Scripture
that underlie this classical view. For Thomas, only perfections
that do not involve any essential limitation can be properly ascribed to God, and even this predication is analogical. Perfections that essentially involve limitation are ascribed to God
metaphorically, as when God is said to be a rock of salvation,
to be angry, etc.

The question arises then whether one is necessarily ascribing
limitation to God if one asserts that he suffers out of compassion with human beings who suffer or is offended when his
freely offered love is rejected through their sins. We would be
ascribing such limitation to God if we implied that because of

[51]*ST* I, 21, 3.

[52]*ST* I-II, 47, 1, ad 1.

[53]See Jean Galot, *Dieu souffre-t-il?* (Paris: P. Le Thielleux, 1976) 148. I com-
mented on this book in *Theological Studies* 38 (1977) 365–367. Also see J. Galot,
"La réalité de la souffrance de Dieu," *Nouvelle revue thélogique* 101 (1979) 224–
245; "Le Dieu trinitaire et la Passion du Christ," ibid., 104 (1982) 70–87; and
Kasper, *The God of Jesus Christ,* 194–197.

his divine being God was dependent upon creatures and specifically human beings, as followers of Hegel and Whitehead seem to think. But this is not the reason Scripture ascribes such suffering to God or the reason we offer, since we hold that creation is a personal, free, and loving divine choice. As we said in reference to the question of change in God, the context for this question is not so much the nature of God as the personal intentionality of God—that he freely chooses human beings to be objects of his love and knowledge. He initiates a personal relation with us that makes a difference not only to us but to him. We recognize that one of the highest of human perfections is the development of a sufficient love for others that we are genuinely engaged with them and for them for their benefit even when it costs us, specifically when such love is purified of egoism. If personal perfection is found in God, must we not say that this care for others is found preeminently in God? In fact, the care we have for others is a pale and remote image of that which God has.

The reason why God suffers is that through his love he freely cares for human beings to such an extent that we make a difference to him. His love is the reason he rejoices in our good, is affected by the suffering we undergo (and particularly, as Scripture shows, by suffering inflicted unjustly upon the weak), and is intrinsically offended by our rejection of his love. We must deny of God any egoistic love, but we must ascribe to him love that is pure and full enough that it leads him to initiate relations of mutuality with human beings so that he in some sense suffers from the pain we inflict on ourselves by sin; he is "vulnerable." Out of his love, he offers us a great gift of union with himself. In some sense then he experiences an emptiness when this is met by our rejection—an emptiness in and for us that cannot leave him indifferent if he loves us greatly. We cannot, however, identify his suffering with our suffering, for as Heschel paraphrases Isaiah 55:8-9: "My pathos is not your pathos. . . . For as the heavens are higher than the earth, so are My ways higher than your ways, and My pathos than your pathos."[54]

[54]Abraham Heschel, *The Prophets,* Vol. II (New York: Harper and Row, 1975 reprint), 56. This is quoted in Warren McWilliams, "Divine Suffering in Contempo-

This does not detract from the perfection of the divine being or even from God's happiness, because even human experience testifies that it is possible to be happy and to suffer with others at the same time. The whole mystery of creation is that God has the fullness of being and yet cares to create; similarly, he has the fullness of happiness and yet cares enough for others so that his relation with them has a note of mutuality and he is affected by what affects them. He suffers not from his lack of happiness, but from the lack of happiness of others. Also, as we said earlier, Scripture indicates that God's purposes will not finally be overthrown by human resistance; the kingdom of God will come in its fullness, even though many whom he invited to partake in it may refuse this gift.

If we consider the divine being as totally actual, we may have difficulty conceiving how he can be passive enough to suffer. But if we consider God as personal and freely offering his love to others, then we have a different perspective and realize that the more fully one person loves another the more the other makes a difference to him or her, to the extent that he or she suffers from what another suffers. To deny to God the capacity for this love is to deny a perfection that Scripture shows him to have; and philosophically this does not seem to be demanded. What is demanded is a change of philosophical perspective from considering God primarily as being to considering God primarily as personal being.

Finally we should add that an essential aspect of an answer to the challenge of evil is that there is a call in it to turn to God for a salvation we cannot gain for ourselves and of ourselves. We will develop this theme briefly in the next chapter, but particularly in the next part of foundational theology.

rary Theology," *Scottish Journal of Theology* 33 (1980) 54.

# 9

## Faith in God, Religion, and Religious Language

In this concluding chapter, we will reflect on what we have done so far. We have been developing a critical reflection on meaning and grounds for belief in God that are, we propose, in accord with the approach of Vatican II and relevant to major difficulties with such faith in the Western world in our time. We have supposed that these difficulties come largely from a widespread modern historical consciousness that is, at least in practice, quite naturalistic, and from a distorted understanding of God. So we have presented meaning and grounds for belief that are related to such difficulties. Now, as a reflection on the meaning and grounds of faith we have given, we ask (I) how faith in God and religion are necessary and transformative for the liberation and fulfillment of human beings in our time, and (II) what the character of the religious languages we have used is. We will conclude by noting the incompleteness of the theme of the present book, and the need of the theme of God's entrance into our lives with his definitive revelation and salvation through Jesus Christ and the Holy Spirit, which belongs to the next part of foundational theology.

### I. Faith and Religion as Necessary for Human Beings in Our Time

To show what we mean by this claim, we should (1) ask what this faith and religion are and how they are essential for us in our time with our characteristic attitudes and problems, (2) reflect on what is distinctive of religion in our time when compared to past ages, and (3) answer some objections that may be posed to our approach from other twentieth-century theological ways of critically mediating faith.

## 1. Faith in God as Necessary for Human Beings in Our Time.

We have attempted to offer meaning and grounds for faith in God that are appropriate to men and women of our time, and so the question arises reflectively about what we mean by saying that faith is perfective and liberating. This of course is a functional question, but since in Christianity men and women are invited to faith because it is salvific, it is not inappropriate to speak about faith in a functional manner. This is not to reduce faith to its functional value. To today's men and women with their somewhat naturalistic interpretation of historical consciousness, we are saying that actually the meaning and assurance of our engagement in history is found only through faith in God; our fulfillment and liberation in our personal and social history is found only through this faith.

What does faith in God mean?[1] We should note that as Christians we believe that it is properly faith in Jesus Christ by which we are saved. The meaning of this specific faith and salvation we will treat in the next part of foundational theology. But we also believe that God wants all people to be saved and gives them an opportunity to be saved, even when the Gospel has not been presented to them in a way adequate to gain their response of faith. Belief in God even when it does not explicitly include belief in Jesus Christ, then, is saving when the lack of explicit inclusion of faith in Jesus does not occur through bad will. This belief is saving, we say, in virtue of Jesus Christ,

---

[1]Besides the documents of the Church referred to in chapter 1, we may refer to Avery Dulles and others, *Toward a Theology of Christian Faith. Readings in Theology* (New York: P.J. Kenedy, 1968); Paul Surlis, ed., *Faith: Its Nature and Meaning* (Dublin: Gill and Macmillan, 1972); Louis Monden, *Faith: Can Man Still Believe?* (New York: Sheed and Ward, 1970); Karl Rahner and Juan Alfaro, "Faith," *Sacramentum Mundi* 2 (New York: Herder and Herder, 1968) 310–326; John O'Donnell, "Faith," *The New Dictionary of Theology,* eds. Joseph Komonchak, M. Collins, and D. Lane (Wilmington, Michael Glazier, Inc., 1987) 375–386.

even when he is not an explicit object of belief. But this is not to deny that it is saving through people's response to whatever of God's revelation is available to them; it is rather to say that this revelation itself looks forward to that which God gives through Jesus Christ and the Holy Spirit and is saving through this relationship. We have reflected on this faith in earlier chapters, particularly when we wrote of Abraham (chapter 3), conversion (chapter 5), and evidence for God's existence as testimonies he gives to evoke faith (chapter 6). And we will analyse it more fully in the second part of foundational theology.

We can recall here several aspects of faith we have already re-flected on critically. It is an act of the human person in re-sponse to God who gives testimonies to himself through our religious tradition and specifically through aspects of this that find critical support in modern experiences of self and the world. God manifests something of himself through the medi-ation of our experience of absolute moral value and through the mediation of the evolving physical world. In fact, if we are open to the testimonies given through these mediations, they point to God as being, as transcendent, as personal, as con-cerned for human beings in motivating, empowering, and di-recting their creative engagement in history to establish a better future—one more in accord with the dignity of the human person and community. Faith is a response to God so revealing himself, a response that is an acceptance of God and his revelation and a commitment in trust to him as revealed. It is a personal act since it is both free and intelligent, and it is a commitment to God as personal. In fact, it is a kind of per-sonal knowledge of God in mystery as distinct from simply philosophical knowledge of God or a moral attitude toward him, since it is an engagement with him through mind and heart. This means too that the primacy of the person's faith and reliance is in God so believed, as distinct from being pri-marily placed in self, in a human community, in some philo-sophical viewpoint, or in an anticipated historical future. Thus it is a surrender of self to God, as we find in many converts to faith in our time. We know from many of these conversion sto-ries how it is in this surrender that men and women experience the *fascinans et tremendum* in their lives in a unique manner.

From the full Christian perspective, we believe that a person accepts God's testimonies of himself and surrenders to him only through God's help—antecedent, concomitant, and following the person's act of faith—that in Christian tradition is called grace.

Why do we say that it is such faith that liberates and fulfills us, oriented as we are to a future in history through our modern historical consciousness? We say this, because for there to be meaning in our engagement in our historical task, it is essential that we accept our horizon, our environment, and ourselves fully rather than seek to gain our historical future through denying and rejecting the fullness of our horizon, environment, and self. We have shown that to be human is to be oriented toward God through our orientation to absolute value and our knowledge of what is, and that this orientation is developmental and dialectical (in the sense of a denial that our fulfillment lies within history) in the individual and essentially involves an orientation to an historical human community. To choose then to be fully human is to act in accord with this good, which fulfills our being. Similarly, we have shown that there is testimony that adequately witnesses to the existence of God as transcendent personal being who is immanent in nature and history as the source, goal, and enabler of our genuine search in history. This then is the only context that can assure the meaning of our engagement in history and our individual personal history and that of the larger societies of which we are members. This is an incomplete analysis of how faith is saving, because it does not reflect explicitly on the Christian belief of the benefits given us through Jesus Christ. Our claim in this book is only that it is a necessary analysis; it is given in preparation for a more adequate analysis, not as a substitute for it.

To accept only the intrahistorical dimension of our life as the meaning of our engagement inevitably leads to a loss of meaning and a distortion of human priorities; and it cannot fulfill the human heart, as Christianity and many religions know so well. Also, such engagement leads to fixations that exclude values essential to assuring this future. To seek such limited goals in a way that excludes larger ones leads to progressively less meaning, so that many people—as we see all too frequently in our time—end up in nihilism or different forms of sedation (e.g., drugs) for the interior pain that results from such rejection of the meaning that is the source and fount of human life. Similarly, unless one progressively accepts one's full dimensions, and that means accepting oneself as a religious being primarily, it is unlikely that one will accept one's dignity and the dignity of others in a way that supports human meaning and community. Human community depends on our acceptance of human rights and duties that flow from this basic human dignity. We cannot accept the limitations that community involves unless we acknowledge that our dignity lies more in our being part of a community than it does in our escaping such limits, and it is impossible to accept interiorly and act externally in a way that consistently acknowledges the dignity of other persons unless we trust that by this we are becoming more deeply ourselves as well as contributing to community. That is, such engagement and commitment does not occur at the cost of a basic diminuition of self, but rather redounds to a becoming more fully ourselves. Our individualistic culture tends to lead people to identify themselves with their possessions, their work, their status, or, in many cases, their physical and psychological experiences. It also leads them, not infrequently, to sacrifice the community and the next generation to preserve their lives, so understood. In more collectivist cultures of our time, on the other hand, individuals are sacrificed for the collectivity.

Perhaps it would be helpful to give one example that illustrates how traditional faith and a re-reading of this in view of the problems of our time are necessary if we are to face the issues that threaten the future of our societies. The religious sociologist Robert Bellah gives such an example when he recalls some threats that the technological revolution in our time brings with it, certain religious resources in the United States and Japan that did modify to some extent the destructive effects of the industrial revolution, and the need to reapply these today in a new or renewed manner. In reference to our earlier modern economic experience, he notes, in agreement with Alexis de Tocqueville, that religion moderated our preoccupation with private betterment and pulled us back to a concern for our fellow men and women. Thus it ameliorated somewhat the harshness of economic competitiveness and supported a more cohesive society. Similarly, in Japan of 100 years ago, Ishida Baigan founded an ethical movement among the merchant class, and argued that their work was equal in dignity to that of the farmer and samurai for they did make a contribution to society. Thus he supported an ethical context for economic life.

In turning to the question whether religion in these countries can offer aid in the technological revolution of our time, he notes, as an example, that "the Catholic bishops' pastoral letter, *Economic Justice for All,* makes an enormous contribution not only in its policy suggestions but even more in its theology. What we need to learn, in the words of the letter, is that 'human life is essentially communitarian'. . . . We will find ourselves only in giving to one another and in concern for the whole world."[2] In reference to Japan, Bellah notes central characteristics of traditional faith and religion there, and how these are essential to that country's present problems, though in a new context:

> To reduce an enormously complex set of phenomena to a very simple formula, I would say that Japanese religion is fundamentally concerned with harmony—harmony among persons and harmony with nature. . . . All three traditions [Shinto, Buddhist, Confucian] are elaborations of the common pattern I am here describing: the harmony of the compassionate dance.
>
> There is enough of this fundamental understanding of life left in Japan to make the surface of life more pleasant than in almost any other culture. But we may doubt that the surface,

[2]Robert Bellah, "Religion and the Technological Revolution in Japan and the United States," University Lecture in Religion at Arizona State University (Tempe: Arizona State Univ., 1987) 10. We can also refer here to Pope John Paul II, *Laborem Exercens (On Human Work),* September 14, 1981. To develop a more humane context for evaluating and resolving issues concerning work in our time, John Paul reflects on the Judaeo-Christian tradition (with particular emphasis on Genesis' account of the creation of human beings) and on the understanding of the human person (since work is an act of a person). I have analyzed and evaluated this encyclical in "Person, Work and Religious Tradition," an article that is forthcoming in George McLean, ed., *The Place of the Person in Social Life* (Washington, D.C.: The Council for Research in Values and Philosophy)

the beautiful form of the practice of many aspects of daily life, really express the ultimate ends of the society. If it did, would the landscape be so ravaged? Would the dignity of the individual be so easily sacrificed to the ends of the group? . . . Rather than setting the ends of life, the pattern of the compassionate dance seems to be used as a means for other purposes. It is useful for socializing individuals into being sensitive to the needs of the group. . . . What would it mean to reverse the process of functionalization of religion, the reduction of the realm of ultimate ends to the status of means?[3]

We are not saying that people cannot have a genuinely communitarian sense without explicit religion, but we are saying that they cannot have this without accepting the absolute moral obligation to respect the dignity of the individual person. And through this experience of conscience God gives testimony to himself that gives grounds for belief in him—a belief that is socially transformative.

Also, unless we accept the environment in which we engage in our personal and social history as larger than the immediate human environment, so that God is engaged in this process too, what trust can we have in the worth and effectiveness of our engagement in history? It is only by accepting God as personal environment and horizon of the human community that we can be assured that what we do for this community will not be lost, since only God has power to assure an enduring future for ourselves and the human community. To accept one's self and one's environment and horizon at this level—the level of the absolute—is an experience of the *fascinans et tremendum* and shows openness to the mystery of self, history, and God. It is all too obvious how ineffectual human plans and intentions are of themselves to influence the course of history for good or to effect its liberation from the evils that afflict it and us. And frequently, the response given by other human beings to even the most beneficial things we can do for society is so minimal, even if it is not outright opposition, that we cannot be sustained in such efforts if these are the full context of our rela-

[3]Bellah, "Religion," 10–11.

tionships. It is only through engaging in our own life and our varied communities in the context of a relationship to God as the final and personal context of our life as horizon and as environment that we can be sustained by a sense of meaning not held hostage to the turns of fortune that beset all human endeavors. And it is only by accepting ourselves on this level that our engagement will redound to our own growth.

It is for these reasons, we propose, that modern men and women with their historical consciousness can find meaning, liberation, and fulfillment only through faith in God as transcendent and immanent personal being related to them in history. Without such faith, their engagement in history falls under the curse of Sisyphus, even though people are able for a while to block out of consciousness the meaninglessness of their efforts. Correlatively, we suggest that a religious relation to God in our time that does not accept historical consciousness, our task in history, and God's relating to a world in change is a counter witness to God, to faith, and to what it means to be human.

## 2. Distinctiveness of Religion in Our Time Compared with Past Ages.

"Religion" has been understood in many different senses.[4] For example, it was understood in Rome of antiquity as rites and cults. It has been understood as the inner attitude of the person who returns to God (re-ligare, rebind), or as a moral

---

[4]On the meaning of religion, see the following: M. Dhavamony, "Self-Understanding of World Religions as Religion," *Gregorianum* 54 (1973) 91–127; L. Dupré, *The Other Dimension. A Search for the Meaning of Religious Attitudes* (New York: Doubleday, 1972); Wilfrid C. Smith, *The Meaning and End of Religion* (New York: New American Library, 1964); J. Goetz and others, "Religion," *New Catholic Encyclopedia,* 12:240–268; Clifford Geertz, "Religion as a Cultural System," ch. 4 in his *The Interpretation of Cultures* (New York: Basic Books, 1973); Mircea Eliade and David Tracy, eds., *What is Religion? An Inquiry for Christian Theology* (*Concilium,* vol. 136, 1980); Frederick Ferré, Joseph Kockelmans, and John E. Smith, eds., *The Challenge of Religion. Contemporary Readings in Philosophy of Religion* (New York: Seabury, 1982); W. Abraham, *An Introduction to the Philosophy of Religion* (Englewood Cliffs: Prentice Hall, 1985); John Thornhill, "Is Religion the Enemy of Faith?", *Theological Studies* 45 (1984) 254–274; Winston King, "Religion," *The Encyclopedia of Religion,* ed. Mircea Eliade (New York: Macmillan, 1987) 12:282–293.

virtue under the cardinal virtue of justice whereby we give God what is his due, or as a system of beliefs, rituals, moral views, etc. associated with one tradition (e.g., Hinduism). It has been taken as human action in counterdistinction to God's, or as including both God's initiative in revealing and offering salvation and human response. And it has been taken as a simple description of all the historical forms of human belief about God or the Ultimate, or as what is normative in our human relation to God. Here we take it as the human response in faith to God and the expression of this in such elements as doctrine, moral action, cult, community, etc. Living faith is its core and rationale; without this, external expressions are without basis, meaningless, and dead. Thus we understand religion without reducing it to human pride and without excluding from it the initiative of God whereby he calls us to respond to him in faith, moral action, cult, community, etc. Obviously, we cannot approve all that goes under the name of religion in history, but we can find in it much that we must acknowledge as having God as its source. Religion needs to be critically evaluated; we have been engaged in that task in this book. Here, we restrict ourselves to a modest task: we will briefly recall something of Mircea Eliade's analysis of religion in pre-modern, particularly archaic, societies through the sacred and myths and then ask how a faith and religion appropriate to our time compares with this.

It is difficult to grasp exactly what is proper to religion in the midst of the vast variety of religious phenomena. We must approach this phenomenon as a whole, not from a part (e.g., economic, social, political), if we wish to understand it. As Eliade writes: "A religious phenomenon will only be recognized as such if it is grasped at its own level, that is to say, if it is studied *as* something religious. . . . The one unique and irreducible element in it—[is] the element of the sacred. . . . At bottom, the only helpful thing one can say of the sacred in general is contained in the very definition of the term: that it is the opposite of the profane."[5]

---

[5]Mircea Eliade, *Patterns in Comparative Religion* (New York: Sheed and Ward, 1958) xi–xii. Also see MacLinscott Ricketts, "In Defense of Eliade," *Religion: Journal of Religion and Religions* 3 (1973) 13–34; articles on Eliade by Ilinca Johnston,

The definition or description of the sacred that many modern students of religion, including Eliade, offer depends in part upon that given by Rudolf Otto in his book, *The Idea of the Holy.* The sacred is *fascinans et tremendum*—that which both attracts and frightens. In accord with this, J. Goetz describes the sacred as follows: "The sacred represents an order of reality, the presence of which commands man's attention and at the same time escapes him; it is simultaneously desired and regarded with awe. In other words, it possesses an essentially ambivalent character, which makes man feel at once irresistibly attracted by its grandeur and frightened by its superiority."[6] The sacred is manifested in a great variety of ways—in rites, myths, divine forms, sacred objects, symbols, cosmologies, consecrated men, animals, sacred places, etc. Eliade calls anything that manifests the sacred a *hierophany.* (Perhaps, in view of some religions' emphasis on the immanence of deity, we could also speak of an *embodiment* of the sacred.) These hierophanies vary vastly from place to place; all of them are historical events in the sense that they occur in some definite situation of time and place. But there are similarities among them, and Eliade analyses them within his morphology of sacred forms. Almost anything can be and has at some time been chosen by a particular group to be the medium of the sacred, and was set aside for this. This implies a choice on the part of the culture, "a clear-cut separation of this thing which manifests the sacred from everything else around it."[7] These hierophanies and religions are relative to the culture of the people. They imply that the sacred is manifesting itself in something profane: "In fact, this paradoxical coming-together of sacred and profane, being and non-being, absolute and relative, the eternal and the becoming, is what every hierophany, even the most elementary, reveals."[8] For a particular people,

Lawrence Sullivan and James Buchanan in *Religious Studies Review* 9 (1983) 11–24; Carl Olson, "The Fore-Structure of Eliade's Hermeneutics," *Philosophy Today* 32 (1988) 43–53; and Douglas Allen, "Eliade and History," *Journal of Religion* 68 (1988) 545–565.

[6] J. Goetz, "Religion," *New Catholic Encyclopedia* 12:241. Also see Eliade, *Patterns,* 462.

[7] Eliade, *Patterns,* 13.

[8] Ibid., 26.

these hierophanies fit into a *system* that includes their religious experiences, myths concerning the origin of the world and the present human condition, religious rites, moral notions, etc. We may add that their religious life implies and expresses a faith.

A hierophany of central importance is found in myths. These are sacred stories relating an event that took place in primordial time. They tell how through actions of supernatural beings reality—the cosmos or a fragment of reality such as a species, a particular kind of human behavior or an institution—came into existence. Myths disclose these beings through their creative activity and reveal the sacredness of their works. They thus constitute the paradigms for all significant human activity. By knowing the myth one knows the origin of things and so can control them or invest one's actions with their sacredness. This knowledge "is not an 'external,' 'abstract' knowledge but a knowledge that one 'experiences' ritually, either by ceremonially recounting the myth or by performing the ritual for which it is the justification; . . . in one way or another one 'lives' the myth, in the sense that one is seized by the sacred, exalting power of the events recollected or re-enacted."[9]

The cosmogony is the exemplary model for every kind of human action. It is presented ritually in the beginning of a new year for the purpose of renewing the world after the model of the cosmogony, by repeating what the supernatural beings did *in illo tempore.* For primitives, it seems that the world has already ended (e.g., in widespread myths of a flood), but this ending is to be repeated in some more or less distant future. Among primitives, "myths referring to an end to come are curiously scarce,"[10] though in India there is belief in an eternal recreation and destruction of the universe. (For the Judaeo-

[9]M. Eliade, *Myth and Reality* (New York: Harper Torchbook ed., 1968) 18–19; see 5–6. B. Malinowski says of myths: "These stories . . . are to the natives a statement of a primeval, greater and more relevant reality, by which the present life, fates and activities of mankind are determined, the knowledge of which supplies man with the motive for ritual and moral actions, as well as with indications as to how to perform them." *Magic, Science and Religion* (New York: 1955 [reprint]) quoted in Eliade, *Myth,* 20.

[10]Eliade, *Myth,* 55.

Christian apocalypses, as we have seen, time is linear and irreversible and there will be an end of this world and the beginning of a renewed world that will be the liberation and triumph of history.) In traditional societies, another manifestation of a return to primordial and sacred time is found in initiation rituals that frequently symbolize a regression to the womb "in order that the beneficiary shall be born into a new mode of being or be regenerated."[11] To go back to the beginnings is to transcend the human condition and regain the non-conditioned state; thus rituals "abolish profane, chronological Time and recover the sacred Time of myth."[12] We see through all of this that:

> On the archaic levels of culture religion maintains the "opening" toward a superhuman world, the world of axiological values. These values are "transcendent," in the sense that they are held to be revealed by Divine Beings or mythical Ancestors. Hence they constitute absolute values, paradigms for all human activities. . . . These models are conveyed by myths. . . . It is the experience of the sacred—that is, an encounter with a transhuman reality—which gives birth to the idea that something *really exists,* that hence there are absolute values capable of guiding man and giving a meaning to human existence. It is, then, through the experience of the sacred that the ideas of *reality, truth,* and *significance* first dawn, to be later elaborated and systematized by metaphysical speculations.[13]

The archaic individual does not feel shut up in his own mode of existence. "He achieves communication with the World because he uses the same language–symbols."[14]

We should note that even when the early philosophers of Greece criticized the gods of their myths as anthropomorphic and substituted a more rational analysis of the world, this rational analysis still interpreted the beginnings as the determi-

[11]Ibid., 79.
[12]Ibid., 140.
[13]Ibid., 139.
[14]Ibid., 143.

native and ultimate reality of the world. It was interpreted by the best of these philosophers—Socrates, Plato, and Aristotle—as form, nature, and being, with divinity as in some way source of this. Transcendence for many of these was gained through breaking out of the realm of time and change into that of the real being and immutability of divinity.[15] As we have seen earlier, the interpretation of the Christian mystery was in part affected for good and for ill by this metaphysical context.

What is characteristic of our age of modern historical consciousness, on the other hand, is a sense that fuller being lies in history and history's future if it is any place at all, and that this future lies in human hands, for we are the creators of history. This fuller being is dependent not so much on a given paradigm in a sacred structure as upon our free choices and our making of ourselves and our political, economic, social, and cultural structures in ways that are appropriate to changing circumstances. Yet this future, many feel, is profoundly threatened in our time by our human capacity for self-destructiveness.

The experience of the sacred has in part changed location with this cultural shift. The traditional world of the past has been shattered. In the developed world particularly, we live today not so much in a world of nature as in a hominized world surrounded by human artifacts, whether these be artifacts of technology or of humanly constructed political, economic, social, and cultural works and systems. We are constantly faced by our own works, which may efface any vital sense of the works of God. Also we live in a world that is in rapid change and that has expanded to embrace many different people and cultures. These peoples are united not through religion, culture, or language, but by science and technology and certain problems that call for action in common—e.g., problems of poverty, the threats of war, ecological degradation, and the need for mutual understanding and acceptance.

Where in this shift is the experience and call of the sacred? I suggest that this experience of *fascinans et tremendum* is found where the absolute is encountered as distinct from the conditioned. The cultural anthropologist Clifford Geertz writes that

[15]Ibid., 147–154.

chaos threatens to break in on the human person "at the limits of his analytic capacities, at the limits of his powers of endurance, and at the limits of his moral insight." Through these experiences, "Bafflement, suffering, and a sense of intractable ethical paradox" come upon us, and they challenge the "proposition that life is comprehensible and that we can . . . orient ourselves effectively within it."[16] There continue to be areas of the experience of the absolute that we have in common with peoples of the past. With peoples of all ages, we experience the absolute when we face the threat of death for ourselves or for others we love; also, the destructive power of nature is still to be reckoned with (e.g., in earthquakes). But we face, too, the sacred in the midst of life. Like people of the past, we experience the absolute in the call of conscience—in the acknowledgement of what we have called a constitutive human good in our individual lives and in community. We still experience the sacred in nature around us; and our ecological awareness calls us to a renewed sense of the sacred in nature and our kinship with it. Together with many others,[17] I suspect that one aspect distinctive of our experience of the sacred in our time is the experience of our lives and our future—individual and social—as freely lying in our hands, though at a depth that recognizes and acknowledges the claims of an absolute upon us. This is distinct from looking at our decisions affecting our individual and communal futures as simply conditioned values, as in simple conflicts of human interests or in market decisions. For us to experience our future as sacred, there must be at some point a dialectical stage that questions an initial acceptance of self and life as having meaning within a secular and temporal context. For example, we face an absolute when we freely acknowledge the unassailable dignity of another per-

---

[16]Clifford Geertz, *The Interpretation of Cultures. Selected Essays,* 100.

[17]L. Gilkey offers one example of a search for ways in which the sacred is experienced in our time; see his books, *Naming the Whirlwind. The Renewal of God-Language* (New York: Bobbs-Merrill, 1969), and *Reaping the Whirlwind. A Christian Interpretation of History* (New York: Seabury, 1976); also see Johannes Metz, *Theology of the World* (New York: Herder and Herder, 1970). We previously noted Antoine Vergote's remarks on pre-religious experiences of modern men and women (see chapter 6). I have sought to interrelate our modern orientation to the future and an initially apocalyptic Christian understanding of salvation in "Trinity as Salvific Mystery," *Monastic Studies* 17 (1986) 81–100.

son and what that entails for us, or when we make a permanent commitment to another in love, as in a marriage unto death, or when we experience the need for some ultimate grounds for human choice, or hope for forgiveness that is beyond us or any other human being, or when we experience profound need for and some basis for hope for the human condition, or the vulnerability of our future or the lack of meaning in life. In part the locus for such experiences has changed for men and women in our non-traditional modern societies, because we seem to hold our lives and our futures more in the risk of free choice than in the encompassing strength and norms of a tradition.

Perhaps from the perspective of this part of foundational theology we can say that there are two primary ways in which people can seek to escape the sacred in our time. One of these is characteristic of those who accept modern historical consciousness and one is characteristic of those who do not accept it. Those who accept it may well consider their lives and their societies, from a practical standpoint, within the context of the human alone—human interests, human making, human market decisions—whether individualist or collectivist. We showed previously that there is in the United States and political liberalism a strong allergy to the absolute—a view that it is the absolute that is the main opponent to democratic societies, because this puts a limit to human hopes placed in manipulation according to our perceived interests and the consequences of our actions. And collectivisms of our time, such as Communism—still very much alive in some places—similarly have fears of an absolute that may challenge their humanly proposed objectives. Both systems and ideologies find a fully accepted recognition of the dignity and freedom of the human person with the rights and duties that this entails deeply threatening, and yet both want to claim such acceptance. On the other hand, there are those who still accept the sacred, but only as this is found in the past of their particular traditional societies and cultures. These identify the sacred with the way it was experienced in the past, and fear an openness to the sacred through an openness to other peoples and to an uncertain, changing, and unmastered future in which certain norms of the past are cast into question, human freedom is accepted, and relationships are enormously extended.[18] These two options are locked in opposition. Each finds the other its greatest enemy. Hence the oppositions between liberalisms and fundamentalisms in their varied forms within and among nations.

What is distinctive of religion in our time then is, we suggest, an acceptance of a new locus for the manifestation of the sacred and its call upon us, without abandoning many earlier manifestations that are of enduring importance because they are rooted in the human and not only in cultural, economic, political, and social environments that are no longer adequate for human needs. This new manifestation of the sacred is found in the intersection between a human mode of transcendence that integrates history and an understanding of God as transcendent personal being and as immanent and related to human beings in history.

We have in previous chapters indicated some implications this has for our religious relation to God; but we cannot indicate here implications this has for aspects of religion such as its institutional forms, relationships, worship, prayer, and the interrelation of worship and work. Suffice it to say that the real context for such reflections is found in the concreteness of a particular religious body, and that much of the Catholic Church's self-reform during and after Vatican II has taken the change in the manifestation and experience of the sacred into consideration. We should, however, note that this manner of facing the sacred needs symbolic expression, so that our engagement in our individual and community histories may genuinely be experiences of integration into a whole where the sacred and the profane interpenetrate.

### 3. *Some Difficulties with Our Critical Mediation of Faith.*

We have in this first part of foundational theology offered a critical mediation of faith in God that we think is in accord with that of Vatican II and the 1967 document of the Faith and Order Commission of the World Council of Churches cited in chapter 2. We propose also that it is in accord with the primary

---

[18]See Geertz, *Interpretation*, chapters 9–12 on new states after World War II and decolonization.

concerns found in varied theological approaches in our century to this question. However, it may well be that representatives of these other approaches would object that it does not do justice to their concerns. Therefore, we should reflect on some possible objections that may be made from their perspectives.

Some who espouse a natural theology may assert that what was important in all the preceding chapters was evidence for the existence of God and answers to those who deny the possibility of metaphysics, because once these are granted it follows that we should honor God through a religious relation to him.

In answer to this, we have not been primarily engaged in metaphysics, even though we have used it. We have been engaged in evaluating critically—though only in part—the meaning and grounds of belief in God as Christians, and specifically the Catholic Church, understand belief in God. Faith is a personal acknowledgement of God and a free commitment to him in response to his testimony to himself, as we have seen in Scripture, in some soundings in Christian tradition, and in instances of conversion in our time. Among other things, this has demanded that we evaluate critically whether human beings appropriately orient themselves toward an absolute dimension of value, whether this very orientation is itself testimony God gives to his existence, and whether God is personal and interacts with human beings.

Some of those who look upon religious affirmations as symbols expressive of religious experience or of the Ultimate known through religious experience may well agree with the anthropological mediation of knowledge of God that we articulated in the preceding chapters, but may have other objections. For example, they may say that since this mediation of knowledge of God is present in all peoples, one cannot find a basis in it to justify the belief in God specific to Western culture, as though this were the privileged belief to which all others had to be assimilated.

In answer, we acknowledge that we begin foundational theology as Christian believers, and that this is the belief we seek to critically evaluate. This belief affirms that God has revealed himself in a uniquely privileged manner through Jesus Christ and his Spirit, but also that he has revealed himself previously in many and partial ways. In evaluating this subordinate dimension of God's self-revelation, we are also in part critically and positively evaluating aspects of the belief of non-Christian peoples. We have understood that God testifies to himself by the cosmos as well as by our experience and reflection on values and conscience, and by this we critically evaluated some earlier Western views of God as inadequate and some views of Buddhists and Hindus as largely true, and thus contributing to a more adequate Christian view of God. We have noted in Scripture particularly many religious affirmations as symbols expressive of the Ultimate, witnesses to our belief in God, and proclamations of God. Since we have critically evaluated this belief by showing that God has given supporting testimonies to himself, we have presented these affirmations as having an objective truth value. On the basis of such testimonies, one can dialogue with and evaluate diverse interpretations of God.

Some followers of Barth may say that faith is a response to God's revelation of himself, and this self-revelation has occurred exclusively through Jesus Christ. Thus in defending faith in God without making Jesus Christ the exclusive mediator of revelation, the present approach is not a Christian approach.

To this we can say that it is true that Jesus Christ is God's definitive Word and revelation; but, as we have seen in Scripture, it is not the Christian view that God has revealed himself exclusively through Jesus. Nor does Scripture restrict salvation to those who explicitly believe in Jesus Christ, for it says, "Anyone who comes to God must believe that he exists, and that he rewards those who seek him" (Heb 11:6). Moreover, it is very unlikely that one will accept God's last word about himself without accepting his lesser and earlier words, for (in words we have quoted before), as Jesus said to Nicodemus, "If you do not believe when I tell you about earthly things, how are you to believe when I tell you about those of heaven?" (John 3:12).

To recall these testimonies God gives of himself antecedent to his revelation through Jesus is not to subordinate this latter revelation to the former and lesser. We have recalled God's testimonies to himself that he gives through the physical world and conscience and, indeed, through the mediations of religions of the world. Vatican II said in reference to the latter that they "often reflect a ray of that truth which enlightens all men."[19] These lesser testimonies can give us a new perspective on God's ultimate testimony to himself, but they do so on the condition that their deliverances are controlled by the meaning of Scripture and tradition. I wrote in an earlier book and another context that "in the application of a correct philosophical analysis of a natural reality to the supernatural mystery, Scripture and tradition are the controlling factor."[20] Of course, with time and changing conditions we can grow in our understanding of the meaning of Scripture and tradition, as Christians have in the past. Also, we saw in chapter 2 that Barth later acknowledged that there were "lights" given to human beings other than Jesus Christ, though these were subordinate to what was given us in Christ.

A follower of Barth may say that the preceding chapters belong to philosophy of religion and seek to establish knowledge of God by a natural theology. They are not an evaluation of faith in God but of knowledge of God by his effects in nature and conscience.

Counter to this, I would say that these chapters are a critical evaluation of the meaning and grounds of faith or belief in God. I wrote them as a Christian believer in God's universal salvific will, in God as personal being who freely gives to all an opportunity for faith and thus gives to them also some revelation of himself and the grace to at least vaguely and implicitly recognize his testimonies to himself and accept them and him through faith. What I try to evaluate is not primarily philosophical knowledge of God but faith in God in some dimensions of what our tradition holds he has revealed about himself. What I use for this purpose is largely philosophical reflection on human experience of the world and the self; without this, the evaluation would not be critical in the manner appropriate to this part of foundational theology. It would not be an intrinsic analysis of these mediations of God's testimonies, nor would it be communication with those whose difficulties in our time are precisely in these areas. This process is not a substitute for God's revelation or his salvific will or the grace he gives us to enable us to respond to him, but is rather

[19]Vatican II, *Nostra Aetate,* 2.
[20]Farrelly, *Predestination,* 156.

secondary to these: a critical evaluation of whether the signs we have support our act of faith as a free and reasonable act. We conduct this evaluation from the belief that God in the present order ordains all human beings to salvation through Jesus Christ, and so from the belief that God's testimonies to himself even through conscience and the physical world are free personal divine testimonies given within this intention.

Bultmann and others may say that in the preceding chapters we have attempted not only to show the meaning of faith in God but grounds for faith in God; but this is counter to the risk of faith, and it confuses faith with knowledge.

Counter to this difficulty, I suggest that experiencing risk and having grounds for faith are not mutually exclusive; we will see in the next section of foundational theology that the early Christians preached the resurrection to show both the meaning of faith and grounds for faith. Faith is a response to God's free personal self-revelation, and so what is primary is this response of acceptance and surrender. The fact that a person has reasons showing that he or she should believe or that it is not a sacrifice of the intellect to believe does not take away the uncertainty in accepting this relationship with God, who remains transcendent, free, and a personal mystery we cannot control. To reflect only on the meaning for us of faith in God may make us subject to a modern critique that faith is wish-fulfillment; to reflect only on grounds for faith may result from assimilating faith too much to the kind of objectivity present in science or classical metaphysics. Faith is personal knowledge of God, and thus we do not critically judge that there are grounds for believing save in the context of acceptance of such a relationship, and we do not critically acknowledge the meaning this has for us save in the context of God's testimonies to himself. Thus, counter to Bultmann, we do not proclaim a faith that lacks grounds; and counter to some statements of Neo-Scholastic theologians and Pannenberg, we do not offer grounds as though people could accept them save as implicitly accepting a commitment of faith and thus under the help of God's grace. The "grounds" can be looked upon as testimony that God gives us in revealing or manifesting himself, or as evidence that God is actually revealing; it would seem inadequate to look upon them exclusively as one or the other.

Perhaps Moltmann may object to us that revelation is promise, specifically as an answer to the problem of evil in the sense of a promise of a transformation of history that leads believers to engage in transforming political, economic, and social conditions. In another way, liberation theologians would accentuate the implications of faith for liberating the oppressed from political, economic, and social injustice. Moltmann presents his viewpoint as opposed to either a cosmological or an existential approach to the question of the existence of God; and liberation theologians present theirs against faith as ideology supporting capitalist individualism.

In answer, we first note that these theologians are speaking about specifically Christian belief. The next section of foundational theology will address the specifically Christian issues they raise. Here, we repeat what we said in reference to Barthian objections. In our world today, it is important to address human difficulties with faith on a human level that shows the meaning and grounds of faith in God; and on this level, Vatican II does not see an opposition between the meaning and grounds of faith that can be called cosmological and existential and the meaning of faith contained in its transformative influence on political and economic structures. In fact, Vatican II seems to think both of these are necessary and mutually corroborating, and I agree. Faith is a personal relation to God that is transformative for the individual and society, though it has all too often not been transformative for either. This has been due in part to a misapprehension of the meaning of person and of God. We have seen that the transcendence of the person includes an opening to society and responsibility for it, and we have seen that God is a transcendent personal being who has personal intentions for human beings in history. God reveals something of himself not only through the physical world around us but through the call of conscience that comes from the demands of the moral good in our own lives and in our societies. Thus a surrender through faith to God entails a commitment to the moral good and an effort to transform our societies so that they reject what is contrary to the dignity of human persons, more effectively guarantee their rights, and call for their fulfillment of their duties. In our age, when so many mutually opposed interpretations of what is human abound, giving grounds for faith in Christian revelation based on the transformative value of faith without addressing the question of what is human and how experience of the human mediates faith in God is to surrender Christian faith to be used ideologically for either individualistic or collectivist purposes.

In conclusion of this section, we recall that this book is a second order study, dependent upon actual conversion in ourselves. The process of conversion itself, as we see in Thomas Merton and others, does not necessarily contain the type of analysis and organization we offer here. There are experiences in life that show the inadequacy of the person's present interpretation of life for his or her deeper needs, an experience of the Christian proclamation or an aspect of this, an act of creative imagination by which the person reimagines himself or herself within this larger theistic and Christian context and an experience of a kind of fit here—that there is something in this newly-opened realm that fulfills a deep human need and liberates one for a much larger and more adequate vision, relationship with the whole, and meaning. This is somewhat similar to the way that people in many pre-modern religions experienced what Eliade calls hierophanies (e.g., myths), inviting inclusion of the self within them and leading to the person's or group's sense that meaning is found through surrender to such inclusion. Thus there are some aspects of this experience comparable to an aesthetic and a pragmatic experience, though if it were confined to these it would never lead to the surrender of faith. In an aesthetic experience people find a life in the aesthetic object with which they sympathize and in which they participate, but their response stops at the object. Thus Kierkegaard was correct in distinguishing the aesthetic stage from the religious stage. And the pragmatic response envisions the object as related to the self and beneficial but it does not include a surrender of the self to the Sacred far greater than the self. What we are speaking of here is similar to what Lonergan calls "affective conversion."[21] I think that Thomas Aquinas'

---

[21]See Bernard Lonergan, *Method in Theology* (New York: Crossroad, 1972) 283–284. Also see J. Mueller, "Appreciative Awareness: The Feeling Dimension in Religious Experience," *Theological Studies* 45 (1984) 57–79.

354    Faith in God, Religion, and Religious Language

words on "connatural knowledge" describe this;[22] we will return to that in the next part of foundational theology.

## II. Religious and Theological Language

We have been using religious and theological language throughout these chapters in different forms, and thus it is appropriate for us now to reflect on this use in view of some modern difficulties with the meaning of religious language and the diversity of interpretations of such language by theologians. As an introduction to our treatment here we can recall something of what this problem is in our time, and what it calls for from us.

We noted two aspects of the problem of the meaning of religious language in the first and second chapters. The first is that much of the contemporary world contests the meaning that Christians assert is found in their religious language. To much of our world, such language is not relevant to what is important for human beings; it does not have meaning that is internally coherent or that is coherent with what we know from elsewhere about the world; and it does not have criteria by which one can distinguish which claims are true and which are false. Thus religious statements have seemed irrelevant, nonsensical, and lacking validation to many people in our time.

This sense of the lack of meaning in religious and metaphysical statements gave rise to schools of linguistic philosophy that attempted to analyse how language means and thus to show why it is that religious and metaphyusical assertions are meaningless. There has been a whole series of such philosophical analyses of language in our century. For example, some philosophers took an interpretation of the way scientific language means as a model for meaning more generally, and so found religious and metaphysical statements meaningless. This at-

[22]See what Thomas Aquinas says of the *instinctus fidei* in *ST* II–II, 2, 9, ad 3; and on the *lumen fidei* in *ST* II–II, 1, 4, ad 3. Also see *ST* I, 1, 6, ad 3; I–II, 45, 2; J. Maritain, "On Knowledge through Connaturality," *Review of Metaphysics* 4 (1950–1951) 483–494; V. White, "Thomism and Affective Knowledge," *Blackfriars* 25 (1944) 321–328; and A. Moreno, "The Nature of St. Thomas's Knowledge *per Connaturalitatem,*" *Angelicum* 47 (1970) 44–62.

tempt to substitute an artificial language for our ordinary language was found to be a misinterpretation of our normal use of language. And so others took the meaning of language from its use in ordinary discourse with its practical purposes. Some philosophers on this basis found metaphysical and religious statements to be meaningless because they divorced language from its ordinary usage. Because of attacks upon the adequacy of these interpretations of the meaning of language, more philosophers have begun to give positive interpretations of religious and even metaphysical language. Some of these have interpreted religious language as non-cognitive (e.g., as though a religious statement was an assertion not of a transcendent reality but rather of an attitude of the speaker, such as love or *agape*). Others have interpreted it as cognitive, in the sense of affirming a disclosure situation (e.g., one that elicits wonder at a deeper dimension of reality opened up to one) and commending an attitude, but still without interpreting it as in part assertive, e.g., of the existence of God. According to others there is cognitive meaning in many religious statements, in the sense that they assert something about reality (called a "locutionary" utterance, with meaning and reference). On the other hand many religious sentences are rather of a performative character, in the sense that they commend, command, forbid, etc., rather than make a statement (these are called 'illocutionary'). Many religious statements, e.g., religious confessions, include both of these elements—an at least implicit assertion about reality and a commitment to such reality.

It is beyond the limits of our study here to review these schools of analytic philosophy.[23] We have attempted to answer difficulties in this matter by reflecting on the fact that people

---

[23]See Jean Ladrière, "Meaning and Truth in Theology," *Proceedings,* Catholic Theological Society of America 42 (1987) 1–15, and (on Ladrière's work in this area) J.-P. Sonnet, "Les langages de la foi. A propos d'un ouvrage récent," *Nouvelle revue théologique* 108 (1986) 404–419. Also see Richard Swinburne, *The Coherence of Theism* (Oxford: Clarendon, 1977); T. W. Tilley, *Talking of God: An Introduction to Philosophical Analysis of Religious Language* (New York: Paulist, 1978); Walter Kasper, *The God of Jesus Christ* (New York: Crossroad, 1984) 87–99; Wolfhart Pannenberg, *Anthropology in Theological Perspective* (Philadelphia: Westminster, 1985) 339–396. I reflected briefly on Wittgenstein, Heidegger, and hermeneutics in *God's Work,* 183–188, 194–200, 207–214.

in our time do find religious language to have relevance to their lives and coherence; by examining the scope of our human transcendence in moral judgment, in knowledge, and in personal horizons, structures, and capacities; by critically evaluating experiences of the self and of the world that lead some people to believe in God; and through articulating something of the resultant meaning of God as transcendent personal being immanent in the world and history and of implications of this for our individual and community lives. But at this point it may still be helpful to reflect on how language is used here; this is simply to make explicit what is already implicit in what we have done so far.

The second aspect of this problem that we face in foundational theology is the mutual opposition among different twentieth-century Christian theologies as they try to mediate faith in our time. We examined this in chapter 2. We have seen, for example, the opposition between a dialogical use of Christian language and a dialectical use of Christian language. One issue here is the question of how God is known. The early Barth asserted that this was only through Christian revelation, while all other supposed knowledge of God was due to religion and thus a prideful attempt to control God. Later he qualified this somewhat, by acknowledging other lights in the world, though he asserted these could be used only after accepting Christian belief. Others asserted that God manifested himself and is known definitively through Christ and the Spirit but also in earlier and less definitive ways through the cosmos or the self—as well as through pre-Christian religions—and, that Christian language makes intrinsic use of these earlier revelations. Some relate this distinction to that between manifestation and proclamation.[24] In reference to interpretations of God's manifestation, there are deep differences between the language of those who stress that this is mediated by the cosmos (e.g., Thomists and Whiteheadians) and those who stress that this is mediated by the self (e.g., Bultmann, Tillich, and Rahner in diverse ways). For the former, religious language is objective, whether it is taken analogically or univocally. For

[24]See David Tracy, *The Analogical Imagination. Christian Theology and the Culture of Pluralism* (New York: Crossroad, 1981) chs. 5 and 6.

the latter, religious language tends to be the objectification of a religious experience or of Holy Being and thus is symbolic. Also, one interpretation of religious language takes its departure from an understanding of religion as a cultural linguistic reality that shapes human existence; in accord with this, religious doctrine is understood as a second order rule about how one appropriately uses religious language within a particular religion.[25] There is a difference also among theologians on the issue of the criteria one uses to mediate faith in God—i.e., whether this mediation is through the transformative impact of Christian belief or through the objective grounds one may give for the fact of divine revelation (e.g., Moltmann versus Pannenberg; some political and liberation theologians versus some more academic forms of theology). We have already sought to answer questions that these differences raise through the approach we have taken in accord with Vatican II. Part of this task remains for us in the next part of foundational theology.

Now in reference to the question of language it remains for us to reflect on what we have already done in this work. After recalling briefly the language characteristic of Judaeo-Christian identity found in Scripture, which is normative for Christians (a normativity that is critically explained and grounded in a later section of foundational theology), we will relate to this the language found in this book's mediation of belief in God by way of modern experience and reflection on it. We do this briefly, because we have largely explained and justified our use of language in the preceding chapters.

## 1. The Language of Scripture.

We noted in chapter 3 that Scripture is a collection of different forms of literature that was written and edited over successive ages, that expressed the beliefs of the Jewish and/or Christian community, that was later recognized as expressing these beliefs, and that was accepted as normative for these religious communities. These texts were put together to constitute

[25]See George Lindbeck, *The Nature of Doctrine. Religion and Theology in a Postliberal Age* (Philadelphia: Westminster, 1984).

a canon. As literature or literary forms, they were constructed by the creative imagination (and thus metaphors) of their authors and editors in the context of their communities. We find this thoughout Scripture, such as in the epic story of the Exodus, the desert period, etc. And we find it in the parables of Jesus and in the Gospels. Logos and life, reason and desire come to juncture in creative imagination and metaphor; and correlatively these appeal to both logos and life, reason and desire. They involve the reader as they did initially the hearer.

Scripture is also specifically religious literature. In this it may be and has been compared and contrasted with other religious literature of the ancient Middle East. We have seen something about religious literature in Eliade's account of myth and symbol, and in our use of Ricoeur's work in chapter 3. Metaphors in Scripture can often be called symbols—religious symbols. The primary language in Scripture as religious is not doctrinal but symbolic—though it is a symbolism that involves doctrine and practice. It speaks of God—and in this case, God is its referent—not so much directly as indirectly—through stories of his interaction with his people, poetry, prophecies, etc. Once more we have an intersection of logos and life, reason and desire, and we have a language that engages the reader or, initially, the hearer. These religious symbols present the Sacred to the reader or hearer in an almost sacramental way—making available its power, transforming, evoking a kind of participative knowledge. This is language that cannot be wholly translated into doctrinal statements without remainder. This is true of Canaanite religious myths and rites and of scriptural language.

In addition, Scripture is specifically Judaeo-Christian religious literature or symbol. What is significant is that these testimonies, in the form of stories, etc., witness to belief in the God of Abraham, the God of Isaac, and the God of Jacob—the God of the Exodus, of the Covenant, of Israel, of David, of Jesus. The God to whom they refer or bear witness is a personal mystery, mediated by his free interventions for the salvation of Israel. What seems central is the *proclamation of God's offer of salvation*—reactualized in succeeding generations by the way that the books were reedited or reinterpreted to make God's salvation actual for changed circumstances. The prophets reflected on the Exodus event to proclaim God's message to the people of succeeding centuries. The New Testament proclaims God's saving presence through Jesus Christ and the Spirit, offering it to people. It calls for their response of faith. Thus Scripture proclaims God as a definite divine personality who has acted freely with specific agents in Israel's past, who has intentions with the Jews, who makes promises, who rebukes as well as blesses. Though there are quite different messages given at different times, and there is a growth and correction with time, God has an identity which can in part be known through these actions; and those called to believe have identity through the one they are called to believe in and the way this one chooses to save them.

This testimony in Scripture to God's words and deeds is presented as mediating God's revelation. Thus the creativity of the human community and the individual author and editor are understood to be responses to and mediations of this divine revelation. We can say then that the ultimate creative imagination at work here as understood by these scriptural authors and by the community of believers is God's. The action, e.g., of the Exodus, has him as its author; and by his words and deeds he performs an act that gives his people access to the Sacred, participation in his saving power, transforming knowledge, etc. And similarly the death and resurrection of Jesus are understood to reflect God's great love for his people: that he would accept the death of his Son and extend his saving power to the people through raising Jesus from the dead and sending the Spirit. In many different metaphors the authors of Scripture mediate God's saving presence and revelation. Testimony is given to these actions and words by which God is present to show the reality and meaning of his saving action. Testimonies are given in ways that indicate what this salvation is (thus once more the juncture of logos and life), involve the people, have implications as to how his people are to act toward God and one another, etc.; but they are also given as grounds for belief in God—e.g., that he has raised his Son from the dead. The Sacred signified here is not so much a universe as a definitive historical intervention by God to save his people and reveal himself to them. In these texts there is both meaning and reference. At this point we are simply trying to clarify what Scripture claims; we defer to the second part of foundational theology a critical reflection on these historical claims as such (e.g., the resurrection of Jesus from the dead).

In Scripture we acknowledge that what is primary is not doctrine but proclamation, and that the language used is not primarily and simply objective but rather metaphoric or symbolic. Objective language and doctrine are present in Scripture, however; for the authors of Scripture, proclamation that makes use of symbol or metaphor conveys and entails objectively affirmed doctrine. Also, doctrine is one literary form that Scripture explicitly uses. Counter to some interpretations of the language of Scripture, the authors' use of metaphor and symbol derives not simply from an objectification of a religious experience or of Holy Being that is manifest through experiences of ultimacy. Rather, it derives—according to the authors—from God's own symbolic acts and deeds. Only symbol or metaphor are proportioned to convey what the authors proclaim, namely—in the New Testament—that God has broken into history through Jesus Christ and his Spirit to offer us his salvation and revelation in a way that is definitive and never to be surpassed, for what is mediated through this proclamation is both logos and life and what it appeals to is both desire and belief—belief in or on and belief that. If doctrine is considered as simply objective talk, it is secondary to this. It does not exhaust what is proclaimed, but without it true proclamation in the manner of the authors of Scripture is not possible. They are saying something objective about God but also something more. Doctrine as a literary form here is, we should note, not properly described as rules for using religious language, but rather as propositional statements about God's relation to human beings and about God himself.

## 2. Theological and Philosophical Language about God

How is the language of Scripture related to the theological and philosophical language we have used, and which Christian tradition has used and still uses? We must recall that the language Scripture used in testimony to God's revelation was related to knowledge and language in the minds of its hearers that preexisted this revelation. This is true of the revelation Scripture asserts was made to Abraham, in the sense that it was related to what Abraham believed about divinity before he received his revelation. It is true, as we saw earlier, of the language used in the Book of Wisdom; and it is true of the Christian proclamation when it was made to the Greeks, as witnessed in Luke's account of Paul's speech at the Areopagus. This relationship has continued in the Church's proclamation to the world, as we saw particularly in chapter 4. The relationship between what Scripture proclaims (and the language it uses) and what preexists it in the mind of its hearers is not simply dialectical, but a dialogue that does have a dialectical moment. In our own attempt to mediate the scriptural proclamation to people of our own time, we have also related it to knowledge and language that derive from elsewhere. We related it to human experience, knowledge, and aspirations of our time. Specifically, we related it to experiences and reflections upon them that, we argued, were testimonies to the existence of God or supportive of faith in God. Here we took two ways, one through our moral experience and the other through the evolving physical world, to help to overcome a dichotomy between some theologians and to be more proportioned to God as personal. We affirmed that the meaning found in these testimonies to the existence of God and the language used of them is intrinsically continued in the language of Christian Scripture and faith, though there it is subsumed within a more adequate understanding of God. It is denied as controlling our understanding of God, but not as intrinsic to our understanding of God.[26] God's meaning that we analysed was not simply what the word "God" signifies, but how God is relevant to and indeed the horizon of our search for meaning and life. Logos and desire are in our reflection because logos and life are in the extra-biblical testimonies on which we reflected.

The *language of being* is called for if we are to reflect on the witness that the world and self give to God. There are several points we should note about this language. First, it is not sim-

---

[26]I expressed this earlier in a review of Eberhard Jüngel, *God as the Mystery of the World* (Grand Rapids, Mich.: Eerdmans, 1983) in *Theological Studies* 45 (1984) 561–563. Also see Ghislain Lafont, *Dieu, le temps et l'être* (Paris: Cerf, 1986).

ply objective language, since being is present to us not only through that which is known intellectually but through the good or what is at issue for us in our lives. Nor is this language simply an objectification of the experience of what is at issue for us or of Presence, since it expresses as well and depends upon objective intellectual knowledge of that which is. In reflecting on God as transcendent personal being, we found that the only sufficient explanation of the language of being used of God here is one that acknowledges the mediation of the experience both of the world and of conscience. This knowledge of God is mediated both by what is and by the impact of the good upon us in the course of our life; and God is known as transcendent agent or One who is and as the absolute good who is the horizon of our life and energizes us and the world. Thus our language referring to God as transcendent personal being is not only objective language but language involving the speaker personally and reflecting such involvement with God through faith. So too with language of God as immanent in the world, free, loving, all-powerful, all-knowing, just, merciful, etc. In brief, language that refers to God, like knowledge of God, is proportioned to the mystery that God is for us and in himself. In metaphysics or theology this language may be used in a simply objective manner, but its origin is not simply objective. And so such philosophy or theology should embrace the full mystery dimensions of what it studies, as Rahner has emphasized so strongly.

Second, this language is used of God *analogically.* What is the meaning of this analogy? In what sense is our talk about God analogical? And what is its validity? Concerning this, there have been disputes not only between some Protestant dialectical theologians on the one hand and Catholic theologians on the other, but also between Catholic theologians and philosophers. We will first reflect on an important aspect of the dispute between some theologians and philosophers who wish to present Thomas' view in a way appropriate to our world today, and then briefly speak to difficulties raised by Barth and some of his followers.

Among theologians and philosophers influenced by Thomas, there is an important controversy between those who interpret analogy as based on the metaphysical foundation of causal similitude between God and creatures, and those who interpret analogy as something language users do to words by the very process of using them to map reality.[27] Some of these latter claim to validate analogical language by a basis other than causal similitude between God and creatures.

I suggest that this controversy comes from the authors' differing understandings of concept formation. Those who relate analogy to the metaphysical foundation of causal similitude are using a classical view of concept formation found, for example, in Thomas; and those who relate analogy to us as language users and do not see the need of establishing causal similitude are using a view of concept formation found in mathematical physics and what may be called "relating logic" and a Galilean mode. I have sought to show earlier that both modes of concept formation are found in our formation of the concept of "being."[28] Thus in reference to the present controversy, I think that there is no contradiction between these interpretations of analogy, unless one mode of concept formation is adopted as a wholly adequate explanation to the exclusion of the other. Here then I would like to present analogy in relation to causal similitude as its basis, and then to show it as related to us as language users in a practical context of life, arguing that, if taken together, these two views can contribute to a richer understanding of the analogical predication of terms between us or the world and God.

There is quite a bit of diversity even in the interpretation of Thomas' view of analogy, but what I present here is broadly accepted as his view and can be defended from the texts.[29] Analogy designates not primarily a relation of similarity between two subjects such as God and creature, but rather a *process* by which we predicate terms or names from one subject to another with a meaning that is partly the same and partly different. Analogy is in contrast to univocal predication on the one hand and equivocal (or equivocal by chance rather than by de-

---

[27]See W. Norris Clarke, *The Philosophical Approach to God. A Thomist Perspective* (Winston-Salem, N.C.; Wake-Forest Univ., 1979) 49–65.

[28]See above, chapter 5, section I; and "Developmental Psychology and Knowledge of Being," in *God's Work*, 287–314.

[29]See particularly, *Summa theologica*, I, Q. 13.

364     *Faith in God, Religion, and Religious Language*

sign) predication on the other. For example, if I say Paul is human and Jude is human, I am predicating the word "human" in a way that has the same meaning in both cases; this predication is univocal. And when I say that what I am writing with is a pen and what is enclosing the pigs in the farm-yard is a pen, I am predicating the word "pen" in ways that have totally disparate meanings. This predication is equivocal by chance, or simply equivocal. If I say that someone is healthy, and then say that a coloring of his face is healthy or a certain food is healthy, I am using the word "healthy" with a sense partly the same and partly different. I am predicating it analogically. Here the different meanings are related through their relation to the health of the body, for this is what the word primarily means. Food and coloration are called healthy through their relation to this health of the body, either as a cause of it or as a sign of it. Here it is only the body that is intrinsically healthy, while this word as applied to food and col-oration designates not something intrinsic to them but their relation to the health of the body.

A word transferred from one subject to another by way of causal relation, however, may designate something *intrinsic* in the second subject of which it is predicated. For example, I may say that the crop is good this year. Then, on the basis of my belief in God, I may say that God is good, because he is the source of this bounty. Initially, my meaning may be simply that God is the source or cause of this good effect. And if this is the extent of my meaning, then I designate God good extrinsically, meaning that he is the cause of something that is good. But be-yond this I may and am likely to mean that God is intrinsically good, because he has freely showered his favors upon us. Here too a causal relation is the basis for my predicating "good" of God, but it is not the meaning of this, since the meaning of the word "good" here is God's own intrinsic goodness. At this point, what may well be predominant is the unity of meaning between the predication of good to creation and to God, though there is a subordinate diversity of meaning. But I may go further, realizing that God's goodness is radically different from that of creation, since the latter is a participated good-ness whereas God's is unlimited and uncreated. In this case, what is predominant is the diversity of meanings of "good" when predicated of God and of creation. This has been called "analogy of proper proportionality," and it is a stage of analogical predication where the diversity between meanings of the word ascribed to the divine being and created being is predominant. Thus the Fourth Council of the Lateran (1215) asserted that "a likeness between creator and creature cannot be noted without a greater dissimilarity having to be noted between them."[30]

This is based on causal similitude between God and creation. However, since God is not a univocal cause (e.g., as one human being in generating another is), but an analogical cause, and since there is no definite proportion between God and his effects, for he infinitely transcends them, we are not by this word saying something or knowing something that is *proper* to God. That is, we do not know what specifies him to be God. The word "good" designates something intrinsic to God, but leaves him uncomprehended. As Thomas writes of another word used of God: "When this word, 'wise', is said of man, it in a way describes and comprehends the thing signified, but not when it is said of God. Here it leaves the thing signified uncomprehended and transcending the meaning of the word."[31] The meaning of our words, such as "good" or "wise," depends upon our initial objects designated by them and concepts formed of them. Thomas obviously thought that we had some real capacity to understand the things about us and ourselves, and thus that the meaning of our words designating such objects through the concepts we formed of them were not totally relative to our culture; and we have defended the validity of this viewpoint. When we, on the basis of Christian faith or on the basis of a causal relation known from elsewhere between God and creation ascribe such terms to God, we deny a mode that they signify which is proper to creatures. Understanding some perfections, such as good, wise, loving, powerful, etc., as simply positive and thus not inherently limited to created beings, we ascribe them to God but without designating the specificity with which God enjoys these perfections; we

---

[30]Denzinger-Schönmetzer, *Enchiridion Symbolorum* (35th ed., Freiburg: Herder, 1973) 806.

[31]*ST* I, 13, 5.

say much more than we mean. We leave God unbounded by our statements, but truly said and known. Such designation of God is, of course, an act of us as personal beings and thus more than simply an intellectual performance. We so designate God because we have a dynamism of mind and heart toward God, and we do so in the context of God's manifestation of himself through the physical world and ourselves and through historical revelation. And, as we said earlier, our designation of God as wise, good, etc., based on the way he manifests himself through self and the world, can be, and has been, profoundly deepened and in part seemingly contradicted by God's further revelations of himself in history. "How great are your works, O Lord! How very deep are your thoughts?" (Ps 92:6). Even Thomas acknowledges that while we know God better through revelation than through reason, still "through the revelation of grace in this life we do not know of God what he is, and thus we are conjoined with him as with one unknown."[32]

We can also consider the analogical process in a way that sees the extended meaning of an analogical term ascribed to God as deriving from what we do as language users rather than from the causal similitude between God and creation.[33] The analogical process is seen here as a series of linguistic moves. Roughly speaking, it is a way of networking, of mapping, that we engage in through language. We initially have a focal meaning of a word dependent on a paradigmatic case, and then we extend this word in sentences to other cases. By a kind of semantic contagion, the word's meaning is differentiated in the process. For example, if I say I am healthy, and then say that this climate is healthy, the word has a different meaning because of its linguistic environment. Thus the analogical meaning of a word comes from what we do to it and with it. In

---

[32]*ST* I, 12, 13, ad 1.

[33]See James Ross, *Portraying Analogy* (Cambridge: Cambridge Univ. Press, 1981) (reviewed in *New Scholasticism* 59 (1985) 347–357); and David Burrell, *Analogy and Philosophical Language* (New Haven: Yale Univ. Press, 1973) (reviewed in *New Scholasticism*, 48 (1974) 386–398). George Lindbeck in his *The Nature of Doctrine: Religion and Theology in a Postliberal Age* (Philadelphia: Westminster, 1984) develops an analysis of Christian doctrine based on an interpretation of language akin to that of Burrell and Ross, not that these philosophers would draw the same conclusions in reference to doctrine. (For reviews of Lindbeck, see *The Thomist* 49 (1985) 392–472; and *Religious Studies Review* 11 (1985) 235–245.)

reference to this interpretation of analogy, we may recall that Piaget explains the development of concepts not by simple abstraction of one attribute of a thing from other attributes of it, but rather by what we do or from our operation on the thing. For example, infants suck on a coverlet and they know it by this process; they also use this action scheme on other things, assimilating them to it and accommodating it to them. By this operation on things they differentiate them. Somewhat similar to this, linguistic philosophers can explain analogy by what we do to our words when we apply them from one subject to another. By a process of assimilation and accommodation, we extend the meaning of a "word scheme" to another object, but in the process accommodate the meaning of the word to its new environment. We organize our world in the process. Within a particular sphere of life, such as law or religion, we form a particular language that is "craftbound" (James Ross' term) so that we know how to get around. We learn how to modify the meaning of our words, e.g., "good," "wise," within this area by a craftbound vocabulary developed by tradition and by continuing changes in our time.

This can be used, I agree, to explain our analogical usage of words. Take, for example, the use of the word "save" of God. Initially, we have an experience of being saved from some danger or saving something or someone from some danger; the word is based on praxis and expresses it. And the word has somewhat different meanings as we map actions of different human subjects in differing circumstances. We then ascribe this to God, e.g., as he leads Israel from Egypt, and in the process the word's meaning changes somewhat because of the subject of which it is predicated and the circumstances in which it is predicated. And this process of change continues through Israel's history, so that eventually the word has an apocalyptic meaning, e.g., in the Book of Daniel and then in the salvation that is proclaimed by Jesus and the early Church, and in early Christian prayer. The basis on which the word is ascribed to God is human action and his action. The meaning of the word differs according to what we do to it, namely the subject to whom and the circumstances in which we ascribe it. This interpretation of analogy perhaps comes from looking at the analogical process as our human action in a practical context for the purpose of mapping our world so that we can find our way around in it.

We can conclude that our analogical predication of words of God derives from God's revelation and the religious experience dependent upon this—an experience that is claimed to be historical and communal in Israel (e.g., when they proclaimed God their savior because they believe he freed them from Egypt through Moses)—from causal similitude (e.g., saying that God is wise and good as manifested in his effects known from the cosmos, the self, and God's actions in history), and from what we do to and with words in our linguistic usage. There is no necessary opposition among these approaches; in fact, each is an integral part in the use of analogical language about God in our response to him in faith and religion. This is exemplified in our use of the word "being" of God in our earlier study of him as transcendent personal being who is also immanent in nature and history. There must be some basis in reality for our "mapping" our relation to God and God's relation to us; and our designation of God by way of causal similitude is within the practical context of faith, religion, and worship.

We should respond to the early Barth's objections to analogy as we previously responded to his critique of religion. He was quite opposed to the scholastic doctrine of the analogy of being, because he thought that it subordinated God and creation within a higher genus of being, thus denying the transcendence of God.[34] Counter to this, we showed that analogy is basically *not* an analogy of being, but rather a way of predicating terms within a proposition. Thomas carried this out in his theology within the context of his faith. Even when he constructed the five ways, he did this within the context of his faith to show something of the God he believed in; thus, counter to the Greeks, he arrived at knowledge of God as a creator. Similarly in defense of faith and not as a substitute for it, Vatican I said that the existence of God *can* be known by the natural light of reason. Here too in foundational theology, we are dealing with this matter from our perspective of faith, i.e.,

[34]See Colman O'Neill, "Analogy, Dialectic and Inter-Confessional Theology," *The Thomist* 47 (1983) 43–65.

as insiders rather than outsiders. Moreover, analogy is of itself not a way of demonstrating God's existence, but a manner of speaking of him when he is known from elsewhere. It is based on a causal similitude, but not as though God is in the same genus of "being" as creation. We explained earlier that there is no larger inclusive reality that subsumes God and creation; all creation participates in the infinite being of God. (Von Balthasar's explanation of analogy in this way did help Barth overcome some objections to it.) Also, analogy demands rather than excludes dialectic. There is a negative moment in the analogical process. For example, in our speech of God mediated by his testimonies through cosmos and conscience, there is a dialectical moment, for we evaluate these testimonies to the point where they witness to the fact that there is One who is not finite reality, not part of the world, not dependent. This dialectical moment is found not only in our human speech about God but in our search for God, as we saw in Thomas Merton and, very graphically, in the Zen Buddhist reflection on Nothing. As Judaeo-Christians we know that God's dialogue and the dialectical moments within it continue in the process of his historical revelation. (This will be even more apparent in the next part of foundational theology, e.g., in the analysis of the stages of the revelation to Peter and other apostles of who Jesus was.) Our understanding of God as transcendent personal being really related to human beings in history shows that further historical revelation is something that would be in accord with such a Being. We would expect even further free revelations on God's part that are appropriate to his loving designs and interaction with humanity, not that we could determine what these would be, thus lessening the wonderment and awe that comes with them. To assert God's transcendence as personal being is to assert his mystery and specifically the mystery of one who is transcendent as personal and free. Counter, however, to some earlier interpretations of God's transcendence, it does not imply that God is not affected by what happens in the history of the individual or of the human community. We proposed that philosophical reflection on human experience does not contest but can support Scripture's presentation of God as both totally perfect and deeply concerned and affected by what happens in history. He is changed and even suffers in his intentional relationship of knowledge and love for those whom he has created, though he does not increase or diminish in perfection. And finally, analogy and dialectic for believers occurs within a context of life, prayer, mystery of suffering, and change rather than within a simply intellectual search.[35]

Finally, an objection that comes from Pannenberg is that analogy really depends upon using a univocal middle term. Moreover, what God is depends on the future, since he is made known by his apocalyptic kingdom and is the power of the future. To use analogy is to define God by what is present, and thus it is inappropriate in the Christian understanding of God revealed through the kingdom to come as the power of the future. It constricts him and does not leave the future free.[36]

It is true that our analogical use of words is controlled by God's revelation of himself through Jesus Christ and the Spirit. But this very revelation presupposes an earlier revelation and even God's testimonies to himself through physical creation and human moral experience. And the words that it uses are taken from words expressing these earlier revelations and testimonies. Even the revelation to Abraham was not in total discontinuity with what he earlier believed about God in

---

[35]For analyses of liturgical language and its relation to doctrine, one can consult, e.g., Geoffrey Wainwright, *Doxology. The Praise of God in Worship, Doctrine and Life* (New York: Oxford Univ. Press, 1980) and David Power, *Unsearchable Riches. The Symbolic Nature of Liturgy* (New York: Pueblo, 1984).

[36]See, e.g., W. Pannenberg, "Analogy and Doxology," *Basic Questions in Theology,* I (Philadelphia: Westminster, 1970), and Elizabeth Johnson, "The Right Way to Speak about God? Pannenberg on Analogy," *Theological Studies* 43 (1982) 673–692. Perhaps Wolfhart Pannenberg's *Metaphysics and the Idea of God* (Grand Rapids, Mich.: Eerdmans, 1990), which I had not read before completing this book, leaves more room for a convergence of views. Pannenberg seeks to integrate time and being, and he points out that there are roots for this in Aristotle: "When one considers that the *telos* is at the same time the reality of the thing, its idea *(eidos),* then one must grant that this *entelecheia* ["completeness"] which is already present in the process of becoming is a form of presence of the thing's essence, although the thing will be completely there only at the end of its becoming" (106). Somewhat similarly, I have sought to integrate being and time, e.g., through using Erikson's analysis of stages of personality development to evaluate Thomas' understanding of the person. This too shows that in some way "the presence of the *entelecheia* in the process of becoming has an anticipatory structure; it implies an anticipatory reality of the *eidos* before its full realization . . . [and a] *retroactive* causality of the *telos* during the course of becoming" (Pannenberg, 106). In the next volume, we shall relate the apocalyptic character of the kingdom of God to this understanding of the human person.

Haran. The Christian experience of God through Christ and the Spirit brought a new meaning to the words previously used, e.g., by the Prophets and the Wisdom literature. But this new meaning was related to the earlier meanings not simply by dialectic but by analogy with a dialectical moment. Since Christians believe that God's definitive revelation came through Jesus, we cannot think that our future experience will simply deny what we already have been given to know about God through Jesus, or that the words we are now justified in using of God through Jesus' revelation will be totally changed in meaning. Our present use of words does not constrict the future revelation God will make of himself, since he has already given us definitive knowledge of him as a gift, but a gift that remains a mystery we cannot encompass. For Christians God is not the power of the future in any way that denies this. Analogy, finally, does depend on there being a moment in the process when the meaning of a word, e.g., "good," ascribed to creature and God is predominantly unitary (though not in a univocal sense), but this process is completed only when there is more difference than unity in the sense of the word. Perhaps Pannenberg's differing interpretation of analogy is influenced by that of Scotus.

In conclusion, we have sought in this book to speak from the fullness of Christian faith in God to those—and this includes us who are believers—who have difficulties with genuine Christian faith in our time because of a pervasive historical consciousness that is frequently naturalistic at least in practice and because of widespread distortions in the understanding of God in our society. We have sought to reflect critically on meaning and grounds for belief in God by recalling something of the Judaeo-Christian understanding of God as one who takes the initiative to offer salvation and revelation to his people in a way that is very relevant to their legitimate concerns for history and who thus makes himself accessible to human knowledge in faith and is relevant to human concerns for liberation and fulfillment. We have sought to show that people in our time do find meaning and grounds to believe in God so proclaimed, and we have critically evaluated such meaning and grounds. This has been a reflection on only a part—and not the most distinctive part—of our Christian belief in God. Such reflection is necessary, both because of difficulties in our time and because we need it to understand what is distinctive of the Christian revelation.

In the second part of foundational theology we will reflect on the meaning and grounds proper for belief in God through Jesus Christ. This will show more adequately what salvation and revelation are as Christians understand them, and reveal grounds for believing in Christ in view of contemporary difficulties. For Christians, what we have said so far is subsumed into a fuller revelation God makes of himself through Jesus Christ and the Spirit. What we have critically reflected on so far is not sufficient at all for our lives, specifically in the midst of the problems of our time. For example, it does not give an answer to the mystery of death, nor does it give us assurance that God's kingdom or salvation will prevail in history, nor does it show us the way of salvation and personal relation to God which he offers us. Thus it is not an adequate understanding of God nor of his relation to us. The full theological reflection on who God is revealed to be in Christian terms and what he offers us is found in the study of the Trinity, and thus not even the next part of foundational theology can claim to be an adequate theological study of the Christian mystery. But a theological study of the Trinity and critical belief in the Trinity are dependent upon what foundational theology itself has to offer. And so even here we contribute modestly to a theological understanding and grounding of the greatest Christian mystery.

# Index of Principal Authors

Anselm, 128–129
Aristotle, 128–129, 134, 137,
140–141, 175, 196, 220–221,
226, 235–236, 243, 299, 344
Augustine, 122–127, 129,
132–133, 139, 171, 236, 314,
323–325

Barrett, W., 182, 189, 191
Barth, K., 38–44, 59, 63,
105–106, 178, 261, 264, 266,
324, 349–350, 368–369
Becker, E., 204
Bellah, R., 21, 336–338
Bernard of Clairvaux, 129
Berry, T., 68–69
Bonaventure, 132–133, 236
Buckley, M., 24, 140, 130
Bultmann, R., 41–44, 63, 80–81,
351, 356
Burrill, D., 255–257

Clarke, W. N., 316, 363
Cobb, J., 58–59, 61–62
Coppens, J., 78, 89–90

Day, D., 174, 176
Descartes, 142–143, 168
Dewey, J., 154–155, 207, 300,
326
Dulles, A., 74, 174–175, 333

Eliade, M., 77–78, 243, 290–293,
322, 340, 353, 358
Erikson, E., 182–201, 270, 275

Feuerbach, L., 154
Fiorenza, F. S., 7, 33, 36, 62,
82
Freud, S., 154–156, 183–187,
189, 193

Gadamer, H. G., 60, 81
Galileo, 142, 226, 363
Galot, J., 319, 329
Geertz, C., 66, 209, 344–345,
347
Gibson, E. and J., 223,
225–226, 256
Gilkey, L., 299–300, 345
Gilson, E., 133–134, 170–171,
174, 175
Griffin, E., 168, 173–178
Griffiths, B., 174

Habermas, J., 210, 310
Hegel, G., 57, 152–154, 158,
300–302, 315, 321, 324, 330
Heidegger, M., 34, 41, 81,
223–224, 229, 268, 281, 323,
355
Heschel, A., 91, 330
Hume, D., 145, 147–148, 161,
196, 223, 229, 244, 255

Irenaeus, 119, 121

Jensen, J., 72, 86, 92
John Paul II, Pope, 22, 190,
    258, 310, 337
John XXIII, Pope, 208, 212–214
Jungel, E., 56, 139, 301, 361
Justin, 118–119, 121

Kant, I., 23, 143, 148–150, 158,
    223, 229, 236, 244, 255
Kasemann, E., 107, 108–109
Kasper, W., 315, 329, 355
Koestler, A., 245–248, 251, 253
Kung, H., 24, 267

Legrand, L. 102–104
Lessing, G., 145–146
Lewis, C. S., 174–176
Lindbeck, G., 357, 360, 366
Livingston, J., 151–158
Lonergan, B., 34, 56, 168,
    223–224, 226, 353
Luther, M., 134, 136–141, 150,
    264, 266

Marx, K., 57, 63, 65, 154–155,
    174, 300–302, 310–312, 326
McLean, G., 14, 82, 181, 193,
    337
Merton, T., 167–178, 217, 219,
    230, 236, 283–284, 306, 322,
    353, 369
Metz, J., 57, 63, 206, 264, 345
Moltman, J., 63–66, 139, 264,
    352

Newman, J. H., 158, 161–164,
    236
Newton, I., 145–146, 148, 151
Nietzsche, F., 25, 154–155
Nishida, K., 278–279
Nishitani, K., 278–281, 287–288

Ockham, 135–136
Osborn, E., 116–121

Panikkar, R., 284–285, 294, 296
Pannenberg, W., 59–63,
    116–118, 120, 190, 264, 351,
    355, 370–371
Paul, 101–112, 235, 243
Pelikan, J., 119, 125, 129, 132,
    136–137, 140, 314
Piaget, J., 184, 193–194,
    223–229, 244, 256, 367
Purcell, E., 206–208
Plotinus, 122–123

Rahner, K., 19, 34–37, 56, 139,
    178, 223–224, 232–233, 236,
    356, 362
Ratzinger, J., 48–49
Reese, J., 96–99
Ricoeur, P., 76–78, 81, 218,
    322–328, 358
Ritschl, A., 157–158
Rousseau, J., 147
Ruether, R., 89, 292–293, 297

Schleiermacher, F., 37–38,
    151–152, 236
Segundo, J., 65

Terrien, S., 87, 88, 90
Tertullian, 120–121, 179,
    313–314
TeSelle, E., 123, 125
Thomas Aquinas, see index of
    subjects
Tillich, P., 43, 268–272, 311,
    356
Tracy, D., 57, 62, 81, 356
Tracy, T., 270–271, 321
Turner, J. 140, 156–157

Vergote, A., 218–219
Voltaire, 146–147

von Balthasar, H. Urs, 39,
    40–41

Waldenfels, H., 278–283,
    287–288
White, R., 193–194
Whitehead, A.N., 57, 59, 244,
251, 261, 270, 300–302, 315,
    321, 330, 356
Wittgenstein, L., 354–355

Yankelovich, D., 182, 189, 191

Zaehner, R., 284–286, 293–296

# Index of Subjects

analogy, 40–41, 61, 77, 98, 119–120, 131, 133, 139, 253, 261, 362–371
apocalyptic, 59–60, 63, 94–95, 108–110, 127, 326, 328
Apologists, the, 116–122
atheism, 17–25, 48, 63, 109–110, 154–156, 159, 171, 326
autonomy, 21, 24, 50, 59, 141, 149–150, 172, 187, 191, 206, 209, 211, 311, 325

being, 34–35, 40, 98, 116, 124, 130, 218–231, 239–241, 249–254, 281, 284, 304, 361–363, 368–369
  see: God, Thomas Aquinas
belief, see: faith
Buddhism, 53, 173, 236, 277–288

causality, 98–99, 110–111, 116–119, 121, 130, 145, 175, 225, 245–258, 273, 297–298
certainty, 32, 142–143, 145, 159–160, 163, 232
Church, 16–17, 217, passim, see: Vatican II
conscience, 48, 111–112, 162–163, 208, 214, 234–243

see: conversion, transcendence, human
conversion, 17, 92, 103, 123, 137, 165–178, 259, 305–306, 322, 328, 353
creative imagination, 80, 171–172, 175, 198, 217–219, 231, 353
creativity, human, 50, 181–183, 194–195, 214, 239–241, 298, 301–302, 304, 308, 328, 358–359

death, 48–49, 168–169, 172, 174, 177, 201, 203–204, 280, 282, 291–292
Deism, 144, 146–147, 162, 261
democracy, 206–214
dialectic, 37–41, 43, 95, 113, 138–139, 152, 174–175, 264, 266, 324, 345, 356, 361, 368–369, 371
dialogue, 11, 27, 31–37, 43, 48, 51, 54, 75, 86, 96–99, 101–105, 112, 174–175, 356, 361, 369

ecology, 68–69, 252–253, 258–259

economic order, 50–51, 64–66, 92, 154, 205, 208, 213, 307–312, 336–338
epistemology, 220–234
*see*: individual authors
eschatology, 121–122, 126–127, 302, 312
*see*: apocalyptic
evil, 18–19, 22, 25, 48–52, 63–66, 94–95, 113, 126, 154–155, 163, 185–186, 243, 280, 289, 305, 312, 321–331, 338
evolution, 68–69, 155–156, 184, 188, 190, 196, 223, 245–255, 298
exitus-reditus, 123–126, 131, 133
experience, 19–26, 41–42, 48–49, 77–79, 139, 170–171, 176, 217–219, 272–274, 280–281, 297, 342, 361
*see*: individual authors, mysticism

faith, as personal knowledge, 217, 242–243, 265, 276
epistemology of, 217–220, 230–234
freedom of, 176, 231–233
need of, 215, 332–339
norm of Christian, 9–10
problems with in our time, 6, 16–26
*see*: conversion, individual authors, Scripture, testimony, Vatican I, Vatican II, passim
feminism, 67–68, 289–299
foundational theology, 1–12, 15–16, 26–29, 70–72, 165, 215–216, 371–372
freedom, human, 48, 141, 154, 170, 176, 180, 187, 194–195, 203, 208, 231–233, 239–242, 305, 311, 317–318, 345–347
future, 228–229, 247, 335–339, 344–347
*see*: apocalyptic, historical consciousness

Gnosticism, 117, 119, 323
God, being itself, 170, 240–241, 263, 268, 273, 276–277
care for all, 93–94, 97
and change in world, 245–255, 303–312
and change in self, 49, 60–61, 63–64, 153, 312–321
distorted modern images of, 24–25
and eternity, 125, 318
existence, evidence for from cosmos, 98–99, 104, 243–258; from moral experience, 111–112, 162–163, 234–243
as father, 100
freedom of, 35, 86, 135
as good, 120, 273, 276, 362, 364–365
as hidden, 25, 39, 87–88, 92–93, 162, 176
as holy, 92, 99
and history, 88, 90, 94–95, 100, 303–312
immanence of, 17, 67–68, 93, 105, 258, 290–299
as immutable, 25, 120, 124–125, 130–131, 289, 313–315, 318
as impassible, 25, 120, 328–329
as ineffable, 119
and justice, 92, 100, 109–110, 328
and his knowledge, 317–320
as loving, 92, 100, 316–321

as mother, 67–68, 93, 289–299
as perfect, 313, 329–331
as personal, 17, 79, 86–87, 119, 260–288, 312–313, 316–317, 362
power of, 93, 98, 100, 135
providence of, 121, 289, 308, 326
as relational, 198, 271–272, 317, 319, 330
as suffering, 64, 91, 153, 328–331
tenderness of, 92, 93, 100
transcendence of, 17, 93, 98–99, 104, 110, 118, 260–288, 313
good, human, 181, 188, 189–198, 221, 224, 239, 284–285, 303–304, 335
*see*: values
grace, 48, 53, 111–112, 120, 132, 135, 138–139, 158, 160–161, 216, 233–234, 335, 350–351
grounds for faith, intellectual, *see*: God, existence

Hellenism, 96–99, 101–105, 115–122
hermeneutics, 28–29, 41–43, 60, 64, 79–84
Hinduism, 53, 171, 236, 241, 293–299
historical consciousness, modern, 17–29, 46–47, 49–51, 54–56, 57–63, 146–147, 151–155, 214, 299–312, 371
and experience of the sacred, 344–347
and faith and meaning in history, 335–339
and human transcendence, 198–205
naturalistic, 6, 17–24, 27, 45, 49–51, 80–81, 150, 154–156, 165–166, 181, 204, 206–208, 299, 325–326, 330, 371
hope, 5, 49, 63–66, 87, 91, 93–95, 338–339, 346
human person, 17–18, 20–23, 28–29, 46–51, 161–163, transcendence of, 28–29, 179–208, 211–214, 232–233, 303–305
*see*: conversion
human rights, 50–51, 208–214, 306–311, 346
humanism, 17–23, 48–49, 139, 154–156, 280

identity, 16–24, 172–173, 179, 194–196
inculturation, 24–29, 45–56, 127, 165, 177, 182, 186–187, 192, 194–195, 309
indifference, religious, 17, 21–23, 181, passim
intentionality, human, in knowledge, 220–230
in personal life, 181–182, 186, 188–189, 198, 238–239, 270–271
in social life, 205–214

Jesus Christ, 13, 16–17, 27, 51–54, 99–100, 121, 265, 321, 324, 349, passim
justice, 18, 50–52, 63–66, 92, 97, 167, 173, 176, 178, 203, 207, 306–310

knowledge, *see*: faith, metaphysics, science, Vatican II, individual authors

language, religious, 12–13, 42–44, 75–81, 139–140, 227, 354–371

liberalism, Protestant, 37–38, 41–44, 156–158, 268–272
Liberation theology, 57, 64–66, 206, 301–302, 311, 327

materialism, 154, 159, 245, 252
mathematics, 142–143, 148, 223–229
meaning, search for
  in personal life, 17–23, 48–50, 169–179, 181–205
  in social existence as such, 205–214, 335–339
mediation, theological, 26–29, 128, 173, 177–178, 217–220
  *see*: individual authors
metaphor, 76–77, 80, 140, 329, 358–360
metaphysics, 23, 25, 148, 190–191, 220–229, 248–257, 348, 354, 361–362
models for mediating belief, 30–72
modernism, 32–33, 55
moral order, 235–253
  in personal life, 48, 189–205, 303–306
  in society as such, 50–51, 205–214, 306–312, 338
  *see*: conversion
mystery, 45, 68, 85–87, 120, 132, 144, 157, 163, 172, 203, 230, 233, 291, 321–322, 326, 331, 334, 338, 344–347, 358, 362, 367, 371
mysticism, 124–125, 129, 132, 136, 170–171, 238, 281, 284, 291, 294
myth, 42, 68, 77–78, 153, 175, 290, 292–293, 298, 322–324, 340–343, 358

natural theology, 33–35, 37, 39, 41, 58–59, 98–99, 110–111, 144, 163, 350

nature, 55–56, 143–144, 151, 174, 218, 221, 243–259, 303, 344
Neo-Scholasticism, 33–34, 80, 161, 178

oppressed, the, 52, 64, 92, 154–155, 156, 172, 186–187, 192, 208–209, 301, 307–333, 327

phenomenology,
  of human knowledge, 223–229
  of personal transcendence, 182–205
  of social transcendence, 205–214
Platonism,
  middle Platonism, 116–122, 313
  Neo-Platonism, 122–127, 314, 344
pluralism, 19–22, 69, 84, 128, 133, 136
political community, 23, 49–50, 64–66, 205–214, 302, 306–312, 327
post-modernism, 23–24, 62
pragmatism, 17–24, 207–208, 240, 306–307, 346, 353
praxis, 50–51, 57–58, 63–66, 133, 154–157, 172–173, 176, 178, 182, 219, 222, 226–227, 276, 301–302, 352
process theology, 57, 58–59, 61–62, 251, 300–301, 304–305, 321
psychology, 176, 275–276
  of cognitive development, 223–229, 238
  of personal development, 182–201

reason, *see*: individual authors,
　dialogue, metaphysics, praxis,
　Vatican I, Vatican II
relativism, 19–20, 25, 69, 192,
　195, 205, 207–208, 272, 365
religion, 19–20, 38–40, 53–54,
　69, 71, 143–144, 146–147,
　149–150, 154–157, 205, 272,
　277, 336–347, passim
revelation, 5, 7, 17, 52–53,
　68–69, 348–350, passim
　　and the Enlightenment,
　　　143–150
　　and Scripture, 74–75, 86,
　　　113, 122, 359–361,
　　　368–369, 372
　　through moral experience,
　　　111–112, 175, 235–243
　　through the physical world,
　　　98–99, 104, 110–112, 121,
　　　144, 243–258, 167
　　*see*: Buddhism, Hinduism,
　　　individual authors, Vati-
　　　can I, Vatican II, passim


Scholasticism, 128–140, 142, 150
Sacred, the, 78–80, 218, 235,
　298, 340–347, 358–359
salvation, 5, 8, 16–17, 51–52,
　65, 68, 79–80, 85, 94–95, 100,
　233, 301–302, 331, 358–360,
　367, 372
science, physical, 23, 142–145,
　148, 150–151, 155–157, 218,
　223–229, 243–248, 267
Scripture, 73–113, 357–360,
　passim
self, 23, 133, 154, 176, 179,
　180–181, 184, 187–188,
　190–196, 199, 201–204,
　217–219, 234–243, 280–282,
　294, 305, 335–339, 361
society, 23, 49–50, 64–66, 89–90,
　104, 182, 186–187, 192,

199–202, 205–214, 306–312,
　335–338
symbols, religious, 23, 45,
　77–80, 87–88, 92, 95, 100,
　133, 150, 153, 189, 217–220,
　230, 290–298, 316, 341–343,
　347–349, 358–360

technological culture, 18, 21,
　165, 207–208, 224, 327
testimony, 75, 167, 216–217,
　230–233, 334–335, 348–351,
　358–361
　　of conscience, 234–243
　　of the physical world,
　　　243–258
Thomas Aquinas, 11–12, 57, 59,
　129–132, 133, 134, 137, 139,
　171, 175
　　on analogy, 362–366,
　　　368–371
　　on being, 180, 197, 202,
　　　250, 263
　　on connatural knowledge,
　　　353–354
　　on epistemology, 220–229
　　on God, as immanent, 289
　　as immutable, 315
　　as impassible, 328–329
　　as transcendent personal
　　　being, 261–264
　　on human person, 179–180,
　　　189–190, 197, 202
　　on relationality, 198
time, 60, 125, 126, 299, 318,
　342–347, 370
transcendence, *see*: human per-
　son, God
Trinity, 9, 11, 13, 16, 64, 97,
　100, 114, 119, 123, 131–133,
　271, 285–288, 296, 319–320,
　372

values, 22–24, 29, 179, 181–182,
　187, 189, 192, 195–196, 199,

205, 217–219, 234–243,
276–277
Vatican Council I, 32, 158–161
Vatican Council II, 7, 15, 20,
46–54, 178, 349–350, 352

women and the image of God,
12–13, 19, 67–68, 89, 93, 194,
199–200, 258, 289–299
World Council of Churches,
54–56, 347

## DATE DUE

| | | | |
|---|---|---|---|
| | | | |
| | | | |
| | | | |
| | | | |
| | | | |
| | | | |
| | | | |
| | | | |
| | | | |
| | | | |
| | | | |
| | | | |
| | | | |
| | | | |
| | | | |
| | | | |
| | | | |
| | | | |

HIGHSMITH 45-220